ANNUAL EDITIONS

Human Development

08/09

Thirty-Sixth Edition

EDITOR

Karen L. Freiberg
University of Maryland, Baltimore County

Dr. Karen Freiberg has an interdisciplinary educational and employment background in nursing, education, and developmental psychology. She received her B.S. from the State University of New York at Plattsburgh, her M.S. from Cornell University, and her Ph.D. from Syracuse University. Dr. Freiberg has worked as a school nurse, a pediatric nurse, a public health nurse for the Navajo Indians, an associate project director for a child development clinic, a researcher in several areas of child development, and a university professor. She is the author of an award-winning textbook, *Human Development: A Life-Span Approach*, which is now in its fourth edition. Dr. Freiberg is currently on the faculty at the University of Maryland, Baltimore County.

 McGraw-Hill **Higher Education**

Boston   Burr Ridge, IL   Dubuque, IA   New York   San Francisco   St. Louis
Bangkok   Bogotá   Caracas   Kuala Lumpur   Lisbon   London   Madrid   Mexico City
Milan   Montreal   New Delhi   Santiago   Seoul   Singapore   Sydney   Taipei   Toronto

Higher Education

ANNUAL EDITIONS: HUMAN DEVELOPMENT, THIRTY-SIXTH EDITION

 This book is printed on recycled, acid-free paper containing 10% postconsumer waste.

1 2 3 4 5 6 7 8 9 0 QPD/QPD 0 9 8 7

ISBN 978–0–07–339751–1
MHID 0–07–339751–2
ISSN 0278–4661

Managing Editor: *Larry Loeppke*
Production Manager: *Beth Kundert*
Developmental Editor: *Dave Welsh*
Editorial Assistant: *Nancy Meissner*
Production Service Assistant: *Rita Hingtgen*
Permissions Coordinator: *Shirley Lanners*
Senior Marketing Manager: *Julie Keck*
Marketing Communications Specialist: *Mary Klein*
Marketing Coordinator: *Alice Link*
Project Manager: *Sandy Wille*
Design Specialist: *Tara McDermott*
Senior Administrative Assistant: *DeAnna Dausener*
Senior Operations Manager: *Pat Koch Krieger*
Cover Graphics: *Maggie Lytle*

Compositor: Laserwords Private Limited
Cover Image: The McGraw-Hill Companies, Inc./Jill Braaten, photographer and Javier Pierini/Brand X Pictures/Jupiterimages

Library in Congress Cataloging-in-Publication Data
Main entry under title: Annual Editions: Human Development. 2008/2009.
  1. Human Development—Periodicals. I. Freiberg, Karen L., *comp.* II. Title: Human Development.
658'.05

www.mhhe.com

Editors/Advisory Board

Members of the Advisory Board are instrumental in the final selection of articles for each edition of ANNUAL EDITIONS. Their review of articles for content, level, currentness, and appropriateness provides critical direction to the editor and staff. We think that you will find their careful consideration well reflected in this volume.

Preface

In publishing ANNUAL EDITIONS we recognize the enormous role played by the magazines, newspapers, and journals of the public press in providing current, first-rate educational information in a broad spectrum of interest areas. Many of these articles are appropriate for students, researchers, and professionals seeking accurate, current material to help bridge the gap between principles and theories and the real world. These articles, however, become more useful for study when those of lasting value are carefully collected, organized, indexed, and reproduced in a low-cost format, which provides easy and permanent access when the material is needed. That is the role played by ANNUAL EDITIONS.

Science, technology, and education have dramatically altered the process of human development in the past millennium. Physical aging has been slowed, and the average survival age lengthened, by improved living conditions, health care, and nutrition. Emotional well-being, stress management, and conflict resolution are the focus of more attention. Social organizations include more tolerance of diversity. The borders separating cultures have blurred due to instant communications and rapid travel opportunities. Even our spiritual development has been transformed by more contemplation of the essence of life. The cognitive revolution of our time allows each of us greater perception of our humanity.

This compendium of articles about human development covers the life span, considering physical, cognitive, psychosocial, and spiritual components. Development should be viewed as a circle of life. Conception begins each new human being, but each unique individual carries genetic materials from biological relatives alive and dead, and may pass them on to future humanity.

Development through infancy proceeds from sensory and motor responses to verbal communication, thinking, conceptualizing, and learning from others. Childhood brings rapid physical growth, improved cognition, and social learning. Adolescence is when the individual begins to test out sexual maturity. Values and identity are questioned. Separation from parents begins. Under the influence of sex hormones the brain undergoes multiple changes. Emotions may fluctuate rapidly.

Early adulthood usually establishes the individual as an independent person. Employment, further education, the beginning of one's own family are all aspects of setting up a distinct life, with both its own characteristics and the characteristics and customs of previous generations.

During middle adulthood persons have new situations to face, new transitions with which to cope. Children grow up and leave home. Signs of aging become apparent. Relationships change, roles shift. New abilities may be found and opportunities created.

Finally, during late adulthood, people assess what they've accomplished. Some are pleased. Some feel they could have done more or lived differently. In the best of instances, individuals accept who they are and are comfortable with themselves.

As you explore this anthology, you will discover that many articles ask questions that have no answers. As a student, I felt frustrated by such writing. I wanted answers, right answers, right away. However, over time I learned that lessons that are necessary to acquire maturity include accepting relativity and acknowledging extenuating circumstances. Life frequently has no right or wrong answers, but rather various alternatives with multiple consequences. Instead of right versus wrong, a more helpful consideration is "What will bring about the greater good for the greater number?" Controversies, whether about terrorism or war, good or evil, stem cells or organ transplants, body-soul separate or unified, can promote healthy discussions. Different viewpoints should be weighed against societal standards. Different philosophies should be celebrated for what they offer in creativity of intellect and human beings' ability to adapt to changing circumstances.

The Greek sophists were philosophers who specialized in argumentation, rhetoric (using language persuasively), and dialectics (finding synthesis or common ground between contradictory ideas). From their skilled thinking came the derogatory term "sophism," suggesting that some argumentation was deceptive or fallacious rather than wise. The term sophomore, which in this era means second-year student, comes from this variation of sophism, combining "sophos" (wise) with "moros" (dull or foolish). "Sophomoric" translates to exhibiting immaturity and lack of judgment, while "sophisticated" translates to having acquired knowledge. Educators strive to have their students move from knowing all the answers (sophomoric) to asking intelligent questions (sophisticated).

This anthology is dedicated to seekers of knowledge and searchers for what is true, right, or lasting. To this end, articles have been selected to provide you with information that will stimulate discussion and that will give your thoughts direction, but not articles that tell you what to think. May you be "seeking" learners all through your own years of human development. May each suggestive answer you discover open your mind to more erudite (instructive) learning, questioning, and sophistication.

Karen Freiberg

Karen Freiberg, Ph.D.
Editor

Contents

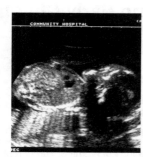

UNIT 1
Genetic and Prenatal Influences on Development

Part A.   Genetic Influences

1. The Identity Dance, Gunjan Sinha, *Psychology Today,* March/April 2004

Identical twins are clones with the same **genetic profiles**. Life experience, therefore, must matter if identical twins develop unlike **emotions**, **health problems**, and **personalities**. This article reports scientific evidence that genes have the equivalent of molecular "switches" that can be turned on or off by **prenatal** and postnatal environmental factors. Several unlike identical twins are described.   **3**

2. The Power to Divide, Rick Weiss, *National Geographic,* July 2005

The United States, under the Bush administration, limits federal funding of **stem cell research**. Some states (e.g., California) and several countries (e.g., Singapore, Korea, United Kingdom) are making progress in therapeutic cloning of cells needed by diabetics, heart attack patients, and others. Some people with regenerated cells are already thriving. Will **ethicists** allow this research to continue? Should they?   **6**

3. What Makes Us Different?, Michael D. Lemonick and Andrea Dorfman, *Time*, October 9, 2006

Chimpanzees and humans share 98 percent of the same **genes**. Chimps use **sign language**, express **emotions**, and have complex **cognition**. The chimpanzee genome was decoded in 2005. Now computers are revealing subtle differences in the species. One gene, active in human **prenatal brain development**, appears to play a major role. This ongoing research has enormous potential for understanding human development.   **12**

Part B.   Prenatal Influences

4. The Age of Genetic Technology Arrives, Leon R. Kass, *The American Spectator*, November/December 2002

The 30,000 human genes have been mapped and biotech businesses are booming. Will **genetic engineering** result in every baby being born without any mental or physical disabilities? Will we eliminate tumors and infections, enhance immunity, and make disease extinct? How much more memory, or years of life, will we add? Will we be fulfilled or dehumanized? Leon Kass addresses these **ethical** issues.   **17**

5. The Mystery of Fetal Life: Secrets of the Womb, John Pekkanen, *Current*, September 2001

Environment affects **prenatal development**. This article reviews known dangers (e.g., **alcohol and drug use**, and viral infections) and recently discovered endocrine disrupters (e.g., chemicals in our air, food, and water). The author gives advice on **exercise**, **nutrition**, and **health maintenance** to optimize the **physical and cognitive status** of our offspring.   **23**

6. The Smallest Patients, Claudia Kalb, *Newsweek*, October 3, 2005

The **health** of a fetus can now be safeguarded with surgery during **pregnancy**. Early detection and intervention has payoffs both for baby and for parents. A **mother**, who is relieved of the **stress**, **anxiety**, and **depression** associated with a **physically** challenged baby, tolerates the surgery well and can go on to deliver the baby normally at term.   **32**

The concepts in bold italics are developed in the article. For further expansion, please refer to the Topic Guide and the Index.

UNIT 2
Development During Infancy and Early Childhood

The concepts in bold italics are developed in the article. For further expansion, please refer to the Topic Guide and the Index.

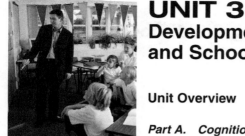

UNIT 3
Development During Childhood: Cognition and Schooling

The concepts in bold italics are developed in the article. For further expansion, please refer to the Topic Guide and the Index.

UNIT 4
Development During Childhood:
Family and Culture

The concepts in bold italics are developed in the article. For further expansion, please refer to the Topic Guide and the Index.

UNIT 5
Development During Adolescence and Young Adulthood

The concepts in bold italics are developed in the article. For further expansion, please refer to the Topic Guide and the Index.

UNIT 6
Development During Middle and Late Adulthood

The concepts in bold italics are developed in the article. For further expansion, please refer to the Topic Guide and the Index.

The concepts in bold italics are developed in the article. For further expansion, please refer to the Topic Guide and the Index.

Topic Guide

This topic guide suggests how the selections in this book relate to the subjects covered in your course. You may want to use the topics listed on these pages to search the Web more easily.

On the following pages a number of Web sites have been gathered specifically for this book. They are arranged to reflect the units of this *Annual Edition*. You can link to these sites by going to the student online support site at *http://www.mhcls.com/online/*.

ALL THE ARTICLES THAT RELATE TO EACH TOPIC ARE LISTED BELOW THE BOLD-FACED TERM.

xv

Internet References

The following Internet sites have been carefully researched and selected to support the articles found in this reader. The easiest way to access these selected sites is to go to our student online support site at *http://www.mhcls.com/online/*.

AE: Human Development 08/09

The following sites were available at the time of publication. Visit our Web site—we update our student online support site regularly to reflect any changes.

General Sources

Association for Moral Education
http://www.amenetwork.org/

This association is dedicated to fostering communication, cooperation, training, curriculum development, and research that links moral theory to educational practices.

Behavior Analysis Resources
http://www.coedu.usf.edu/behavior/bares.htm

Dedicated to promoting the experimental, theoretical, and applied analysis of behavior, this site encompasses contemporary scientific and social issues, theoretical advances, and the dissemination of professional and public information.

Healthfinder
http://www.healthfinder.gov

Healthfinder is a consumer health site that contains the latest health news, prevention and care choices, and information about every phase of human development.

UNIT 1: Genetic and Prenatal Influences on Development

American Academy of Pediatrics (AAP)
http://www.aap.org

AAP provides data on optimal physical, mental, and social health for all children. The site links to professional educational sources and current research.

Basic Neural Processes
http://psych.hanover.edu/Krantz/neurotut.html

An extensive tutorial on brain structures is provided here.

Evolutionary Psychology: A Primer
http://www.psych.ucsb.edu/research/cep/

A link to an evolutionary psychology primer is available on this site. Extensive background information is included.

Genetics Education Center
http://www.kumc.edu/gec/

The University of Kansas Medical Center provides information on human genetics and the human genome project at this site. Included are a number of links to research areas.

MedlinePlus Health Information/Prenatal Care
http://www.nlm.nih.gov/medlineplus/prenatalcare.html

On this site of the National Library of Medicine and the National Institutes of Health, you'll find prenatal-related sections such as General Information, Diagnosis/Symptoms, Nutrition, Organizations, and more.

UNIT 2: Development During Infancy and Early Childhood

BabyCenter
http://www.babycenter.com

This well-organized site offers quick access to practical information on a variety of baby-related topics that span the period from preconception to toddlerhood.

Children's Nutrition Research Center (CNRC)
http://www.bcm.tmc.edu/cnrc/

CNRC is dedicated to defining the nutrient needs of healthy children, from conception through adolescence, and of pregnant and nursing mothers.

Early Childhood Care and Development
http://www.ecdgroup.com

Child development theory, programming and parenting data, and research can be found on this site of the Consultative Group. It is dedicated to the improvement of conditions of young children at risk.

Zero to Three: National Center for Infants, Toddlers, and Families
http://www.zerotothree.org

Zero to Three is dedicated solely to infants, toddlers, and their families. Organized by recognized experts in the field, it provides technical assistance to communities, states, and the federal government.

UNIT 3: Development During Childhood: Cognition and Schooling

Children Now
http://www.childrennow.org

Children Now focuses on improving conditions for children who are poor or at risk. Articles include information on education, the influence of media, health, and security.

Council for Exceptional Children
http://www.cec.sped.org

This is the home page of the Council for Exceptional Children, which is dedicated to improving education for exceptional children and the gifted child.

Educational Resources Information Center (ERIC)
http://www.eric.ed.gov/

Sponsored by the U.S. Department of Education, this site will lead to numerous documents related to elementary and early childhood education.

www.mhcls.com/online/

Federation of Behavioral, Psychological, and Cognitive Science
http://federation.apa.org

The federation's mission is fulfilled through legislative and regulatory advocacy, education, and information dissemination to the scientific community. Hotlink to the National Institutes of Health's Project on the Decade of the Brain.

The National Association for the Education of Young Children (NAEYC)
http://www.naeyc.org

NAEYC is the nation's largest organization of early childhood professionals. It is devoted to improving the quality of early childhood education programs for children from birth through the age of eight.

Project Zero
http://pzweb.harvard.edu

Following 30 years of research on the development of learning processes in children and adults, Project Zero is now helping to create communities of reflective, independent learners; to enhance deep understanding within disciplines; and to promote critical and creative thinking.

UNIT 4: Development During Childhood: Family and Culture

Childhood Injury Prevention Interventions
http://depts.washington.edu/hiprc/

Systematic reviews of childhood injury prevention and interventions on such diverse subjects as adolescent suicide, child abuse, accidental injuries, and youth violence are offered on this site.

Families and Work Institute
http://www.familiesandwork.org/index.html

The Families and Work Institute conducts policy research on issues related to the changing workforce, and it operates a national clearinghouse on work and family life.

Parentsplace.com: Single Parenting
http://www.parentsplace.com/

This resource focuses on issues concerning single parents and their children. The articles range from parenting children from infancy through adolescence.

UNIT 5: Development During Adolescence and Young Adulthood

ADOL: Adolescent Directory On-Line
http://education.indiana.edu/cas/adol/adol.html

The ADOL site contains a wide array of Web documents that address adolescent development. Specific content ranges from mental health issues to counselor resources.

AMA—Adolescent Health On-Line
http://www.ama-assn.org/ama/pub/category/1947.html

This AMA adolescent health initiative describes clinical preventive services that primary care physicians and other health professionals can provide to young people.

American Academy of Child and Adolescent Psychiatry
http://www.aacap.org/

Up-to-date data on a host of topics that include facts for families, public health, and clinical practice may be found here.

UNIT 6: Development During Middle and Late Adulthood

Alzheimer's Disease Research Center
http://alzheimer.wustl.edu/

ADRC facilitates advanced research on clinical, genetic, neuropathological, neuroanatomical, biomedical, neuropsychological, and psychosocial aspects of Alzheimer's disease and related brain disorders.

Lifestyle Factors Affecting Late Adulthood
http://www.school-for-champions.com/health/lifestyle_elderly.htm

The way a person lives his or her life in the later years can affect the quality of life. Find here information to improve a senior's lifestyle plus a few relevant links.

National Aging Information Center (NAIC)
http://www.aoa.dhhs.gov/naic/

This service by the Administration on Aging is a central source of data on demographic, health, economic, and social status of older Americans.

We highly recommend that you review our Web site for expanded information and our other product lines. We are continually updating and adding links to our Web site in order to offer you the most usable and useful information that will support and expand the value of your Annual Editions. You can reach us at: *http://www.mhcls.com/annualeditions/.*

UNIT 1

Genetic and Prenatal Influences on Development

Unit Selections

Key Points to Consider

- Will genetic technology result in more attempts to alter genes than environment in the 21st century? Will life experiences still conspire to switch new DNA sequences on or off?

- Will the United States become a laggard in body-part replacement research using stem cells? Why do many people oppose this life-saving technology?

- Does a specific period of prenatal development determine the cognitive abilities of the future human? Can, or should this time frame be manipulated?

- Why should embryonic development become a political priority in the 21st century?

- Describe the long-term effects of health status during pregnancy on the development of mental abilities in infants and children.

- Is it possible for surgeons to correct heart defects before a fetus is born? Is such an operating procedure safe?

- How does maternal depression affect a developing fetus? Can depression be safely treated during pregnancy?

Student Web Site
www.mhcls.com/online

Internet References
Further information regarding these Web sites may be found in this book's preface or online.

American Academy of Pediatrics (AAP)
   http://www.aap.org
Basic Neural Processes
   http://psych.hanover.edu/Krantz/neurotut.html
Evolutionary Psychology: A Primer
   http://www.psych.ucsb.edu/research/cep/
Genetics Education Center
   http://www.kumc.edu/gec/
MedlinePlus Health Information/Prenatal Care
   http://www.nlm.nih.gov/medlineplus/prenatalcare.html

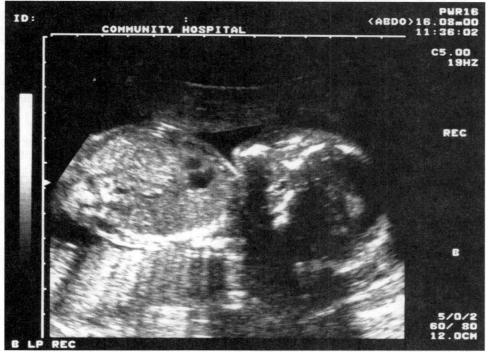

The total human genome was fully mapped in 2003. This knowledge of the human complement of twenty-three pairs of chromosomes with their associated genes in the nucleus of every cell has the potential for allowing genetic manipulation. The use of stem cells (undifferentiated embryonic cells) in animal research has documented the possibility of morphing stem cells into any kind of human cells. Stem cells will turn into desired tissue cells when the gene sequences of cytosine, adenine, thymine, and guanine (CATG) of the desired tissues are expressed. Scientists may eventually use their knowledge of the human genome, plus embryonic stem cells, to alter behavior or cure diseases. Cloning (complete reproduction) of a human already exists when one egg fertilized by one sperm separates into identical twins. Monozygotic twin research suggests that one's genetic CATG sequencing does not determine human behaviors, diseases, and traits without environmental input. Nature versus nurture is better phrased nature plus nurture. Genes appear to have mechanisms by which environmental factors can turn them on, or leave them dormant.

Genetic precursors of human development and the use of stem cells, morphing, and cloning will be hot topics of the next several years as genetic manipulation becomes feasible. As DNA sequences associated with particular human traits (genetic markers) are uncovered, pressure will appear to alter these traits. Will the focus be on altering the CATG sequencing, or altering the environmental factors that will "operate" on the genes?

Human embryology (the study of the first through seventh weeks after conception) and human fetology (the study of the eighth week of pregnancy through birth) have given verification to the idea that behavior precedes birth. The genetic hardwiring of CATG directs much of this behavior. However, the developing embryo/fetus reacts to the internal and external environments provided by the mother as well. Substances diffuse through the placental barrier from the mother's body. The embryo reacts to toxins (viruses, antigens) that pass through the umbilical cord. The fetus reacts to an enormous number of other stimuli, such as the sounds from the mother's body (digestive rumblings, heartbeat) and the mother's movements, moods, and medicines. How the embryo/fetus reacts (weakly to strongly, positively to negatively) depends, in large part, on his or her genetic preprogramming. Genes and environment are so inextricably intertwined that the effect of each cannot be studied separately. Prenatal development always has strong environmental influences and vice versa.

The three articles in the genetic influences section of this unit are state-of-the-science expositions on how decoding of the human genome will affect our future views about human development. The information in them is central to many ongoing discussions of human development. The potentialities for altering structures and behaviors, by altering the CATG messages of DNA on chromosomes within cells or by cloning humans, are massive. We all need to understand what is happening. We need to make knowledgeable and well-thought-out choices for our futures.

The first article, "The Identity Dance," addresses the interplay of genes and environment. It presents research on identical twins suggesting that life factors conspire to switch genetic sequences of CATG on, or off, to create personality traits, diseases, and other human behaviors. What will we, the human race, choose to do with the technology in our hands: alter gene sequences or alter environment? The author poses several questions about human twins which should stimulate lively debates.

The second article, "The Power to Divide," explains how stem cell research could launch an era of body part replacement. Tissues and organs can be custom made for recipients. Will the political/moral movers of different countries allow this to take place? What are the objections to, and dangers of, creating new body parts for individuals with diseased tissues and/or organs? Which countries are moving ahead with this technology? Will the United States continue to be a cell-replacement laggard?

The third article, "What Makes Us Different?," compares the newly mapped chimpanzee genome to the human genome. It explains how dark matter (junk DNA) governs how very similar genes result in very different species. The intellect of humans may be linked to a gene active only in a specific prenatal period. This has major implications for understanding prenatal influences on cognition.

The fifth article, "The Mystery of Fetal Life: Secrets of the Womb," answers questions on fetal psychological development. Human behaviors such as intelligence and personality may be profoundly influenced by the environment of the mother's uterus. Nurture occurs before and after birth. John Pekkanen addresses issues such as over-the-counter drugs, caffeine, infections, pets, and environmental pollutants. He reviews what is known about fetal memory, including the much misunderstood "Mozart effect."

The sixth article, "The Smallest Patients," discusses the ability to surgically correct heart defects in unborn fetuses. The success rate of this procedure is about 75 percent. A few decades ago most babies with heart defects died in infancy. What other prenatally diagnosed defects will be repaired before birth in the future? Will prenatal surgery become a highly skilled specialty?

The last article discusses depression as a factor in about one out of five pregnancies, a frequently concealed truth. The importance of a healthy pregnancy cannot be overemphasized. Depression is a health risk which can, and should be revealed and treated. The article describes therapy alternatives.

The Identity Dance

The battle between genes and the environment is over. As the dust settles, scientists piece together how DNA and life experience conspire to create personality.

GUNJAN SINHA

Sandra and Marisa Peña, 32-year-old identical twins, seem to be exactly the same. They have the same thick dark hair, the same high cheekbones, the same habit of delicately rubbing the tip of the nose in conversation. They had the same type of thyroid cyst at the same age (18) in the same place (right side). When San Diego is mentioned, they both say, simultaneously and with the same intonation, "Oh, I love San Diego!" They live together, work one floor away from each other at MTV, wear the same clothes, hang out with the same friends. They even have the same dreams.

The sisters are as alike as two people can be. At the same time, they are opposites. Sandra is outgoing and confident; Marisa is reserved. They have the same pretty face, but those cheekbones make shy Marisa look mysterious and brooding, while Sandra looks wholesome and sweet. Sandra tends to speak for her sister: "Marisa's always been more quiet, more subdued, an introvert"; Marisa nods her assent. They see themselves as a duo—but more like complementary photo negatives rather than duplicates of each other. "I think we balance each other out," says Sandra. "Definitely," Marisa chimes in. Sandra begins, "In every family photo, I'm smiling, she's—" " 'I'm not," Marisa says with a laugh.

When their father passed away ten years ago from pancreatic cancer and their mother died soon after, the deeper differences between the two became obvious. Their family had been very loving and protective, and the sisters were traumatized by the sudden loss. But as Marisa sank into a depression, Sandra picked up and changed her life. She left San Antonio for Germany to live with her boyfriend. Marisa stayed put, catatonic with sadness. It was the first time the two had ever been apart.

Then, after a few months in Germany, Sandra headed to New York City—the buzzing metropolis in which she had dreamed of living since she was a teenager. Marisa soon followed Sandra, but when she arrived in New York, "She just couldn't let go of [her sadness]," says Sandra. "I didn't know what to do with her."

In recent years, we've, come to believe that genes influence character and personality more than anything else does. It's not just about height and hair color—DNA seems to have its clutches on our very souls. But spend a few hours with identical twins, who have exactly the same set of genes, and you'll find that this simplistic belief crumbles before your eyes. If DNA dictates all, how can two people with identical genes—who are living, breathing clones of each other—be so different?

To answer such questions, scientists have begun to think more broadly about how genes and life experience combine to shape us. The rigid idea that genes determine identity has been replaced with a more flexible and complex view in which DNA and life experience conspire to mold our personalities. We now know that certain genes make people susceptible to traits like aggression and depression. But susceptibility is not inevitability. Gene expression is like putty: Genes are turned on and off, dialed up or down both by other genes and by the ups and downs of everyday life. A seminal study last year found that the ideal breeding ground for depression is a combination of specific genes *and* stressful triggers—simply having the gene will not send most people into despair. Such research promises to end the binary debate about nature vs. nurture—and usher in a revolution in understanding who we are.

We've come to believe genes influence character more than anything else—DNA seems to have its clutches on our souls.

"While scientists have been trying to tease apart environmental from genetic influences on diseases like cancer, this is the first study to show this effect [for a mental disorder]," says Thomas Insel, director of the National Institute of Mental Health. "This is really the science of the moment."

About ten years ago, technological advances made it possible to quickly identify human genes. That breakthrough launched a revolution in human biology—and in psychiatry. Not only were scientists rapidly discovering genes linked to illnesses such as cancer and birth defects like dwarfism, they also found genes associated with such traits as sexual preference and aggression as well as mental illnesses such as schizophrenia.

Genetic discoveries transformed the intellectual zeitgeist as well, marking a decisive shift from the idea that environment alone shapes human personality. Nurture-heavy theories about behavior dominated in the 1960s and 1970s, a reaction in part to the legacy of Nazi eugenics. By the 1990s, the genome was exalted as "the human blueprint," the ultimate dictator of our attributes. Behavioral geneticists offered refreshingly simple explanations for human identity—and for social problems. Bad parenting, poor neighborhoods or amoral television didn't cause bad behavior; genes did. No wonder all those welfare programs weren't working.

"People really believed that there must be something exclusively genetically wrong with people who are not successful. They were exhausted with these broken-hearted liberals saying that it's all social," says Andreas Heinz, professor of psychiatry at Humboldt and Freie University in Berlin, who has been studying the influence of genes and environment on behavior for years. The idea that violent behavior in particular might be genetically "set" was so accepted that in 1992, the director of the agency overseeing the National Institute of Mental Health compared urban African-American youth with "hyperaggressive" and "hypersexual" monkeys in a jungle.

Behavioral genetics had a simple argument: Bad parenting, poor neighborhoods or TV didn't cause bad behavior. Genes did.

Genetic explanations for behavior gained ground in part through great leaps in our understanding of mood disorders. In the early 1990s, research at the federal labs of Stephen Suomi and Dee Higley found that monkeys with low levels of serotonin—now known to be a major player in human anxiety and depression—were prone to alcoholism, anxiety and aggression. Around the same time, Klaus-Peter Lesch at the University of Würtzburg in Germany identified the serotonin transporter gene, which produces a protein that ferries serotonin between brain cells. Prozac and other drugs work by boosting levels of serotonin in the brain, so this gene seemed like an obvious target in the search for the genetic roots of depression.

Lesch, who was working on the connection between this gene and psychiatric disorders, later found that people who had at least one copy of the short version of this gene were much more likely to have an anxiety disorder. Short and long versions of genes function much like synonymous words: Different lengths, or "spellings," generate subtle but critical differences in biology.

Genetics couldn't explain why some people bounce back from terrible trauma that shatters others, or why some people are ruthlessly ambitious and others laid-back.

Despite these groundbreaking insights, it quickly became clear that complex human behaviors couldn't be reduced to pure genetics. Apart from a few exceptions, scientists couldn't find a gene that directly caused depression or schizophrenia or any other major mental of mood disorder. The new research also failed to answer a lot of common-sense questions: If identical twins are genetically indistinguishable, how could just one end up schizophrenic or homosexual? And it couldn't address subtler questions about character and behavior. Why do some people bounce back from terrible trauma that shatters others? Why are some people ruthlessly ambitious and others laid-back?

Thanks to misfit monkeys like George, a rhesus macaque living in a lab in Maryland, researchers have clues to the missing element. In most ways, George is a typical male monkey. He's covered in sandy fur and has a rubbery, almost maniacal grin. But a couple of things set George apart. After he was born, Higley and Suomi's team separated George from his mother, raising him instead in a nursery with other macaque infants his own age. George has another strike against him: a short version of the serotonin transporter gene (monkeys, like people, can have either a short form or a long form of the gene).

But the most notable thing about George is that he is an alcoholic. Each day, George and his simian chums have happy hour, with alcohol freely available in their cage for one hour. Unlike his buddies, George drinks like the resident barroom lush—he sways and wobbles and can't walk a straight line.

And his problems go beyond the bottle. He's reluctant to explore new objects, and he is shy around strangers. He always seems to be on edge and tends to get aggressive and impulsive quickly. In short, he's a completely different animal from his cousin Jim, who also has the short version of the transporter gene but was raised by his biological mom. Jim's "normal" upbringing seems to have protected him from the gene: This monkey is laid-back and prefers sugar water to booze.

After studying 36 family-raised monkeys and 79 nursery-raised animals, the team found that the long version of the gene seems to help the animals shrug off stress. The short form of the gene, by contrast, doesn't directly *cause* alcoholism: Monkeys with the short gene and a normal family upbringing have few personality problems. But the short version of the gene definitely puts the animals at a disadvantage when life gets tough. Raised without the care and support of their mothers, their predisposition toward anxiety and alcoholism comes to the fore.

"Maternal nurturing and discipline seem to buffer the effect of the serotonin gene," says Suomi. "If they don't have good mothers, then the [troubled] behavior comes out loud and clear."

The implications of this research are tantalizing, since people also carry long and short versions of the transporter gene. These variants, unlike those that have been identified as making people susceptible to diseases like breast cancer or Alzheimer's, are very common: Among Caucasians, about one-fifth of the population has two copies of the short gene (everyone gets one copy from Mom and the other from Dad), and another third have two copies of the long gene. The rest have one of each. (The gene has not yet been studied in other populations.) The evidence indicated that this gene was related to resilience and depression in humans. Why, then, had researchers thus far failed to find a convincing correlation between the gene and the risk of depression?

Terrie Moffitt and Avshalom Caspi, a husband-and-wife team of psychologists at King's College in London, had the insight that environmental influences might be the missing part of the puzzle. Moffitt and Caspi turned to a long-term study of almost 900 New Zealanders, identified these subjects' transporter genes and interviewed the subjects about traumatic experiences in early adulthood—like a major breakup, death in the family or serious injury—to see if the difficulties brought out an underlying genetic tendency toward depression.

The results were striking: 43 percent of subjects who had the short genes and who had experienced four or more tumultuous events became clinically depressed. By contrast, only 17 percent of the long-gene people who had endured four or more stressful events wound up depressed—no more than the rate of depression in the general population. People with the short gene who experienced no stressful events fared pretty well too—they also became depressed at the average rate. Clearly, it was the combination of hard knocks and short genes that more than doubled the risk of depression.

Caspi and Moffitt's study, published last summer, was one of the first to examine the combined effects of genetic predisposition and experience on a specific trait. Psychiatrists were delighted. "It's just a wonderful story," says Insel. "It changed the way we think about genes and psychiatric disorders."

Moffitt and Caspi have found a similar relationship between another gene and antisocial behavior. Abused and neglected children with a gene responsible for low levels of monoamine oxidase in the brain were nine times more likely to engage in violent of other antisocial behavior as adults than were people with the same gene who were not mistreated. Finnish scientists have since found similar effects on genes for novelty seeking— a trait associated with attention deficit hyperactivity disorder. Children who had the genes and who were also raised by strict, emotionally distant parents were much more likely to engage in risky behavior and make impulsive decisions as adults than children with the same genes who were raised in more tolerant and accepting environments.

While scientists don't exactly know how genes are influenced by environment at the molecular level, there are clues that genes have the equivalent of molecular "switches" and can be programmed—turned on or off, up or down—very early. Both Lesch and Suomi have shown that the level of biochemicals such as the serotonin transporter molecule can be "set" as early as in the womb, at least in mice and monkeys.

Mothers of multiples will tell you their babies were distinct the moment they were born.

The prenatal environment also has a major influence on differences between identical twins. Mothers of multiples will tell you that their babies were distinct the moment they were born, and research backs them up. Twins experience different environments even in the womb, as they compete with each other for nutrients. One can beat out the other, which is why they often have different birth weights: Marisa Pena is a bit taller and heavier than her sister.

Prenatal experiences are just the first in a lifetime of differentiating factors. Only about 50 percent of the characteristics twins have in common are due to genes alone. Researchers now believe that an illness suffered by only one twin, or different amounts of attention from peers or parents, can set the stage for personality differences. This makes it easier to understand why the Pena sisters reacted as they did: By the time their parents died, "these twins had had a lifetime of experiences which might have made them react differently," says Moffitt. "In addition, some pairs of identical twins individuate themselves in early childhood. They seem to take on the roles of 'the shy one' and 'the outgoing one' and then live up to those roles." in other words, they customize their environment, and the world treats them accordingly.

The new science of nature *and* nurture isn't as straightforward as the DNA-is-destiny mantra, but it is more accurate. "People have a really hard time understanding the probabilistic nature of how genes impact traits like depression," says Kenneth Kendler, director of the Virginia Institute for Psychiatric and Behavioral Genetics at Virginia Commonwealth University, who heads a major twin registry. "They think that if something is heritable, then it can't be modified by the environment." The knowledge that the traits we inherit are also contingent on what the world does to us promises more insight into why people act and feel differently—even when they look exactly the same.

GUNJAN SINHA is an award-winning science writer based in Frankfurt, Germany.

Additional reporting by Jeff Grossman.

The Power to Divide

Stem cells could launch a new era of medicine, curing deadly diseases with custom-made tissues and organs. But science may take a backseat to politics in deciding if—and where—that hope will be realized.

RICK WEISS

In the beginning, one cell becomes two, and two become four. Being fruitful, they multiply into a ball of many cells, a shimmering sphere of human potential. Scientists have long dreamed of plucking those naive cells from a young human embryo and coaxing them to perform, in sterile isolation, the everyday miracle they perform in wombs: transforming into all the 200 or so kinds of cells that constitute a human body. Liver cells. Brain cells. Skin, bone, and nerve.

The dream is to launch a medical revolution in which ailing organs and tissues might be repaired—not with crude mechanical devices like insulin pumps and titanium joints but with living, homegrown replacements. It would be the dawn of a new era of regenerative medicine, one of the holy grails of modern biology.

Revolutions, alas, are almost always messy. So when James Thomson, a soft-spoken scientist at the University of Wisconsin in Madison, reported in November 1998 that he had succeeded in removing cells from spare embryos at fertility clinics and establishing the world's first human embryonic stem cell line, he and other scientists got a lot more than they bargained for. It was the kind of discovery that under most circumstances would have blossomed into a major federal research enterprise. Instead the discovery was quickly engulfed in the turbulent waters of religion and politics. In church pews, congressional hearing rooms, and finally the Oval Office, people wanted to know: Where were the needed embryos going to come from, and how many would have to be destroyed to treat the millions of patients who might be helped? Before long, countries around the world were embroiled in the debate.

Most alarmed have been people who see embryos as fully vested, vulnerable members of society, and who decry the harvesting of cells from embryos as akin to cannibalism. They warn of a brave new world of "embryo farms" and "cloning mills" for the cultivation of human spare parts. And they argue that scientists can achieve the same results using adult stem cells—immature cells found in bone marrow and other organs in adult human beings, as well as in umbilical cords normally discarded at birth.

Immature and full of potential, stem cells haven't yet differentiated into the specialized cells that form body parts, like the museum specimens stacked in the Berlin lab of pathologist Rudolf Virchow. He pioneered the idea, in the 1800s, that disease begins at the cellular level.

Advocates counter that adult stem cells, useful as they may be for some diseases, have thus far proved incapable of producing the full range of cell types that embryonic stem cells can. They point out that fertility clinic freezers worldwide are bulging with thousands of unwanted embryos slated for disposal. Those embryos are each smaller than the period at the end of this sentence. They have no identifying features or hints of a nervous system. If parents agree to donate them, supporters say, it would be unethical not to do so in the quest to cure people of disease.

Few question the medical promise of embryonic stem cells. Consider the biggest United States killer of all: heart disease. Embryonic stem cells can be trained to grow into heart muscle cells that, even in a laboratory dish, clump together and pulse in spooky unison. And when those heart cells have been injected into mice and pigs with heart disease, they've filled in for injured or dead cells and sped recovery. Similar studies have suggested stem cells' potential for conditions such as diabetes and spinal cord injury.

Critics point to worrisome animal research showing that embryonic stem cells sometimes grow into tumors or morph into unwanted kinds of tissues—possibly forming, for example, dangerous bits of bone in those hearts they are supposedly repairing. But supporters respond that such problems are rare and a lot has recently been learned about how to prevent them.

The arguments go back and forth, but policymakers and governments aren't waiting for answers. Some countries, such as Germany, worried about a slippery slope toward unethical human experimentation, have already prohibited some types of stem cell research. Others, like the U.S., have imposed severe limits on government funding but have left the private sector to do what it wants. Still others, such as the U.K., China, Korea, and Singapore, have set out to become the epicenters of stem cell research, providing money as well as ethical oversight to encourage the field within carefully drawn bounds.

In such varied political climates, scientists around the globe are racing to see which techniques will produce treatments soonest. Their approaches vary, but on one point, all seem to agree: How humanity handles its control over the mysteries of embryo development will say a lot about who we are and what we're becoming.

For more than half of his seven years, Cedric Seldon has been fighting leukemia. Now having run out of options, he is about to become a biomedical pioneer—one of about 600 Americans last year to be treated with an umbilical cord blood transplant.

Cord blood transplants—considered an adult stem cell therapy because the cells come from infants, not embryos—have been performed since 1988. Like bone marrow, which doctors have been transplanting since 1968, cord blood is richly endowed with a kind of stem cell that gives rise to oxygen-carrying red blood cells, disease-fighting white blood cells, and other parts of the blood and immune systems. Unlike a simple blood transfusion, which provides a batch of cells destined to die in a few months, the stem cells found in bone marrow and cord blood can—if all goes well—burrow into a person's bones, settle there for good, and generate fresh blood and immune cells for a lifetime.

Propped on a hospital bed at Duke University Medical Center, Cedric works his thumbs furiously against a pair of joysticks that control a careening vehicle in a Starsky and Hutch video game. "Hang on, Hutch!" older brother Daniel shouts from the bedside, as a nurse, ignoring the screeching tires and gunshots, sorts through a jumble of tubes and hangs a bag of cord blood cells from a chrome pole. Just an hour ago I watched those cells being thawed and spun in a centrifuge—awakening them for the first time since 2001, when they were extracted from the umbilical cord of a newborn and donated by her parents to a cell bank at Duke. The time has come for those cells to prove their reputed mettle.

For days Cedric has endured walloping doses of chemotherapy and radiation in a last-ditch effort to kill every cancer cell in his body. Such powerful therapy has the dangerous side-effect of destroying patients' blood-making stem cells, and so is never applied unless replacement stem cells are available. A search of

every bone marrow bank in the country had found no match for Cedric's genetic profile, and it was beginning to look as if he'd run out of time. Then a computer search turned up the frozen cord blood cells at Duke—not a perfect match, but close enough to justify trying.

"Ready?" the nurse asks. Mom and dad, who have spent hours in prayer, nod yes, and a line of crimson wends its way down the tube, bringing the first of about 600 million cells into the boy's body. The video game's sound effects seem to fade behind a muffling curtain of suspense. Although Cedric's balloon-laden room is buoyant with optimism, success is far from certain.

"Grow, cells, grow," Cedric's dad whispers.

His mom's eyes are misty. I ask what she sees when she looks at the cells trickling into her son.

"Life," she says. "It's his rebirth."

It will be a month before tests reveal whether Cedric's new cells have taken root, but in a way he's lucky. All he needs is a new blood supply and immune system, which are relatively easy to re-create. Countless other patients are desperate to regenerate more than that. Diabetics need new insulin-producing cells. Heart attack victims could benefit from new cardiac cells. Paraplegics might even walk again if the nerves in their spinal cords could regrow.

In a brightly lit laboratory halfway across the country from Cedric's hospital room, three teams of scientists at the University of Wisconsin in Madison are learning how to grow the embryonic stem cells that might make such cures possible. Unlike adult stem cells, which appear to have limited repertoires, embryonic stem cells are pluripotent—they can become virtually every kind of human cell. The cells being nurtured here are direct descendants of the ones James Thomson isolated seven years ago.

For years Thomson and his colleagues have been expanding some of those original stem cells into what are called stem cell lines—colonies of millions of pluripotent cells that keep proliferating without differentiating into specific cell types. The scientists have repeatedly moved each cell's offspring to less crowded laboratory dishes, allowing them to divide again and again. And while they worked, the nation struggled to get a handle on the morality of what they were doing.

It took almost two years for President Bill Clinton's administration to devise ethics guidelines and a system for funding the new field. George W. Bush's ascension prevented that plan from going into effect, and all eyes turned to the conservative Texan to see what he would do. On August 9, 2001, Bush announced that federal funds could be used to study embryonic stem cells. But to prevent taxpayers from becoming complicit in the destruction of human embryos, that money could be used only to study the stem cell lines already in the works as of that date—a number that, for practical reasons, has resulted in about two dozen usable lines. Those wishing to work with any of the more than a hundred stem cell lines created after that date can do so only with private funding.

Every month scientists from around the world arrive in Madison to take a three-day course in how to grow those approved cells. To watch what they must go through to keep the cells happy is to appreciate why many feel hobbled by the Bush doctrine. For one thing—and for reasons not fully understood—the surest way to keep these cells alive is to place them on a layer of other cells taken from mouse embryos, a time-consuming requirement. Hunched over lab benches, deftly handling forceps and pipettes with blue latex gloves, each scientist in Madison spends the better half of a day dissecting a pregnant mouse, removing its uterus, and prying loose a string of embryos that look like little red peas in a pod. They then wash them, mash them, tease apart their cells, and get them growing in lab dishes. The result is a hormone-rich carpet of mouse cells upon which a few human embryonic stem cells are finally placed. There they live like pampered pashas.

If their scientist-servants don't feed them fresh liquid nutrients at least once a day, the cells die of starvation. If each colony is not split in half each week, it dies from overcrowding. And if a new layer of mouse cells is not prepared and provided every two weeks, the stem cells grow into weird and useless masses that finally die. By contrast, scientists working with private money have been developing embryonic stem cell lines that are hardier, less demanding, and not dependent on mouse cells. Bypassing the use of mouse cells is not only easier, but it also eliminates the risk that therapeutic stem cells might carry rodent viruses, thereby potentially speeding their approval for testing in humans.

Here in the Madison lab, scientists grumble about how fragile the precious colonies are. "They're hard to get to know," concedes Leann Crandall, one of the course's instructors and a co-author of the 85-page manual on their care and feeding. "But once you get to know them, you love them. You can't help it. They're so great. I see so many good things coming from them."

A few American scientists are finding it is easier to indulge their enthusiasm for stem cells overseas. Scores of new embryonic stem cell lines have now been created outside the U.S., and many countries are aggressively seeking to spur the development of therapies using these cells, raising a delicate question: Can the nation in which embryonic stem cells were discovered maintain its initial research lead?

"I know a lot of people back in the U.S. who would like to move into embryonic stem cell work but who won't because of the political uncertainties," says Stephen Minger, director of the Stem Cell Biology Laboratory at King's College in London, speaking to me in his cramped and cluttered office. "I think the United States is in real danger of being left behind."

Minger could be right. He is one of at least two high-profile stem cell scientists to move from the U.S. to England in the past few years, something less than a brain drain but a signal, perhaps, of bubbling discontent.

The research climate is good here, says Minger. In 2003 his team became the first in the U.K. to grow colonies of human embryonic stem cells, and his nine-person staff is poised to nearly double. He's developing new growth culture systems that won't rely on potentially infectious mouse cells. He's also figuring out how to make stem cells morph into cardiac, neural, pancreatic, and retinal cells and preparing to test those cells in animals. And in stark contrast to how things are done in the U.S., Minger says, he's doing all this with government support—and oversight.

The Human Fertilisation and Embryology Authority (HFEA), the government agency that has long overseen U.K. fertility clinics, is now also regulating the country's embryonic stem cell research. In closed-door meetings a committee of 18 people appointed by the National Health Service considers all requests to conduct research using embryos. The committee includes scientists, ethicists, lawyers, and clergy, but the majority are lay people representing the public.

To an American accustomed to high security and protesters at venues dealing regularly with embryo research, the most striking thing about the HFEA's headquarters in downtown London is its ordinariness. The office, a standard-issue warren of cubicles and metal filing cabinets, is on the second floor of a building that also houses the agency that deals with bankruptcy. I ask Ross Thacker, a research officer at the authority, whether the HFEA is regularly in need of yellow police tape to keep protesters at bay.

"Now that you mention it," he says, "there was a placard holder outside this morning . . ."

Aha!

". . . but he was protesting something about the insolvency office."

Thacker politely refrains from criticizing U.S. policy on embryo research, but he clearly takes pride in the orderliness of the British system. The committee has approved about a dozen requests to create stem cell lines in the past 18 months, increasing the number of projects to 35. Most were relatively routine—until a strong-willed fertility doctor named Alison Murdoch decided to ask for permission to do something nobody had done before: create cloned human embryos as sources of stem cells.

As controversial as embryonic stem cell research can be, cloning embryos to produce those stem cells is even thornier. Much of the world became familiar with cloning in 1997, when scientists announced they'd cloned a sheep named Dolly. The process involves creating an animal not from egg and sperm but by placing the nucleus of a cell inside an egg that's had its nucleus removed. It's since been used to replicate mice, rabbits, cats, and cattle, among others.

As in many other countries and a few U.S. states, it's illegal in the U.K. to create cloned human babies (called reproductive cloning), because of concerns that clones may be biologically abnormal and because of ethical issues surrounding the creation of children who would be genetic replicas of their one-and-only "parent."

In 2001 the British Parliament made it legal to create cloned human embryos—as opposed to babies—for use in medical research (called therapeutic cloning). Still, no one on the HFEA was completely comfortable with the idea. The fear was that some rogue scientist would take the work a step further, gestate

How Many Lines Exist?

Since President Bush banned U.S. government funding for the study of embryonic stem cell lines created after August 9, 2001, the number of lines worldwide has doubled, though reliable data are hard to come by. Biologist Douglas Melton of Harvard says many lines approved for federal dollars "are old fuddy-duddies that have lost potential" because of how they were cultured. "That's why we need new lines," he says.

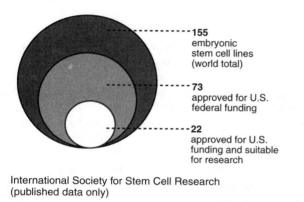

155
embryonic
stem cell lines
(world total)

73
approved for U.S.
federal funding

22
approved for U.S.
funding and suitable
for research

International Society for Stem Cell Research
(published data only)

the embryo in a woman's womb, and make the birth announcement that no one wanted to hear.

But Murdoch, of the University of Newcastle upon Tyne, made a compelling case. If replacement tissues grown from stem cells bore the patient's exact genetic fingerprint, they would be less likely to be rejected by a patient's immune system, she told the committee. And what better way to get such a match than to derive the cells from an embryo cloned from the patient's own DNA? Disease research could also benefit, she said. Imagine an embryo—and its stem cells—cloned from a person with Lou Gehrig's disease, a fatal genetic disorder that affects nerves and muscles. Scientists might learn quite a bit, she argued, by watching how the disease damages nerve and muscle cells grown from those stem cells, and then testing various drugs on them. It's the kind of experiment that could never be done in a person with the disease.

The HFEA deliberated for five months before giving Murdoch permission to make human embryo clones in her lab at the Centre for Life in Newcastle, a sprawling neon-illuminated complex of buildings that strikes a decidedly modern note in the aging industrial hub. But there was a catch: It takes an egg to make a clone. And under the terms of HFEA approval, Murdoch is allowed to use only those eggs being disposed of by the center's fertility clinic after they failed to fertilize when mixed with sperm.

It's not a perfect arrangement, Murdoch says. After all, eggs that have failed to fertilize are almost by definition of poor quality. "They're not brilliant," she says of the eggs. "But the U.K. has decided at the moment that these are the most ethical sort to use. So that's really all we can work with." As of April the group hadn't managed to clone any embryos, despite numerous attempts.

No such obstacle faced Woo-Suk Hwang and his colleagues at Seoul National University in February 2004 when they became the world's first to clone human embryos and extract stem cells from them. The South Korean government allows research on human embryos made from healthy eggs—in this case, donated by 16 women who took egg-ripening hormones.

Cloning is an arduous process that requires great patience and almost always ends in failure as cells burst, tear, or suffer damage to their DNA, but the Koreans are expert cloners, their skills sharpened in the country's state-funded livestock-cloning enterprise. In Hwang's lab alone, technicians produce more than 700 cloned pig or cattle embryos every day, seven days a week, in a quest to produce livestock with precise genetic traits. "There is no holiday in our lab," Hwang told me with a smile.

But there is something else that gives Koreans an edge over other would-be cloners, Hwang says. "As you know, Asian countries use chopsticks, but only the Koreans use steel chopsticks," he explains. "The steel ones are the most difficult to use. Very slippery." I look at him, trying to tell if he's kidding. A lifetime of using steel chop sticks makes Koreans better at manipulating tiny eggs? "This is not simply a joke," he says.

Time will tell whether such skill will be enough to keep Korea in the lead as other countries turn to cloning as a source of stem cells. The competition will be tough. China has pioneered a potentially groundbreaking technique that produces cloned human embryos by mixing human skin cells with the eggs of rabbits, which are more easily obtained than human eggs. A few privately funded researchers in the U.S. are also pursuing therapeutic cloning.

Yet the biggest competition in the international race to develop stem cell therapies may ultimately come from one of the smallest of countries—a tiny nation committed to becoming a stem cell superpower. To find that place, one need only track the migration patterns of top scientists who've been wooed there from the U.S., Australia, even the U.K. Where they've been landing, it turns out, is Singapore.

Amid the scores of small, botanically rich but barely inhabited islands in the South China Sea, Singapore stands out like a post-modern mirage. The towering laboratory buildings of its Biopolis were created in 2001 to jump-start Singapore's biotechnology industry. Like a scene from a science fiction story, it features futuristic glass-and-metal buildings with names like Matrix, Proteos, and Chromos, connected by skywalks that facilitate exchanges among researchers.

Academic grants, corporate development money, laws that ban reproductive cloning but allow therapeutic cloning, and a science-savvy workforce are among the lures attracting stem cell researchers and entrepreneurs. Even Alan Colman—the renowned cloning expert who was part of the team that created Dolly, the cloned sheep—has taken leave of his home in the U.K. and become the chief executive of ES Cell International, one of a handful of major stem cell research companies blossoming in Singapore's fertile environs.

"You don't have to fly from New York to San Diego to see what's going on in other labs," says Robert Klupacs, the firm's previous CEO. "You just walk across the street. Because Singapore is small, things can happen quickly. And you don't have to go to Congress at every turn."

The company's team of 36, with 15 nationalities represented, has taken advantage of that milieu. It already owns six stem cell lines made from conventional, noncloned embryos that are approved for U.S. federal funding. Now it is perfecting methods of turning those cells into the kind of pancreatic islet cells that diabetics need, as well as into heart muscle cells that could help heart attack patients. The company is developing new, mouse-free culture systems and sterile production facilities to satisfy regulators such as the U.S. Food and Drug Administration. It hopes to begin clinical tests in humans by 2007.

Despite its research-friendly ethos—and its emphasis on entrepreneurial aspects of stem cell science—Singapore doesn't want to be known as the world's "Wild West" of stem cell research. A panel of scientific and humanitarian representatives spent two years devising ethical guidelines, stresses Hwai-Loong Kong, executive director of Singapore's Biomedical Research Council. Even the public was invited to participate, Kong says—an unusual degree of democratic input for the authoritarian island nation. The country's policies represent a "judicious balance," he says, that has earned widespread public support.

Widespread, perhaps, but not universal. After my conversation with Kong, a government official offered me a ride to my next destination. As we approached her parked car, she saw the surprise on my face as I read the bumper sticker on her left rear window: "Embryos—Let Them Live. You Were Once an Embryo Too!"

Where are they?

The U.S. still leads in the number of embryonic stem cell lines, despite the restrictions on federal funding; states such as California are investing in research to create new and better lines. But the U.K. and rising Asian economies, such as South Korea and Singapore, are pouring funds into their research labs in an effort to catch up—with government oversight and financial support.

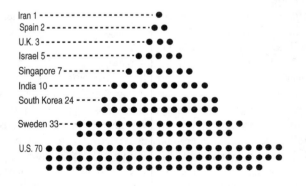

International Society for Stem Cell Research
(published data only)

"I guess this is not completely settled," I said. "No," she replied, choosing not to elaborate.

That bumper sticker made me feel strangely at home. I am an American, after all. And no country has struggled more with the moral implications of embryonic stem cell research than the U.S., with its high church attendance rates and pockets of skepticism for many things scientific. That struggle promises to grow in the months and years ahead. Many in Congress want to ban the cloning of human embryos, even in those states where it is currently legal and being pursued with private funding. Some states have already passed legislation banning various kinds of embryo research. And federally backed scientists are sure to become increasingly frustrated as the handful of cell colonies they're allowed to work with becomes an ever smaller fraction of what's available.

Yet one thing I've noticed while talking to stem cell experts around the world: Whenever I ask who is the best in the field, the answers are inevitably weighted with the names of Americans. The work of U.S. researchers still fills the pages of the best scientific journals. And while federal policy continues to frustrate them, they are finding some support. Following the lead of California, which has committed 300 million dollars a year for embryonic stem cell research for the next decade, several states are pushing initiatives to fund research, bypassing the federal restrictions in hopes of generating well-paying jobs to boost their economies. Moves like those prompt some observers to predict that when all is said and done, it will be an American team that wins the race to create the first FDA-approved embryonic stem cell therapy.

Tom Okarma certainly believes so, and he intends to be that winner. Okarma is president of Geron, the company in Menlo Park, California, that has been at the center of the embryonic stem cell revolution from the beginning. Geron financed James Thomson's discovery of the cells in Wisconsin and has since developed more than a dozen new colonies. It holds key patents on stem cell processes and products. And now it's laying the groundwork for what the company hopes will be the first controlled clinical trials of treatments derived from embryonic stem cells. Moreover, while others look to stem cells from cloned embryos or newer colonies that haven't come into contact with mouse cells, Okarma is looking no further than the very first colonies of human embryonic stem cells ever grown: the ones Thomson nurtured back in 1998. That may seem surprising, he acknowledges, but after all these years, he knows those cells inside out.

"We've shown they're free of human, pig, cow, and mouse viruses, so they're qualified for use in humans," Okarma says at the company's headquarters. Most important, Geron has perfected a system for growing uniform batches of daughter cells from a master batch that resides, like a precious gem, in a locked freezer. The ability to produce a consistent product, batch after batch, just as drug companies do with their pills is what the FDA wants—and it will be the key to success in the emerging marketplace of stem cell therapies, Okarma says. "Why do you think San Francisco sourdough bread is so successful?" he asks. "They've got a reliable sourdough culture, and they stick with it."

Geron scientists can now make eight different cell types from their embryonic lines, Okarma says, including nerve cells, heart cells, pancreatic islet cells, liver cells, and the kind of brain cells that are lost in Parkinson's disease. But what Geron wants most at this point is to develop a treatment for spinal cord injuries.

Okarma clicks on a laptop and shows me a movie of white rats in a cage. "Pay attention to the tail and the two hind legs," he says. Two months before, the rats were subjected to spinal cord procedures that left their rear legs unable to support their weight and their tails dragging along the floor. "That's a permanent injury," he says. He flips to a different movie: white rats again, also two months after injury. But these rats received injections of a specialized nervous system cell grown from human embryonic stem cells. They have only the slightest shuffle in their gait. They hold their tails high. One even stands upright on its rear legs for a few moments.

"It's not perfect," Okarma says. "It's not like we've made a brand new spinal cord." But tests show the nerves are regrowing, he says. He hopes to get FDA permission to start testing the cells in people with spinal cord injuries in 2006.

Those experiments will surely be followed by many others around the world, as teams in China, the U.K., Singapore, and other nations gain greater control over the remarkable energy of stem cells. With any luck the political and ethical issues may even settle down. Many suspect that with a little more looking, new kinds of stem cells may be found in adults that are as versatile as those in embryos.

At least two candidates have already emerged. Catherine Verfaillie, a blood disease specialist at the University of Minnesota, has discovered a strange new kind of bone marrow cell that seems able to do many, and perhaps even all, the same things human embryonic stem cells can do. Researchers at Tufts University announced in February that they had found similar cells. While some scientists have expressed doubts that either kind of cell will prove as useful as embryonic ones, the discoveries have given birth to new hopes that scientists may yet find the perfect adult stem cell hiding in plain sight.

Maybe Cedric Seldon himself will discover them. The stem cells he got in his cord blood transplant did the trick, it turns out. They took root in his marrow faster than in anyone his doctors have seen. "Everyone's saying, 'Oh my God, you're doing so well'" his mother says.

That makes Cedric part of the world's first generation of regenerated people, a seamless blend of old and new—and, oddly enough, of male and female. His stem cells, remember, came from a girl, and they've been diligently churning out blood cells with two X chromosomes ever since. It's a detail that will not affect his sexual development, which is under the control of his hormones, not his blood. But it's a quirk that could save him, his mother jokes, if he ever commits a crime and leaves a bit of blood behind. The DNA results would be unambiguous, she notes correctly. "They'll be looking for a girl."

What Makes Us Different?

Not very much, when you look at our DNA. But those few tiny changes made all the difference in the world.

MICHAEL D. LEMONICK AND ANDREA DORFMAN

You don't have to be a biologist or an anthropologist to see how closely the great apes—gorillas, chimpanzees, bonobos and orangutans—resemble us. Even a child can see that their bodies are pretty much the same as ours, apart from some exaggerated proportions and extra body hair. Apes have dexterous hands much like ours but unlike those of any other creature. And, most striking of all, their faces are uncannily expressive, showing a range of emotions that are eerily familiar. That's why we delight in seeing chimps wearing tuxedos, playing the drums or riding bicycles. It's why a potbellied gorilla scratching itself in the zoo reminds us of Uncle Ralph or Cousin Vinnie—and why, in a more unsettled reaction, Queen Victoria, on seeing an orangutan named Jenny at the London Zoo in 1842, declared the beast "frightful and painfully and disagreeably human."

It isn't just a superficial resemblance. Chimps, especially, not only look like us, they also share with us some human-like behaviors. They make and use tools and teach those skills to their offspring. They prey on other animals and occasionally murder each other. They have complex social hierarchies and some aspects of what anthropologists consider culture. They can't form words, but they can learn to communicate via sign language and symbols and to perform complex cognitive tasks. Scientists figured out decades ago that chimps are our nearest evolutionary cousins, roughly 98% to 99% identical to humans at the genetic level. When it comes to DNA, a human is closer to a chimp than a mouse is to a rat.

Yet tiny differences, sprinkled throughout the genome, have made all the difference. Agriculture, language, art, music, technology and philosophy—all the achievements that make us profoundly different from chimpanzees and make a chimp in a business suit seem so deeply ridiculous—are somehow encoded within minute fractions of our genetic code. Nobody yet knows precisely where they are or how they work, but somewhere in the nuclei of our cells are handfuls of amino acids, arranged in a specific order, that endow us with the brainpower to outthink and outdo our closest relatives on the tree of life. They give us the ability to speak and write and read, to compose symphonies, paint masterpieces and delve into the molecular biology that makes us what we are.

Until recently, there was no way to unravel these crucial differences. Exactly what gives us advantages like complex brains and the ability to walk upright—and certain disadvantages, including susceptibility to a particular type of malaria, AIDS and Alzheimer's, that don't seem to afflict chimps—remained a mystery.

But that's rapidly changing. Just a year ago, geneticists announced that they had sequenced a rough draft of the chimpanzee genome, allowing the first side-by-side comparisons of human and chimpanzee DNA. Already, that research has led to important discoveries about the development of the human brain over the past few million years and possibly about our ancestors' mating behavior as well.

And sometime in the next few weeks, a team led by molecular geneticist Svante Pääbo of the Max Planck Institute for Evolutionary Anthropology, in Leipzig, Germany, will announce an even more stunning achievement: the sequencing of a significant fraction of the genome of Neanderthals—the human-like species we picture when we hear the word caveman—who are far closer to us genetically than chimps are. And though Neanderthals became extinct tens of thousands of years ago, Pääbo is convinced he's on the way to reconstructing the entire genome of that long-lost relative, using DNA extracted, against all odds, from a 38,000-year-old bone.

Laid side by side, these three sets of genetic blueprints—plus the genomes of gorillas and other primates, which are already well on the way to being completely sequenced—will not only begin to explain precisely what makes us human but could lead to a better understanding of human diseases and how to treat them.

First Glimmerings

Scientists didn't need to wait for the chimp genome to begin speculating about the essential differences between humans and apes, of course. They didn't even need to know about

DNA. Much of the vitriol directed at Charles Darwin a century and a half ago came not from his ideas about evolution in general but from his insulting but logical implication that humans and the African apes are descended from a common ancestor.

As paleontologists have accumulated more and more fossils, they have compiled data on a long list of anatomical features, including body shape, bipedalism, brain size, the shape of the skull and face, the size of canine teeth, and opposable thumbs. Using comparative analyses of these attributes, along with dating that shows when various features appeared or vanished, they have constructed increasingly elaborate family trees that show the relationships between apes, ancient hominids and us. Along the way they learned, among other things, that Darwin, even with next to no actual data, was close to being right in his intuition that apes and humans are descended from a single common ancestor—and, surprisingly, that the ability to walk upright emerged millions of years before the evolution of our big brains.

But it wasn't until the 1960s that details of our physical relationship to the apes started to be understood at the level of basic biochemistry. Wayne State University scientist Morris Goodman showed, for example, that injecting a chicken with a particular blood protein from a human, a gorilla or a chimp provoked a specific immune response, whereas proteins from orangutans and gibbons produced no response at all. And by 1975, the then new science of molecular genetics had led to a landmark paper by two University of California, Berkeley, scientists, Mary-Claire King and Allan Wilson, estimating that chimps and humans share between 98% and 99% of their genetic material.

Zeroing in on the Genes

Even before the chimp genome was published, researchers had begun teasing out our genetic differences. As long ago as 1998, for example, glycobiologist Ajit Varki and colleagues at the University of California, San Diego, reported that humans have an altered form of a molecule called sialic acid on the surface of their cells. This variant is coded for by a single gene, which is damaged in humans. Since sialic acids act in part as a docking site for many pathogens, like malaria and influenza, this may explain why people are more susceptible to these diseases than, say, chimpanzees are.

3 billion—Number of base pairs in the human genome
1.23%—Percent that are different in the chimp genome

A few years later, a team led by Pääbo announced that the human version of a gene called FOXP2, which plays a role in our ability to develop speech and language, evolved within the past 200,000 years—after anatomically modern humans first appeared. By comparing the protein coded by the human FOXP2 gene with the same protein in various great apes and in mice, they discovered that the amino-acid sequence that makes up the human variant differs from that of the chimp in just two locations out of a total of 715—an extraordinarily small change that may nevertheless explain the emergence of all aspects of human speech, from a baby's first words to a Robin Williams monologue. And indeed, humans with a defective FOXP2 gene have trouble articulating words and understanding grammar.

Then, in 2004, a team led by Hansell Stedman of the University of Pennsylvania identified a tiny mutation in a gene on chromosome 7 that affects the production of myosin, the protein that enables muscle tissue to contract. The mutant gene prevents the expression of a myosin variant, known as MYH16, in the jaw muscles used in biting and chewing. Since the same mutation occurs in all of the modern human populations the researchers tested—but not in seven species of nonhuman primates, including chimps—the researchers suggest that lack of MYH16 made it possible for our ancestors to evolve smaller jaw muscles some 2 million years ago. That loss in muscle strength, they say, allowed the braincase and brain to grow larger. It's a controversial claim, one disputed by anthropologist C. Owen Lovejoy of Kent State University. "Brains don't expand because they were permitted to do so," he says. "They expand because they were selected"—because they conferred extra reproductive success on their owners, perhaps by allowing them to hunt more effectively than the competition.

Beyond the Genes

Still, the principle of gene-by-gene comparison remains a powerful one, and just a year ago geneticists got hold of a long-awaited tool for making those comparisons in bulk. Although the news was largely overshadowed by the impact of Hurricane Katrina, which hit the same week, the publication of a rough draft of the chimp genome in the journal *Nature* immediately told scientists several important things. First, they learned that overall, the sequences of base pairs that make up both species' genomes differ by 1.23%—a ringing confirmation of the 1970s estimates—and that the most striking divergence between them occurs, intriguingly, in the Y chromosome, present only in males. And when they compared the two species' proteins—the large molecules that cells construct according to blueprints embedded in the genes—they found that 29% of the proteins were identical (most of the proteins that aren't the same differ, on average, by only two amino-acid substitutions).

The genetic differences between chimps and humans, therefore, must be relatively subtle. And they can't all be due simply to a slightly different mix of genes. Even before the human genome was sequenced back in 2000, says biologist Sean Carroll of the University of Wisconsin, Madison, "it was estimated that humans had 100,000 genes. When we got the genome, the estimate dropped to 25,000. Now we know the overall number is about 22,000, and it might even come down to 19,000."

This shockingly small number made it clear to scientists that genes alone don't dictate the differences between species; the changes, they now know, also depend on molecular switches that tell genes when and where to turn on and off. "Take the genes involved in creating the hand, the penis and the vertebrae," says Lovejoy. "These share some of the same structural genes. The pelvis is another example. Humans have a radically different pelvis from that of apes. It's like having the blueprints for two different brick houses. The bricks are the same, but the results are very different."

Those molecular switches lie in the noncoding regions of the genome—once known dismissively as junk DNA but lately rechristened the dark matter of the genome. Much of the genome's dark matter is, in fact, junk—the residue of evolutionary events long forgotten and no longer relevant. But a subset of the dark matter known as functional noncoding DNA, comprising some 3% to 4% of the genome and mostly embedded within and around the genes, is crucial. "Coding regions are much easier for us to study," says Carroll, whose new book, *The Making of the Fittest: DNA and the Ultimate Forensic Record of Evolution,* delves deep into the issue. "But it may be the dark matter that governs a lot of what we actually see."

What causes changes in both the dark matter and the genes themselves as one species evolves into another is random mutation, in which individual base pairs—the "letters" of the genetic alphabet—are flipped around like a typographical error. These changes stem from errors that occur during sexual reproduction, as DNA is copied and recombined. Sometimes long strings of letters are duplicated, creating multiple copies in the offspring. Sometimes they're deleted altogether or even picked up, turned around and reinserted backward. A group led by geneticist Stephen Scherer of the Hospital for Sick Children in Toronto has identified 1,576 apparent inversions between the chimp and human genomes; more than half occurred sometime during human evolution.

When an inversion, deletion or duplication occurs in an unused portion of the genome, nothing much changes—and indeed, the human, chimp and other genomes are full of such inert stretches of DNA. When it happens in a gene or in a functional noncoding stretch, by contrast, an inversion or a duplication is often harmful. But sometimes, purely by chance, the change gives the new organism some sort of advantage that enables it to produce more offspring, thus perpetuating the change in another generation.

What the Apes Can Teach Us

A striking example of how gene duplication may have helped propel us away from our apelike origins appeared in *Science* last month. A research team led by James Sikela of the University of Colorado at Denver and Health Sciences Center, in Aurora, Colo., looked at a gene that is believed to code for a piece of protein, called DUF1220, found in areas of the brain associated with higher cognitive function. The gene comes in

multiple copies in a wide range of primates—but, the scientists found, humans carry the most copies. African great apes have substantially fewer copies, and the number found in more distant kin—orangutans and Old World monkeys—drops off even more.

Another discovery, first published online by *Nature* two months ago, describes a gene that appears to play a role in human brain development. A team led by biostatistician Katherine Pollard, now at the University of California, Davis, and Sofie Salama, of U.C. Santa Cruz, used a sophisticated computer program to search the genomes of humans, chimps and other vertebrates for segments that have undergone changes at substantially accelerated rates. They eventually homed in on 49 discrete areas they dubbed human accelerated regions, or HARS.

The region that changed most dramatically from chimps to humans, known as HAR1, turns out to be part of a gene that is active in fetal brain tissue only between the seventh and 19th weeks of gestation. Although the gene's precise function is unknown, that happens to be the period when a protein called reelin helps the human cerebral cortex develop its characteristic six-layer structure. What makes the team's research especially intriguing is that all but two of the HARs lie in those enigmatic functional noncoding regions of the genome, supporting the idea that much of the difference between species happens there.

Sex with Chimps?

Comparisons of primitive genomes have also led to an astonishing, controversial and somewhat disquieting assertion about the origin of humanity. Along with several colleagues, David Reich of the Broad Institute in Cambridge, Mass., compared DNA from chimpanzees and humans with genetic material from gorillas, orangutans and macaques. Scientists have long used the average difference between genomes as a sort of evolutionary clock because more closely related species have had less time to evolve in different directions. Reich's team measured how the evolutionary clock varied across chromosomes in the different species. To their surprise, they deduced that chimps and humans split from a common ancestor no more than 6.3 million years ago and probably less than 5.4 million years ago. If they're correct, several hominid species now considered to be among our earliest ancestors—*Sahelanthropus tchadensis* (7 million years old), Orrorin tugenensis (about 6 million years old) and *Ardipithecus kadabba* (5.2 to 5.7 million years old)—may have to be re-evaluated.

And that's not the most startling finding. Reich's team also found that the entire human X chromosome diverged from the chimp's X chromosome about 1.2 million years later than the other chromosomes. One plausible explanation is that chimps and humans first split but later interbred from time to time before finally going their separate evolutionary ways. That could explain why some of the most ancient fossils now considered human ancestors have such striking mixtures of chimp and human traits some could actually have been hybrids. Or they might have simply coexisted with, or even predated, the last common ancestor of chimps and humans.

All of that depends in part on the accuracy of fossil dating and the reliability of using genetic variation as a clock. Both methods currently carry big margins of error. But the more primate genomes that geneticists can lay side by side, the more questions they will be able to answer. "We have rough sequences for humans, orangutans, chimps, macaques," says Eric Lander, director of the Broad Institute and a leader of the research team that decoded the chimpanzee genome. "But we don't have the entire gorilla genome yet. Lemurs are coming along, and so are gibbons."

Decoding Neanderthals

Also coming along, thanks to two independent teams of researchers, is the genome of the closest relative of all: the Neanderthal. Ancestors of Neanderthals first appeared some 500,000 years ago, and for a long time it was a toss-up whether that lineage would outlive our own species, at least in Europe and western Asia—or whether, bizarre as it seems today, they would both survive indefinitely. The Neanderthals held out for hundreds of thousands of years. A discovery published online by *Nature* last month suggests Neanderthals may have made their last stand in Gibraltar, on the southern tip of the Iberian Peninsula, surviving until about 28,000 years ago—and possibly even longer.

The Neanderthals weren't nearly as primitive as many assume, observes Eddy Rubin, director of the Department of Energy's Joint Genome Institute in Walnut Creek, Calif. "They had fire, burial ceremonies, the rudiments of what we would call art. They were advanced—but nothing like what humans have done in the last 10,000 to 15,000 years." We eventually out-competed them, and the key to how we did so may well lie in our genes. So two years ago, Svante Pääbo, the man who deconstructed the FOXP2 language gene and has done considerable research on ancient DNA, launched an effort to re-create the Neanderthal genome. Rubin, meanwhile, is tackling the same task using a different technique.

The job isn't an easy one. Like any complex organic molecule, DNA degrades over time, and bones that lie in the ground for thousands of years become badly contaminated with the DNA of bacteria and fungi. Anyone who handles the fossils can also leave human DNA behind. After probing the remains of about 60 different Neanderthals out of the 400 or so known, Pääbo and his team found only two with viable material. Moreover, he estimates, only about 6% of the genetic material his team extracts from the bones turns out to be Neanderthal DNA.

As a result, progress is maddeningly slow. And while he can't reveal details, Pääbo says he'll soon be announcing in a major scientific journal the sequencing of 1 million base pairs of the Neanderthal genome. And he says he has 4 million more in the bag. Rubin, meanwhile, is also poised to publish his results, but refuses to divulge specifics. "Pääbo's team has significantly

more of a sequence than we do," he says. "Some of the dates will differ, but the conclusions are largely similar."

Although Pääbo admits that he still hasn't learned much about what distinguishes us from our closest cousins, simply showing he can reconstruct significant DNA sequences from such long-dead creatures is an important proof of concept. Both he and Rubin agree that within a couple of years a reasonably complete Neanderthal genome should be available. "It will tell us about aspects of biology, like soft tissue, that we can't say anything about right now," Rubin notes. "It could tell us about disease susceptibility and immunity. And in places where the sequence overlaps that of humans, it will enable us to compare a prehistoric creature with chimps." Someday it may even be possible to insert equivalent segments of human and Neanderthal DNA into different laboratory mice in order to see what effects they produce.

What It All Means

Precisely how useful this information will be is hard to assess. Indeed, a few experts are dismissive of the whole project. "I'm not sure what Neanderthals will tell us," says Kent State's Lovejoy. "They're real late [in terms of human evolution]. And they represent, at best, a little environmental isolate in Europe. I can't imagine we're going to learn much about human evolution by studying them." Lovejoy is even more dismissive about claims that ancestors of chimps and humans interbred, arguing that using mutation rates in the genome to time evolutionary changes is extraordinarily imprecise.

In fact, even the most ardent proponents of genome-comparison research acknowledge that pretty much everything we know so far is preliminary. "We're interested in traits that really distance us from other organisms," says Wisconsin's Carroll, "such as susceptibility to diseases, big brains, speech, walking upright, opposable thumbs. Based on the biology of other organisms, we have to believe that those are very complex traits. The development of form, the increase in brain size, took place over a long period of time, maybe 50,000 generations. It's a pretty complicated genetic recipe."

But even the toughest critics acknowledge that these studies have enormous potential. "We will eventually be able to pinpoint every difference between every animal on the planet," says Lovejoy. "And every time you throw another genome, like the gorilla's, into the mix, you increase the chances even more."

Some of the differences could have enormous practical consequences. Since his discovery that human cells lack one specific form of sialic acid, which was accomplished even before the human genome was decoded, Varki and his collaborators have determined that 10 of the 60 or so genes that govern sialic-acid biology show major differences between chimps and humans. "And in every case," says Varki, "it's humans who are the odd one out." Such revelations could probably lead to a better understanding of such devastating diseases as malaria, AIDS and viral hepatitis and likely do so faster than by studying the human genome alone.

For most of us, though, it's the grand question about what it is that makes us human that renders comparative genome studies so compelling. As scientists keep reminding us, evolution is a random process in which haphazard genetic changes interact with random environmental conditions to produce an organism somehow fitter than its fellows. After 3.5 billion years of such randomness, a creature emerged that could ponder its own origins—and revel in a Mozart adagio. Within a few short years, we may finally understand precisely when and how that happened.

The Age of Genetic Technology Arrives

LEON R. KASS

As one contemplates the current and projected state of genetic knowledge and technology, one is astonished by how far we have come in the less than fifty years since Watson and Crick first announced the structure of DNA. True, soon after that discovery, scientists began seriously to discuss the futuristic prospects of gene therapy for genetic disease and of genetic engineering more generally. But no one then imagined how rapidly genetic technology would emerge. The Human Genome Project, disclosing the DNA sequences of all thirty thousand human genes, is all but completed. And even without comprehensive genomic knowledge, biotech business is booming. According to a recent report by the research director for GlaxoSmithKline, enough sequencing data are available to keep his researchers busy for the next twenty years, developing early-detection screening techniques, rationally designed vaccines, genetically engineered changes in malignant tumors leading to enhanced immune response, and, ultimately, precise gene therapy for specific genetic diseases. The age of genetic technology has arrived.

Genetic technology comes into existence as part of the large humanitarian project to cure disease, prolong life, and alleviate suffering. As such, it occupies the moral high ground of compassionate healing. Who would not welcome personal genetic profiling that would enable doctors to customize the most effective and safest drug treatments for individuals with hypertension or rheumatoid arthritis? Who would not welcome genetic therapy to correct the defects that lead to sickle cell anemia, Huntington's disease, and breast cancer, or to protect against the immune deficiency caused by the AIDS virus?

And yet genetic technology has also aroused considerable public concern, for it strikes most people as different from other biomedical technologies. Even people duly impressed by the astonishing genetic achievements of the last decades and eager for the medical benefits are nonetheless ambivalent about these new developments. For they sense that genetic technology, while in some respects continuous with the traditional medical project of compassionate healing, also represents something radically new and disquieting. Often hard-pressed to articulate the precise basis of their disquiet, they talk rather in general terms about the dangers of eugenics or the fear of "tampering with human genes" or, for that matter, "playing God."

Enthusiasts for genetic technology, made confident by their expertise and by their growing prestige and power, are often impatient with the public's disquiet. Much of it they attribute to ignorance of science: "If the public only knew what we know, it would see things our way and give up its irrational fears." For the rest, they blame outmoded moral and religious notions, ideas that scientists insist no longer hold water and only serve to obstruct scientific progress.

In my own view, the scientists' attempt to cast the debate as a battle of beneficial and knowledgeable cleverness versus ignorant and superstitious anxiety should be resisted. For the public is right to be ambivalent about genetic technology, and no amount of instruction in molecular biology and genetics should allay its—our—legitimate human concerns. Rightly understood, these worries are, in fact, in touch with the deepest matters of our humanity and dignity, and we ignore them at our peril.

I will not dispute here which of the prophesied technologies will in fact prove feasible or how soon.[1] To be sure, as a practical matter we must address the particular ethical issues raised by each new technical power as it comes into existence. But the moral meaning of the entire enterprise does not depend on the precise details regarding what and when. I shall proceed by raising a series of questions, the first of which is an attempt to say how genetic technology is different.

Is Genetic Technology Special?

What is different about genetic technology? At first glance, not much. Isolating a disease-inducing aberrant gene looks fairly continuous with isolating a disease-inducing intracellular virus. Supplying diabetics with normal genes for producing insulin has the same medical goal as supplying them with insulin for injection.

Nevertheless, despite these obvious similarities, genetic technology is also decisively different. When fully developed, it will wield two powers not shared by ordinary medical practice. Medicine treats only existing individuals, and it treats them only remedially, seeking to correct deviations from a more or less stable norm of health. By contrast, genetic engineering will, first of all, deliberately make changes that are transmissible into succeeding generations and may even alter in advance specific *future* individuals through direct "germ-line" or embryo interventions. Secondly, genetic engineering may be able, through so-called genetic enhancement, to create new human capacities and, hence, new norms of health and fitness.[2]

For the present, it is true, genetic technology is hailed primarily for its ability better to diagnose and treat *disease* in *existing* individuals. Confined to such practices, it would raise few questions (beyond the usual ones of safety and efficacy). Even intrauterine gene therapy for existing fetuses with diagnosable genetic disease could be seen as an extension of the growing field of fetal medicine.

But there is no reason to believe that the use of gene-altering powers can be so confined, either in logic or in practice. For one thing, "germ-line" gene therapy and manipulation, affecting not merely the unborn but also the unconceived,[3] is surely in our future. The practice has numerous justifications, beginning with the desire to reverse the unintended dysgenic effects of modern medical success. Thanks to medicine, for example, individuals who would have died from diabetes now live long enough to transmit their disease-producing genes. Why, it has been argued, should we not reverse these unfortunate changes by deliberate intervention? More generally, why should we not effect precise genetic alteration in disease-carrying sperm or eggs or early embryos, in order to prevent in advance the emergence of disease that otherwise will later require expensive and burdensome treatment? In short, even before we have had more than trivial experience with gene therapy for existing individuals—none of it successful—sober people have called for overturning the current (self-imposed) taboo on germ-line modification. The line between somatic and germ-line modification cannot hold.

Despite the naive hopes of many, neither will we be able to defend the boundary between therapy and genetic enhancement. Will we reject novel additions to the human genome that enable us to produce, internally, vitamins or amino acids we now must get in our diet? Will we decline to make alterations in the immune system that will increase its efficacy or make it impervious to HIV? When genetic profiling becomes able to disclose the genetic contributions to height or memory or intelligence, will we deny prospective parents the right to enhance the potential of their children?[4] Finally, should we discover—as no doubt we will—the genetic switches that control our biological clock and that very likely influence also the maximum human life expectancy, will we opt to keep our hands off the rate of aging or our natural human life span? Not a chance.

We thus face a paradox. On the one hand, genetic technology really *is* different. It can and will go to work directly and deliberately on our basic, heritable, life-shaping capacities at their biological roots. It can take us beyond existing norms of health and healing—perhaps even alter fundamental features of human nature. On the other hand, precisely because the goals it will serve, at least to begin with, will be continuous with those of modern high-interventionist medicine, we will find its promise familiar and irresistible.

This paradox itself contributes to public disquiet: rightly perceiving a powerful difference in genetic technology, we also sense that we are powerless to establish, on the basis of that difference, clear limits to its use. The genetic genie, first unbottled to treat disease, will go its own way, whether we like it or not.

How Much Genetic Self-Knowledge Is Good for Us?

Quite apart from worries about genetic engineering, gaining genetic knowledge is itself a legitimate cause of anxiety, not least because of one of its most touted benefits—the genetic profiling of individuals. There has been much discussion about how knowledge of someone's genetic defects, if leaked to outsiders, could be damaging in terms of landing a job or gaining health or life insurance, and legislative measures have been enacted to guard against such hazards. Little attention has been paid, however, to the implications of genetic knowledge for the person himself. Yet the deepest problem connected with learning your own genetic sins and unhealthy predispositions is neither the threat to confidentiality nor the risk of "genetic discrimination" in employment or insurance, important though these practical problems may be.[5] It is, rather, the various hazards and deformations in living your life that will attach to knowing in advance your likely or possible medical future. To be sure, in some cases such foreknowledge will be welcome, if it can lead to easy measures to prevent or treat the impending disorder, and if the disorder in question does not powerfully affect self-image or self-command. But will and should we welcome knowledge that we carry a predisposition to Alzheimer's disease or schizophrenia, or genes that will definitely produce, at an unknown future time, a serious but untreatable disease?

Still harder will it be for most people to live easily and wisely with less certain information—say, where multigenic traits are involved. The recent case of a father who insisted that ovariectomy and mastectomy be performed on his ten-year-old daughter because she happened to carry the BRCA-1 gene for breast cancer dramatically shows the toxic effective of genetic knowledge.

Less dramatic but more profound is the threat to human freedom and spontaneity, a subject explored twenty-five years ago by the philosopher Hans Jonas, one of our wisest commentators on technology and the human prospect. As Jonas observed, "Knowledge of the future, especially one's own, has always been excepted [from the injunction to 'Know thyself'] and the attempt to gain it by whatever means (astrology is one) disparaged—as futile superstition by the enlightened, but as sin by theologians." Everyone remembers that Prometheus was the philanthropic god who gave fire and the arts to humans. But it is often forgotten that he gave them also the greater gift of "blind hopes"—"to cease seeing doom before their eyes"—precisely because he knew that ignorance of one's own future fate was indispensable to aspiration and achievement. I suspect that many people, taking their bearings from life lived open-endedly rather than from preventive medicine practiced rationally, would prefer ignorance of the future to the scientific astrology of knowing their genetic profile. In a free society, that would be their right.

Or would it? This leads us to the third question.

What About Freedom?

Even people who might otherwise welcome the growth of genetic knowledge and technology are worried about the coming power of geneticists, genetic engineers and, in particular, governmental authorities armed with genetic technology.[6] Precisely because we have been taught by these very scientists that genes hold the secret of life, and that our genotype is our essence if not quite our destiny, we are made nervous by those whose expert knowledge and technique touch our very being. Even apart from any particular abuses and misuses of power, friends of human freedom have deep cause for concern.

C. S. Lewis, no friend of ignorance, put the matter sharply in *The Abolition of Man*:

> If any one age really attains, by eugenics and scientific education, the power to make its descendants what it pleases, all men who live after it are the patients of that power. . . . But even within this master generation (itself an infinitesimal minority of the species) the power will be exercised by a minority smaller still. Man's conquest of Nature, if the dreams of some scientific planners are realized, means the rule of a few hundreds of men over billions upon billions of men.

Most genetic technologists will hardly recognize themselves in this portrait. Though they concede that abuses or misuses of power may occur, especially in tyrannical regimes, they see themselves not as predestinators but as facilitators, merely providing increased knowledge and technique that people can freely choose to use in making decisions about their health or reproductive choices. Genetic power, they tell us, serves not to limit freedom, but to increase it.

But as we can see from the already existing practices of genetic screening and prenatal diagnosis, this claim is at best self-deceptive, at worst disingenuous. The choice to develop and practice genetic screening and the choices of which genes to target for testing have been made not by the public but by scientists—and not on liberty-enhancing but on eugenic grounds. In many cases, practitioners of prenatal diagnosis refuse to do fetal genetic screening in the absence of a prior commitment from the pregnant woman to abort any afflicted fetus. In other situations, pregnant women who still wish *not* to know prenatal facts must withstand strong medical pressures for testing.

In addition, economic pressures to contain health-care costs will almost certainly constrain free choice. Refusal to provide insurance coverage for this or that genetic disease may eventually work to compel genetic abortion or intervention. State-mandated screening already occurs for PKU (phenylketonuria) and other diseases, and full-blown genetic screening programs loom large on the horizon. Once these arrive, there will likely be an upsurge of economic pressure to limit reproductive freedom. All this will be done, of course, in the name of the well-being of children.

Already in 1971, geneticist Bentley Glass, in his presidential address to the American Association for the Advancement of Science, enunciated "the right of every child to be born with a sound physical and mental constitution, based on a sound genotype." Looking ahead to the reproductive and genetic technologies that are today rapidly arriving, Glass proclaimed: "No parents will in that future time have a right to burden society with a malformed or a mentally incompetent child." It remains to be seen to what extent such prophecies will be realized. But they surely provide sufficient and reasonable grounds for being concerned about

restrictions on human freedoms, even in the absence of overt coercion, and even in liberal polities like our own.

What about Human Dignity?

Here, rather than in the more-discussed fears about freedom, lie our deepest concerns, and rightly so. For threats to human dignity can—and probably will—arise even with the free, humane, and "enlightened" use of these technologies. Genetic technology, the practices it will engender, and above all the scientific teachings about human life on which it rests are not, as many would have it, morally and humanly neutral. Regardless of how they are practiced or taught, they are pregnant with their own moral meanings and will necessarily bring with them changes in our practices, our institutions, our norms, our beliefs, and our self-conception. It is, I submit, these challenges to our dignity and humanity that are at the bottom of our anxiety over genetic science and technology. Let me touch briefly on four aspects of this most serious matter.

"Playing God"

Paradoxically, worries about dehumanization are sometimes expressed in the fear of superhumanization, that is, that man will be "playing God." This complaint is too facilely dismissed by scientists and nonbelievers. The concern has meaning, God or no God.

Never mind the exaggeration that lurks in this conceit of man's playing God. (Even at his most powerful, after all, man is capable only of *playing* God.) Never mind the implicit innuendo that nobody has given to others this creative and judgmental authority, or the implicit retort that there is theological warrant for acting as God's co-creator in overcoming the ills and suffering of the world. Consider only that if scientists are seen in this godlike role of creator, judge, and savior, the rest of us must stand before them as supplicating, tainted creatures. Despite the hyperbolic speech, that is worry enough.

Practitioners of prenatal diagnosis, working today with but a fraction of the information soon to be available from the Human Genome Project, already screen for a long list of genetic diseases and abnormalities, from Down syndrome to dwarfism. Possession of any one of these defects, they believe, renders a prospective child unworthy of life. Persons who happen still to be born with these conditions, having somehow escaped the spreading net of detection and eugenic abortion, are increasingly regarded as "mistakes," as inferior human beings who should not have been born.[7] Not long ago, at my own university, a physician making rounds with medical students stood over the bed of an intelligent, otherwise normal ten-year-old boy with spina bifida. "Were he to have been conceived today," the physician casually informed his entourage, "he would have been aborted." Determining who shall live and who shall die—on the basis of genetic merit—is a godlike power already wielded by genetic medicine. This power will only grow.

Manufacture & Commodification

But, one might reply, genetic technology also holds out the premise of redemption, of a *cure* for these life-crippling and life-forfeiting disorders. Very well. But in order truly to practice their salvific power, genetic technologists will have to increase greatly their manipulations and interventions, well beyond merely screening and weeding out. True, in some cases genetic testing and risk management aimed at prevention may actually cut down on the need for high-tech interventions aimed at cure. But in many other cases, ever-greater genetic scrutiny will lead necessarily to ever more extensive manipulation. And, to produce Bentley Glass's healthy and well-endowed babies, let alone babies with the benefits of genetic enhancement, a new scientific obstetrics will be necessary, one that will come very close to turning human procreation into manufacture.

This process was already crudely begun with in vitro fertilization. It is now taking giant steps forward with the ability to screen in vitro embryos before implantation (so-called pre-implantation genetic diagnosis). And it will come to maturity with interventions such as cloning and, eventually, with precise genetic engineering. Just follow the logic and the aspirations of current practice: the road we are traveling leads all the way to the world of designer babies—reached not by dictatorial fiat, but by the march of benevolent humanitarianism, and cheered on by an ambivalent citizenry that also dreads becoming merely the last of man's manmade things.

Make no mistake: the price to be paid for producing optimum or even only genetically sound babies will be the transfer of procreation from the home to the laboratory. Such an arrangement will be profoundly dehumanizing, no matter how genetically good or healthy the resultant children. And let us not forget the powerful economic interests that will surely operate in this area; with their advent, the commodification of nascent human life will be unstoppable.

Standards, Norms, & Goals

According to Genesis, God, in His creating, looked at His creatures and saw that there were *good*—intact, complete, well-working wholes, true to the spoken idea that guided their creation. What standards will guide the genetic engineers?

For the time being, one might answer, the norm of health. But even before the genetic enhancers join the party, the standard of health is being deconstructed. Are you healthy if, although you show no symptoms, you carry genes that will definitely produce Huntington's disease? What if you carry, say, 40 percent of the genetic markers thought to be linked to the appearance of Alzheimer's disease? And what will "healthy" and "normal" mean when we discover your genetic propensities for alcoholism, drug abuse, pederasty, or violence?[8] The idea of health progressively becomes at once both imperial and vague: medicalization of what have hitherto been mental or moral matters paradoxically brings with it the disappearance of any clear standard of health itself.

Once genetic *enhancement* comes on the scene, standards of health, wholeness, or fitness will be needed more than ever, but just then is when all pretense of standards will go out the window. "Enhancement" is, of course, a euphemism for "improvement," and the idea of improvement necessarily implies a good, a better, and perhaps even a best. If, however, we can no longer look to our previously unalterable human nature for a standard or norm of what is good or better, how will anyone know what constitutes an improvement? It will not do to assert that we can

extrapolate from what we like about ourselves. Because memory is good, can we say how much more memory would be better? If sexual desire is good, how much more would be better? Life is good, but how much extension of the life span would be good for us? Only simplistic thinkers believe they can easily answer such questions.[9]

More modest enhancers, like more modest genetic therapists and technologists, eschew grandiose goals. They are valetudinarians, not eugenicists. They pursue not some faraway positive good, but the positive elimination of evils: diseases, pain, suffering, the likelihood of death. But let us not be deceived. Hidden in all this avoidance of evil is nothing less than the quasi-messianic goal of a painless, suffering-free and, finally, immortal existence. Only the presence of such a goal justifies the sweeping-aside of any opposition to the relentless march of medical science. Only such a goal gives trumping moral power to the principle "cure disease, relieve suffering."

"Cloning human beings is unethical and dehumanizing, you say? Never mind: it will help us treat infertility, avoid genetic disease, and provide perfect materials for organ replacement." Such, indeed, was the tenor of the June 1997 report of the National Bioethics Advisory Commission, *Cloning Human Beings*. Notwithstanding its call for a temporary ban on the practice, the only moral objection the commission could agree upon was that cloning "is not safe to use in humans at this time," because the technique has yet to be perfected.[10] Even this elite ethical body, in other words, was unable to muster any other moral argument sufficient to cause us to forgo the possible health benefits of cloning.[11]

The same argument will also justify creating and growing human embryos for experimentation, revising the definition of death to increase the supply of organs for transplantation, growing human body parts in the peritoneal cavities of animals, perfusing newly dead bodies as factories for useful biological substances, or reprogramming the human body and mind with genetic or neurobiological engineering. Who can sustain an objection if these practices will help us live longer and with less overt suffering?

It turns out that even the more modest biogenetic engineers, whether they know it or not, are in the immortality business, proceeding on the basis of a quasi-religious faith that all innovation is by definition progress, no matter what is sacrificed to attain it.

The Tragedy of Success

What the enthusiasts do not see is that their utopian project will not eliminate suffering but merely shift it around. Forgetting that contentment requires that our desires do not outpace our powers, they have not noticed that the enormous medical progress of the last half-century has not left the present generation satisfied. Indeed, we are already witnessing a certain measure of public discontent as a paradoxical result of rising expectations in the health care field: although their actual health has improved substantially in recent decades, people's *satisfaction* with their current health status has remained the same or declined. But that is hardly the highest cost of success in the medical/humanitarian project.

As Aldous Huxley made clear in his prophetic, *Brave New World,* the road chosen and driven by compassionate humaneness paved by biotechnology, if traveled to the end, leads not to human fulfillment but to human debasement. Perfected bodies are achieved at the price of flattened souls. What Tolstoy called "real life"—life in its immediacy, vividness, and rootedness—has been replaced by an utterly mediated, sterile, and disconnected existence. In one word: dehumanization, the inevitable result of making the essence of human nature the final object of the conquest of nature for the relief of man's estate. Like Midas, bioengineered man will be cursed to acquire precisely what he wished for, only to discover—painfully and too late—that what he wished for is not exactly what he wanted. Or, worse than Midas, he may be so dehumanized he will not even recognize that in aspiring to be perfect, he is no longer even truly human. To paraphrase Bertrand Russell, technological humanitarianism is like a warm bath that heats up so imperceptibly you don't know when to scream.

The main point here is not the rightness or wrongness of this or that imagined scenario; all this is, admittedly, highly speculative. I surely have no way of knowing whether my worst fears will be realized, but you surely have no way of knowing they will not. The point is rather the plausibility, even the wisdom, of thinking about genetic technology like the entire technological venture, under the ancient and profound idea of tragedy in which success and failure are inseparably grown together like the concave and the convex. What I am suggesting is that genetic technology's way of approaching human life, a way spurred on by the utopian promises and perfectionist aims of modern thought and its scientific crusaders, may well turn out to be inevitable, heroic, and doomed. If this suggestion holds water, then the question regarding genetic technology is not "triumph *OR* tragedy," because the answer is "both together."

In the nineteenth and early twentieth century, the challenge came in the form of Darwinism and its seeming opposition to biblical religion, a battle initiated not so much by the scientists as by the beleaguered defenders of orthodoxy. In our own time, the challenge comes from molecular biology, behavioral genetics, and evolutionary psychology, fueled by their practitioners' overconfident belief in the sufficiency of their reductionist explanations of all vital and human phenomena. Never mind "created in the image of God"; what elevated *humanistic* view of human life or human goodness is defensible against the belief, asserted by most public and prophetic voices of biology, that man is just a collection of molecules, an accident on the stage of evolution, a freakish speck of mind in a mindless universe, fundamentally no different from other living—or even nonliving—things? What chance have our treasured ideas of freedom and dignity against the reductive notion of "the selfish gene" (or, for that matter, of "genes for altruism"), the belief that DNA is the essence of life, or the teaching that all human behavior and our rich inner life are rendered intelligible only in terms of their contributions to species survival and reproductive success?

These transformations are, in fact, welcomed by many of our leading scientists and intellectuals. In 1997 the luminaries of the International Academy of Humanism—including biologists Crick, Dawkins, and Wilson, and humanists Isaiah Berlin, W. V. Quine, and Kurt Vonnegut—issued a statement in defense of cloning research in higher mammals and human beings. Their reasons were revealing:

> Views of human nature rooted in humanity's tribal past ought not to be our primary criterion for making moral decisions about cloning. . . . The potential benefits of cloning may be so immense that it would be a tragedy if ancient theological scruples should lead to a Luddite rejection of cloning.

In order to justify ongoing research, these intellectuals were willing to shed not only traditional religious views, but any view of human distinctiveness and special dignity, their own included. They failed to see that the scientific view of man they celebrated does more than insult our vanity. It undermines our self-conception as free, thoughtful, and responsible beings, worthy of respect because we alone among the animals have minds and hearts that aim far higher than the mere perpetuation of our genes.

The problem may lie not so much with scientific findings themselves, but with the shallow philosophy that recognizes no other truths but these and with the arrogant pronouncements of the bioprophets. For example, in a letter to the editor complaining about a review of his book *How the Mind Works,* the well-known evolutionary psychologist and popularizer Stephen Pinker rails against any appeal to the human soul:

> Unfortunately for that theory, brain science has shown that the mind is what the brain does. The supposedly immaterial soul can be bisected with a knife, altered by chemicals, turned on or off by electricity, and extinguished by a sharp blow or a lack of oxygen. Centuries ago it was unwise to ground morality on the dogma that the earth sat at the center of the universe. It is just as unwise today to ground it on dogmas about souls endowed by God.

One hardly knows whether to be more impressed by the height of Pinker's arrogance or by the depth of his shallowness. But he speaks with the authority of science, and few are able and willing to dispute him on his own grounds.

There is, of course, nothing novel about reductionism, materialism, and determinism of the kind displayed here; these are doctrines with which Socrates contended long ago. What is new is that, as philosophies, they seem (to many people) to be vindicated by scientific advance. Here, in consequence, is perhaps the most pernicious result of our technological progress, more dehumanizing than any actual manipulation or technique, present or future: the erosion, perhaps the final erosion, of the idea of man as noble, dignified, precious, or godlike, and its replacement with a view of man, no less than of nature, as mere raw material for manipulation and homogenization.

Hence our peculiar moral crisis. We are in turbulent seas without a landmark precisely because we adhere more and more to a view of human life that both gives us enormous power and, *at the same time,* denies every possibility of nonarbitrary standards for guiding its use. Though well equipped, we know not who we are or where we are going. We triumph over nature's unpredictability only to subject ourselves, tragically, to the still greater unpredictability of our capricious wills and our fickle opinions. Engineering the engineer as well as the engine, we race our train we know not where. That we do not recognize our predicament is itself a tribute to the depth of our infatuation with scientific progress and our naive faith in the sufficiency of our humanitarian impulses.

Does this mean that I am therefore in favor of ignorance, suffering, and death? Of killing the goose of genetic technology even before she lays her golden eggs? Surely not. But unless we mobilize the courage to look foursquare at the full human meaning of our new enterprise in biogenetic technology and engineering, we are doomed to become its creatures if not its slaves. Important though it is to set a moral boundary here, devise a regulation there, hoping to decrease the damage caused by this or that little rivulet, it is even more important to be sober about the true nature and meaning of the flood itself.

That our exuberant new biologists and their technological minions might be persuaded of this is, to say the least, highly unlikely. For all their ingenuity, they do not even seek the wisdom that just might yield the kind of knowledge that keeps human life human. But it is not too late for the rest of us to become aware of the dangers—not just to privacy or insurability, but to our very humanity. So aware, we might be better able to defend the increasingly beleaguered vestiges and principles of our human dignity, even as we continue to reap the considerable benefits that genetic technology will inevitably provide.

Notes

1. I will also not dispute here the scientists' reductive understanding of life and their treatment of rich vital activities solely in terms of the interactions of genes. I do, however, touch on the moral significance of such reductionism toward the end of this essay.

2. Some commentators, in disagreement with these arguments, insist that genetic technology differs only in degree from previous human practices that have existed for millennia. For example, they see no difference between the "social engineering" of education, which works on the next generation through speech or symbolic deed, and biological engineering, which inscribes its effects, directly and irreversibly, into the human constitution. Or they claim to see no difference between the indirect genetic effects of human mate selection and deliberate, direct genetic engineering to produce offspring with precise biological capacities. Such critics, I fear, have already bought into a reductionist view of human life and the relation between the generations. And they ignore the fact that most people choose their mates for reasons different from stud farming.

3. Correction of a genetically abnormal egg or sperm (that is, of the "germ cells"), however, worthy an activity, stretches the meaning of "therapy" beyond all normal uses. Just who is the "patient" being "treated"? The potential child-to-be that might be formed out of such egg or sperm is, at the time of the treatment, at best no more than a hope and a hypothesis. There is no medical analogue for treatment of nonexistent patients.

4. To be sure, not all attempts at enhancement will require genetic alterations. We have already witnessed efforts to boost height with supplementary growth hormone or athletic performance with steroids or "blood doping." Nevertheless, the largest possible changes in what is "normally" human are likely to come about only with the help of genetic alterations or the joining of machines (for example, computers) to human beings.

5. I find it odd that it is these issues that have been put forward as the special ethical problems associated with genetic technology and the Human Genome Project. Issues of privacy and risks of discrimination related to medical conditions are entirely independent of whether the medical condition is genetic in origin. Only if a special stigma were attached to having an inherited disease—for example, only if having thalassemia or sickle cell anemia were more shameful than having gonorrhea or lung cancer—would the genetic character of a disease create special or additional reasons for protecting against breaches of confidentiality or discrimination in the workplace.

6. Until the events of September 11 and the anthrax scare that followed, they did not worry enough. It is remarkable that most bioethical discussions of genetic technology had naively neglected its potential usefulness in creating biological weapons, such as, to begin with, antibiotic-resistant plague bacteria, or later, aerosols containing cancer-inducing or mind-scrambling viral vectors. The most outstanding molecular geneticists were especially naive in this area. When American molecular biologists convened the 1975 Asilomar Conference on recombinant DNA research, which called for a voluntary moratorium on experiments until the biohazards could be evaluated, they invited Soviet biologists to the meeting who said virtually nothing but who photographed every slide that was shown.

7. One of the most worrisome but least appreciated aspects of the godlike power of the new genetics is its tendency to "redefine" a human being in terms of his genes. Once a person is decisively characterized by his genotype, it is but a short step to justifying death solely for genetic sins.

8. Many scientists suspect that we have different inherited propensities for these and other behavioral troubles, though it is almost certain that there is no single "gene for x" that is responsible.

9. This strikes me as the deepest problem with positive eugenics: less the threat of coercion, more the presumption of thinking we are wise enough to engineer "improvements" in the human species.

10. This is, of course, not an objection to cloning itself but only to hazards tied to the technique used to produce the replicated children.

11. I forbear mentioning what is rapidly becoming another trumping argument: increasing the profits of my biotech company and its shareholders, an argument often presented in more public-spirited dress: if we don't do it, other countries will, and we will lose our competitive edge in biotechnology.

LEON R. KASS, M.D. is professor in social thought at the University of Chicago, Hertog fellow at the American Enterprise Institute, and chairman of the President's Council on Bioethics. Excerpted from Life, Liberty and the Defense of Dignity. Published by Encounter Books, San Francisco, October 2002. Reprinted with permission.

The Mystery of Fetal Life: Secrets of the Womb

JOHN PEKKANEN

In the dim light of an ultrasound room, a wand slides over the abdomen of a young woman. As it emits sound waves, it allows us to see into her womb. The video screen brightens with a grainy image of a 20-week-old fetus. It floats in its amniotic sac, like an astronaut free of gravity.

The fetal face stares upward, then turns toward us, as if to mug for the camera. The sound waves strike different tissues with different densities, and their echoes form different images. These images are computer-enhanced, so although the fetus weighs only 14 ounces and is no longer than my hand, we can see its elfin features.

Close up, we peek into the fetal brain. In the seconds we observe, a quarter million new brain cells are born. This happens constantly. By the end of the nine months, the baby's brain will hold 100 billion brain cells.

The sound waves focus on the chest, rendering images of a vibrating four-chambered heart no bigger than the tip of my little finger. The monitor tells us it is moving at 163 beats a minute. It sounds like a frightened bird fluttering in its cage.

We watch the rib cage move. Although the fetus lives in an airless environment, it "breathes" intermittently inside the womb by swallowing amniotic fluid. Some researchers speculate that the fetus is exercising its chest and diaphragm as its way of preparing for life outside the womb.

The clarity of ultrasound pictures is now so good that subtle abnormalities can be detected. The shape of the skull, brain, and spinal cord, along with the heart and other vital organs, can be seen in breathtaking detail.

In this ultrasound exam, there are no hints to suggest that anything is abnormal. The husband squeezes his wife's hand. They both smile.

The fetus we have just watched is at the midpoint of its 40-week gestation. At conception 20 weeks earlier, it began as a single cell that carried in its nucleus the genetic code for the human it will become.

After dividing and redividing for a week, it grew to 32 cells. Like the initial cell, these offspring cells carry 40,000 or so genes, located on 23 pairs of chromosomes inherited from the mother and father. Smaller than the head of a pin, this clump of cells began a slow journey down the fallopian tube and attached itself to the spongy wall of the uterus.

Once settled, some embryonic cells began to form a placenta to supply the embryo with food, water, and nutrients from the mother's bloodstream. The placenta also filtered out harmful substances in the mother's bloodstream. The embryo and mother exchange chemical information to ensure that they work together toward their common goal.

Instructed by their genes, the cells continued to divide but didn't always produce exact replicas. In a process still not well understood, the cells began to differentiate to seek out their own destinies. Some helped build internal organs, others bones, muscles, and brain.

At 19 days postconception, the earliest brain tissues began to form. They developed at the top end of the neural tube, a sheath of cells that ran nearly the entire length of the embryo.

The human brain requires virtually the entire pregnancy to emerge fully, longer than the other organ systems. Even in the earliest stage of development, the fetus knows to protect its brain. The brain gets the most highly oxygenated blood, and should there be any shortage, the fetus will send the available blood to the brain.

Extending downward from the brain, the neural tube began to form the spinal cord. At four weeks, a rudimentary heart started to beat, and four limbs began sprouting. By eight weeks, the two-inch-long embryo took human form and was more properly called a fetus. At 10 to 12 weeks, it began moving its arms and legs, opened its jaws, swallowed, and yawned. Mostly it slept.

"We are never more clever than we are as a fetus," says Dr. Peter Nathanielsz, a fetal researcher, obstetrician, and professor of reproductive medicine at Cornell University. "We pass far more biological milestones before we are born than we'll ever pass after we're born."

Not long ago, the process of fetal development was shrouded in mystery. But through the power of scanning techniques, biotechnology, and fetal and animal studies, much of the mystery of fetal life has been unveiled.

We now know that as the fetus matures it experiences a broad range of sensory stimulation. It hears, sees, tastes, smells, feels, and has rapid eye movement (REM) sleep, the sleep stage we associate with dreaming. From observation of its sleep and wake cycles, the fetus appears to know night from day. It learns and remembers, and it may cry. It seems to do everything in utero that it will do after it is born. In the words of one researcher, "Fetal life is us."

Studies now show that it's the fetus, not the mother, who sends the hormonal signals that determine when a baby will be born. And we've found out that its health in the womb depends in part on its mother's health when she was in the womb.

Finally, we've discovered that the prenatal environment is not as benign, or as neutral, as once thought. It is sensitive to the mother's health, emotions, and behavior.

The fetus is strongly affected by the mother's eating habits. If the mother exercises more than usual, the fetus may become temporarily short of oxygen. If she takes a hot bath, the fetus feels the heat. If she smokes, so does the fetus. One study has found that pregnant women exposed to more sunlight had more outgoing children.

We now know that our genes do not encode a complete design for us, that our "genetic destiny" is not hard-wired at the time of conception. Instead, our development involves an interplay between genes and the environment, including that of the uterus. Because genes take "cues" from their environment, an expectant mother's physical and psychological health influences her unborn child's genetic well-being.

Factors such as low prenatal oxygen levels, stress, infections, and poor maternal nutrition may determine whether certain genes are switched on or off. Some researchers believe that our time in the womb is the single most important period of our life.

"Because of genetics, we once thought that we would unfold in the womb like a blueprint, but now we know it's not that simple," says Janet DiPietro, an associate professor of maternal and child health at the Johns Hopkins School of Public Health and one of a handful of fetal-behavior specialists. "The mother and the uterine environment she creates have a major impact on many aspects of fetal development, and a number of things laid down during that time remain with you throughout your life."

The impact of the womb on our intelligence, personality, and emotional and physical health is beginning to be understood. There's also an emerging understanding of something called fetal programming, which says that the effects of our life in the womb may be not felt until decades after we're born, and in ways that are more powerful than previously imagined.

Says Dr. Nathanielsz, whose book *Life in the Womb* details the emerging science of fetal development: "It's an area of great scientific importance that until recently remained largely unknown."

"I'm pregnant. Is it okay to have a glass of wine? Can I take my Prozac? What about a Diet Coke?"

Years ago, before she knew she was pregnant, a friend of mine had a glass of wine with dinner. When she discovered she was pregnant, she worried all through her pregnancy and beyond.

She feels some guilt to this day, even though the son she bore turned out very well.

Many mothers have experienced the same tangled emotions. "There's no evidence that a glass of wine a day during pregnancy has a negative impact on the developing fetus," says Dr. John Larsen, professor and chair of obstetrics and gynecology at George Washington University. Larsen says that at one time doctors gave alcohol by IV to pregnant women who were experiencing preterm labor; it relaxed the muscles and quelled contractions.

Larsen now sometimes recommends a little wine to women who experience mild contractions after a puncture from an amniocentesis needle, and some studies suggest that moderate alcohol intake in pregnancy may prevent preterm delivery in some women.

Even though most experts agree with Larsen, the alcohol message that most women hear calls for total abstinence. Experts worry that declaring moderate alcohol intake to be safe in pregnancy may encourage some pregnant women to drink immoderately. They say that pregnant women who have an occasional drink should not think they've placed their baby at risk.

What is safe? Some studies show children born to mothers who consumed three drinks a day in pregnancy averaged seven points lower on IQ tests than unexposed children. There is evidence that six drinks a day during pregnancy puts babies at risk of fetal alcohol syndrome (FAS), a constellation of serious birth defects that includes mental retardation. The higher the alcohol intake, the higher the FAS risk.

Are there drugs and drug combinations that women should avoid or take with caution during pregnancy? Accutane (isotretinoin), a prescription drug for acne and psoriasis, is known to cause birth defects. So too are some anticonvulsant drugs, including Epitol, Tegretol, and Valproate. Tetracycline, a widely prescribed antibiotic, can cause bone-growth delays and permanent teeth problems for a baby if a mother takes it during pregnancy.

Most over-the-counter drugs are considered safe in pregnancy, but some of them carry risks. Heavy doses of aspirin and other nonsteroidal anti-inflammatory drugs such as ibuprofen can delay the start of labor. They are also linked to a life-threatening disorder of newborns called persistent pulmonary hypertension (PPHN), which diverts airflow away from the baby's lungs, causing oxygen depletion. The March issue of the journal *Pediatrics* published a study linking these nonprescription painkillers to PPHN, which results in the death of 15 percent of the infants who have it.

OTC Drugs

In 1998, researchers at the University of Nebraska Medical Center reported dextromethorphan, a cough suppressant found in 40 or more OTC drugs including Nyquil, Tylenol Cold, Dayquil, Robitussin Maximum Strength, and Dimetapp DM, caused congenital malformations in chick embryos. The research was published in *Pediatric Research* and supported by the National Institutes of Health.

Although no connection between dextromethorphan and human birth defects has been shown, the Nebraska researchers noted that similar genes regulate early development in virtually all species. For this reason, the researchers predicted that dextromethorphan, which acts on the brain to suppress coughing, would have the same harmful effect on a human fetus.

Many women worry about antidepressants. Some need them during pregnancy or took them before they knew they were pregnant. A study published in the *New England Journal of Medicine* found no association between fetal exposure to antidepressants and brain damage. The study compared the IQ, temperament, activity level, and distractibility of more than 125 children whose mothers took antidepressants in pregnancy with 84 children whose mothers took no drugs known to harm the fetus.

The two groups of children, between 16 months and eight years old when tested, were comparable in every way. The antidepressants taken by the mothers included both tricyclates such as Elavil and Tofranil and selective serotonin reuptake inhibitors such as Prozac.

Not all mood-altering drugs may be safe. There is some evidence that minor tranquilizers taken for anxiety may cause developmental problems if taken in the first trimester, but there is no hard proof of this. Evidence of fetal damage caused by illegal drugs such as cocaine is widely accepted, as is the case against cigarette smoking. A 1998 survey found that 13 percent of all mothers who gave birth smoked. Evidence is striking that cigarette smoking in pregnancy lowers birth weight and increases the risks of premature birth, attention deficit hyperactive disorder, and diminished IQ.

A long-running study based on information from the National Collaborative Perinatal Project found that years after they were born, children were more apt to become addicted to certain drugs if their mother took them during delivery.

"We found drug-dependent individuals were five times more likely to have exposure to high doses of painkillers and anesthesia during their delivery than their nonaddicted siblings," says Stephen Buka of the Harvard School of Public Health. Buka suspects this is caused by a modification in the infant's brain receptors as the drugs pass from mother to child during an especially sensitive time.

Caffeine

Coffee consumption has worried mothers because there have been hints that caffeine may be harmful to the fetus. Like most things in life, moderation is the key. There's no evidence that 300 milligrams of caffeine a day (about three cups of coffee, or four or five cups of most regular teas, or five to six cola drinks) harms a developing baby. Higher caffeine consumption has been weakly linked to miscarriage and difficulty in conceiving.

Expectant mothers concerned about weight gain should be careful of how much of the artificial sweetener aspartame they consume. Marketed under brand names such as NutraSweet and Equal, it's found in diet soft drinks and foods.

The concern is this: In the body, aspartame converts into phenylalanine, a naturally occurring amino acid we ingest when we eat protein. At high levels, phenylalanine can be toxic to brain cells.

When we consume phenylalanine in protein, we also consume a number of other amino acids that neutralize any ill effects. When we consume it in aspartame, we get none of the neutralizing amino acids to dampen phenylalanine's impact. And as it crosses the placenta, phenylalanine's concentrations are magnified in the fetal brain.

If a fetal brain is exposed to high levels of phenylalanine because its mother consumes a lot of aspartame, will it be harmed? One study found average IQ declines of ten points in children born to mothers with a fivefold increase of phenylalanine blood levels in pregnancy. That's a lot of aspartame, and it doesn't mean an expectant mother who drinks moderate amounts of diet soda need worry.

Researchers say consuming up to three servings of aspartame a day—in either diet soda or low-calorie foods—appears to be safe for the fetus. However, a pregnant woman of average weight who eats ten or more servings a day may put her unborn baby at risk. In testimony before Congress, Dr. William Pardridge, a neuroscience researcher at UCLA, said it's likely that the effect of high phenylalanine levels in the fetal brain "will be very subtle" and many not manifest until years later.

One wild card concerns the 10 to 20 million Americans who unknowingly carry a gene linked to a genetic disease called phenylketonuria (PKU), which can lead to severe mental retardation. Most carriers don't know it, because PKU is a recessive genetic disorder, and both mother and father must carry the defective gene to pass PKU on to their child. A carrier feels no ill effects. According to researchers, a pregnant woman who unknowingly carries the PKU gene might place her unborn child at risk if she consumes even relatively moderate amounts of aspartame. There is no hard evidence that this will happen, but it remains a serious concern. PKU can be detected in the fetus by amniocentesis; a restrictive diet can prevent the worst effects of PKU on the child.

How does a mother's getting an infection affect her unborn baby? And should she be careful of cats?

Many experts think pregnant women should be more concerned about infections and household pets than a glass of wine or can of diet drink. There's overwhelming evidence of the potential harm of infections during pregnancy. We've known for a long time that rubella (German measles), a viral infection, can cause devastating birth defects.

More worrisome are recent studies showing that exposure to one of the most common of winter's ills—influenza—may put an unborn child at risk of cognitive and emotional problems. If flu strikes in the second trimester, it may increase the unborn baby's risk of developing schizophrenia later in life. While the flu may be a trigger, it's likely that a genetic susceptibility is also needed for schizophrenia to develop.

Some evidence exists that maternal flu may also lead to dyslexia, and suspicions persist that a first-trimester flu may cause fetal neural-tube defects resulting in spina bifida. The common cold, sometimes confused with the flu, has not been linked to any adverse outcomes for the baby.

"Infections are probably the most important thing for a pregnant woman to protect herself against," says Lise Eliot, a developmental neurobiologist at the Chicago Medical School. "She should always practice good hygiene, like washing her hands frequently, avoiding crowds, and never drinking from someone else's cup." She adds that the flu vaccine has been approved for use during pregnancy.

Some researchers recommend that pregnant women avoid close contact with cats. Toxoplasmosis, a parasitic infection, can travel from a cat to a woman to her unborn child.

Most humans become infected through cat litter boxes. An infected woman might experience only mild symptoms, if any, so the illness usually goes undetected. If she is diagnosed with the infection, antiparasitic drugs are helpful, but they don't completely eliminate the disease. The infection is relatively rare, and the odds of passing it from mother to child are only one in five during the first two trimesters, when the fetal harm is most serious. The bad news is that a fetus infected by toxoplasmosis can suffer severe brain damage, including mental retardation and epilepsy. Some researchers also suspect it may be a latent trigger for serious mental illness as the child grows older.

Cerebral Palsy

An expectant mother may not realize she has potentially harmful infections. The prime suspects are infections in the reproductive tract. Researchers suspect most cerebral-palsy cases are not caused by delivery problems, as has been widely assumed. There's strong evidence that some cases of cerebral-palsy may be linked to placental infections that occur during uterine life. Other cerebral-palsy cases may be triggered by oxygen deprivation in early development, but very few appear to be caused by oxygen deprivation during delivery. It's now estimated that only 10 percent of cerebral-palsy cases are related to delivery problems.

Maternal urinary-tract infections have been linked to lower IQs in children. Another infection, cytomegalovirus (CMV), has been linked to congenital deafness. Sexually transmitted diseases such as chlamydia are suspected to be a trigger for preterm birth. Despite the serious threat posed to developing babies, infections during pregnancy remain poorly understood.

"We just don't know right now when or how the uterine infections that really make a difference to the fetus are transmitted in pregnancy," says Dr. Karin Nelson, a child neurologist and acting chief of the neuro-epidemiology branch of the National Institute of Neurologic Disorders and Stroke at NIH. "Nor do we know all the potential problems they may cause."

Because of this, researchers offer little in the way of recommendations other than clean living and careful sex. They recommend that any woman contemplating pregnancy get in her best physical condition, because a number of studies have found that a woman's general health before she becomes pregnant is vital to fetal health. They also recommend a thorough gynecological exam because it may detect a treatable infection that could harm the fetus.

Rachel Carson was right about pesticides. So if you're pregnant, how careful should you be about what you eat?

In her book *Silent Spring,* author Rachel Carson noted that when pregnant mammals were exposed to synthetic pesticides, including DDT and methoxychlor, the pesticides caused developmental abnormalities in offspring. Carson, a scientist, noted that some pesticides mimicked the female hormone estrogen and caused the male offspring to be feminized.

About the time of Carson's 1962 book, another story was emerging about diethylstilbestrol (DES), a man-made female hormone administered in the 1940s and '50s to prevent miscarriages. In the 1960s it became clear that many young daughters of DES mothers were turning up reproductive malformations and vaginal cancers. Sons born to DES mothers suffered reproductive problems, including undescended testicles and abnormal sperm counts.

Endocrine Disrupters

Over the years, suspicion grew from both animal and human studies that something in the environment was disrupting fetal development. In the 1990s it was given a name—endocrine disruption. The theory was that DES and the pesticides cited by Carson caused defects in offspring because they disrupted the normal endocrine process. They did this by mimicking hormones inside the human body.

It's now clear that DDT and DES are the tip of the iceberg. Today more than 90,000 synthetic chemicals are used, most made after World War II. New chemicals are produced every week. They are used in everything from pesticides to plastics.

How many of these man-made chemicals might act as endocrine disrupters? More than 50 have been identified, and hundreds more are suspects.

To understand the threat from endocrine disrupters, it helps to understand what human hormones do. Secreted by endocrine glands, these tiny molecules circulate through the bloodstream to the organs. They include estrogen, adrenalin, thyroid, melatonin, and testosterone. Each is designed to fit only into a specific receptor on a cell, like a key that fits only one lock. When a hormone connects with the cell receptor, it enters the cell's nucleus. Once there, the hormone acts as a signaling agent to direct the cell's DNA to produce specific proteins.

During fetal life, the right type and concentration of hormones must be available at the right time for normal fetal development to occur. Produced by both mother and fetus, hormones are involved in cell division and differentiation, the development of the brain and reproductive organs, and virtually everything else needed to produce a baby.

"We know from animal experiments and wildlife observations that periods in development are very sensitive to alterations in the hormone levels," says Robert Kavlock, director of reproductive toxicology for the Environmental Protection Agency.

The damage is done when chemical mimickers get into cells at the wrong time, or at the wrong strength, or both. When this happens, something in the fetus will not develop as it should.

After years of witnessing the harmful impact on wildlife, we now know that humans are not immune to endocrine disrupters. More troubling, because of the pervasiveness of these chemicals, is that we can't escape them. We get them in the food we eat, the water we drink, the products we buy.

One of the most dramatic examples came to light in the 1970s when researchers wanted to find out why so many babies born in the Great Lakes region suffered serious neurological defects. They found the answer in polychlorinated biphenyls (PCBs), organic chemicals once used in electrical insulation and adhesives. Heavy PCB contamination of Great Lakes fish eaten by the mothers turned out to be the cause.

It is not clear how PCBs cause fetal brain damage, but it's believed to happen when they disrupt thyroid hormones. Severe thyroid deficiency in pregnancy is known to cause mental retardation. Another study found reduced penis size in boys born to mothers exposed to high levels of PCBs.

The U.S. manufacture of PCBs ended in 1977. PCB levels found in the mothers and the fish they ate suggested at the time that only very high exposure caused a problem for developing babies. Now we know this isn't true.

Because PCBs don't break down, they've remained a toxin that continues to enter our bodies through the food we eat. They have leached into soil and water and are found in shellfish and freshwater fish and to a smaller degree in ocean fish. Bottom-feeding freshwater fish, such as catfish and carp, have the highest PCB concentrations.

PCBs store in fat tissue and are found in dairy products and meats. Fatty meats, especially processed meats like cold cuts, sausages, and hot dogs, are usually heaviest in PCBs. They get into these products because farm animals graze on PCB-contaminated land. However, eating fish from PCB-contaminated water remains the primary way we get these chemicals into our systems. In pregnant women, PCBs easily cross the placenta and circulate in the fetus.

PCBs are ubiquitous. They've been detected in the Antarctic snow. If you had detection equipment sensitive enough, you'd find them in the milk at the supermarket.

What concerns experts are findings from studies in the Netherlands and upstate New York that found even low maternal PCB exposures pose risk to a fetus.

The Dutch study followed 418 children from birth into early childhood. In the final month of pregnancy, researchers measured the maternal PCB blood levels, and at birth they measured PCB levels in the umbilical cord. None of the mothers was a heavy fish eater or had any history of high PCB exposure, and none of their PCB levels was considered high by safety standards.

At 3½ years of age, the children's cognitive abilities were assessed with tests. After adjusting for other variables, the researchers found that maternal and cord blood PCB levels correlated with the children's cognitive abilities. As the PCB blood levels went up, the children suffered more attention problems and their cognitive abilities went down. It should be noted that the brain damage in these Dutch children was not devastating. They were not retarded or autistic. But on a relative scale, they had suffered measurable harm.

The Dutch researchers concluded that the in utero PCB exposure, and not any postnatal exposure, caused the children's brain damage. The study also revealed that these children had depressed immune function.

"All we can say now," says Deborah Rice, a toxicologist at the EPA's National Center for Environmental Assessment in Washington, "is we have strong evidence that PCB levels commonly found among women living in industrialized society can cause subtle neurological damage in their offspring." But one of the difficulties, according to Rice, is that we really don't yet know what an unsafe maternal PCB level might be.

"I think the bottom line is that women should be aware of PCBs and aware of what they're putting in their mouth," adds Rice.

The Dutch study is a warning not only about the potential impact of low levels of PCBs but about the potential harm from low levels of other endocrine disrupters.

More news arrived in March when the results from the federal government's on-going Fourth National Health and Nutrition Examination Survey (NHANES) became public. The survey of 38,000 people revealed that most of us have at least trace levels of pesticides, heavy metals, and plastics in our body tissues. In all, NHANES tested for 27 elements.

The survey found widespread exposure to phthalates, synthetic chemicals used as softeners in plastics and other products. Phthalates are one of the most heavily produced chemicals and have been linked in animal studies to endocrine disruption and birth defects. The likely sources of human exposure are foods and personal-care products such as shampoos, lotions, soaps, and perfumes; phthalates are absorbed through the skin.

Dr. Ted Schettler, a member of the Greater Boston Physicians for Social Responsibility, suspects endocrine disrupters may be linked to increases in the three hormone-driven cancers—breast, prostate, and testicular. The rate of testicular cancer among young men has nearly doubled in recent years, and the rates of learning disabilities and infertility also have increased.

"We can't blame all that is happening on toxic chemicals," says Schettler, who coauthored *In Harm's Way,* a report on how chemical contaminants affect human health. "But we need to ask ourselves if we're seeing patterns that suggest these chemicals are having a major impact on fetal development and human populations. We also need to ask what level of evidence we're going to need before we take public-health measures. That's a political question."

The EPA's Kavlock says, "We don't know the safe or unsafe levels for many of these chemicals." Nor do we know how many of the thousands of man-made chemicals in the environment will turn out to be endocrine disrupters or cause human harm. The EPA received a mandate from Congress in 1996 to find the answers, but it will be a long wait.

"If we devoted all the toxicology testing capacity in the entire world to look for endocrine-disrupting chemicals, we couldn't do all the chemicals. There's just not enough capacity," Kavlock says. "So we are focusing on 500 to 1,000 chemicals that are the major suspects. It will take many years and a lot of money just to understand how they interact with hormonal-system and fetal development."

What is all this bad stuff we can get from eating fish or from microwaving food in plastics? Do vitamins help?

Methylmercury is a heavy metal that can cause fetal brain damage. NHANES revealed that 10 percent of American women of child-bearing age—a representative sample of all American women—had methylmercury blood and hair levels close to "potentially hazardous levels." The EPA and some non-government experts consider these existing methylmercury levels already above what is safe.

Dr. Jill Stein, an adolescent-medicine specialist and instructor at Harvard Medical School, has studied methylmercury's toxicity. She says the acceptable levels of methyl-mercury in the NHANES report were too high and that many more women are in the danger zone. "The NHANES data tells me that more than 10 percent of American women today are carrying around enough mercury to put their future children at risk for learning and behavior problems," she says.

Like PCBs and other toxic chemicals, mercury is hard to avoid because it is abundant in our environment. It comes from natural and man-made sources, chiefly coal-fired power plants and municipal waste treatment. Each year an estimated 160 tons of mercury is released into the nation's environment. In water, mercury combines with natural bacteria to form methyl-mercury, a toxic form of the metal. It is easily absorbed by fish. When a pregnant woman consumes the contaminated fish, methylmercury crosses the placenta and the fetal blood-brain barrier.

The world became aware of methylmercury's potential for harm more than 40 years ago in the fishing village of Minamata in Japan. People there were exposed to high levels of the heavy metal from industrial dumping of mercury compounds into Minamata Bay. The villagers, who ate a diet heavy in fish caught in the bay, experienced devastating effects. The hardest hit were the unborn. Women gave birth to babies with cerebral-palsy-like symptoms. Many were retarded.

Mercury

Fish are the major source of mercury for humans. The Food and Drug Administration recommends that pregnant women not eat swordfish, king mackerel, shark, and tilefish. These fish are singled out because large oceangoing fish contain more methyl-mercury. Smaller ocean fish, especially cod, haddock, and pollock, generally have low methylmercury levels. A whitefish found off the coast of Alaska, pollock is commonly found in fish sticks and fast-food fish. Salmon have low methylmercury

levels, but they are a fatty fish and apt to carry higher levels of PCBs.

Like the Dutch PCB studies, recent studies of maternal methylmercury exposure have turned up trouble. They've shown that the so-called "safe" maternal levels of the metal can cause brain damage during fetal development.

One study was carried out in the 1990s by a Danish research team that studied 917 children in the Faroe Islands, where seafood is a big part of the diet. Children were grouped into categories depending on their level of maternal methylmercury exposure; they were assessed up to age seven by neurological tests. None of the children's methylmercury exposure levels was considered high, yet many of the children had evidence of brain damage, including memory, attention, and learning problems.

"Subtle effects on brain function therefore seem to be detectable at prenatal methylmercury exposure levels currently considered safe," the study concluded. In a follow-up report published in a 1999 issue of the *Journal of the American Medical Association,* the authors said the blood concentrations of methylmercury found in the umbilical cord corresponded with the severity of the neurological damage suffered by the children.

In a study of 237 children, New Zealand researchers found similar neurological harm, including IQ impairment and attention problems, in children whose mothers' exposure to methylmercury came from fish they ate during pregnancy.

"The children in these studies were not bathed in methylmercury," notes Rita Schoeny, a toxicologist in the EPA's Office of Water. "Can people in the U.S. be exposed to the same levels of mercury in the course of their dietary practice? We think so."

Jill Stein and other experts worry that the more scientific studies we do, the more we'll realize that in fetal development there may be no such thing as a "safe" maternal level for methylmercury, PCBs, and scores of other synthetic chemicals.

"We keep learning from studies that these chemicals are harmful to fetal development at lower and lower doses," Stein says. "It's what we call the declining threshold of harm."

What about canned tuna? It has been assumed to contain low methylmercury levels because most of it comes from smaller fish. The FDA offers no advisories about it. But according to EPA researchers, a recent State of Florida survey of more than 100 samples of canned tuna found high levels of methylmercury. The more-expensive canned tuna, such as albacore and solid white tuna, usually carried higher methylmercury levels, according to the survey. This apparently is because more expensive canned tuna comes from larger tuna. In some of the canned tuna, the methylmercury levels were high enough to prevent their export to several countries, including Canada.

Some of the methylmercury levels were "worrisomely high," according to Kathryn Mahaffey, a toxicologist and director of the division of exposure assessment at the EPA. They were high enough to cause concern for pregnant women.

"A big problem is the tremendous variability out there in the tuna supply," adds Stein. "You have no idea when you're eating a can of tuna how much methylmercury you're getting."

"Even if you ate just a small serving of some of these canned tunas each day," says Mahaffey, "you'd be substantially above a level we would consider safe."

Mahaffey and Stein agree that an expectant mother who ate even a few servings a week with methylmercury levels found in some of the canned tuna would put her developing baby at risk of brain and other neurological damage.

Now that we know a developing fetus is sensitive to even low levels of toxic chemicals, women can exercise some basic precautions to help protect their developing babies.

Don't microwave food that is wrapped in plastic or is still in plastic containers. "There are endocrine-disrupting chemicals in these plastics," Schettler says, "that leach right into the food when it's microwaved. This has been well documented and measured." Studies suggest that even at very low levels these chemicals can have an adverse effect on the fetus's hormonal system.

The EPA's Kavlock considers the fruits and vegetables you buy at the supermarket to be safe in pregnancy, but Schettler says you should try to eat organic foods to avoid even trace amounts of pesticides. Wash fruits and vegetables before eating them. Avoid pesticides or insecticide use around the house during pregnancy as well as the use of chemical solvents for painting or remodeling.

Herbicides and pesticides have leached into reservoirs that supply home drinking water, and filtration plants can't remove them all. Some are known to be endocrine disrupters. Home water filters can reduce contaminants; the best ones use active charcoal as a filtering agent.

Experts agree that a pregnant woman, or a woman who may get pregnant, can eat fish but should be careful about the kind she eats and how much of it. EPA's Rice cautions any woman who is pregnant or thinking of becoming pregnant to avoid eating any sport fish caught in a lake or river.

Vegetable Fats

Rice adds that the PCB risk with fish can be reduced. "Trim the fish of fat and skin, and broil or grill it," see says. "That way you cook off fat and minimize your PCB exposure." There is not much you can do to reduce the methylmercury levels in fish because it binds to protein.

"Fat is important for a baby's neurological development before and after birth, so pregnant women should consider vegetable fats like olive oil and flaxseed oil as a source," Rice adds. She says low fat dairy and meat products carry fewer PCBs than higher-fat ones.

The EPA has issued a PCB advisory for the Potomac River in the District, Virginia, and Maryland, citing in particular catfish and carp. You can go to *www.epa.gov/ost/fish/epafish.pdf* for EPA advisories on PCB and methylmercury environmental contamination. From there you can connect to state Web sites for advisories on local waters and specific fish.

Women can help prevent neurological and other birth defects by taking vitamin supplements before pregnancy. A daily dose of 400 micrograms of folic acid can reduce the risk of such problems as spina bifida by more than 70 percent as well as prevent brain defects and cleft lip and palate. Indirect evidence from a study published last year in the *New England Journal of Medicine* suggests that folic acid may also help prevent congenital heart defects.

To be effective, folic acid should be taken before pregnancy to prevent developmental defects. Folic acid comes in multivitamins and prenatal vitamins and is found naturally in legumes, whole-wheat bread, citrus fruits, fortified breakfast cereal, and leafy green vegetables. Despite the proven value of folic acid, a recent March of Dimes survey found that only 32 percent of American women of childbearing age—including pregnant women—took folic-acid supplements.

What can a fetus learn in the womb? And does playing Mozart make a baby lots smarter?

Developmental psychologist Anthony DeCasper wanted to answer two questions: What does a fetus know, and when does it know it?

DeCasper's aim was to find out if a fetus could learn in utero and remember what it learned after it was born. He enlisted the help of 33 healthy expectant mothers and asked each to tape-record herself reading passages from Dr. Seuss's *The Cat in the Hat* or from another children's book, *The King, the Mice, and the Cheese*. The mothers were randomly assigned to play one of these readings, each of which lasted two or three minutes, to their unborn children three times a day during the final three weeks of their pregnancies.

DeCasper, a professor of developmental psychology at the University of North Carolina at Greensboro, could do the experiment because it was known that fetuses could hear by the third trimester and probably earlier. DeCasper had shown earlier that at birth, babies preferred their mother's voice to all other voices. Studies in the early 1990s found that fetuses could be soothed by lullabies and sometimes moved in rhythm to their mother's voice. Fetuses hear their mother's voice from the outside, just as they can hear any other voice, but they hear the mother's voice clearer and stronger through bone conduction as it resonates inside her.

A little more than two days after birth, each of the newborns in DeCasper's study was given a specially devised nipple. The device worked by utilizing the baby's sucking reflex. When the baby sucked on the nipple, it would hear its mother's voice. But if it paused for too long a time between sucks, it would hear another woman's voice. This gave the baby control over whose voice it would hear by controlling the length of its pause between sucks.

DeCasper also placed small earphones over the infant's ears through which it could hear its mother's voice read from the books.

"Now two days or so after it was born, the baby gets to choose between two stories read by its own mother," DeCasper said. "One was the story she'd recited three times a day for the last three weeks of pregnancy, and the other is one the baby's never heard before, except for the one day his mother recorded it. So the big question was: Would the babies prefer the story they'd heard in the womb, or wouldn't they? The answer was a clear yes—the babies preferred to hear the familiar story."

DeCasper did a second experiment by having women who were not the baby's mothers recite the same two stories. The babies again showed a strong preference for the story they'd heard in the womb.

"These studies not only tell us something about the fidelity with which the fetal ear can hear," DeCasper says, "but they also show that during those two or three weeks in the womb, fetal learning and memory are occurring."

British researchers observed expectant mothers who watched a TV soap opera. The researchers placed monitors on the mother's abdomens to listen in on fetal movements when the program aired. By the 37th week of pregnancy, the babies responded to the show's theme music by increasing their movements, an indication they remembered it.

Soon after the babies were born, the researchers replayed the theme music to them. This time, instead of moving more, the babies appeared to calm down and pay attention to the music. The researchers considered this a response to familiar music.

Fetal Memory

"The fact that we find evidence of fetal memory doesn't mean fetuses carry conscious memories, like we remember what we ate for breakfast," explains Lise Eliot, author of *What's Going On in There?*, a book on early brain development. "But we now know there is a tremendous continuity from prenatal to postnatal life, and the prenatal experience begins to shape a child's interaction with the world it will confront after birth. Babies go through the same activity patterns and behavioral states before and after birth. Well before it is born, the baby is primed to gravitate to its mother and its mother's voice."

Some researchers speculate a baby's ability to remember in the womb may be a way of easing its transition from prenatal life to postnatal life. A baby already accustomed to and comforted by its mother's voice may be reassured as it enters a new world of bright lights, needle pricks, curious faces, and loud noises.

The question arises: Can the uterine environment affect a baby's intelligence? Twins studies have shown that genes exert an all-powerful influence on IQ. The role of environment in IQ has traditionally meant the nurturance and stimulation the baby receives after birth.

Bernie Devlin, a biostatistician and assistant professor of psychiatry at the University of Pittsburgh, did an analysis of 212 twins studies on intelligence. In a paper published in *Nature,* he concluded that the accepted figure of 60 to 80 percent for IQ heritability is too high. It should be closer to 50 percent, he says, which leaves more room for environmental factors. Devlin says the one environmental factor that's been missing in understanding human intelligence is time in the womb.

"I'm surprised that the impact of fetal life on a child's intelligence had not been accounted for in these IQ studies," Devlin says. "I know it's very complicated, but it's surprising that people who study the heritability of intelligence really haven't considered this factor."

What is the impact of life in the womb on intelligence? Devlin thinks it's equal to if not greater than the impact of a child's upbringing. In other words, it's possible a mother may have more influence over her child's intelligence before birth than after.

As the brain develops in utero, we know it undergoes changes that affect its ultimate capacity. Nutritional and hormonal influences from the mother have a big impact. And twins studies show that the heavier twin at birth most often has the higher IQ.

A number of studies from the United States and Latin America also found that a range of vitamins, as well as sufficient protein in the mother's prenatal diet, had an impact on the child's intelligence.

Links between specific vitamins and intelligence have been borne out in two studies. An animal study conducted at the University of North Carolina and published in the March issue of *Developmental Brain Research* found that rats with a choline deficiency during pregnancy gave birth to offspring with severe brain impairments. Choline, a B-complex vitamin involved in nerve transmission, is found in eggs, meat, peanuts, and dietary supplements.

The August 1999 issue of the *New England Journal of Medicine* reported that expectant mothers with low thyroid function gave birth to children with markedly diminished IQs as well as motor and attention deficits. The study said one cause of hypothyroidism—present in 2 to 3 percent of American women—is a lack of iodine in the American diet. Women whose hypothyroidism was detected and treated before pregnancy had children with normal test scores. Hypothyroidism can be detected with a blood test, but expectant mothers who receive little or late prenatal care often go undiagnosed or are diagnosed too late to help their child.

Although most American women get the nutrition they need through diet and prenatal vitamins, not all do. According to a National Center for Health Statistics survey, more than one in four expectant mothers in the U.S. received inadequate prenatal care.

Devlin's *Nature* article took a parting shot at the conclusions reached in the 1994 book *The Bell Curve,* in which Richard J. Herrnstein and Charles Murray argued that different social classes are a result of genetically determined, and therefore unalterable, IQ levels. The lower the IQ, the argument goes, the lower the social class.

Not only does the data show IQ to be far less heritable than that book alleges, Devlin says, but he suspects improvements in the health status of mostly poor expectant mothers would see measurable increases in the IQs of their offspring.

Devlin's argument is supported by Randy Thornhill, a biologist at the University of New Mexico. Thornhill's research suggests that IQ differences are due in part to what he calls "heritable vulnerabilities to environmental sources of developmental stress." In other words, vulnerable genes interact with environmental insults in utero resulting in gene mutations that affect fetal development. Thornhill says environmental insults may include viruses, maternal drug abuse, or poor nutrition.

"The developmental instability that results," Thornhill says, "is most readily seen in the body's asymmetry when one side of the body differs from the other. For example, on average an individual's index fingers will differ in length by about two millimeters. Some people have much more asymmetries than others."

But the asymmetries we see on the outside also occur in the nervous system. When this happens, neurons are harmed and memory and intelligence are impaired. Thornhill says the more physical asymmetries you have, the more neurological impairment you have. He calculates that these factors can account for as much as 50 percent of the differences we find in IQ.

Thornhill adds that a fetus that carries these genetic vulnerabilities, but develops in an ideal uterine environment, will not experience any serious problems because the worrisome mutations will not occur.

"The practical implications for this are tremendous," Thornhill says. "If we can understand what environmental factors most disrupt fetal development of the nervous system, then we'll be in a position to remove them and have many more intelligent people born."

Studies on fetal IQ development suggest that the current emphasis on nurturance and stimulation for young children be rethought. The philosophy behind initiatives such as Zero to Three and Early Head Start makes sense. The programs are based on evidence that the first three years are very important for brain development and that early stimulation can effect positive changes in a child's life. But Devlin and Thornhill's research suggests a stronger public-health emphasis on a baby's prenatal life if we are to equalize the opportunities for children.

Does that mean unborn babies need to hear more Mozart? Companies are offering kits so expectant mothers can play music or different sounds to their developing babies—the prenatal "Mozart effect." One kit promises this stimulation will lead to "longer new-born attention span, better sleep patterns,

accelerated development, expanded cognitive powers, enhanced social awareness and extraordinary language abilities." Will acceptance to Harvard come next?

"The number of bogus and dangerous devices available to expectant parents to make their babies smarter constantly shocks me," says DiPietro. "All these claims are made without a shred of evidence to support them."

Adds DeCasper: "I think it is dangerous to stimulate the baby in the womb. If you play Mozart and it remembers Mozart, is it going to be a smarter baby? I haven't got a clue. Could it hurt the baby? Yes, I think it could. If you started this stimulation too early and played it too loud, there is evidence from animal studies that you can destroy the ear's ability to hear sounds in a particular range. That's an established fact. Would I take a risk with my fetus? No!"

DeCasper and other researches emphasize that no devices or tricks can enhance the brainpower of a developing baby. Their advice to the expectant mother: Take the best possible care of yourself.

"The womb is a quiet, protective place for a reason," DiPietro concludes. "Nature didn't design megaphones to be placed on the abdomen. The fetus gets all the stimulation it needs for its brain to develop."

MR. PEKKANEN is a contributing editor to *The Washingtonian*. From "Secrets of the Womb," by John Pekkanen, The Washingtonian, August 2001, pages 44–51, 126–135.

The Smallest Patients

To help babies with heart defects, doctors can now operate in the womb.

CLAUDIA KALB

Melissa Paske was 29 weeks pregnant with a girl when she asked her doctor for a second ultrasound. Her belly had been scanned at 24 weeks, and there was no medical reason to take additional images. But, says Paske, "something in me felt that I needed to see her again." That something turned out to be a devastating diagnosis for her baby: a badly clogged aortic valve, which doctors feared could lead to a massively underdeveloped left side of the heart, a condition called hypoplastic left heart syndrome (HLHS). The news, says Paske, "was like a truck backing up over me."

Babies with HLHS typically undergo a complex series of surgeries after birth to compensate for the defect. But a team of doctors at Children's Hospital Boston and neighboring Brigham and Women's Hospital offered Melissa Paske and her husband, Travis, of Spokane, Wash., something new: a revolutionary procedure performed while their baby was still floating in Melissa's womb. Within days the Paskes were flying across the country. In her 30th week of pregnancy, doctors inserted a needle through Melissa's uterus into her fetus's heart, where they dilated a balloon and opened the blocked valve. Six weeks later the Paskes' daughter, Camryn, was born HLHS-free. Last week the slender little girl with eight tiny teeth and a mop of light brown hair celebrated her 1st birthday. "She's just beautiful," says Melissa.

She's also a medical pioneer. Thirty years ago, babies diagnosed with HLHS were doomed to die within the first days to weeks of life. Today, thanks to earlier detection through ultrasound and postnatal surgery, the majority of the 1,500-plus HLHS babies born every year now survive; the oldest are in their early 20s. The medical journey, however, is far from easy. Ten to 25 percent of infants die during or after their first operation, and those who do make it require lifelong care; some will need pacemakers or even heart transplants. The condition is so severe that many couples choose to terminate their pregnancies. The Boston team is now trying to change all that by waging a pre-emptive strike through fetal intervention. The procedure is experimental, but the potential payoff is huge: warding off HLHS before it even develops. It's way too early to claim victory, but Dr. Jim Lock, Children's cardiologist in chief, is optimistic: "This is clearly the wave of the future."

Development of the human heart is nothing short of anatomical wizardry. The organ starts out as a narrow tube, then twists and turns during the first eight weeks of gestation to create its elegant final design: four chambers, four valves, two walls or septums and an assortment of veins and arteries. The two lower chambers of the heart operate as pumping stations: the right ventricle squeezes blood out to the lungs, and the left—responsible for the lion's share of the work—pumps to the rest of the body. Nobody knows precisely what causes HLHS, but one key factor is the plumbing problem that Camryn suffered early on in development: a narrowing of the aortic valve. The malfunction causes blood to back up in the left ventricle, forcing the developing heart muscle to squeeze extra hard. Eventually the muscle tires, stops pumping and growing, and withers. The outcome is dire: babies with HLHS have one working ventricle instead of two, making their hearts incapable of sustaining life.

As of now, the best treatment for HLHS is a three-stage open-heart surgery—performed at birth, at 6 months and around the age of 2 or 3—which re-engineers the heart's plumbing, making the right side take on the pumping job of the left side as well. (A complete heart transplant is also an option, but few infant hearts are available for donation.) "We don't fix the heart," says Dr. Jack Rychik, director of the Fetal Heart Program at Children's Hospital of Philadelphia (CHOP). "We cheat nature by redirecting the blood." Since it was first attempted in the early 1980s, the procedure has been a godsend, saving the lives of thousands. But it's not a cure. The goal among fetal experts is to redirect the heart toward normal development and get rid of HLHS altogether.

Operating in the womb raises the surgical stakes. For starters, there are two patients—mother and fetus—and one of them is floating in fluid. A team of doctors, including anesthesiologists (both mother and fetus are given medication to relieve pain), echocardiographers, obstetricians, radiologists and cardiologists, must work together, using snowy ultrasound images as their only road map. A needle must be carefully guided through the mother's abdomen and uterine wall into the grape-size fetal heart and then on to the aortic valve, about the diameter of spaghetti, where doctors dilate a balloon to stretch the opening. Along with the technical challenges come operational dangers.

Both mother and fetus are susceptible to complications from anesthesia. The mother could develop blood clots or an infection or go into premature labor. Her fetus could be injured by the needle, suffer cardiac distress, even die in utero. "There are risks with no guarantee that the intervention will work," says Lock's colleague Dr. Wayne Tworetzky, who counsels prospective parents. "We have to be very straightforward with families."

A needle is guided into the grape-size fetal heart.

Since 2000, the Boston team has performed just over 50 procedures. Most have been aortic-valve dilations, but the team is using a similar approach to try to fix blocked pulmonary valves, which can lead to a mirror image of HLHS called hypoplastic right heart syndrome. And the team is intervening in an even more dangerous problem that strikes some fetuses who have already developed HLHS: a blockage in the atrial septum, which divides the two upper chambers of the heart. In addition to withered left hearts, these babies are susceptible to lung damage. Not all the procedures have been technically successful—the needle hasn't gone in properly or the balloon hasn't dilated. Some of the sickest babies have died despite the intervention; others have developed HLHS. But seven babies who had successful aortic-valve dilations have been spared the syndrome, a home run in congenital heart disease. "We now have significant evidence that we can remodel hearts before birth," says Lock. "This represents a major potential breakthrough in the field."

There are still challenges ahead. The womb is new territory, the learning curve is steep and the parents, desperate to help their babies, are vulnerable. Doctors can't predict with certainty which babies will benefit from the procedure, making patient selection tricky. And even if a procedure does seem warranted, there's no guarantee that the baby's outcome will be better than what standard surgery now offers. CHOP's Rychik believes more research is needed on the evolution of congenital heart disease before those dilemmas can be solved. "I'm encouraged by the Boston experience, and I applaud it," says Rychik, who is launching a nationwide study to document fetal heart development, but "we're still very early in all of this." Other clinics are taking the plunge, albeit in very small numbers. Doctors at the University of California, San Francisco, have performed one fetal procedure; the Cleveland Clinic has completed two. "We're seeing the fetus as a patient, and we're prepared to do everything in our power to make things better," says Cleveland's Dr. Stephen Emery.

Fetal intervention is still in its infancy. The number of affected babies is small, and the technique requires highly skilled doctors at topnotch clinics. But the odds for sick babies could improve immediately simply through better detection of abnormalities during pregnancy. Alex Osborne of Lebanon, Pa., is proof of that. His heart defect was identified during a routine 19-week ultrasound, allowing his parents, Julie and David, to seek out cardiac experts at CHOP well before their baby's due date. Doctors were able to counsel the couple about Alex's condition—he had HLHS complicated by a blocked atrial septum—and prepare them for surgical intervention. And a team of experts, including obstetricians, pediatric cardiologists and cardiac surgeons, could be assembled for Julie's delivery, ready to provide immediate care. "We delivered him and rushed him to the OR," says Rychik. Just two hours after birth, Alex had his first surgery. Today he's 7 years old and a four-foot-tall, 50-pound budding paleontologist. "It's unlikely he would have survived if we hadn't known about his condition ahead of time," says Rychik.

Alex, however, is in the minority. Today more than 90 percent of women receive midtrimester ultrasounds, and yet only 20 to 30 percent of congenital heart defects are picked up, says Dr. Lisa Hornberger, director of UCSF's Fetal Cardiovascular Program. That means doctors are delivering babies with ticking time bombs inside: they look perfectly healthy at birth, then suddenly crash, gasping for air. Ultrasound works, says Hornberger; "the problem is, people don't know what to look for." Today Hornberger is conducting seminars for obstetricians and other diagnosticians, teaching them to identify the earliest signs of trouble. Once they do, babies can be scheduled for surgery after birth, or perhaps even referred for fetal intervention. "We're at the tip of the iceberg," she says. "We need to be improving detection, or we're not going to be making a difference."

Camryn Paske is making a difference in her own little 1-year-old way. "She's crawling and getting into everything," says Melissa. "I call her my 'terror on knees'." She's also laughing and playing around with pet beagles Copper and Bagel. Camryn's heart isn't perfect. She takes three medications a day to make sure it pumps efficiently, and one day she may need her damaged aortic valve repaired or replaced. But she's been spared the worst. "I feel so fortunate and indebted to the doctors," says Melissa. Her family may live in Spokane, but "we're Red Sox fans now," she says. Rooting not just for baseball—but for every fragile little heart that makes its way to Boston.

Not Always 'the Happiest Time'

**Pregnancy and depression: a new understanding
of a difficult—and often hidden—problem.**

LISA MILLER AND ANNE UNDERWOOD

Let's just say that you are among the millions of women for whom pregnancy was not bliss. You may have felt cranky or anxious, exhausted or fat, moody, stressed, nauseated, overwhelmed, isolated or lonely. You may even have felt bad about feeling bad. Now let's say that you, like Marlo Johnson, are a veteran of depression, someone who has battled the illness on and off for years. Then pregnancy can feel like the worst thing that ever happened to you. Johnson, 35 years old and from Brentwood, Calif., felt her mood plummet almost as soon as she conceived. But she put a brave face on it at work, with her family—even with her own therapist. The only time she cried was when she visited her obstetrician. Every time. Johnson's doctor encouraged her to look on the bright side. " 'Just think, at the end you're going to have this beautiful baby, the most beautiful gift'," Johnson recalls her saying, "and I said, 'I don't care. I don't want it. It doesn't matter to me'."

Contrary to conventional wisdom and medical lore, pregnancy does not necessarily equal happiness, and its hormones are not protective against depression. Doctors estimate that up to 20 percent of women experience symptoms of depression at some point during their pregnancy—about the same as women who are not pregnant. Even as postpartum depression has become morning-television fodder, the problem of depression during pregnancy has remained hidden—largely because most people still assume that pregnancy is or should be the realization of every woman's dream. When she was training as a psychiatric resident in the 1980s, Katherine Wisner, now a professor of psychiatry and Ob-Gyn at the University of Pittsburgh, remembers being told not to worry about pregnant patients who were, in her view, "very ill." Pregnant women, her teachers said, are "psychologically fulfilled."

Finally, pregnancy-linked depression is coming into the open. A series of studies, published this year in medical journals, is looking at all aspects of the problem—with special focus on the effects of anti-depressants on the health of pregnant women and newborn babies. These studies have launched, for the first time, a serious debate among doctors on the risks and benefits of treating pregnant women with medication. "There are still unanswered questions" about SSRIs and pregnancy, says Lee Cohen, a psychiatrist at Mass General Hospital in Boston and author of one of the recent studies. "But the doctors—the psychiatrists, the OBs—can't be cavalier, and can't presume that [without treatment] things are going to be fine."

Pregnancy probably doesn't cause depression, per se, but just like a divorce or a death in the family, it can trigger it in women who may already be genetically predisposed. And the hormones don't help. The relationship between estrogen, progesterone and mood is not well understood, but scientists believe it is the *changes* in hormonal levels, rather than the levels themselves, that affect people's moods. In a series of experiments published in *The New England Journal of Medicine* in 1998, psychiatrists Peter Schmidt and David Rubinow found that women who were prone to mild depression associated with premenstrual syndrome felt better only when their hormonal cycles were artificially shut down. They guess that the same is probably true with pregnancy: massive hormonal changes affect mood, but only in susceptible women. "In some women it may be the dramatic drop in hormones at childbirth that is the trigger," says Rubinow. "In others, it may be the elevated levels at the end of pregnancy."

It's difficult to detect depression in a pregnant woman, doctors say, because so few of them admit they're depressed—and because so many of the symptoms, such as sluggishness and sleeplessness, look alike. But Linda Worley, a psychiatrist at the University of Arkansas, who has a $250,000 federal grant to raise awareness about pregnancy and depression, says too many doctors don't ask pregnant patients about their mood or administer routine screening tests; some are too busy, some assume it isn't a problem and a few—not knowing where to refer such a patient—are afraid to hear the answer. According to preliminary results of a survey Worley received from 145 obstetrical providers, more than 80 percent rely on patients to self-report depression.

Treating a pregnant woman for depression is a delicate balancing act, a constant weighing of risks and benefits to the mother and to the fetus. But intervention is critical: a recent study by Columbia's Myrna Weissman shows that a mother's mental health directly affects the mental health of her children. Without aggressive treatment, "the whole family will suffer," Weissman says. Cohen's study, in *The Journal of the American Medical Association,* showed without a doubt that depressed mothers-to-be do better on SSRIs. Women who continued taking medication while pregnant were five times less likely to have a relapse of their illness than women who didn't. This is important—and not only because it improves the mother's health. Depressed women are far likelier to smoke, drink and miss doctors' appointments; depressed mothers give birth more often to under-weight babies. Faced with these facts, Claudia Crain of Newburyport, Mass., decided to continue taking her antidepressants: "The more research I did, the better I felt about what, in the end, was my personal decision." Her twins are due this month.

Most people assume that pregnancy is the realization of every woman's dream.

At the same time, no one would argue that antidepressants are good for growing fetuses. Two new studies help people assess the risks for themselves. In one, published in *The New England Journal of Medicine,* researchers found that newborns whose mothers took Prozac, Paxil or Zoloft in the third trimester had six times the risk of persistent pulmonary hypertension, a rare blood-pressure condition that is potentially fatal.

In another, smaller study, 30 percent of infants whose mothers took SSRIs showed symptoms of neonatal abstinence syndrome, a kind of supercrankiness linked to withdrawal. Most got better within days.

Therapy is a good alternative, especially for women with mild or moderate symptoms. In today's world, where families live far apart and everyone works all the time, many pregnant women say they feel isolated. This can be alleviated by talking. Margaret Spinelli, a psychiatrist at Columbia University, was surprised to find in a 2003 study that depressed pregnant women had a 60 percent recovery rate with interpersonal psychotherapy, a short-term, focused treatment—about the same rate as with antidepressants. "We just don't have the networks of close-by girlfriends and sisters and neighbors and moms that provide support," adds Pittsburgh's Wisner.

One of the reasons Marlo Johnson kept her depression hidden was that she didn't want to take antidepressants during her second pregnancy, as she had during her first. "I don't like being on medication; I kept telling myself I could handle it," she says. But finally Johnson's doctor took action. She ordered her to take a leave from work and to come clean with her therapist; Johnson's husband, who was working hundreds of miles away, came home. On March 20, Carter Patrick Johnson was born, weighing more than eight pounds. Mom says she loves the baby, "but I'm still depressed," and is back on medication. Sometimes even happy stories have bittersweet endings.

With Joan Raymond

UNIT 2

Development During Infancy and Early Childhood

Unit Selections

Key Points to Consider

- What purposes are served by involving babies in hectic activity schedules and introducing them to academics as early as possible?

- How much do babies understand at birth? What emotions do they feel? Are there social and emotional "milestones" to help caregivers watch progress?

- Are there inexpensive and easy ways to boost a baby's brain power? Can any caregiver incorporate them into daily activities?

- Should the United States provide preschool to every child? What would be the advantages of this expensive undertaking?

- Should preschools focus on pre-reading and pre-math skills? If so, how much? What else should good preschools provide for their charges?

- When should children know right from wrong? How is it learned?

Student Web Site

www.mhcls.com/online

Internet References

Further information regarding these Web sites may be found in this book's preface or online.

BabyCenter
 http://www.babycenter.com
Children's Nutrition Research Center (CNRC)
 http://www.bcm.tmc.edu/cnrc/
Early Childhood Care and Development
 http://www.ecdgroup.com
Zero to Three: National Center for Infants, Toddlers, and Families
 http://www.zerotothree.org

Development during infancy and early childhood is more rapid than in any other life stage, excluding prenatal development. Newborns are quite well developed in some areas, and incredibly deficient in others. Babies' cerebral hemispheres already have their full complement of neurons (worker cells). The neuroglia (supportive cells) are almost completely developed and will reach their final numbers by age one. In contrast, babies' legs and feet are tiny, weak, and barely functional. Look at newborns from another perspective, however, and their brains seem somewhat less superior. The neurons and neuroglia present at birth must be protected. We may discover ways to make more cerebral neurons in the future, but such knowledge now is in its infancy and does not go very far. By contrast, the cells of the baby's legs and feet (skin, fat, muscles, bones, blood vessels) are able to replace themselves by mitosis indefinitely. Their numbers will continue to grow through early adulthood; then

their quantity and quality can be regenerated through advanced old age.

The developing brain in infancy is a truly fascinating organ. At birth it is poorly organized. The lower (primitive) brain parts (brain stem, pons, medulla, cerebellum) are well enough developed to allow the infant to live. The lower brain directs vital organ systems (heart, lungs, kidneys, etc.). The higher (advanced) brain parts (cerebral hemispheres) have allocated neurons, but the nerve cells and cell processes (axons, dendrites) are small, underdeveloped, and unorganized. During infancy, these higher (cerebral) nerve cells (that allow the baby to think, reason, and remember) grow at astronomical rates. They migrate to permanent locations in the hemispheres, develop myelin sheathing (insulation), and conduct messages. Many 20th century researchers, including Jean Piaget, the father of cognitive psychology, believed that all brain activity in the newborn was reflexive, based on instincts for survival. They were wrong. New research has documented that fetuses can learn and newborns can think as well as learn.

The role played by electrical and chemical activity of neurons in actively shaping the physical structure of the brain is particularly awe-inspiring. The neurons are produced prenatally. After birth, the flood of sensory inputs from the environment (sights, sounds, smells, tastes, touch, balance, and kinesthetic sensations) drives the neurons to form circuits and become wired to each other. Trillions of connections are established in a baby's brain. During childhood the connections that are seldom or never used are eliminated or pruned. The first three years are critical for establishing these connections. Environments that provide both good nutrition and lots of sensory stimulation really do produce richer, more connected brains.

The first selection on infancy asks and partially answers the question, "Who's Raising Baby?" Anne Pierce discusses the challenges to modern day parenting from a mother's-eye view. Contemporary parents seem to be on a competitive merry-go-round to have their offspring involved in as many "enriching" activities as their neighbors, friends, coworkers, etc. What is the purpose of all this activity? The article cites the opinions of renowned child psychologists such as David Elkind and Stanley Greenspan that this race for supremacy is not healthy. In infancy, emotional learning and the ability to relate to others are more important than literacy. Home life is valuable. The author believes lessons learned at home supercede those obtained in daycare.

The second selection on infancy, "Reading Your Baby's Mind," addresses a concern of many parents: "How much does this baby understand?" With electroencephalography and laser eye tracking, scientists are providing surprising answers. In short, a lot! They feel empathy when others are stressed, as well as fear and contentment from birth onwards. This article explains how infant minds develop, the role of environment, and gives milestones of progress in the first 18 months of life.

To complete the infancy section, Alice Honig suggests "20 Ways to Boost Your Baby's Brain Power." These ideas are easily put into practice without a great deal of time or money. They really work, too!

The first early childhood article addresses "Long-Term Studies of Preschool." Many industrialized nations subsidize high-quality early childhood education. The United States does not. Long-term studies of three excellent preschool programs in the United States have documented long-lasting benefits. While national preschool funding would be an expensive investment, the authors argue that it would be worth the costs.

Deborah Stipek, in the second early childhood article, "Accountability Comes to Preschool," gives sketches of what a good preschool can do, and what will happen if the nonacademic aspects of preschools are dropped in favor of a narrow set of reading and math skills. Young children, advises Stipek, need preschool programs that emphasize social skills, emotional well-being, and health habits, as well as an enthusiasm for learning. Preschools should not evolve into the kindergartens or first grades of yesteryear.

The last article in this unit discusses how parents can instill and nurture moral values and behaviors in young children. Although states vary in the ages that they hold children legally accountable for knowing right from wrong, child developmentalists believe that preschoolers can grasp, and should be taught, moral values.

Who's Raising Baby?
Challenges to Modern-Day Parenting

ANNE R. PIERCE

Drive through the empty streets of our neighborhoods and ask yourself not merely where the children have gone but where childhood has gone. It is most unlikely you will see such once-familiar scenes as these: a child sitting under a tree with a book, toddlers engaged in collecting leaves and sticks, friends riding bikes or playing tag, parents and their offspring working together in the yard, families (in no hurry to get anywhere) strolling casually along. Today's children are too busy with other things to enjoy the simple pleasures children used to take for granted. Preoccupied with endless "activities" and diversions, they have little time for simply going outside.

Where are the children and what are they doing? They are in day-care centers, now dubbed "learning centers." They are in "early childhood programs" and all-day kindergarten. They are acquiring new skills, attending extracurricular classes, and participating in organized sports. They are sitting in front of the computer, the TV, and the Play Station. They are not experiencing the comfortable ease of unconditional love, nor the pleasant feeling of familiarity. They are not enjoying a casual conversation, nor are they playing. They are working—at improving their talents, at competing with their peers, at "beating the enemy" in a video game, at just getting by, at adapting to the new baby-sitter or coach, at not missing Mom or Dad. They, like their computers, are "on." Being, for them, is doing, adjusting, coping. Parenting, for us, is providing them with things to do.

Young children expend their energy on long days in group situations, in preschool and after-school programs, in music and athletic lessons. For much-needed relaxation, they collapse in front of the TV or computer, the now-defining features of "homelife." Relaxation no longer signifies quiet or repose. The hyperactive pace of children's television shows and video games, always accompanied by driving music, exacerbates and surpasses the fast pace of modern life. Children stare at the screen, though the inanity, violence, and doomsday sociopolitical messages of the programming are anything but reassuring.

From doing to staring, from staring to doing. There is little room in this scenario for idle contentment, playful creativity, and the passionate pursuit of interests. Alternatives to this framework for living are provided neither in thought nor in deed by busy parents who, themselves, end their rushed days with television and escapism.

Before nursery school starts, most children who can afford it have attended "classes," from gymnastics to ballet, piano, or swimming. Infant "swim lessons," in which an instructor in diving gear repeatedly forces screaming babies underwater so that they are forced to swim, are now commonplace. Day-care centers claim to give toddlers a head start in academic advancement and socialization. Increasing numbers of bright young children spend time with tutors or at the learning center to attain that ever-elusive "edge."

Children in elementary school now "train" and lift weights in preparation for their sports. Football and track are new options for first-graders. A recent trend in elementary athletic programs is to recruit professional coaches, due to the supposed competitive disadvantage of amateur coaching done by parents. It is more common for young children to "double up," participating in two team sports at a time. A constantly increasing selection of stimulating activities lures modern families, making downtime more elusive.

What used to be "time for dinner" (together) is, more often than not, time for family members to rush and scatter in different directions. A typical first-grade soccer team practices two evenings a week, from 6:00 to 7:30. The stress involved in getting six-year-olds fed and in gear by practice time and, after practice, bathed and in bed at an appropriate hour is obvious. And yet, if you attend a first-grade soccer game, you'll likely find parents eager to discover the activities of other people's children and anxious to sign their children up for—whatever it might be. Some parents appear to be jealous of the activities others have discovered.

The New Conformism— Afraid of Missing Out

In asking scores of parents about the purpose of all this activity, I have never received a clear or, to my mind, satisfactory answer. The end, apparently, is unclear apart from the idea, often expressed, that if one's child starts activities later than other children, he (or she) will be "left behind." Some of the more cohesive explanations I have received are these: A mother described herself as being "swept along by the inevitable"; she didn't want her young daughter to be "the only one missing out." A couple explained their determination to expose their toddler to a wide variety of opportunities so that he would know which sports he excelled in "by the time things get competitive." A father said, simply, that he saw his role in terms of making sure his children were "the best at something," and with all the other kids starting activities at such an early age, this meant that his kids "had to start even earlier."

In effect, this is the "do what everyone else does, only sooner and more intensely" theory of child rearing. This theory creates a constant downward pressure upon children of a younger and younger age. This was evident to me when my youngest son entered kindergarten and I discovered he was within a small minority of boys who had not *already* participated in team sports. Only five years earlier, my oldest son was within the sizable majority of kindergartners whose parents had decided kindergarten was a little too early for such endeavors. (First grade was then the preferred starting point.)

The more families subscribe to this "lifestyle," the more there is another reason for pushing kids off to the races: If no children are around to play with, then, especially for only children, organized activities become their only opportunity to "play" with other kids. Playing is thus thoroughly redefined.

The philosophy of child rearing as a race and of homelife as oppressive for women compels families toward incessant action. Love, nurture, and, concomitantly, innocence have been demoted as compared to experience and exposure. The family is viewed as a closedness to experience, the nurturing role within the family as the most confining of all. Indeed, busyness supplants togetherness in many modern families.

One legacy of Freud, Piaget, Pavlov, and the behaviorists, neodevelopmentalists, and social scientists who followed them has been the decreasing respect for the child's being and the increasing emphasis upon his "becoming." The child is seen as "socializable" and is studied as a clinical object whose observable response to this or that "environmental stimulus" becomes more important than his deeper, more complicated features. With the clinical interpretation of childhood, social engineering projects and "activities" that make the child's world more stimulating gain momentum.

Conformism, convenience, and new interpretations of childhood are, then, contributing factors in the hectic existence and the premature introduction to academics that parents prescribe for their children.

In addition to the advantage that all this activity supposedly gives children, there is also the element of convenience. If parents are too busy to supervise their children, it behooves them to keep the kids so busy and under the auspices of so many (other) adults that they are likely to "stay out of trouble." Such is the basis of many modern choices. Children spend much of their time exhausted by activities, the purposes of which are ill construed.

Conformism, convenience, and new interpretations of childhood are, then, contributing factors in the hectic existence and the premature introduction to academics that parents prescribe for their children. For example, before the 1960s, it was generally believed that placing young children in out-of-home learning programs was harmful. The concern for the harmfulness of such experiences was abandoned when these learning programs became convenient and popular.

Education as 'Socialization'

In *Miseducation: Preschoolers at Risk*, David Elkind expressed dismay at the fact that age-inappropriate approaches to early education have gained such momentum despite the undeniable evidence that pushing children into formal academics and organized activities before they are ready does more harm than good. He lamented, "In a society that prides itself on its preference for facts over hearsay, on its openness to research, and on its respect for 'expert' opinion, parents, educators, administrators, and legislators are ignoring the facts, the research and the expert opinion about how young children learn and how best to teach them. . . . When we instruct children in academic subjects, or in swimming, gymnastics, or ballet, at too early an age, we miseducate them; we put them at risk for short-term stress and long-term personality damage for no useful purpose."

Elkind pointed to the consistent result of reputable studies (such as that conducted by Benjamin Bloom) that a love of learning, not the inculcation of skills, is the key to the kind of early childhood development that can lead to great things. These findings, warned Elkind, point to the fallacy of early instruction as a way of producing children who will attain eminence. He noted that with gifted and talented individuals, as with children in general, the most important thing is an excitement about learning: "Miseducation, by focusing on skills to the detriment of motivation, pays an enormous price for teaching infants and young children what amounts to a few tricks."

He further observed that those advocating early instruction in skills and early out-of-home education rely upon youngsters who are very disadvantaged to tout early education's advantages. "Accordingly, the image of the competent child introduced to remedy the understimulation of low-income children now serves as the rationale for the overstimulation of middle-class children."

Dr. Jack Westman of the Rockford Institute, renowned child psychiatrist Dr. Stanley Greenspan, and brain researcher Jane Healy are among the many unheeded others who warn of the implications of forcing the "childhood as a race" approach upon young children. Laments Westman, "The result is what is now referred to as the 'hothousing movement' for infants and toddlers devoted to expediting their development. This is occurring in spite of the evidence that the long-term outcomes of early didactic, authoritarian approaches with younger children relate negatively to intellectual development."

In an interview for "Parent and Child" magazine, Dr. Greenspan insisted that young children suffer greatly if there is inadequate "emotional learning" in their daily lives.

In an interview for *Parent and Child* magazine, Dr. Greenspan insisted that young children suffer greatly if there is inadequate "emotional learning" in their daily lives. Such learning, he explained, is both a requisite for their ability to relate well with others and the foundation of cognitive learning. "Emotional development and interactions form the foundation for all children's learning—especially in the first five years of life. During these years, children abstract from their emotional experiences constantly to learn even the most basic concepts. Take, for example, something like saying hello or learning when you can be aggressive and when you have to be nice—and all of these are cues by emotions."

In *Endangered Minds: Why Children Don't Think and What We Can Do About It*, Healy states the case for allowing young children to play with those who love them before requiring them to learn academic skills. She intones, "Driving the cold spikes of inappropriate pressure into the malleable heart of a child's learning may seriously distort the unfolding of both intellect and motivation. This self-serving intellectual assault, increasingly condemned by teachers who see its warped products, reflects a more general ignorance of the growing brain. . . . Explaining things to children won't do the job; they must have the chance to experience, wonder, experiment, and act it out for themselves. It is this process, throughout life, that enables the growth of intelligence."

Healy goes so far as to describe the damaging effect on the "functional organization of the plastic brain" in pushing too hard too soon: "Before brain regions are myelinated, they do not operate efficiently. For this reason, trying to 'make' children master academic skills for which they do not have the requisite maturation may result in mixed-up patterns of learning. . . . It is possible to force skills by intensive instruction, but this may cause a child to use immature, inappropriate neural networks and distort the natural growth process."

Play is a way for children to relish childhood, prepare for adulthood, and discover their inner passions.

Play is important for intellectual growth, the exploration of individuality, and the growth of a conscience. Play is a way for children to relish childhood, prepare for adulthood, and discover their inner passions. Legendary psychoanalyst D.W. Winnicott warned us not to underestimate the importance of play. In *The Work and Play of Winnicott*, Simon A. Grolnick elucidates Winnicott's concept of play.

Play in childhood and throughout the life cycle helps to relieve the tension of living, helps to prepare for the serious, and sometimes for the deadly (e.g., war games), helps define and redefine the boundaries between ourselves and others, helps give us a fuller sense of our own personal and bodily being. Playing provides a trying-out ground for proceeding onward, and it enhances drive satisfaction. . . . Winnicott repeatedly stressed that when playing becomes too drive-infested and excited, it loses its creative growth-building capability and begins to move toward loss of control or a fetishistic rigidity. . . . Civilization's demands for controlled, socialized behavior gradually, and sometimes insidiously, supersedes the psychosomatic and aesthetic pleasures of open system play.

When we discard playtime, we jeopardize the child's fresh, creative approach to the world. The minuscule amount of peace that children are permitted means that thinking and introspection are demoted as well. Thought requires being, not always doing. Children who are not allowed to retreat once in a while into themselves are not allowed to find out what is there. Our busy lives become ways of hiding from the recesses of the mind. Teaching children to be tough and prepared for the world, making them into achieving doers instead of capable thinkers, has its consequences. Children's innate curiosity is intense. When that natural curiosity has no room to fulfill itself, it burns out like a smothered flame.

In an age when "socialization" into society's ideals and mores is accepted even for babies and toddlers, we should remember that institutionalized schooling even for older children is a relatively new phenomenon. Mass education was a post-Industrial Revolution invention, one that served the dual purposes of preparing children for work and freeing parents to contribute fully to the industrial structure. No longer was work something that families did together, as a unit.

The separation of children from the family's work paved the way for schools and social reformers to assume the task of preparing children for life. This is a lofty role. As parents, we need to inform ourselves as to what our children are being prepared *for* and *how* they are being prepared.

Although our children's days are filled with instruction, allowing them little time of their own, we seem frequently inattentive as to just what they are learning. As William Bennett, Allan Bloom, and others have pointed out, recent years have been characterized by the reformulation of our schools, universities, and information sources according to a relativist, left-leaning ideology saturated with cynicism. This ideology leaves students with little moral-intellectual ground to stand on, as they are taught disrespect not only for past ideas and literary works but for the American political system and Judeo-Christian ethics. Such works as *The Five Little Peppers and How They Grew* and *Little Women* are windows into the soul of a much less cynical (and much less hectic) time.

Teaching children about the great thinkers, writers, and statesmen of the past is neglected as the very idea of greatness and heroism is disputed. Thus, the respect for greatness that might have caused children to glance upward from their TV show or activity and the stories about their country's early history that might have given them respect for a time when computer games didn't exist are not a factor in their lives. The word *preoccupied* acquires new significance, for children's minds are stuffed with the here and now.

The Devaluation of Homelife

The busyness of modern child rearing and the myopia of the modern outlook reinforce each other. The very ideas that education is a race and that preschool-age children's participation in beneficial experience is more important than playing or being with the family are modern ones that continually reinforce themselves for lack of alternatives. Our busy lives leave insufficient time to question whether all this busyness is necessary and whether the content of our childrens' education is good.

The possibility that children might regard their activities less than fondly when they are older because these activities were forced upon them is not addressed. The possibility that they may never find their own passionate interests is not considered. (I came across an interesting television show that discussed the problem middle-school coaches are having with burned-out and unenthusiastic participants in a wide range of sports. The coaches attributed this to the fact that children had already been doing these sports for years and were tired of the pressure.)

One needs time to be a thinker, freedom to be creative, and some level of choice to be enthusiastic. Families can bestow upon children opportunities for autonomy while at the same time giving them a stable base to fall back upon and moral and behavioral guidelines. Having a competitive edge is neither as important nor as lasting as the ability to lead a genuine, intelligently thought-out, and considerate life.

Some of the best learning experiences happen not in an institution, not with a teacher, but in a child's independent "research" of the world at hand.

Some of the best learning experiences happen not in an institution, not with a teacher, but in a child's independent "research" of the world at hand. As the child interprets the world around her, creates new things with the materials available to her, and extracts new ideas from the recesses of her mind, she is learning to be an active, contributing participant in the world. She occupies her physical, temporal, and intellectual space in a positive, resourceful way. Conversely, if she is constantly stuffed with edifying "opportunities," resentment and lack of autonomy are the likely results.

In *The Erosion of Childhood*, Valerie Polakow insists upon the child's ability to "make history" as opposed to simply receiving it. Lamenting the overinstitutionalization of children in day care and school, she warns, "Children as young as a year old now enter childhood institutions to be formally schooled in the ways of the social system and emerge eighteen years later to enter the world of adulthood having been deprived of their own history-making power, their ability to act upon the world in significant and meaningful ways." She adds, "The world in which children live—the institutional world that babies, toddlers and the very young have increasingly come to inhabit and confront—is a world in which they become the objects, not the subjects of history, a world in which history is being made of them."

Day care provides both too much stimulation of the chaotic, disorganized kind, which comes inevitably from the cohabitation of large numbers of babies and toddlers, and too much of the organized kind that comes, of necessity, from group-centered living. It provides too little calm, quiet, space, or comfort and too little opportunity to converse and relate to a loving other.

Imagine, for example, a parent sitting down with her child for a "tea party." As she pours real tea into her own cup and milk into her child's, the "how to do things" is taken seriously. The child is encouraged to say "thank you" and to offer cookies to his mother, and their chat begins. Although they are pretending to be two adults, the ritual is real; it occurs in a real home setting; it provides the child with real food and a real opportunity for "mature" conversation. The mother says, "I'm so glad to be here for tea. How have you been?" The child, enjoying the chance to play the part of his mother's host, answers, "Fine! Would you like another cookie?" "Oh yes, thank you," answers his mother. "These cookies are delicious!" The child is learning about civilized behavior.

Children living in the new millennium need a refuge from the impersonal, the mechanical, and the programmed. We must provide them with more than opportunities for skill learning, socialization, and competition.

Then, picture the toy tea set at the learning center. Two children decide "to have tea." They fight over who has asked whom over. When one child asks, "How have you been?" the other loses interest and walks away. Too much of this peer-centered learning and not enough of adult-based learning clearly has negative implications for social development. The child simply cannot learn right from wrong, proper from improper, from other children who themselves have trouble making these distinctions.

Homelife that provides a break from group action has innumerable advantages for older children as well. Think of the different learning experiences a child receives from sitting down at the dinner table with his family and from gulping down a hamburger on the way to a nighttime game. In one case, the child has the opportunity to learn about manners and conversation. In the other, he is given another opportunity to compete with peers. (This is not to deny the benefits of being part of a team but simply to state that homelife itself is beneficial.) I hear many parents of high-school students complain about the competitive, selfish manner of today's students. And, yet, most of these students have not a moment in their day that is not competitive.

How can we expect children to value kindness and cooperation when their free time has been totally usurped by activities wherein winning is everything? At home, winning is not everything (unless the child expends all his time trying to "beat the enemy" in a video game). At home, a child is much more likely to be reprimanded for not compromising with his siblings than for not "defeating" them. If homelife provides children with time to define their individuality and interact with family members (and all the give-and-take implied), then it is certainly an invaluable aspect of a child's advancement.

Children living in the new millennium need a refuge from the impersonal, the mechanical, and the programmed. We must provide them with more than opportunities for skill learning, socialization, and competition. Otherwise, something will be missing in their humanness. For to be human is to have the capacity for intimate attachments based upon love (which can grow more intimate because of the closeness that family life provides); it is to reason and to have a moral sense of things; it is to be capable of a spontaneity that stems from original thought or from some passion within.

We must set our children free from our frenetic, goal-oriented pace. We must create for them a private realm wherein no child-rearing "professional" can tread. Within this secure space, the possibilities are endless. With this stable base to fall back upon, children will dare to dream, think, and explore. They will compete, learn, and socialize as the blossoming individuals that they are, not as automatons engineered for results.

ANNE R. PIERCE is an author and political philosopher who lives in Cincinnati with her husband and three children. As a writer, she finds that bringing up children in the modern world gives her much food for thought.

Reading Your Baby's Mind

New research on infants finally begins to answer the question: what's going on in there?

Pat Wingert and Martha Brant

Little Victoria Bateman is blond and blue-eyed and as cute a baby as there ever was. At 6 months, she is also trusting and unsuspecting, which is a good thing, because otherwise she'd never go along with what's about to happen. It's a blistering June afternoon in Lubbock, Texas, and inside the Human Sciences lab at Texas Tech University, Victoria's mother is settling her daughter into a high chair, where she is the latest subject in an ongoing experiment aimed at understanding the way babies think. Sybil Hart, an associate professor of human development and leader of the study, trains video cameras on mother and daughter. Everything is set. Hart hands Cheryl Bateman a children's book, "Elmo Pops In," and instructs her to engross herself in its pages. "Just have a conversation with me about the book," Hart tells her. "The most important thing is, do not look at [Victoria.]" As the two women chat, Victoria looks around the room, impassive and a little bored.

After a few minutes, Hart leaves the room and returns cradling a lifelike baby doll. Dramatically, Hart places it in Cheryl Bateman's arms, and tells her to cuddle the doll while continuing to ignore Victoria. "That's OK, little baby," Bateman coos, hugging and rocking the doll. Victoria is not bored anymore. At first, she cracks her best smile, showcasing a lone stubby tooth. When that doesn't work, she begins kicking. But her mom pays her no mind. That's when Victoria loses it. Soon she's beet red and crying so hard it looks like she might spit up. Hart rushes in. "OK, we're done," she says, and takes back the doll. Cheryl Bateman goes to comfort her daughter. "I've never seen her react like that to anything," she says. Over the last 10 months, Hart has repeated the scenario hundreds of times. It's the same in nearly every case: tiny babies, overwhelmed with jealousy. Even Hart was stunned to find that infants could experience an emotion, which, until recently, was thought to be way beyond their grasp.

And that's just for starters. The helpless, seemingly clueless infant staring up at you from his crib, limbs flailing, drool oozing, has a lot more going on inside his head than you ever imagined. A wealth of new research is leading pediatricians and child psychologists to rethink their long-held beliefs about the emotional and intellectual abilities of even very young babies.

In 1890, psychologist William James famously described an infant's view of the world as "one great blooming, buzzing confusion." It was a notion that held for nearly a century: infants were simple-minded creatures who merely mimicked those around them and grasped only the most basic emotions—happy, sad, angry. Science is now giving us a much different picture of what goes on inside their hearts and heads. Long before they form their first words or attempt the feat of sitting up, they are already mastering complex emotions—jealousy, empathy, frustration—that were once thought to be learned much later in toddlerhood.

They are also far more sophisticated intellectually than we once believed. Babies as young as 4 months have advanced powers of deduction and an ability to decipher intricate patterns. They have a strikingly nuanced visual palette, which enables them to notice small differences, especially in faces, that adults and older children lose the ability to see. Until a baby is 3 months old, he can recognize a scrambled photograph of his mother just as quickly as a photo in which everything is in the right place. And big brothers and sisters beware: your sib has a long memory—and she can hold a grudge.

Babies yet to utter an INTELLIGENT SYLLABLE are now known to feel a range of COMPLEX EMOTIONS like envy and empathy.

The new research is sure to enthrall new parents—See, Junior *is* a genius!—but it's more than just an academic exercise. Armed with the new information, pediatricians are starting to change the way they evaluate their youngest patients. In addition to tracking physical development, they are now focusing much more deeply on emotional advancement. The research shows how powerful emotional well-being is to a child's future health. A baby who fails to meet certain key "emotional milestones" may have trouble learning to speak, read and, later, do well in school. By reading emotional responses, doctors have begun to discover ways to tell if a baby as young as 3 months is showing early signs of possible psychological disorders, including depression, anxiety, learning disabilities and perhaps autism. "Instead of just asking if they're crawling or sitting, we're asking more questions about how they share their world with their caregivers," says Dr. Chet Johnson, chairman of the American Academy of Pediatrics' early-childhood committee. "Do they point to things? When they see a new person, how do they react? How children do on social and emotional and language skills are better predictors of success in adulthood than motor skills are." The goal: in the not-too-distant future, researchers hope doctors will routinely identify at-risk kids years earlier than they do now—giving parents crucial extra time to turn things around.

One of the earliest emotions that even tiny babies display is, admirably enough, empathy. In fact, concern for others may be hard-wired into babies' brains. Plop a newborn down next to another crying infant, and chances are, both babies will soon be wailing away. "People have always known that babies cry when they hear other babies cry," says Martin Hoffman, a psychology professor at New York University who did the first studies on infant empathy in the 1970s. "The question was, why are they crying?" Does it mean that the baby is truly concerned for his fellow human, or just annoyed by the racket? A recent study conducted in Italy, which built on Hoffman's own work, has largely settled the question. Researchers played for infants tapes of other babies crying. As predicted, that was enough to start the tears flowing. But when researchers played babies recordings of their own cries, they rarely began crying themselves. The verdict: "There is some rudimentary empathy in place, right from birth," Hoffman says. The intensity of the emotion tends to fade over time. Babies older than 6 months no longer cry but grimace at the discomfort of others. By 13 to 15 months, babies tend to take matters into their own hands. They'll try to comfort a crying playmate. "What I find most charming is when, even if the two mothers are present, they'll bring their own mother over to help," Hoffman says.

Part of that empathy may come from another early-baby skill that's now better understood, the ability to discern emotions from the facial expressions of the people around them. "Most textbooks still say that babies younger than 6 months don't recognize emotions," says Diane Montague, assistant professor of psychology at LaSalle University in Philadelphia. To put that belief to the test, Montague came up with a twist on every infant's favorite game, peekaboo, and recruited dozens of 4-month-olds to play along. She began by peeking around a cloth with a big smile on her face. Predictably, the babies were delighted, and stared at her intently—the time-tested way to tell if a baby is interested. On the fourth peek, though, Montague emerged with a sad look on her face. This time, the response was much different. "They not only looked away," she says, but wouldn't look back even when she began smiling again. Refusing to make eye contact is a classic baby sign of distress. An angry face got their attention once again, but their faces showed no pleasure. "They seemed primed to be alert, even vigilant," Montague says. "I realize that's speculative in regard to infants

. . . I think it shows that babies younger than 6 months find meaning in expressions."

This might be a good place to pause for a word about the challenges and perils of baby research. Since the subjects can't speak for themselves, figuring out what's going on inside their heads is often a matter of reading their faces and body language. If this seems speculative, it's not. Over decades of trial and error, researchers have fine-tuned their observation skills and zeroed in on numerous consistent baby responses to various stimuli: how long they stare at an object, what they reach out for and what makes them recoil in fear or disgust can often tell experienced researchers everything they need to know. More recently, scientists have added EEGs and laser eye tracking, which allow more precise readings. Coming soon: advanced MRI scans that will allow a deeper view inside the brain.

When infants near their first birthdays, they become increasingly sophisticated social learners. They begin to infer what others are thinking by following the gaze of those around them. "By understanding others' gaze, babies come to understand others' minds," says Andrew Meltzoff, a professor of psychology at the University of Washington who has studied the "gaze following" of thousands of babies. "You can tell a lot about people, what they're interested in and what they intend to do next, by watching their eyes. It appears that even babies know that . . . This is how they learn to become expert members of our culture."

Meltzoff and colleague Rechele Brooks have found that this skill first appears at 10 to 11 months, and is not only an important marker of a baby's emotional and social growth, but can predict later language development. In their study, babies who weren't proficient at gaze-following by their first birthday had much less advanced-language skills at 2. Meltzoff says this helps explain why language occurs more slowly in blind children, as well as children of depressed mothers, who tend not to interact as much with their babies.

In fact, at just a few months, infants begin to develop superpowers when it comes to observation. Infants can easily tell the difference between human faces. But at the University of Minnesota, neuroscientist Charles Nelson (now of Harvard) wanted to test how discerning infants really are. He showed a group of 6-month-old babies a photo of a chimpanzee, and gave them time to stare at it until they lost interest. They were then shown another chimp. The babies perked up and stared at the new photo. The infants easily recognized each chimp as an individual—they were fascinated by each new face. Now unless you spend a good chunk of your day hanging around the local zoo, chances are you couldn't tell the difference between a roomful of chimps at a glance. As it turned out, neither could babies just a few months older. By 9 months, those kids had lost the ability to tell chimps apart; but at the same time, they had increased their powers of observation when it came to human faces.

Nelson has now taken his experiment a step further, to see how early babies can detect subtle differences in facial expressions, a key building block of social development. He designed a new study that is attempting to get deep inside babies' heads by measuring brain-wave activity. Nelson sent out letters to the parents of nearly every newborn in the area, inviting them to participate. Earlier this summer it was Dagny Winberg's turn. The 7-month-old was all smiles as her mother, Armaiti, carried her into the lab, where she was fitted with a snug cap wired with 64 sponge sensors. Nelson's assistant, grad student Meg Moulson, began flashing photographs on a screen of a woman. In each photo, the woman had a slightly different expression—many different shades of happiness and fear. Dagny was given time to look at each photo until she became bored and looked away. The whole time, a computer was closely tracking her brain activity, measuring her mind's minutest responses to the different photos. Eventually, after she'd run through 60 photos, Dagny had had enough of the game and began whimpering and fidgeting. That ended the session. The point of the experiment is to see if baby brain scans look like those of adults. "We want to see if babies categorize emotions in the ways that adults do," Moulson says. "An adult can see a slight smile and categorize it as happy. We want to know if babies can do the same." They don't have the answer yet, but Nelson believes that infants who display early signs of emotional disorders, such as autism, may be helped if they can develop these critical powers of observation and emotional engagement.

Halfway across the country, researchers are working to dispel another baby cliché: out of sight, out of mind. It was long believed that babies under 9 months didn't grasp the idea of "object permanence"—the ability to know, for instance, that when Mom leaves the room, she isn't gone forever. New research by psychologist Su-hua Wang at the University of California, Santa Cruz, is showing that babies understand the concept as early as 10 weeks. Working with 2- and 3-month-olds, she performs a little puppet show. Each baby sees a duck on a stage. Wang covers the duck, moves it across the stage and lifts the cover. Sometimes the duck is there. Other times, the duck disappears beneath a trapdoor. When they see the duck has gone missing, the babies stare intently at the empty stage, searching for it. "At 2½ months," she says, "they already have the idea that the object continues to exist."

A strong, well-developed ability to connect with the world—and with parents in particular—is especially important when babies begin making their first efforts at learning to speak. Baby talk is much more than mimickry. Michael Goldstein, a psychologist at Cornell University, gathered two groups of 8-month-olds and decked them out in overalls rigged up with wireless microphones and transmitters. One group of mothers was told to react immediately when their babies cooed or babbled, giving them big smiles and loving pats. The other group of parents was also told to smile at their kids, but randomly, unconnected to the babies' sounds. It came as no surprise that the babies who received immediate feedback babbled more and advanced quicker than those who didn't. But what interested Goldstein was the way in which the parents, without realizing it, raised the "babble bar" with their kids. "The kinds of simple sounds that get parents' attention at 4 months don't get the same reaction at 8 months," he says. "That motivates babies to experiment with different sound combinations until they find new ones that get noticed."

A decade ago Patricia Kuhl, a professor of speech and hearing at the University of Washington and a leading authority on early language, proved that tiny babies have a unique ability to learn a foreign language. As a result of her well-publicized findings, parents ran out to buy foreign-language tapes, hoping their little Einsteins would pick up Russian or French before they left their cribs. It didn't work, and Kuhl's new research shows why. Kuhl put American 9-month-olds in a room with Mandarin-speaking adults, who showed them toys while talking to them. After 12 sessions, the babies had learned to detect subtle Mandarin phonetic sounds that couldn't be heard by a separate group of babies who were exposed only to English. Kuhl then repeated the experiment, but this time played the identical Mandarin lessons to babies on video- and audiotape. That group of babies failed to learn any Mandarin. Kuhl says that without the emotional connection, the babies considered the tape recording just another background noise, like a vacuum cleaner. "We were genuinely surprised by the outcome," she says. "We all assumed that when infants stare at a television, and look engaged, that they are learning from it." Kuhl says there's plenty of work to be done to explain why that isn't true. "But at first blush one thinks that people—at least babies—need people to learn."

So there you have it. That kid over there with one sock missing and smashed peas all over his face is actually a formidable presence, in possession of keen powers of observation, acute emotional sensitivity and an impressive arsenal of deductive powers. "For the last 15 years, we've been focused on babies' abilities—what they know and when they knew it," says the University of Washington's Meltzoff. "But now we want to know what all this predicts about later development. What does all this mean for the child?"

Some of these questions are now finding answers. Take shyness, for instance. It's long been known that 15 to 20 percent of children are shy and anxious by nature. But doctors didn't know why some seemed simply to grow out of it, while for others it became a debilitating condition. Recent studies conducted by Nathan Fox of the University of Maryland show that shyness is initially driven by biology. He proved it by wiring dozens of 9-month-olds to EEG machines and conducting a simple experiment. When greeted by a stranger, "behaviorally inhibited" infants tensed up, and showed more activity in the parts of the brain associated with anxiety and fear. Babies with outgoing personalities reached out to the stranger. Their EEG scans showed heightened activity in the parts of the brain that govern positive emotions like pleasure.

Just because your baby is MORE PERCEPTIVE than you thought doesn't mean she'll be DAMAGED if she cries for a minute.

But Fox, who has followed some of these children for 15 years, says that parenting style has a big impact on which kind of adult a child will turn out to be. Children of overprotective parents, or those whose parents didn't encourage them to overcome shyness and childhood anxiety, often remain shy and anxious as adults. But kids born to confident and sensitive parents who gently help them to take emotional risks and coax them out of their shells can often overcome early awkwardness. That's an important finding, since behaviorally inhibited kids are also at higher risk for other problems.

Stanley Greenspan, clinical professor of psychiatry and pediatrics at George Washington University Medical School, is one of the leaders in developing diagnostic tools to help doctors identify babies who may be at risk for language and learning problems, autism and a whole range of other problems. He recently completed a checklist of social and emotional "milestones" that babies should reach by specific ages (graphic). "I'd like to see doctors screen babies for these milestones and tell parents exactly what to do if their babies are not mastering them. One of our biggest problems now is that parents may sense intuitively that something is not right," but by the time they are able to get their child evaluated, "that family has missed a critical time to, maybe, get that baby back on track."

So what should parents do with all this new information? First thing: relax. Just because your baby is more perceptive than you might have thought doesn't mean she's going to be damaged for life if she cries in her crib for a minute while you answer the phone. Or that he'll wind up quitting school and stealing cars if he witnesses an occasional argument between his parents. Children crave—and thrive on—interaction, one-on-one time and lots of eye contact. That doesn't mean filling the baby's room with "educational" toys and posters. A child's social, emotional, and academic life begins with the earliest conversations between parent and child: the first time the baby locks eyes with you; the quiet smile you give your infant and the smile she gives you back. Your child is speaking to you all the time. It's just a matter of knowing how to listen.

With T. Trent Gegax, Margaret Nelson, Karen Breslau, Nadine Joseph and Ben Whitford

20 Ways to Boost Your Baby's Brain Power

ALICE STERLING HONIG, PH.D.

At birth, your baby's brain contains 100 billion neurons (as many as there are stars in the Milky Way)! During his first years, he will grow trillions of brain-cell connections, called neural synapses.

The rule for brain wiring is "use it or lose it." Synapses that are not "wired together" through stimulation are pruned and lost during a child's school years. Although an infant's brain does have some neurological hard wiring (such as the ability to learn any language), it is more pliable and more vulnerable than an adult's brain. And, amazingly, a toddler's brain has twice as many neural connections as an adult's.

When you provide loving, language-enriched experiences for your baby, you are giving his brain's neural connections and pathways more chances to become wired together. In turn, he will acquire rich language, reasoning, and planning skills.

1. **Give your baby a physically healthy start before he is born.** Stay healthy while you are pregnant, and be aware that certain drugs can be destructive to your baby's brain in utero. Many children who were drug-abused in the womb struggle with severe learning problems and suddenly act with unprovoked aggressive behaviors. Studies have also revealed that cigarette smoking during pregnancy causes lower fourth-grade reading scores.

2. **Have meaningful conversations.** Respond to infant coos with delighted vocalizations. Slowly draw out your syllables in a high-pitched voice as you exclaim, "Pretty baby!" This talk is called "parentese." The areas in the brain for understanding speech and producing language need your rich input.

3. **Play games that involve the hands** (Patty-cake, Peekaboo, This Little Piggy). Babies respond well to learning simple sequential games.

4. **Be attentive.** When your baby points, be sure to follow with your gaze and remark on items or events of interest to her. This "joint attention" confirms for your baby how important her interests and observations are to you.

5. **Foster an early passion for books.** Choose books with large and colorful pictures, and share your baby's delight in pointing and making noises—say, the animal sounds to go along with farm pictures. Modulate the tone of your voice; simplify or elaborate on story lines; encourage toddlers to talk about books. Remember that building your baby's "receptive" language (understanding spoken words) is more important than developing his "expressive" language (speaking) in infancy.

6. **Use diaper time to build your baby's emotional feelings** of having a "lovable body." Stroke your baby's tummy and hair. Studies have shown that babies who are not often touched have brains that are smaller than normal for their age. Also, when diapering your baby, you are at the ideal 12 to 18 inches from her eyes to attract attention to your speech.

7. **Choose developmentally appropriate toys** that allow babies to explore and interact. Toys such as a windup jack-in-the-box or stackable blocks help your baby learn cause-and-effect relationships and "if-then" reasoning. If a baby stacks a big block on a smaller one, the top block falls off. If he successfully stacks a small block on a bigger one, he "wires in" the information.

8. **Respond promptly when your baby cries.** Soothe, nurture, cuddle, and reassure him so that you build positive brain circuitry in the limbic area of the brain, which relates to emotions. Your calm holding and cuddling, and your day-to-day intimate engagement with your baby, signal emotional security to the brain.

9. **Build trust by being attentive and focused.** Babies who are securely attached to you emotionally will be able to invest more life energy in the pleasures of exploration, learning, and discovery.

10. **Use body massage** to decrease your infant's stress and enhance her feelings of well-being and emotional security. Loving touches promote growth in young babies. Research has shown that premature babies who are massaged three times daily are ready to leave the hospital days earlier than babies who do not receive massages.

11. **Enlist help from your toddler at clean-up times**—a good way to practice categorization. Toddlers learn that stuffed animals have one place to go for "night-night"

time; cars, trucks, and other vehicles also have their special storage place. Children need to learn about sorting into categories and seriation (placing things in order; for example, from littlest to biggest) as part of their cognitive advancement in preschool.

12. **Set up a safe environment** for your crawling baby or toddler. Spatial learning is important, and your mobile child will begin to understand parameters such as under, over, near, and far. He will be able to establish mental maps of his environment and a comfortable relationship with the world in which he lives.

13. **Sing songs** such as "Itsy Bitsy Spider" and "Ring-Around-the-Rosy." The body motions and finger play will help your baby integrate sounds with large and small motor actions. Songs also enhance your child's learning of rhythms, rhymes, and language patterns.

14. **Match your tempo to your child's temperament.** Some children adjust easily to strange situations, some are bold and impulsive, and some are quite shy. Go with the flow as you try to increase a shy child's courage and comfort level. Help a highly active child safely use his wonderful energy while learning impulse control. Your acceptance will give him the comfort he needs to experiment and learn freely.

15. **Make meals and rest times positive.** Say the names of foods out loud as your baby eats. Express pleasure as she learns to feed herself, no matter how messy the initial attempts may be. This will wire in good associations with mealtime and eating. Battles and nagging about food can lead to negative emotional brain patterns.

16. **Provide clear responses to your baby's actions.** A young, developing brain learns to make sense of the world if you respond to your child's behavior in predictable, reassuring, and appropriate ways. Be consistent.

17. **Use positive discipline.** Create clear consequences without frightening or causing shame to your child. If your toddler acts inappropriately, such as by hitting another child, get down to his eye level, use a low, serious tone of voice, and clearly restate the rule. Keep rules simple, consistent, and reasonable for your child's age. Expecting a toddling baby not to touch a glass vase on a coffee table is not reasonable. Expecting a toddler to keep sand in the sandbox and not throw it is reasonable!

18. **Model empathic feelings** for others. Use "teachable moments" when someone seems sad or upset to help your toddler learn about feelings, caring, sharing, and kindness. The more brain connections you create for empathic responses and gentle courtesies, the more these brain circuits will be wired in. This helps not only with language and cognitive learning, but with positive emotional skills, too!

19. **Arrange supervised play** with messy materials, such as water, sand, and even mud. This will teach your toddler about the physics and properties of mixtures and textures, liquids and solids. During bath time, the brain wires in knowledge about water, slippery soap, and terry towel textures. Sensory experiences are grist for the learning brain.

20. **Express joy and interest in your baby.** Let your body language, your shining eyes, your attentiveness to babbling and baby activities, and your gentle caresses and smiles validate the deeply lovable nature of your little one.

ALICE STERLING HONIG, Ph.D., professor emerita at Syracuse University, is the author, with **H. BROPHY**, of *Talking With Your Baby: Family as the First School.*

Long-Term Studies of Preschool: Lasting Benefits Far Outweigh Costs

Mr. Bracey and Mr. Stellar summarize the findings of three studies that provide strong evidence of long-term positive outcomes for high-quality preschool programs. All that remains now, they argue, is for the U.S. to make a commitment to universal, free preschool.

GERALD W. BRACEY AND ARTHUR STELLAR

The November 2001 issue of the *Kappan* contained a special section offering a cross-national perspective on early childhood education and day care. Day-care programs in England, Italy, and Sweden were described and contrasted with day care in the U.S. The other countries, especially Sweden, have coherent, comprehensive programs based on a set of assumptions about the positive outcomes of early education. In the U.S., by contrast, there is a "nonsystem." Sharon Lynn Kagan and Linda Hallmark wrote that, in the U.S., "not only has early childhood never been a national priority, but decades of episodic, on-again, off-again efforts have yielded a set of uncoordinated programs and insufficient investment in the infrastructure. Often, the most important components of high-quality education and care—financing, curriculum development, and teacher education—are neglected."[1]

According to Kagan and Hallmark, the U.S. has historically resisted major government intrusions into the early years of education because such intervention would signal a failure on the part of the family. This resistance has produced a vicious circle: parents resist government intervention in the education of young children on ideological grounds; the government, for its part, doesn't produce high-quality day care; parental resistance to government day care solidifies because of the low quality of the care. Today, the ideology that seeks to keep government out of family matters is still very much alive. David Salisbury of the Cato Institute put it this way: "The key to producing intelligent, healthy children does not lie in putting more of them in taxpayer-funded preschools. . . . Instead of forcing mothers into the workplace through heavy taxation, the government should reduce the tax burden on families and, thereby, allow child care to remain in the capable hands of parents."[2]

This view of day care is most unfortunate, as evidence is now strong that high-quality day care produces long-term positive outcomes. Three studies of specific programs provide the evidence.

The "granddaddy" of these three studies is known as the High/Scope Perry Preschool Project.[3] In the mid-1960s, African American children whose parents had applied to a preschool program in Ypsilanti, Michigan, were randomly assigned to receive the program or not. Those who tested the children, interviewed the parents, or were the children's teachers once they reached school age did not know to which group the children had been assigned. Random assignment eliminates any systematic bias between the groups, although it cannot *guarantee* that they will be the same. By keeping the information on group assignment confidential, the experimenters sought to minimize any kind of Pygmalion effects stemming from expectations about the children who had been in preschool and those who had not. Few preschool programs existed at the time, and children in the control group remained at home.

Parents of the preschool children had completed an average of 9.4 years of school. Only 20% of the parents had high school diplomas, compared to 33% of all African American adults at the time of the study. The children attended preschool for a half day for eight months. The first group of children, entering in 1962, received one year of the preschool program; later groups received two. The program also included weekly, 90-minute home visits by members of the project staff.

The vision of childhood underlying the High/Scope Program was shaped by Piaget and other theorists who viewed children as active learners. Teachers asked questions that allowed children to generate conversations with them. Those who developed the program isolated 10 categories of preschool experience that they deemed important for developing children: creative representation, language and literacy, social relations and personal initiative, movement, music, classification, seriation (creating series and patterns), number, space, and time. Children partici-pated in individual, small-and large-group activities. The cur-riculum and instruction flowed from both constructivist and cognitive/developmental approaches.[4]

Teachers rarely assessed the children's specific knowledge. This approach stood in marked contrast to another preschool curriculum, Direct Instruction (DI). DI attempts to impart spe-cific bits of knowledge through rapid-fire drill and highly pro-grammed scripts.

A study of the Perry preschoolers and controls at age 40 is in progress. Other studies took place when the subjects reached ages 19 and 27. At age 19, the preschoolers had higher gradua-tion rates and were less likely to have been in special education. The graduation rate effect, though, was limited to females. The preschoolers also had higher scores on the Adult Performance Level Survey, a test from the American College Testing Pro-gram that simulates real-life problem situations.

By the time the two groups turned 27, 71% of the preschool group had earned high school diplomas or GEDs, compared to 54% of the control group. The preschoolers also earned more, were more likely to own their own homes, and had longer and more stable marriages. Members of the control group were arrested twice as often, and five times as many members of the control group (35%) had been arrested five or more times.

The second study is called the Abecedarian Project and has been run out of the University of North Carolina, Chapel Hill, since 1972.[5] The study identified children at birth and provided them full-day care, 50 weeks a year, from birth until they entered school. Adults would talk to the children, show them toys or pictures, and offer them opportunities to react to sights and sounds in the environment. As the children grew, these adult/child interactions became more concept and skill oriented. For older preschoolers, they also became more group oriented. Some children continued in the program until age 8, while another group of children began to receive an enrichment program after they started school.

Although the children were randomly assigned, it is impor-tant to note that children in the "control" group were not without assistance. To reduce the chances that any differences might come from nutritional deficiencies affecting brain growth, the researchers supplied an enriched baby formula. Social work and crisis intervention services were also available to families in the control group. If the researchers' assessments indicated that the children were lagging developmentally, the families were referred to a relevant social agency. As a consequence of these policies and services, four of the children in the control group were moved to the head of the waiting list for what the researchers called "scarce slots in other quality community child centers."

In the decade following the start of the Perry Project, early childhood education became more prevalent, especially in uni-versity areas like Chapel Hill. Thus some of the families in the control group sent their children to other preschool programs. It seems likely, therefore, that some children in the control group received benefits similar to those provided to the children in the experimental group. These benefits would tend to reduce the differences seen between experimental and control groups.

A 1988 follow-up study of the subjects at age 21 found that young adults who had taken part in the Abecedarian Project completed more years of schooling than the controls (12.2 ver-sus 11.6). As with the Perry Project, this difference was most evident among the females in the study. More members of the experimental group were still in school (42% versus 20%), and more had enrolled in four-year colleges (35.9% versus 13.7%). Forty-seven percent of the experimental group worked at skilled jobs, such as electrician, compared to just 27% of the control group. The subjects who had attended the Abecedarian preschool were less likely to smoke or to use marijuana, but they were no less likely to use alcohol or to indulge in binge drinking.

The researchers administered reading and math tests at ages 8, 12, 15, and 21. Subjects who had been in the program for eight years showed much better reading skills than those in the control group. The "effect sizes" obtained for reading ranged from 1.04 at age 8 to .79 at age 21. Effect sizes for math ranged from .64 at age 8 to .42 at age 21. Judgment must be used in interpreting effect sizes, but all researchers would consider these to be large, with the possible exception of the .42 for math at age 21, which might be considered "medium."

For subjects who had terminated the program when they entered school, the reading effect sizes ran from .75 at age 8 to .28 at age 21. The impact of math for the same group actually grew over time, from .27 at age 8 to .73 at age 21. In general, it appears that participants who continued with the Abecedarian program into the elementary grades were affected more than those who stopped at the end of preschool.

Subjects who received the school-only program showed smaller effect sizes. For reading, the effect size was .28 at age 8 and dwindled to just .11 at age 21. Once again, math showed increased impact over time, from .11 at age 8 to .26 at age 21.

The third major long-term study of preschool outcomes is known as the Chicago Child-Parent Center Program (CPC).[6] It was a much larger study than the Perry or Abecedarian project, but the children were not randomly assigned to experimental and control groups. The CPC was also much more diffuse than the other projects, taking place in some 20 centers, and initially teachers had more latitude over what kinds of materials were incorporated. Later, all centers adopted a program developed through the Chicago Board of Education that emphasized three major areas: body image and gross motor skills, perceptual/motor and arithmetic skills, and language.

As with the other projects, extensive parent involvement was emphasized. Project staff members visited the homes of partici-pants, and parents often accompanied children on field trips. In a 2000 follow-up study, subjects at age 21 who had taken part in the project had lower crime rates, higher high school comple-tion rates, and fewer retentions in grade.

Quality Concerns

There is now some evidence to suggest that even diffuse pro-grams that are broad in scope, such as Head Start, produce increases in high school graduation rates and in college atten-dance.[7] It seems clear, though, that high-quality programs are more effective. As laid out by Steven Barnett of Rutgers University, to be high quality, programs should have the following characteristics:

- low child/teacher ratios,
- highly qualified and well-paid teachers,
- intellectually rich and broad curricula,
- parents engaged as active partners with the program, and
- starting dates at or before the child reaches age 3.[8]

According to Kagan and Hallmark, many programs in the U.S. do not meet these criteria. Samuel Meisels of the Erikson Institute posits that the proposed "national reporting system" for Head Start will not bring such qualities to Head Start, either.[9] Indeed, Meisels worries that the system might reduce the quality of Head Start and psychologically damage children.

Costs and Benefits

The three preschool programs discussed here cost money, substantially more money than Head Start and even more than most preschools provided by private companies. The question arises as to whether the benefits from the programs are worth these costs. Cost-benefit analyses on all three conclude that they are.

A recent analysis of the Abecedarian Project by Leonard Masse and Steven Barnett of Rutgers University concluded that the benefit/cost ratio for the program was 4 to 1.[10] That is, society received four dollars in return for every dollar invested. This is not as high as analyses suggested for the Perry and Chicago projects. These yielded benefit/cost ratios on the order of 7 to 1. As we noted, though, a number of children in the Abecedarian project control groups attended some other preschools, and this could have reduced the differences between the groups.

Masse and Barnett estimated that children who took part in the program would earn $143,000 more over their lifetimes than those who did not. Their mothers would earn $133,000 more. The latter figure might surprise readers at first, but Masse and Barnett cite other studies finding that given stable, continuous child care, mothers are able to effectively reallocate their time to allow them to establish better, longer-term, and more productive relationships with employers.

Masse and Barnett also infer that the children of the children who participated in high-quality preschool programs will earn more as a consequence. Although it is difficult to quantify such projected earnings increases, they estimate a lifetime increase of $48,000 for the children of the participants. Although clearly conjectural, the logic is straightforward: the children who participated will experience outcomes, such as higher educational attainment, that are associated with higher earnings for future generations.

The cost-benefit analysts warn that these programs can be expensive. They estimated the cost of the Perry Project at $9,200 per child, per year, while the Abecedarian cost figure comes in at $13,900 (both estimates in constant 2002 dollars). This compares to $7,000 for Head Start. They worry that governments might experience "sticker shock" if they try to replicate these projects on a large-scale basis, but they caution that "costs alone offer little guidance. The costs of a program must be compared against the benefits that the program generates. Benefit/cost ratios that are greater than one indicate that a program is worthy of consideration regardless of the absolute level of program costs."[11]

The programs described in this article all involved children living in poverty. Little if any research exists on long-term benefits for middle-class children. Masse and Barnett argue that, if we limit the programs to children under age 5 and assume that 20% of those children live in poverty, the annual cost for high-quality preschool for those 20% would be $53 billion per year.

Governments, however, appear to be looking at absolute costs. The Education Commission of the States reports that eight states have cut back on funds available for preschool in 2002–03. Moreover, today, in early 2003, state government budgets are in their worst shape since World War II. Still, sentiment for universal preschool is growing. After reviewing the evidence on the impact of early childhood education, the Committee for Economic Development led off a monograph as follows:

> The Committee for Economic Development (CED) calls on the federal and state governments to undertake a new national compact to make early education available to all children age 3 and over. To ensure that all children have the opportunity to enter school ready to learn, the nation needs to reform its current, haphazard, piecemeal, and underfunded approach to early learning by linking programs and providers to coherent state-based systems. The goal should be universal access to free, high-quality prekindergarten classes, offered by a variety of providers for all children whose parents want them to participate.[12]

Such a program makes much more sense to us than a program that tests all children in reading, math, and science in grades 3 through 8. Alas, Chris Dreibelbis of the CED reports that, while the CED monograph has been well received in both the education and business communities, there is little movement that might make its proposal a reality.[13]

Notes

1. Sharon L. Kagan and Linda G. Hallmark, "Early Care and Education Policies in Sweden: Implications for the United States," *Phi Delta Kappan*, November 2001, p. 241.

2. David Salisbury, "Preschool Is Overhyped," *USA Today*, 18 September 2002.

3. John R. Berrueta-Clement et al., *Changed Lives: The Effects of the Perry Preschool Program on Youths Through Age 19* (Ypsilanti, Mich.: High/ Scope Press, 1984); and Lawrence J. Schweinhart, Helen V. Barnes, and David P. Weikart, *Significant Benefits: The High/Scope Perry Preschool Study Through Age 27* (Ypsilanti, Mich.: High/Scope Press, 1993).

4. Mary Hohmann and David P. Weikart, *Educating Young Children: Active Learning Practices for Preschool and Child Care Programs* (Ypsilanti, Mich.: High/Scope Press, 1995).

5. Frances A. Campbell et al., "Early Childhood Education: Young Adult Outcomes for the Abecedarian Project," *Applied Developmental Science*, vol. 6, 2002, pp. 42–57; and

Frances A. Campbell, "The Development of Cognitive and Academic Abilities: Growth Curves from an Early Childhood Experiment," *Developmental Psychology*, vol. 37, 2001, pp. 231–42.

6. Arthur J. Reynolds et al., "Age 21 Benefit-Cost Analysis of the Chicago Child-Parent Center Program," paper presented to the Society for Prevention Research, Madison, Wis., 21 May–2 June 2001; and idem, "Long-Term Effects of an Early Childhood Intervention on Educational Achievement and Juvenile Arrest," *Journal of the American Medical Association*, 9 May 2001.

7. Eliana Garces, Duncan Thomas, and Janet Currie, "Longer Term Effects of Head Start," Working Paper No. 8054, National Bureau of Economic Research, December 2000, available at www.nber.org/papers/w8054; and Janet Currie and Duncan Thomas, "School Quality and the Longer-Term Effects of Head Start," *Journal of Human Resources*, Fall 2000, pp. 755–74.

8. W. Steven Barnett, "Early Childhood Education," in Alex Molnar, ed., S*chool Reform Proposals: The Research Evidence* (Greenwich, Conn.: Information Age Publishing, 2002),

available at www.asu.edu/educ/epsl. Click on Education Policy Research Unit, then, under "archives," click on "research and writing."

9. Samuel J. Meisels, "Can Head Start Pass the Test?," *Education Week*, 19 March 2003, p. 44.

10. Leonard N. Masse and W. Steven Barnett, *Benefit Cost Analysis of the Abecedarian Early Childhood Intervention Project* (New Brunswick, N.J.: National Institute for Early Childhood Research, Rutgers University, 2002).

11. Ibid., p. 14.

12. *Preschool for All: Investing in a Productive and Just Society* (New York: Committee for Economic Development, 2002), p. 1.

13. Personal communication, 3 February 2003.

GERALD W. BRACEY is an associate for the High/Scope Educational Research Foundation, Ypsilanti, Mich., and an associate professor at George Mason University, Fairfax, Va. He lives in the Washington, D.C., area. **ARTHUR STELLAR** is president and CEO, High/Scope Educational Research Foundation, Ypsilanti, Mich.

Accountability Comes to Preschool

Can We Make It Work for Young Children?

Early childhood educators are justifiably concerned that demands for academic standards in preschool will result in developmentally inappropriate instruction that focuses on a narrow set of isolated skills. But Ms. Stipek believes that teaching preschoolers basic skills can give them a good foundation for their school careers, and she shows that it is possible to do this in ways that are both effective and enjoyable.

Deborah Stipek

Pressures to raise academic achievement and to close the achievement gap have taken a firm hold on elementary and secondary schools. Now, preschools are beginning to feel the heat. Testing for No Child Left Behind isn't required until third grade. But as elementary schools ratchet up demands on children in the early grades and as kindergarten becomes more academic, children entering school without basic literacy and math skills are at an increasingly significant disadvantage.

Accountability is also beginning to enter the preschool arena. Both the House and Senate versions of the Head Start reauthorization bill require the development of educational performance standards based on recommendations of a National Academy of Sciences panel. Head Start programs would then be held accountable for making progress toward meeting these goals, and their funding would be withdrawn after some period of time if they failed. States and districts are likely to follow with initiatives designed to ensure that children in publicly funded early childhood education programs are being prepared academically to succeed in school.

There are good reasons for the increased attention to academic skills in preschool, especially in programs serving economically disadvantaged children. Children from low-income families enter kindergarten on average a year to a year and a half behind their middle-class peers in terms of school readiness. And the relatively poor cognitive skills of low-income children at school entry predict poor achievement in the long term. Meredith Phillips, James Crouse, and John Ralph estimated in a meta-analysis that about half of the total black/white gap in math and reading achievement at the end of high school is explained by the gap between blacks and whites at school entry.[1] Preschool education can give children from economically disadvantaged homes a better chance of succeeding in school by contributing to their cognitive skills. Moreover, all young children are capable of learning far more than is typically believed, and they enjoy the process.

Until recently, kindergarten was a time for children to *prepare* for school. Today, it *is* school.

This new focus on academic preparation will undoubtedly have significant implications for the nature of preschool programs, and it could have negative consequences. Until recently, kindergarten was a time for children to *prepare* for school. Today, it *is* school—in most places as focused on academic skill as first grade used to be. Will the same thing happen to preschool? We need to think hard about how we will balance the pressure to prepare young children academically with their social/emotional needs. How will we increase young children's academic skills without undermining their enthusiasm for learning or reducing the attention we give to the many other domains of development that are important for their success?

The early childhood education community has resisted a focus on academic skills primarily because experts are worried that it will come in the form of whole-group instruction, rigid pacing, and repetitive, decontextualized tasks—the kind of "drill and kill" that is becoming commonplace in the early elementary grades and that is well known to suffocate young children's natural enthusiasm for learning. My own recent observations in preschools suggest that these concerns are well founded.

I am seeing children in preschool classrooms counting by rote to 10 or 20 in a chorus. When I interview the children, many have no idea what an 8 or a 10 is. They can't tell me, for example, how many cookies they would have if they started with 7 and I gave them one more, or whether 8 is more or less than 9. I am seeing children recite the alphabet, call out letters shown on flashcards, and identify letter/sound connections on worksheets (e.g., by drawing a line from a *b* to a picture of a ball). Some can read the word *mop* but have no idea that they are referring to a tool for cleaning floors, and they are not able to retell in their own words a simple story that had been read to them.[2] I am seeing young children recite by rote the days of the week and the months of the year while the teacher points to the words written on the board—without any understanding of what a week or a month is and without even a clear understanding that the written words the teacher points to are connected to the words they are saying. In these classrooms every child in the class gets the same task or is involved in the same activity, despite huge variability in their current skill levels. Some children are bored because they already know what is being taught; others are clueless.

Alternatives to Drill and Kill

The good news is that young children can be taught basic skills in ways that engage rather than undermine their motivation to learn. Motivating instruction must be child-centered—adapted to the varying skills and interests of children.

Good teachers embed instruction in activities that make sense to young children. They teach vocabulary, for example, by systematically using and reinforcing the meaning of new words in the context of everyday activities. When children are blowing bubbles, the teacher might introduce different descriptive terms (e.g., "shimmer") or names of shapes (e.g., "oval" versus "round"). Teachers promote oral language by reading stories, encouraging story making, joining in role play, asking children to explain how things work, giving children opportunities to share experiences, helping them to expand what they say, and introducing and reinforcing more complex sentence structures. Comprehension and analytic skills can be developed by reading to children and asking them to predict what will happen next and to identify patterns and draw conclusions. Print awareness is promoted by creating a book area, having materials and other things in the classroom labeled, and pointing out features of books being read to children. Phonics can be taught through songs, rhyming games, and language play. Early writing skills can be encouraged and developed in the context of pretend play (e.g., running a restaurant or post office) and by having children dictate stories or feelings to an adult and gradually begin to write some of the words themselves.

Good teachers are busy asking questions, focusing children's attention, helping them document and interpret what they see, and providing scaffolds and suggestions.

Young children develop basic number concepts best by actively manipulating objects, not by rote counting.[3] Mathematics, like literacy, can be learned in the context of playful activities. A pretend restaurant can provide many opportunities for learning math. Children can match one straw for each glass for each person, count out amounts to pay for menu items (five poker chips for a plastic pizza,

four chips for a glass of apple juice, and so on), tally the number of people who visit the restaurant, or split the pizza between two customers. Questions about relative quantities (less and more, bigger and smaller) can be embedded in restaurant activities and conversations. (Who has *fewer* crackers or *more* juice left in her glass?) Children can categorize and sort objects (e.g., put all the large plates on this shelf and the tall glasses on the shelf below). Measurement of weight and even a basic notion of fractions can be learned by cooking for the restaurant (a half cup of milk, a quarter cup of sugar); volume can be learned by pouring water from measuring cups into larger containers.

Effective teaching of young children cannot be delivered through a one-size-fits-all or scripted instructional program, in part because teachers need to be responsive to children's individual skills and interests. Good teachers know well what each child knows and understands, and they use that knowledge to plan appropriate and varied learning opportunities. For example, whereas one child may dictate a few sentences to the teacher for his journal each day, another might actually write some of the words herself. While some children are asked to count beans by ones, others are asked to count them by twos or by fives.

Teaching in the kinds of playful contexts mentioned above can be direct and explicit. Young children are not left to their own devices—to explore aimlessly or to invent while the teacher observes. To the contrary, effective and motivating teaching requires a great deal of active teacher involvement. Teachers need to have clear learning goals, plan activities carefully to achieve those goals, assess children's learning regularly, and make modifications when activities are not helping children learn.

Good teachers are busy asking questions, focusing children's attention, helping them document and interpret what they see, and providing scaffolds and suggestions. Which object do you think will float, the small metal ball or the block of wood? Why do you think the wood floated and the ball didn't, even though the wood block is bigger? On the paper, let's put an "F" for float after the pictures of the objects that float and an "S" after the pictures of the objects that sink. Then we can look at our summary of findings to figure out how the floating objects and the sinking objects are different from each other. Teachers need to assess children's understanding and skill levels both informally—as they listen to children's replies and comments during classroom activities—and more formally—interacting with each child individually for a few minutes every few weeks. And teachers need to use what they learn from their assessments to plan instructional interventions that will move *each child* from where he or she is to the next step.

Effective teachers also maintain children's enthusiasm for learning by being vigilant and seizing opportunities to use children's interests to teach. I once observed a brilliant teacher turn a child's comment about new shoes (which most teachers would have found distracting) into a multidisciplinary lesson. She asked the students to take off one shoe and use it to measure the length of their leg, from their waist to their ankle. Some had to learn how to find their waist and ankle to accomplish the task (physiology and vocabulary). They also had to count each time they turned the shoe and keep track of where they ended up (math). The teacher then led a conversation about who had the longest and the shortest leg (comparisons). Then they measured arms and talked about whether arms were shorter or longer than legs and by how much (introduction to subtraction and idea of averages). The conversation finally turned to other objects that could be used as measuring instruments.

This teacher didn't always rely on spontaneous teaching opportunities. She had a very well-planned instructional program. But she also took good advantage of children's interests and seized opportunities to build academic lessons out of them.

Beyond Academic Skills

Ironically, to achieve high academic standards, we need to be more, not less, concerned about the nonacademic aspects of children's development. Children's social skills and dispositions toward learning, as well as their emotional and physical well-being, directly affect their academic learning.

Fortunately, efforts to promote development on important nonacademic dimensions need not reduce the amount of time children spend learning academic skills. As I describe below, efforts to support positive social, emotional, and physical development can be embedded in the academic instructional program and the social climate of the classroom.

Social skills. Children who have good social skills—who are empathic, attentive to others' needs, helpful, respectful, and able to engage in sustained social interactions—achieve academically at a higher level than children who lack social skills or are aggressive.[4] The higher achievement results in part because children who are socially adept develop positive relationships with teachers and peers. They are motivated to work hard to please their teachers, and they feel more comfortable and secure in the classroom. Aggressive and disruptive children develop conflictual relationships with teachers and peers and spend more time being disciplined (and thus less time engaged in academic tasks).

Social skills can be taught in the context of classroom routines and activities designed to teach academic skills. Lessons about appropriate social behavior can be provided as stories that are read to children and discussed. Opportunities to develop skills in collaboration can be built into tasks and activities designed to teach literacy and math skills. Teachers can encourage children to develop social problem-solving skills when interpersonal conflicts arise by helping them solve the problem themselves—"Is there another way you could have let Sam know that you wanted to play with the airplane?"—rather than solving the problem for them—"Sam, give the airplane to Jim. It's his turn."

A program called "Cool Tools," designed to promote social and academic skills, begins with preschoolers at the UCLA laboratory elementary school—the Corinne A. Seeds University Elementary School. Children create an alphabet that decorates the walls of their classroom: "S" is for "share," "K" is for "kindness," "H" is for "help," "C" is for "cooperation." Teachers also take advantage of events in the world and in the community. Following the tsunamis in Southeast Asia, the children made lists of what survivors might need. They donated the coins they had collected for their study of money in mathematics to a fund for survivors, and they made muffins and granola and sold them to parents and friends to raise additional funds. Thus literacy and math instruction, and a little geography, were embedded in activities designed to promote feelings of responsibility and generosity.

Dispositions toward learning. Children's beliefs about their ability to learn also affect their learning. Children who develop perceptions of themselves as academically incompetent and expect

to fail don't exert much effort on school tasks, and they give up as soon as they encounter difficulty. Engagement in academic tasks is also affected by students' sense of personal control. Children enjoy schoolwork less and are less engaged when they feel they are working only because they have to, not because they want to.[5]

Luckily, much is known about practices that foster feelings of competence and expectations for success. These beliefs are not "taught" directly. Rather, they are influenced by the nature and difficulty level of the tasks children are asked to complete and by the kind of evaluation used and the nature of the feedback they receive. Children's self-confidence is maintained by working on tasks that require some effort (so that when they complete them they have a sense of satisfaction and achievement). However, the tasks must not be so difficult that the children cannot complete them even if they try. The huge variability in children's skill levels is why rigidly paced instruction is inappropriate; if all children are asked to do the same task, it will invariably be too easy (and thus boring) for some students or too difficult (and thus discouraging) for others.

Classroom climate is also important. Self-confidence is engendered better in classrooms in which all children's academic achievements are celebrated than in classrooms in which only the best performance is praised, rewarded, or displayed on bulletin boards. Effective teachers encourage and praise children for taking on challenges and persisting when they run into difficulty, and they invoke no negative consequences for failure. ("You didn't get it this time, but I bet if you keep working on these kinds of problems, by lunch, you'll have figured out how to do them.")

The nature of evaluation also matters. Evaluation that tells children what they have learned and mastered and what they need to do next, rather than how their performance compares to that of other children, fosters self-confidence and high expectations. ("You are really good at consonants, but it looks like you need to practice vowels a little more.") All children can learn and will stay motivated if they see their skills developing, but only a few can perform better than their peers, and many will become discouraged if they need to compete for rewards.

We also know how to foster a feeling of autonomy. Clearly children cannot be given carte blanche to engage in any activity they want and be expected to master a set of skills and understandings adults believe to be important. But children can be given choices in what they do and how and when they do it, within a constrained set of alternatives. Even modest choices (whether to use beans or chips for a counting activity; which puzzle to work on) promote interest and engagement in learning.[6]

Emotional well-being and mental health. Children's emotional well-being and mental health (a clear and positive sense of the self; a positive, optimistic mood; the ability to cope with novel and challenging situations) have an enormous impact on how well they learn. Students who are depressed, anxious, or angry are not effective learners. Feeling disrespected, disliked, or disconnected from the social context can also promote disengagement—from academic work in the short term and, eventually for many students, from school altogether. Paying close attention to the social and emotional needs of students and creating a socially supportive environment can go a long way toward promoting social/emotional and mental well-being. It can also reduce the need for special services.

Substantial research suggests that the school social climate is also critical to mental health. A respectful and caring social context that ensures close, personal relationships with adults, that is orderly and predictable, and that promotes feelings of self-determination and autonomy in students can contribute substantially to students' emotional well-being. Peers affect the social context as much as teachers, and thus they have to be taught the effects of their behavior on other children. The "Cool Tools" program, for example, teaches 4-year-olds about "put-ups" and "put-downs," noting that it takes five put-ups to repair one put-down. Children also play games that illustrate how the same comment can be heard differently, depending on the volume and tone of voice and body posture.

Physical development. Lack of exercise and consumption of too much sugar are two behaviors that have immediate negative effects on children's ability to focus on academic work. We need to provide children with opportunities—such as outdoor play time and healthy snacks—to engage in positive behavior while they are at school. And we need to help them develop healthy habits—such as brushing teeth, washing hands, and exercising—that will contribute to their well-being.

Teachers can talk to children about how exercise affects their bodies in the context of a science lesson on physiology. (Why do we need a heart? How are muscles different from fat?) And compelling and visible messages can be given through science experiments, such as observing what happens to two pieces of bread several days after one piece was touched with a dirty hand and the other with a clean one.

Programs serving children from low-income families should also make an effort to work with community agencies to ensure access to dentists and physicians. Even a trip to the doctor or dentist can be used to promote academic skills. Children can develop communication skills by being asked to describe their experience, they can learn vocabulary, and they can develop the cultural knowledge that we now know is necessary for becoming a proficient reader. (It's hard to make sense of a sentence with the word "stethoscope" in it if you've never seen one used.)

Educating Children

Educational leaders need to take seriously the accountability demands made on them. By paying more attention to academic skills in preschool, we can help close the achievement gap, and we can give all children a chance to expand their intellectual skills. But we need to avoid teaching strategies that take all the joy out of learning. This will not, in the end, help students achieve the high standards being set for them.

We also need to resist pressures to prepare children only to perform on tests that assess a very narrow set of academic outcomes. Attention to other domains of development is also important if we want children to be effective learners as well as effective citizens and human beings. Policy makers should demand that if assessments for accountability are to be used in early childhood programs, they measure genuine understanding and the nonacademic skills and dispositions that we want teachers to promote. We have learned from No Child Left Behind that, if the tools used for accountability focus on a narrow set of skills, so will the educational program.

Finally, teaching young children effectively takes a great deal of skill. If we want teachers to promote students' learning and motivation, we need to invest in their training. States vary considerably in their credentialing requirements for early childhood education teachers. Few require a sufficient level of training. On-the-job opportunities for collegial interactions focused on teaching and learning and professional development are also critical. Preschools that are good learning environments for adults are likely to be good learning environments for children.

An investment in preschool education could help us achieve the high academic standards to which we aspire. Let's make sure we provide it in a way that does more good than harm.

Notes

1. Meredith Phillips, James Crouse, and John Ralph, "Does the Black-White Test Score Gap Widen After Children Enter School?," in Christopher Jencks and Meredith Phillips, eds., *The Black-White Test Score Gap* (Washington, D.C.: Brookings Institution Press, 1998), pp. 229–72.

2. A story recounted to me by a researcher who was assessing a young child's reading skill illustrates what can happen if decoding is overemphasized. The child read a brief passage flawlessly but was unable to answer a simple question about what he had read. He complained to the researcher that he had asked him to read the passage, not to understand it. Clearly this child had learned that reading was synonymous with decoding sounds.

3. See, for example, Barbara Bowman, M. Suzanne Donovan, and M. Susan Burns, eds., *Eager to Learn: Educating Our Preschoolers* (Washington, D.C.: National Academy Press, 2001); and Douglas Clements, Julie Sarama, and Ann-Marie DiBiase, *Engaging Young Children in Mathematics: Standards for Early Childhood Mathematics Education* (Mahwah, N.J.: Erlbaum, 2003).

4. See, for example, David Arnold, "Co-Occurrence of Externalizing Behavior Problems and Emergent Academic Difficulties in Young High-Risk Boys: A Preliminary Evaluation of Patterns and Mechanisms," *Journal of Applied Developmental Psychology,* vol. 18, 1997, pp. 317–30; Nancy Eisenberg and Richard A. Fabes, "Prosocial Development," in William Damon and Nancy Eisenberg, eds., *Handbook of Child Psychology,* 5th ed., vol. 3 (New York: Wiley, 1997), pp. 701–78.

5. For a review, see Deborah Stipek, *Motivation to Learn: Integrating Theory and Practice,* 4th ed. (Needham Heights, Mass.: Allyn & Bacon, 2002).

6. See, for example, Leslie Gutman and Elizabeth Sulzby, "The Role of Autonomy-Support Versus Control in the Emergent Writing Behaviors of African-American Kindergarten Children," *Reading Research & Instruction,* vol. 39, 2000, pp. 170–83; and Richard Ryan and Jennifer La Guardia, "Achievement Motivation Within a Pressured Society: Intrinsic and Extrinsic Motivations to Learn and the Politics of School Reform," in Timothy Urdan, ed., *Advances in Motivation and Achievement: A Research Annual,* vol. II (Greenwich, Conn.: JAI Press, 1999), pp. 45–85.

DEBORAH STIPEK is a professor of education and dean of the School of Education at Stanford University, Stanford, Calif.

From *Phi Delta Kappan,* June 2006, pp. 740–744, 747. Copyright © 2006 by Phi Delta Kappan. Reprinted by permission of the publisher and Deborah Stipek.

Raising a Moral Child

**For many parents, nothing is more important than teaching kids
to know right from wrong. But when does a sense of morality begin?**

KAREN SPRINGEN

Nancy Rotering beams as she recalls how her 3-year-old son Jack recently whacked his head against a drawer hard enough to draw blood. It's not that she found the injury amusing. But it did have a silver lining: Jack's wails prompted his 2-year-old brother, Andy, to offer him spontaneous consolation in the form of a cup of water and a favorite book, "Jamberry." "Want 'Berry' book, Jack?" he asked. Nancy loved Andy's "quick-thinking act of sympathy." "I was thrilled that such a tiny person could come up with such a big thought," she says. "He stepped up and offered Jack refreshment—and entertainment—to take his mind off the pain."

All parents have goals for their children, whether they center on graduating from high school or winning the Nobel Prize. But for a great many, nothing is more important than raising a "good" child—one who knows right from wrong, who is empathetic and who, like Andy, tries to live by the Golden Rule, even if he doesn't know yet what it is. Still, morality is an elusive—and highly subjective—character trait. Most parents know it when they see it. But how can they instill and nurture it in their children? Parents must lead by example. "The way to raise a moral child is to be a moral person," says Tufts University psychologist David Elkind. "If you're honest and straightforward and decent and caring, that's what children learn." Humans seem innately inclined to behave empathetically; doctors talk about "contagious crying" among newborns in the hospital nursery. And not all children of murderers or even tax cheats follow in their parents' footsteps. "What's surprising is how many kids raised in immoral homes grow up moral," says New York psychiatrist Alvin Rosenfeld.

81% of mothers and 78% of fathers say they plan eventually to send their young child to Sunday school or some other kind of religious training

Parents have always been preoccupied with instilling moral values in their children. But in today's fast-paced world, where reliable role models are few and acts of violence by children are increasingly common, the quest to raise a moral child has taken on new urgency.

Child criminals grow ever younger; in August, a 6-year-old California girl (with help from a 5-year-old friend) smothered her 3-year-old brother with a pillow. Such horrific crimes awaken a dark, unspoken fear in many parents: Is my child capable of committing such an act? And can I do anything to make sure that she won't?

There are no guarantees. But parents are increasingly aware that even very young children can grasp and exhibit moral behaviors—even if the age at which they become "morally accountable" remains under debate. According to the Roman Catholic Church, a child reaches "the age of reason" by 7. Legally, each state determines how old a child must be to be held responsible for his acts, ranging from 7 to 15. Child experts are reluctant to offer a definitive age for accountability. But they agree that in order to be held morally responsible, children must have both an emotional and a cognitive awareness of right and wrong—in other words, to know in their heads as well as feel in their hearts that what they did was wrong. Such morality doesn't appear overnight but emerges slowly, over time. And according to the latest research, the roots of morality first appear in the earliest months of an infant's life. "It begins the day they're born, and it's not complete until the day they die," says child psychiatrist Elizabeth Berger, author of "Raising Children with Character."

It's never too early to start. Parents who respond instantly to a newborn's cries lay an important moral groundwork. "You work to understand what the baby's feeling," says Barbara Howard, a specialist in developmental behavioral pediatrics at the Johns Hopkins University School of Medicine. "Then the baby will work to understand what other people are feeling." Indeed, empathy is among the first moral emotions to develop. Even before the age of 2, children will try to comfort an upset child—though usually in an "egocentric" way, says Marvin Berkowitz, professor of character education at the University of Missouri-St. Louis: "I might give them *my* teddy even though your teddy is right there." To wit: Andy Rotering brought his brother his own favorite book.

Morality consists of not only caring for others but also following basic rules of conduct. Hurting another child, for instance, is never OK. But how you handle it depends on your child's age. If a 1-year-old is hitting or biting, "you simply say 'no' firmly, and you remove the child from the situation," says Craig Ramey, author of "Right From Birth." But once a child acquires language skills, parents can provide more detail. "You can say, 'We don't hit in this family'," says David Fassler, chairman of the American Psychiatric Association's council on children, adolescents and their families. "You can say, 'Everyone feels like hitting and biting from time to time. My job is to help you figure out what to do with those kinds of feelings'." Suggest alternatives—punching a pillow, drawing a sad picture or lying quietly on a bed.

Children grow more moral with time. As Lawrence Kohlberg of Harvard University has said, kids go through progressive stages of moral development. Between 1 and 2, children understand that there are rules—but usually follow them only if an adult is watching, says Barbara Howard. After 2, they start obeying rules—inconsistently— even if an adult isn't there. And as any adult who has ever driven faster than 65 mph knows, people continue "circumstantial" morality throughout life, says Howard. "People aren't perfect, even when they know what the right thing to do is."

Though all children are born with the capacity to act morally, that ability can be lost. Children who are abused or neglected often fail to acquire a basic sense of trust and belonging that influences how people behave when they're older. "They may be callous because no one has ever shown them enough of the caring to put that into their system," says Howard. Ramey argues that "we come to expect the world to be the way we've experienced it"—whether that means cold and forbidding or warm and loving. According to Stanford developmental psychologist William Damon, morality can also be hampered by the practice of "bounding"—limiting children's contact with the world only to people who are like them—as opposed to "bridging," or exposing them to people of different backgrounds. "You can empathize with everyone who looks just like you and learn to exclude everyone who doesn't," says Damon. A juvenile delinquent may treat his sister gently—but beat up an old woman of another race. "The bridging approach ends up with a more moral child," says Damon.

No matter how hard you try, you can't force your child to be moral. But there are things you can do to send him in the right direction:

If you're honest, straightforward, decent and caring, that's what children learn

• Decide what values—such as honesty and hard work—are most important to you. Then do what you want your children to do. "If you volunteer in your community, and you take your child, they will do that themselves," says Joseph Hagan, chairman of the American Academy of Pediatrics' committee on the psychosocial aspects of child and family health. "If you stub your toe, and all you can say is the F word, guess what your child is going to say when they stub their toe?"

Always help your child see things from the other person's point of view

• Praise children liberally. "You have to ignore the behaviors you don't want and highlight the behaviors you do want," says Kori Skidmore, a staff psychologist at Children's Memorial Hospital in Chicago. Rather than criticizing a toddler for his messy room, compliment him on the neat corner, recommends Darien, Ill., pediatrician Garry Gardner. Use "no" judiciously, otherwise "a child starts to feel like 'I'm always doing something wrong'," says the APA's Fassler. "If you're trying to teach a child to share, then praise them when they share. Don't just scold them when they're reluctant to."

• Take advantage of teachable moments. When Gardner's kids were 3 and 4, they found a $10 bill in front of a store. Gardner talked to them about the value of the money—and they agreed to give it to the shopkeeper in case someone returned for it. They mutually decided "finders keepers" shouldn't apply to anything worth more than a quarter. "Certainly you wouldn't go back and say, 'I found a penny'," says Gardner. Parents can also use famous parables, like "The Boy Who Cried Wolf," or Bible stories to illustrate their point.

• Watch what your child watches. TV and computer games can glorify immoral behavior. "If children are unsupervised, watching violence or promiscuity on TV, they're going to have misguided views about how to treat other people," says Karen Bohlin, director of Boston University's Center for the Advancement of Ethics and Character. "Children by nature are impulsive and desperately need guidance to form good habits. That can come only from a loving caregiver who's by their side, teaching them how to play nicely, safely, fairly, how to take turns, how to put things back where they belong, how to speak respectfully."

• Discuss consequences. Say, " 'Look how sad Mary is because you broke her favorite doll'," explains Berkowitz. Parents can also ask their children to help them pick fair punishments—for example, no TV. "They're learning that their voice is valued," says Berkowitz. Allowing kids to make choices—even about something as trivial as what to have for lunch—will enable them to make moral ones later. "If they don't learn peanut butter and jelly at 2, how are they going to decide about drinking when they're 14?" asks family physician Nancy Dickey, editor in chief of Medem, an online patient-information center.

• Always help them see things from the other person's point of view. If a child bops his new sibling, try to reflect the newborn's outlook. Say, " 'Oh, my, that must hurt. How would you feel if someone did that to you?'" says Howard. Gardner encourages parents whose kids find stray teddy bears to ask their children how sad they would feel if they lost their favorite stuffed animal—and how happy they would be if someone returned it. "It's one thing to hear about it at Sunday school," he says. And another to live the "do unto others" rule in real life.

• In the end, the truest test of whether a parent has raised a moral child is how that young person acts when Mom or Dad is not around. With a lot of love and luck, your child will grow up to feel happy and blessed—and to want to help others who aren't as fortunate. Now, *that's* something to be proud of.

UNIT 3

Development During Childhood: Cognition and Schooling

Unit Selections

Key Points to Consider

- What is authentic learning? Why is it vanishing in contemporary classrooms? Should it be restored?

- Why should foreign language instruction be emphasized in American education before high school?

- What has the No Child Left Behind (NCLB) legislation done for American education? What are its weaknesses? How can it be improved?

- Should school teachers emphasize students' strengths instead of weaknesses? What might be the consequences of such a practice?

- Are achievement tests necessary to make sure first graders acquire sufficient reading and math skills. Should 5- and 6-year-old children have homework? Should they be tutored if they fall behind their peers? What impact will this have?

Student Web Site
www.mhcls.com/online

Internet References
Further information regarding these Web sites may be found in this book's preface or online.

Children Now
http://www.childrennow.org
Council for Exceptional Children
http://www.cec.sped.org
Educational Resources Information Center (ERIC)
http://www.eric.ed.gov/
Federation of Behavioral, Psychological, and Cognitive Science
http://federation.apa.org
The National Association for the Education of Young Children (NAEYC)
http://www.naeyc.org
Project Zero
http://pzweb.harvard.edu

Nw research in 2007 suggested that human brain stem cells may make new neurons as they migrate to the olfactory bulb. While the outcome of these new brain cells for human cognition is yet to be learned, the smell-sensing mechanism can help children learn and adapt in some areas (e.g., safe smells, dangerous odors).

The mental process of knowing—cognition—includes aspects such as sensing, understanding, associating, and discriminating. Cognitive research has been hampered by the limitations of trying to understand what is happening inside the minds of living persons without doing harm. It has also been challenged by problems with defining concepts such as intuition, unconsciousness, unawareness, implicit learning, incomprehension, and all the aspects of knowing situated behind our sensations and perceptions (metacognition). Many kinds of achievement that require cognitive processes (awareness, perception, reasoning, judgment) cannot be measured with intelligence tests or with achievement tests.

Intelligence is the capacity to acquire and apply knowledge. It is usually assumed that intelligence can be measured. The ratio of tested mental age to chronological age is expressed as an intelligence quotient (IQ). For years, schoolchildren have been classified by IQ scores. The links between IQ scores and school achievement are positive, but no significant correlations exist between IQ scores and life success. Consider, for example, the motor coordination and kinesthetic abilities of Hall of Fame baseball player Cal Ripken, Jr. He had a use of his body that surpassed the capacity of most other athletes and nonathletes. Is knowledge of kinesthetics a form of intelligence? Many people believe it is.

Some psychologists have suggested that uncovering more about how the brain processes various types of intelligences will soon be translated into new educational practices. Today's tests of intelligence only measure abilities in the logical/mathematical, spatial, and linguistic areas of intelligence, which is what schools now teach. Jean Piaget, the Swiss founder of cognitive psychology, was involved in the creation of the world's first intelligence test, the Binet-Simon Scale. He became disillusioned with trying to quantify how much children knew at different chronological ages. He was much more intrigued with what they did not know, what they knew incorrectly, and how they came to know the world as they did. He started the Centre for

Genetic Epistemology in Geneva, Switzerland, where he began to study the nature, extent, and validity of children's knowledge. He discovered qualitative, rather than quantitative, differences in cognitive processes over the life span. Infants know the world through their senses and their motor responses. After language develops, toddlers and preschoolers know the world through their language/symbolic perspectives. Piaget likened early childhood cognitive processes to bad thought, or thought akin to daydreams. By school age, children know things in concrete terms, which allows them to number, seriate, classify, conserve, think backwards and forwards, and think about their own thinking (metacognition). However, Piaget believed that children do not acquire the cognitive processes necessary to think abstractly and to use clear, consistent, logical patterns of thought until early adolescence. Their moral sense and personal philosophies of behavior are not completed until adulthood.

The first article in this unit, "A Time and a Place for Authentic Learning," considers the difficulties in contemporary educational processes. The current focus on test preparation leaves little time for the application of knowledge, or for learning by doing. The authors state the fears that creativity and innovative ideas (that have long characterized Americans) will decrease as teachers are required to teach for the test. Authentic learning changes the focus of the student from lesson-learner to inquirer, and the role of the teacher from fact-giver to mentor and resource person. Authentic learning offers the chance to make both teachers and students excited about education in engaging, enjoyable, enriching classrooms. It is worth our efforts to find more time and place for it.

The second article, "Why We Need 'The Year of Languages,'" opens the door for discussing early emphasis on second-language learning in contemporary schooling. Are American children linguistically ignorant? What effect will this have in the global economy? Why are languages acquired more rapidly before puberty? Why do females acquire languages more rapidly than males? Should our American schoolchildren be taught languages important in global economy: Chinese? Arabic?

In the first article of "Schooling," the author gives examples of how students can succeed if given options and high expectations.

"Ten Big Effects of the No Child Left Behind Act on Public Schools" explains the findings of a four-year, comprehensive review of the implementation of NCLB. The ten effects are broad generalizations drawn from all 50 states. While test scores are rising and low-performing schools are being restructured across the United States, there are problems. Many relate to rising costs, staffing, quality teaching, high-stakes testing, and accountability requirements for children with exceptionalities.

The next article in the schooling section of this unit addresses the power of teaching students using strengths. Gloria Henderson discusses her conscious efforts to change her teaching style from remediation to abilities guidance. Students achieved at higher levels when they were led to improve their preexisting skills.

The final article of this unit address "The New First Grade: Too Much Too Soon?" Pressure to succeed academically is very high for first-grade students in many American schools. While some parents are propelling the movement for more education at earlier ages, other parents are resisting the pressures. Many experts worry that the stress on achievement may impede a lifelong love of learning. Too much pushing can lead to frustration and eventual emotional-behavioral disorders.

A Time and a Place for Authentic Learning

Challenge students to solve everyday problems in meaningful contexts, and the learning will take care of itself.

JOSEPH S. RENZULLI, MARCIA GENTRY, AND SALLY M. REIS

Each week, all the students at the Bret Harte Middle School in Oakland, California, leave their classrooms to participate in interest-based enrichment clusters. Under a teacher's guidance, one group of students is identifying, archiving, and preserving documents from the 1800s that were found in a suitcase belonging to the first pharmacist in Deadwood, South Dakota. Another group with strong interests in media, technology, and graphic arts is converting the archives into digital format and making the students' research available on a Web site.

These crossgrade clusters are scheduled on a rotating basis during the fall months. They usually last for eight weeks, generally meeting weekly for a double-period time block, with a new series scheduled in the spring. A medium-sized school might typically offer 15 to 20 clusters. The number of students in each cluster varies depending on student interest in the topic and teacher requirements for effective student participation. Teachers develop the clusters around their own strengths and interests, sometimes working in teams that include parents and community members.

Numerous schools across the United States have developed the enrichment cluster concept to deal with what many education leaders believe is a crisis in our schools. The focus on test preparation has squeezed more authentic kinds of learning out of the curriculum, thereby minimizing the one aspect of U.S. education that contributes to the innovativeness and creative productivity of the nation's culture, economy, and leadership role in the world. Improved test scores are important, but it's the *application* of knowledge in authentic learning situations—not perpetual memorization and testing—that characterizes a progressive education system.

What Is Authentic Learning?

All learning exists on a continuum that ranges from deductive and prescriptive learning on one end to inductive, self-selected, and investigative learning on the other. The essence of inductive or high-end learning is applying relevant knowledge and skills to solving real problems. Such learning involves finding and focusing on a problem; identifying relevant information; categorizing, critically analyzing, and synthesizing that information; and effectively communicating the results.

Real-life problems share four criteria. First, a real-life problem has a personal frame of reference. In other words, the problem must involve an emotional or internal commitment on the part of those involved in addition to a cognitive interest. Second, no agreed-on solutions or prescribed strategies for solving the problem exist. If they do, the process would more appropriately be classified as a training exercise because its main purpose would be to teach predetermined content or thinking skills.

Third, real-life problems motivate people to find solutions that change actions, attitudes, or beliefs. A group of students might gather, analyze, and report on data about the community's television-watching habits, causing people in that community to think critically about the television-viewing habits of young people. Last, real-life problems target a real audience. For example, students working on a local oral history project— a biographical study of Connecticut residents who died in Vietnam—initially presented their findings to their classmates, mainly to rehearse presentation skills. Their authentic audience consisted of members of a local historical society, members of veterans groups, family members of servicemen and servicewomen, attendees at a local commemoration of Vietnam veterans, and community members who had read about the research in the local newspaper.

Enrichment clusters are *not* mini-courses. There are no predetermined content or process objectives. The nature of the problem guides students toward using just-in-time knowledge, appropriate investigative techniques or creative production skills, and professional methods for communicating results. In this type of learning, students assume roles as investigators, writers, artists, or other types of practicing professionals.

Authentic learning is the vehicle through which everything from basic skills to advanced content and processes come together in the form of student-developed products and services. The student's role changes from lesson-learner to firsthand inquirer, and the role of the teacher changes from instructor and disseminator of knowledge to coach, resource procurer, and mentor. Although products play an important role in creating authentic learning, students learn principally from the cognitive, affective, and motivational processes involved.

A Different Approach

Developing an authentic enrichment cluster draws on skills that most teachers already possess, especially if they have been involved in clubs or other extracurricular activities. As you begin the process of developing your own cluster, keep in mind the following:

- *Reverse the teaching equation.* Your role in planning and facilitating an enrichment cluster differs from the teacher's traditional role. Too much preplanning on your part may push the cluster toward deductive rather than inductive teaching and learning. Enrichment clusters develop just-in-time knowledge that has immediate relevance in resolving the problem. Students typically move to higher levels of knowledge than grade-level textbooks support.

- *Reverse the role of students.* Young people working on an original piece of historical research, creative writing, or play production become young historians, authors, scenery designers, and stage managers. Instead of teaching lessons, you will begin to think about how to help a young poet get work published, how to get the shopping mall manager to provide space for a display of models of historically significant town buildings, and how to engineer a presentation by young environmentalists to the state wildlife commission.

- *Create a unique enrichment cluster.* As long as you follow the guidelines for inductive teaching, there is no wrong way to plan and facilitate an enrichment cluster. Differences in interests, personalities, and styles among cluster facilitators contribute to the uniqueness of this type of learning. Experience in an inductive learning environment will help you hone the skills that will become a natural part of your teaching repertoire both in clusters and in your classroom.

- *When in doubt, look outward.* To mirror real-world situations, examine conditions outside the classroom for models of planning, teaching, and organizing. Athletic coaches, advisors for the drama club or the school newspaper, and 4-H Club leaders make excellent enrichment cluster facilitators. Similarly, tasks and organizational patterns should resemble the activities that take place in a small business, a social service agency, a theater production company, or a laboratory.

Guidelines for Developing an Enrichment Cluster
Select a Topic

Base enrichment clusters on topics in which you have a strong interest. Make a list of topics that fascinate you. Reflect on your choices, discuss your list with colleagues—there may be possibilities for collaboration—and prioritize the topics to help you decide on the focus of your first enrichment cluster.

Focus on Key Questions

Develop enrichment clusters around the following six key questions:

- What do people with an interest in this topic or area of study do?
- What products do they create, and what services do they provide?
- What methods do they use to carry out their work?
- What resources and materials are needed to produce high-quality products and services?
- How and with whom do they communicate the results of their work?
- What steps do cluster participants need to take to have an impact on an intended audience?

These questions do not need to be answered immediately, sequentially, or comprehensively at this stage. As your cluster develops, have students discuss the questions and allow them to reach their own conclusions about the activities, resources, and products that professionals pursue in particular areas of study. If you have all the answers ready before the cluster begins, the excitement of pure inquiry will be lost.

Students assume roles as investigators, writers, artists, or other types of practicing professionals.

Explore the Topic

The most obvious way to learn about the work of a professional is to discuss the key questions with someone working in the field. A cartoonist, landscape architect, or fashion designer will give you the lay of the land and offer some recommended resources. When talking with professionals, keep in mind that you want to learn what they routinely do in their jobs, how they do it, and what they produce. This background material will help you plan the cluster, but students should also pursue the same questions with professionals after the cluster commences. Such interaction dramatically increases motivation and engagement.

Almost all professionals belong to professional associations. A quick Internet search turns up approximately 3,500 professional organizations. To learn about the work that genealogists do, one teacher went to the Association of Professional Genealogists Web site (www.apgen.org) and found a treasure trove of resources on careers in the field, conferences, publications, places where family records can be found, and local chapters. She also located a directory of members by state. Association membership lists can suggest speakers, mentors, or enrichment cluster cofacilitators. By clicking on *Connecticut*, the teacher found the names, addresses, and phone numbers of 13 professional genealogists in the state, one of whom lived in close proximity to the school.

Another way to explore the key questions as you develop cluster content is to obtain resource books on the methodology of a particular field. A visit to the Genealogical Publishing Company Web site yielded an extensive list of potential resources: 423 titles, to be exact. Librarians and college bookstores can also help locate methodological resource books.

In the real world, almost all work is intended to have an impact on at least one targeted audience. In finding target audiences, you will be serving as a referral agent, promoter, or marketing manager of student work. In school, fellow students and parents are obvious audiences for whom students can practice and perfect performances and presentations, but young people will begin to view themselves in a much more professional role when you help them seek audiences outside the school. The students themselves should make the contacts and be prepared to answer questions.

Local newspapers, city or state magazines, and literary reviews—especially those that target young authors—are excellent places to submit written work. Public buildings and business offices are often receptive to requests to display student artwork. Local or state organizations—such as historical societies, writers clubs, civic groups, environmental preservation organizations, and advocacy groups—also provide opportunities for young entrepreneurs to present their work. Young dramatists can take their performances on the road to senior citizen centers, day-care centers, religious groups, or professional organizations. One group of students who wrote and produced a legal thriller presented a synopsis of the plot at a county bar association meeting.

The essence of inductive or high-end learning is applying relevant knowledge and skills to solving real problems.

Contests and competitions are also great outlets. Most teachers are familiar with science fairs, National History Day, and Math League, but thousands of other competitions take place in such areas as photography, fashion design, inventions, drama, and Web design. Searching for outlets and audiences; writing query letters and submitting work for possible publication, presentation, or display; and receiving replies—both positive and negative—are all part of the creative process and motivate aspiring writers, scientists, and artists.

Write Your Enrichment Cluster Description

The enrichment cluster description should convey, in no more than 100 words, the essence of the experience. Use verbs that emphasize the explorative nature of the cluster by conveying action and illustrating tasks. For example, in a cluster that involves building and marketing compost bins, you might use such verbs as *design, field-test, construct, advertise, market, contact, display*, and *sell*.

You might also pose questions about potential student interests and possible types of involvement: Do you like to express your feelings by writing poetry or short stories? Are you concerned about finding better ways to protect wildlife? Would you like to try your hand at designing fashions for teens? Each of these questions relates to a topic around which a cluster might be developed, yet they are all open-ended enough to encompass a broad range of activities in specific interest areas.

Launch Your Enrichment Cluster

Although students who have signed up for your cluster have expressed an interest in the topic, it may take them some time to understand the cluster's approach to learning. Displaying products or tools that professionals in your topic area typically use is always a good way to begin. In a cluster on archaeology, entitled *The Trash Heaps of Mankind*, the facilitator showed slides of famous and local archaeological discoveries. She opened a Mystery Box in the front of the room to reveal a trowel, a sieve, a pair of gloves, a dust brush, pegs and string, a marking pen, and a camera. She pointed out that these were the main tools of the archaeologist and that an examination of material found in garbage dumps was one of the ways in which archaeologists analyzed past and present cultures. A short videotape of a dig in the students' own state heightened student interest in the work of practicing archaeologists.

Escalate Content and Process

One of the problems we encountered in our research on enrichment clusters was a failure on the part of some facilitators to escalate the level of content and methodology pursued within a cluster. Indeed, critics may point out that clusters are nothing more than fun and games or that students carry out their work using existing skills rather than acquiring more advanced ones. You can guard against these criticisms by examining each cluster with an eye toward providing authentic and rigorous content within the topic area.

In a cluster on research about political opinion, for example, students evaluated archived news articles and editorials from the World War II and Vietnam War eras to analyze and compare public support for these wars. Students in an ecology and evolutionary biology cluster studied the survival prospects of tropical plants grown in the school's greenhouse and conducted experiments to explore optimal conditions for propagation. Content and process objectives evolve as a result of the investigations that students conduct, and this is one factor that highly differentiates the clusters from regular instruction.

Gathering Original Data

During many years of working with students in authentic learning situations, we have discovered that there is a certain magic associated with gathering original data and using that information to create new knowledge. This knowledge may not be new for all humankind, but it may be original to students and their local audiences. A group of elementary students spent an entire school year gathering and analyzing samples of rainwater for sulfur and nitrogen oxide emissions, the main pollutants responsible for acid rain. The students then prepared a report concerning the extent of acid rainfall in their region of the country. Their teacher helped them obtain a standard rain gauge and a kit for testing acidity.

Additional resources enabled these students to prepare statistical and graphic summaries of their data; compare their findings with data from national and regional reports that were easily accessed on the Internet; and design maps showing acid rain trends over time and across geographic regions. The data provided participants with the excitement and motivation to study environmental and health problems associated with various types of pollution. The students found receptive audiences for their work among state environmental protection groups, the U.S. Environmental Protection Agency, and the National Weather Bureau.

Putting It All Together

Most teachers have had a vision, at one time or another, about what they thought teaching would entail. They pictured themselves in classrooms with interested and excited students dramatizing dangerous midnight journeys on the Underground Railroad, conducting science experiments to find out how things work, or experiencing the exhilaration that occurs when a student-developed board game unlocks the relationships between a set of numbers and everyday experiences.

Real-life problems target a real audience.

Many teachers, however, experience a disconnect between their vision of a challenging and rewarding career and the day-to-day grind of test preparation. What is most ironic about the separation between the ideal and the reality of today's classrooms is that most teachers actually have the skills and motivation to do the kinds of teaching they dream of. Unfortunately, lists, regulations, and other people's requirements have resulted in both a prescriptive approach to teaching and a barrier to creating a challenging and exciting classroom. Overprescribing the work of teachers has, in some cases, lobotomized good teachers and denied them the creative teaching opportunities that attracted them to the profession in the first place.

Freedom to teach still exists, as does the possibility of making learning enjoyable, engaging, and enriching. You can find both in enrichment clusters, where authentic learning is in the driver's seat.

JOSEPH S. RENZULLI is Director of the National Research Center on the Gifted and Talented at the University of Connecticut, Storrs, Connecticut; joseph.renzulli@uconn.edu. MARCIA GENTRY is Associate Professor of Education Studies at Purdue University, West Lafayette, Indiana. SALLY M. REIS is Professor and Chair of the Educational Psychology Department at the University of Connecticut, Storrs, Connecticut.

From Educational Leadership, 62(1), September 2004, pp. 73–77. Copyright © 2004 by ASCD. Reprinted by permission. The Association for Supervision and Curriculum Development is a worldwide community of educators advocating sound policies and sharing best practices to achieve the success of each learner. To learn more, visit ASCD at www.ascd.org.

Why We Need "The Year of Languages"

"2005: The Year of Languages" will focus on educating the U.S. public about the benefits of learning another language.

SANDY CUTSHALL

Q: What do you call a person who speaks three languages?
A: Trilingual.
Q: What do you call a person who speaks two languages?
A: Bilingual.
Q: What do you call a person who speaks one language?
A: An American.

The late Paul Simon, senator from Illinois and a champion of foreign language learning, once called the United States "linguistically malnourished" compared with other nations (Simon, 1980). People from different cultural and linguistic backgrounds have always come together to season the American melting pot, yet we have nevertheless held monolingualism in English as the gold standard of U.S. citizenship for immigrants, often at the expense of heritage languages.

Sadly, a chronic case of *xenoglossophobia*—the fear of foreign languages—has marked U.S. history. Only a few generations back, 22 states had restrictions prohibiting the teaching of foreign languages; it was not until 1923 that the U.S. Supreme Court overturned those laws. In 1954, only 14.2 percent of U.S. high school students were enrolled in foreign language classes; most public high schools (56 percent) offered no foreign language instruction at all (Clifford, 2004).

Studies have frequently reported on this area of national weakness. In 1979, the President's Commission on Foreign Language and International Studies noted that "Americans' incompetence in foreign languages is nothing short of scandalous, and it is becoming worse" (Clifford, 2004). Two decades later, a senior Department of Defense official said that the United States' greatest national challenge was its "general apathy toward learning foreign languages" (Clifford, 2004). In August 2001—one month before the September 11 terrorist attacks against the United States—the National Foreign Language Center at the University of Maryland noted that the country faced "a critical shortage of linguistically competent professionals across federal agencies and departments responsible for national security" (Simon, 2001).

This apathy plays out in the education landscape as well. Fewer than 1 in 10 students at U.S. colleges major in foreign languages, and most of those language majors choose French, German, Italian, or Spanish. Only 9 percent learn Arabic, Chinese, Japanese, Russian, or Indonesian—languages that are spoken by the majority of the planet's people (Strauss, 2002).

The current lack of accurate U.S. intelligence has heightened awareness of our lack of foreign language prowess. Many are hoping that the United States will finally change its priorities and find new and better ways to encourage and support language learning. Multilingualism carries many benefits. Individuals who speak, read, and understand more than one language can communicate with more people, read more literature, and benefit more fully from travel to other countries. Further, people who can communicate in at least two languages are a great asset to the communities in which they live and work. Jobs today are increasingly requiring workers who can interact with those who speak languages other than English and who can adapt to a wide range of cultural backgrounds. Every year, more than 200,000 Americans lose out on jobs because they do not know another language (Simon, 1980).

Allen Over Geld

So are we putting our money where our "tongues" are? Total federal funding for foreign language education was approximately $85 million for 2003, which represents less than one-sixth of 1 percent of the overall Department of Education budget. This means that for every $100 spent by the Department of Education in 2003, approximately $0.15 went to foreign language education (Keatley, 2004).

According to Thomas Keith Cothrun, president of the American Council on the Teaching of Foreign Languages (ACTFL), there is clearly a disconnect in the government: On one hand, the military and intelligence communities decry the lack of language experts; on the other hand, the Department of Education underemphasizes the importance of language learning. A recent study by the Council for Basic Education (CBE) indicates that the No Child Left Behind Act (NCLB) has forced a narrow focus on reading, math, and science at the expense of languages. Instruction time in foreign languages has decreased—particularly in schools serving minority populations—as a direct result of NCLB (CBE, 2004). The National Association of State Boards of Education (NASBE) also recently reported that both arts and foreign language education are increasingly at risk of being eliminated from the core curriculum (NASBE, 2003).

Non è Facile

Foreign language learning is not something that happens overnight; it takes a commitment of time and money. U.S. schools compound the problem by waiting too long to start foreign language instruction. According to ACTFL Professional Programs Director Elvira Swender, U.S. students often start learning foreign languages at puberty, "an age at which their brains are least receptive to language learning." Swender also notes the relative unimportance that schools assign to languages. "It doesn't occur to anyone that we should wait to teach students math," she points out, "so why do we wait with foreign languages?"

ACTFL recommends that elementary school language programs include classes three to five days a week for 30 to 40 minutes; middle schools should hold classes daily for 40 to 50 minutes. Few public schools do this even in Spanish and French, the most commonly taught languages (Strauss, 2002).

Further, some of the languages that are most crucial for Americans to learn are the most challenging for English speakers, thus requiring the greatest commitment of time and effort. Research estimates that it takes between 2,400 and 2,760 hours of instruction for someone with a superior aptitude for languages to attain the highest level of achievement in Arabic, for example (Strauss, 2002).

Quel est le Problème?

It's not that people in the United States don't want to learn languages; rather, they often believe that they are unable to do so or that they simply don't need to. As ACTFL Executive Director Bret Lovejoy points out,

> This perception that languages are too difficult to learn can often be traced to the fact that a person didn't start early enough, didn't have enough time devoted to the language, or had a difficult time in a language course in the past. (Personal communication, April 7, 2004)

People in the United States may travel hundreds of miles in their own nation and never hear a language other than English spoken, a decidedly different situation from that of European countries, whose citizens live in much more multilingual world. In addition, the widespread perception of English as the international language of business has contributed to a pervasive belief in the United States that everyone should learn English and that Americans simply don't need to learn another language. In fact, the international language of business is always the language of the client or customer. If businesses in the United States don't speak the language of their customers, those businesses end up at a competitive disadvantage.

Beginning language learning at an early age is crucial to increasing our language capabilities. A primary difference between the United States and nations that boast greater language strengths is the latter countries' emphasis on learning languages at younger ages. The Center for Applied Linguistics (CAL) issued a report on approaches to language learning that compared the United States with 22 other nations. Seven countries—Australia, Austria, Germany, Italy, Luxembourg, Spain, and Thailand—had widespread or compulsory education in additional languages by age 8, and another eight—Canada, the Czech Republic, Denmark, Finland, Israel, Kazakhstan, Morocco, and the Netherlands—introduced a foreign language in the upper elementary grades. In many cases, a *second* foreign language was offered or required in the elementary grade.

In stark contrast, the majority of students in the United States do not start studying foreign language until age 14 (Pufahl, Rhodes, & Christian, 2000). Most foreign language study in the United States takes place in grades 9–12, during which time more than one-third (39 percent) of students study a foreign language. Only 6 percent of U.S. students study a foreign language in grades 1–6.

The shortage of language teachers in the United States is yet another challenge. Because early language learning has not been part of the traditional U.S. education model and most communities don't have access to foreign languages in elementary schools, there is a lack of well-trained language teachers at these levels.

People who can communicate in at least two languages are a great asset to the communities in which they live and work.

El Año de Lenguas

Language learning is a complex, long-term issue. In a culture unfortunately known for its short attention span, we need to do something dramatic to draw sustained attention to this issue.

Enter "2005: The Year of Languages," a national public awareness campaign that may be our best hope to put language learning in the spotlight and engage in a fruitful national conversation about the relationship between Americans and foreign language learning. Under the guidance and stewardship of ACTFL, 2005: The Year of Languages advances the concept that every person in the United States should develop proficiency in at least one language in addition to English. Each month of the yearlong endeavor will focus on a different area—such as language policy, higher education, language advocacy, heritage languages, and early language learning—with specific events reflecting the monthly focus.

For example, in February—the month that will tackle international engagement—a panel of Fulbright Exchange participants and representatives from other international programs will discuss the importance of study-abroad programs. There are currently more than 3,000 study-abroad programs for U.S. students to choose from. Although the number of U.S. students studying abroad for credit doubled in the past decade to more than 150,000 in the 2000-2001 school year, this number represents only 1 percent of college enrollments (Institute of International Education, 2003). Many students lack access to study-abroad programs through their institutions.

July's focus will be on languages and communities; during that month, the annual Folk Life Festival sponsored by the Smithsonian Institution will feature communities within and outside the United States and their respective languages and cultures. October will emphasize the benefits of early language learning: Activities cosponsored by the National Council of PTAs will provide parents with information on the benefits of learning languages at an early age and will feature K-12 programs that highlight language learning.

Language teachers in a school or district may choose to meet as a group to brainstorm ideas for promoting foreign language awareness, using the official Year of Languages Calendar of Events as a starting point. The calendar (available at www.yearoflanguages.org) may be used as a guide in planning local school events. ACTFL state and regional organizations have also coordinated plans for 2005: The Year of Languages and can serve as a local resource for schools to get involved with activities planned in their areas.

Alle Sind Optimistisch

There is great hope that the 2005: The Year of Languages campaign will not only draw U.S. attention to the important issue of foreign language learning but also inspire actions like those that resulted from a similar European effort in 2001, such as an ongoing annual National Language Day/Week, a national language agenda, and an official language policy.

With so much at stake—international relations, global competitiveness, support for internal diversity, and national security—it may well be time for everyone involved in education to think about what they can personally do to make this a successful Year of Languages.

References

Clifford, R. (2004, Jan. 16). Remarks at *National briefing on language and national security*, National Press Club, Washington, DC. Available: www.ndu.edu/nsep/january16_briefing.htm

Council for Basic Education. (2004). *Academic atrophy: The condition of the liberal arts in America's public schools.* Washington, DC: Author.

Institute of International Education. (2003). *Open doors 2003: Report on international educational exchange.* New York: Author.

Keatley, C. (2004, March). Who is paying the bills? The federal budget and foreign language education in U.S. schools and universities. *The Language Resource Newsletter.* Available: www.nclrc.org/caidlr82.htm#no2

National Association of State Boards of Education. (2003). *The complete curriculum: Ensuring a place for the arts and foreign languages in America's schools.* Alexandria, VA: Author.

Pufahl, I., Rhodes, N., & Christian, D. (2000, December). *Foreign language teaching: What the United States can learn from other countries.* Washington, DC: Center for Applied Linguistics. Available: www.cal.org/resources/countries.html

Simon, P. (1980). *The tongue-tied American: Confronting the foreign language crisis.* New York: Continuum.

Strauss, V. (2002, May 28). Mastering Arabic's nuances no easy mission. *The Washington Post,* p. A9.

SANDY CUTSHALL is Managing Editor of *Foreign Language Annals*, the quarterly journal of the American Council on the Teaching of Foreign Languages, and a teacher of English as a second language to adults in Mountain View, California.

Author's note—Thomas Keith Cothrun, Bret Lovejoy, Mary Louise Pratt, Nancy Rhodes, and Elvira Swender contributed to this article. For more information about 2005: The Year of Languages, visit www.yearoflanguages.org or contact the American Council on the Teaching of Foreign Languages (ACTFL) at 703-894-2900.

Choosing to Learn

Students in all classrooms have always had the power to make the most basic choice about their learning: they may choose to engage in learning or to disengage. Our goal, the authors point out, is to inspire them to choose to engage. In short, we want students to choose to learn and choose in order to learn.

BOBBY ANN STARNES AND CYNTHIA PARIS

H igh school English and Spanish teacher Susan Moon stood near a thick pad of chart paper. Her class of juniors and seniors sat casually around the room. On the chalkboard were the state curriculum mandates. They had been through this process before, so they were prepared.

"Okay," Susan said, "this is what we have to demonstrate that we know. Any ideas how we are going to do that?"

With almost no lapse, the kids began to throw out ideas and to argue the merits of each proposal until they identified a project they believed would permit each student to meet the state requirements. Once Susan felt confident that their choices would allow them to do well, she asked, "Okay, you're going to need money to do this. How are you going to get it?"

Once again, the kids took over. Before I left, they had identified how they would meet or exceed state mandates, raise money to support their plans, and demonstrate what they had learned. They were energized. I was exhausted from trying to keep up with them.

Will they meet their goals? If their history bears out, they will. . . . Typically, kids in Susan's classes score in the 90th percentile on state achievement tests. And this is no wealthy suburban school district. It is a rural school serving a population in which teen pregnancy and dropout rates are high. It is a school where one might not expect to find this kind of teaching and learning going on.

—Trip Log, September 1996

Some might say that Susan is unique, that she is part of an elite club of exceptional teachers, or that hers is a one-of-a-kind classroom. But our experience has shown us that there are many Susans in many schools around the country—places where, without fanfare and often where one might least expect it, teachers go about their work and do remarkable things in spite of challenges and barriers. Foxfire works with some of these teachers—in both small schools and massive urban campuses in 37 states, from the border town of Calexico, California, to a school at the end of the road in Elk City, Idaho; from South Central Los Angeles to rural Alabama; from the suburbs of Princeton, New Jersey, to the inner-city neighborhoods of Seattle, Washington. Across grade levels, across content areas, across cultures and races and economic levels, these teachers create dynamic learning environments.

Like Susan, many teachers believe learners will meet high expectations when they are actively involved in making meaningful choices about how they will learn. Such teachers have worked in isolation, in small groups, and in regional or national networks to define, develop, and construct means to put their beliefs into practice. Through their efforts and their individual and collective decisions, they have found ways to provide their students opportunities to succeed academically and, at the same time, to engage in classroom experiences that make them active decision makers and partners in their own educations.

To achieve success, these teachers balance the demands of their school systems and their own deeply held beliefs. They involve learners in making significant decisions about how they will learn, how they will assess what they learn, and how they will use what they have learned in meaningful ways. In this way, they create active, learner-centered teaching and learning steeped in the ideas and ideals of democratic principles. Moreover, their work together creates rich, interactive relationships between teachers, learners, and the curriculum.

Regardless of experience or the school context, they adapt their work in proactive ways, creating learning environments that are unique, yet similar. And though they share these powerful beliefs, most of these teachers have never met or talked, or even know there are others with whom they share a vision.

Including learners in making decisions that affect them and *still* meeting high academic standards strikes many in the popular and professional media as incompatible, if not mutually exclusive. Yet, these teachers know they are not. They know that including learners increases their determination to do well, to meet high standards. Our work has taught us that learners of all ages can and will make good choices and contribute meaningfully when they are regularly given—with proper preparation and within developmentally-appropriate boundaries—the opportunity to participate in making the decisions that affect them. The climate that emerges from a decision-making classroom allows the learners, in collaboration with the teacher, to solve emerging problems as they address the curriculum. In this way, learners are supported in the development of their ability to solve problems and accept responsibility. At the same time, teachers who share these beliefs accept their responsibility to ensure that the academic integrity of all classroom experiences is clear. These teachers share their high expectations, taking away the mystery of what they are "supposed" to learn. Then, through collaborative planning, students engage in learning experiences that allow them to meet or exceed the mandates.

We know that access to educational, economic, and career opportunities is more available to those who have mastered a set of basic academic skills in such areas as reading, writing, speaking, math, and science. Therefore, teachers have a moral and ethical responsibility to ensure that learners acquire these skills and develop the traits that provide access to a broad array of life choices.

Teachers who include their students in devising a learning plan for the class that ensures that all learners achieve academic success have the ability to integrate these two, seemingly divergent ideals. Through the experiences of such teachers, we have learned that, taken together, these practices contribute to the development of independent, self-assured, self-directed citizens with the intelligence and personal power to think and act independently, both as individuals and as members of a larger community.

"Taken together" is both the key and the challenge. One without the other diminishes the richness and possibility of education. To permit learners to make choices that deprive them of the opportunity to build the skills they need in order to obtain access to learning opportunities is to act irresponsibly. To slight learners' development as good decision makers or self-governing young adults is just as irresponsible.

Yet the history of our profession has been one of either/ors and pendulum swings from "soft" progressivism to "tough" back-to-basics movements. It is not surprising, then, that many teachers see academic integrity and learner choice as incompatible. And teachers who see them as incompatible but value both are faced with an interesting dilemma. Some teachers resolve the conflict by retaining for themselves decisions regarding the curriculum, discipline, grades, and classroom learning activities. Learners are left to make small choices, such as whether they use green paint or red. Other teachers resolve this conflict by providing choice during free time or after the "work" is done.

John Dewey leads us to see the spaces between these either/ors as places of possibility. In such spaces, we can explore the ways in which learner choice creates conditions in which academic integrity can flourish. And we can do so with a confidence bred of our own experience and that of many others.

Over half a century ago, this kind of dynamic interdependence between choice and academic integrity was explored in the Eight-Year Study (Aiken, 1942). This study confirmed that students who had attended schools in which they were partners

The Foxfire Core Practices

1. The work teachers and learners do together is infused from the beginning with learner choice, design, and revision.
2. The role of the teacher is that of facilitator and collaborator.
3. The academic integrity of the work teachers and learners do together is clear.
4. The work is characterized by active learning.
5. Peer teaching, small-group work, and teamwork are all consistent features of classroom activities.
6. Connections between the classroom work, the surrounding communities, and the world beyond the community are clear.
7. There is an audience beyond the teacher for learner work.
8. New activities spiral gracefully out of the old, incorporating lessons learned from past experiences, building on skills and understandings that can now be amplified.
9. Imagination and creativity are encouraged in the completion of learning activities.
10. Reflection is an essential activity that takes place at key points throughout the work.
11. The work teachers and learners do together includes rigorous, ongoing assessment and evaluation.

in curriculum planning met and even exceeded expectations for academic achievement in college. Teachers and learners in those schools engaged in creating curricula that were grounded in the learners' interests and experiences and directed toward the achievement of academic goals. Projects and theme studies focusing on learners' concerns were the vehicles for acquiring the necessary academic skills and knowledge.

Alfie Kohn's (1993) synthesis of more recent classroom research has demonstrated the applicability of the findings of the Eight-Year Study's findings to education today. Among other things, Kohn found that learners given opportunities to make choices about how they would learn worked longer, produced more creative work, missed fewer days of school, and scored higher on standardized tests.

In the sections that follow, we examine the concepts of learner choice and academic integrity as teachers and learners who use the Foxfire approach have come to understand them over the years. Using excerpts from logs we have kept of classroom visits over the years as well as published remarks, we hope to show that learner choice and academic integrity are, by necessity, interwoven concepts.

Learner Choice

. . . [T]he choice thing just doesn't work with these kids. . . . [I agree] kids should be allowed to make choices . . . but these kids make bad choices. . . .

"The other day I was working with a reading group, and I told the rest of the class they could choose what to do. One boy

chose to crawl around the room and make loud whooping noises. We couldn't get our work done because he was making so much noise. But it was his choice, so I couldn't do anything about it."
I was stunned.

—Trip Log, September 1996

The most damaging misinterpretation of the notion of learner choice is that adopting it leads to an "anything goes" classroom. Of course, such an interpretation invites anarchy. If students are permitted to make decisions without boundaries, without coaching, and without respect for the rights of others, effective learning, the development of democratic principles, and the developmental process are seriously impaired.

Still, confusion about the difference between democratic principles and anarchy is not unusual. It may be difficult for those with limited experience participating in environments shaped by democratic principles to see the differences between freedom and license and to see the need for boundaries within which choices must be made.

Over the years, teachers have documented learners' engagement, achievement, and pride in mastering skills that permit them to complete tasks they have set for themselves and helped design. Through their reports, we have come to understand the nature and implications of making student choice a pivotal piece of teaching practice. Typical of these reports is Carol Coe's (1997) description of students in her sophomore composition class after they decided they would write a book in order to meet their required curriculum goals:

The book idea had definitely captured their interest and without any of my ideas appearing to light the class fire. . . . I noticed an immediate surge in energy and mood among the students, with ideas bubbling forth. . . . Students willingly volunteered their time and talents . . . Why hadn't I noticed this wealth of creative energy and talent before? Clearly it had been there all along, but I hadn't seen it. This previously untapped potential now became a driving force propelling us forward.[3]

With their interests engaged and potential revealed, Coe's students completed this challenging academic task.

John Dewey offers us some insight into what might be at work here. He claimed that there are conditions that must be met for school activities to be truly educative. The first is interest. An activity must "lay hold on the emotions and desires" and "offer an outlet for energy that means something to the individual."[4] Such an activity "arouses curiosity, strengthens initiative, and sets up desires and purposes sufficient to carry a person over the dead places."[5]

Potential "dead places" litter the path to learning. They may be the seemingly endless revisions before a piece of writing meets the author's standards, or they may be the necessary but often tedious and frustrating struggle to master skills necessary to accomplish a task. Clearly, neither Dewey nor teachers we write about here are saying that *everything* learners do must be solely their choice. Both acknowledge the significance and reality of dead places.

Diane Sanna describes a child whose personal interests and desires carried him through these places:

I was having a difficult time finding a way to reach Craig. Then it happened one day; Craig found something that was uniquely meaningful to him, the spark that would launch him forward academically . . . a children's book about the *Titanic*. . . . Although the book was at a reading level that was challenging for him, Craig stuck with it for two days, reading every chance he got. . . . Eager to discover the magic the book had for Craig, I asked him why it was interesting to him. He told me he had once watched a TV program about the *Titanic* with his father. Craig was connecting . . . something that was interesting to him [in school] to his life outside the classroom.[6]

This is all well and good, but professional wisdom and humility require us to concede that we cannot know what engages the interest of each and every one of our students. Nor can we presume to know what life has offered or demanded of each learner in our increasingly diverse classrooms. Well-meaning attempts to anticipate learners' interests and purposes with flashy teaching units on teddy bears or dinosaurs or poetry introduced through rap music often miss the mark. If we hope to arouse and engage learners' interests, we must help *them* discover and pursue what *they* care about, what excites *them,* and what arouses *their* curiosity. We cannot guess it for them.

Craig's teacher summed up her story with this thought: "The best we can do is provide meaningful experiences and wait and watch their eyes light up and they're off and running, and determined and motivated to learn."[7]

Now, all interests, in and of themselves, are not educative. Neither are all choices. Good choices are those that have a purpose or what Dewey refers to as an "end view."[8] Good choices are purposeful on at least two levels. Good choices allow learners to pursue interests of personal significance, while building on past knowledge and experience, stretching toward greater understanding and skill, and meeting required learning objectives.

Making good choices is an acquired skill. It demands, among other things, the higher-order thinking skills to evaluate options against standards. When choices are offered to learners, the question posed is seldom "What shall we learn?" Curricular mandates most often guide the "what." Rather, the question is "How shall we learn?" Together, teachers and learners construct a plan for meeting the requirements that allows all learners to be involved at their individual achievement levels of and that includes opportunities for individual choice.

"Together" is key here. Choices are made *in collaboration* with the teacher—a mature, responsible decision maker who deliberately models decision making for learners and coaches them in the skills of making good choices.

This point can best be illustrated by taking a close look at Harold Brown's sophomore English classroom. He has carefully prepared his students, and, although he remains outside the discussion reported here, he is a fully attentive and active member of the decision-making activity.

This is a really big day in Harold Brown's sophomore English class near the California-Mexico border. It is the day he turns over decision making to his students for the first time. Harold spent a semester preparing the students for this day—helping them learn to make good choices, providing opportunities for them to assess their work, creating a learning community, setting high standards, and making the curriculum mandates explicit.

Standing in front of the room, he begins. "These are the givens," he says pointing to a long list. Moving his hand down the list, he continues by identifying those requirements mandated by the state and school, those determined by his teaching team, those he will require, and those that the class has developed.

"Now the question is," he says, "how are we going to make sure that we meet these requirements in the next nine weeks? Your job today is to figure out how we do that."

Before moving their chairs into the discussion circle, the students briefly review the class norms. Finally, Harold explains that he will not participate in the discussion. "You will need to talk to each other to solve the problem," he explains.

The students are silent. This is a bigger challenge than Harold has posed before. Some seem skeptical that they will really be given so much responsibility.

Once in the circle, they sit quietly for a few moments. Then one takes the lead. Another goes to the chalkboard to write their ideas. For the next 30 minutes, the students talk among themselves, making decisions about homework, journal entries, use of class time, responsibility. At first timidly, students begin to take charge. By the end of the discussion period, they are on the edge of their seats, even the most skeptical waving his hand wildly to add to the conversation.

Early in the discussion, Harold's role was tested. "Mr. Brown," one student asked, "Can we decide to do our journal entries for homework?" Harold remained silent, raising his arms to point back at the group. After a pause, the student looked away from Harold to the group and asked, "So, can we decide to do the journals for homework?"

Harold's only comment during the discussion came after the students' first vote. "Remember, now, that although almost all of you agree, some people do not." The students take the cue, and a discussion begins that gives time for those with minority opinions to speak their minds. Sometimes the minority sways the group. Other times they're convinced to go along. But in each case, those with divergent views are heard and respected.

This is the first such meeting for this class. There will be many more. These students are now crafters of their own learning experiences. For months before this meeting, they learned to choose. Now they are choosing to learn.

—Trip Log, January 1998

During the study, Harold and his students will revisit the plan periodically, assess its effectiveness, and make revisions based on the plan's success in meeting objectives. Issues may arise that challenge the ability of the teacher and learners to implement their plans. Whether students are dealing with unforeseen obstacles (e.g., school closings that make deadlines unattainable) or management problems (e.g., inappropriate or nonproductive behavior disrupting others' efforts), any issues that affect the learners will be solved collaboratively. Throughout the planning and implementation of learning experiences, emphasis will be placed on providing opportunities for learners to make individual and group choices about how they will address curricular mandates. Through this process, learners will construct experiences that build on their personal and group concerns and interests.

Such carefully constructed experiences lead learners to assume responsibility for their learning and to see a clear purpose in all they do. As they see that they can make good decisions and that their participation in planning and implementing learning experience is valued, learners become more connected to the content. Through this process, they become ever more capable of participating in the development of learning experiences. By assuming more ownership, their commitment to meeting curricular objectives rises, and their sense of personal power and their concern for the group increase. As a result, it becomes possible to build a true community of learners.

Learners will often not bring with them well-developed decision-making skills. They may see decision making as the teacher's responsibility. Nevertheless, learners can develop decision-making skills. Still, it is important for teachers to assess learners' developmental levels and match the complexity of decisions to be made to the learners' abilities. Just as teachers work to move curricular skills to higher levels, so do they work to build and move to higher levels individual and group decision-making skills.

When learners in Harold Brown's class make significant choices about how they will learn the required curriculum, how they will use what they learn, and how they will assess what they have learned, they are able to engage the personal interests, curiosities, questions, goals, and experiences that will support solid academic learning. Furthermore, they are given opportunities to develop the abilities necessary to take an active, informed role in making important life decisions.

Academic Integrity

Susan explained that she had made some leaps of faith—that the kids could learn basic Spanish skills by following the plan they had devised: planning lessons and teaching Spanish to younger children. It felt risky, and she worried all year long. As the teacher across the hall finished chapter after chapter in the Spanish textbook, her anxiety grew. At the end of the year, the kids took the state Spanish tests. Her kids scored first in the state in Spanish 2 and second in Spanish 1.

—Trip Log, September 1996

In spite of Susan Moon's success and the success of her students, the lingering suspicion that Spanish should be learned by covering chapters plagues her. She struggles against a taken-for-granted notion that good teaching and learning must rise from one of two choices: either "soft" liberalism or "tough" conservatism. For some reason and in spite of evidence to the contrary, there is a persistent notion that to fall into one of these camps ensures "good teaching" and to fall into the other ensures failure. We believe this notion is false; effective and ineffective teachers reside in both camps.

We propose a discussion of academic integrity that transcends the black-and-white definitions. Simply stated, we believe that teaching and learning with academic integrity can only mean that learners achieve at consistently high levels, meeting and even exceeding mandated goals. Regardless of the approach used, teaching that does not provide learners with the skills they need to make choices for their futures or prepare them to be fully participating citizens is unacceptable.

To teachers who embrace the practice of integrating choice and academic standards, merely fulfilling curriculum mandates is not enough. They believe that education requires more. They recognize that the rich experiences they create open doors to a wide variety of learning opportunities that build strong, assertive, and self-directed learners who know how to learn and how to use what they learn.

The classrooms of teachers who integrate choice and high academic expectations are highly conceptualized and operate to meet the unique interests and needs of the teachers and learners who inhabit them. Yet, a striking commonality among these teachers is the explicit nature of expectations and mandates. As in Harold Brown's classrooms, learners know they are required to learn. By making the curricular and teacher "givens" explicit, teachers can involve learners in building exciting learning opportunities within which, in collaboration with the teacher and to the extent appropriate, the learners assume responsibility and are accountable for their own learning.

Most often, teachers present curriculum requirements and teacher expectations to the class or to individual learners and work with them to develop the means for meeting these givens. When learners and teachers make decisions about learning experiences, they do so with curricular goals and objectives clearly in mind. While many options may be proposed, teachers and learners weigh each one carefully and jointly select those that are most likely to lead to mastery of curriculum goals. By making the expectations and mandates explicit, the appropriateness of potential learning activities can be measured against the givens.

A curriculum with academic integrity, then, not only teaches mandated skills. It also teaches a rich array of life skills, from decision making to responsibility, from respect for self to respect for others, and from strong individuality to a powerful sense of belonging to a group larger than the self.

In keeping with this expanded definition of academic integrity, learning can be seen to spring from and lead back to learners' own homes and communities. It is so alive and vital that learners can readily see uses for it in their own lives. Emphasis is placed on helping learners to identify the ways in which the subject matter relates to their lives, to their communities, and to the world beyond. Learners are helped to see the curriculum as an integrated whole. Skills learned in one content area open doors for new explorations in other areas of the curriculum. Students learn to articulate how their current focus of study relates to other content areas. They are aware of what they are learning, why they are learning it, and how mastering the curriculum will affect their lives outside the classroom.

Early in the century, Alfred North Whitehead (1929) warned against an education that presents learners with "inert ideas" handed down by teachers in small disconnected portions, a theorem here, a historical fact there. Life, he argued, is conducted each day as a whole, drawing on skills and knowledge from various subject areas simultaneously. And life—the here-and-now lives of learners—should be the context, motivation, and

proving ground for learning. Whitehead argued that expecting learners to participate in studies for which they can imagine no purpose in their immediate experience couldn't lead to true and lasting learning. Instead, this kind of learning leads to a mere performance of meaningless and trivial "intellectual minuets."[9]

Teachers and learners share responsibility for meeting and exceeding curriculum goals and for connecting the curriculum with learners' lives and across disciplinary lines. Learners experience the difference between freedom and license and learn responsibility for the decisions they make. These experiences support social and emotional growth and create the basis for the development of skilled, active, and responsible membership in society, be it the society of the school, the community, or the country.

Keeping the Faith

In spite of research that documents the broad gains learners make when they are given power to make choices about their learning, a group of learners lacking decision-making skills can create a dilemma for teachers. Sometimes teachers feel they must "play it safe" and revert to more teacher-directed practices. But teachers who persist testify to the rewards of "keeping the faith." To them, trusting the process and focusing on teaching children to choose wisely is so fundamental that meeting the challenges of learners unprepared to choose to learn is one they accept. Judy Bryson's story provides a final example of how involving learners in the decisions that affect them, even if slowly at first, leads to significant educational gains, along with growth in responsibility, involvement, creativity, and attitude. And, coincidentally, it improves test scores.

In an article title "Learning in a Forest," Judy Bryson (1996, pp. 22–26) tells the story of one of her most challenging classes. She was an accomplished and experienced teacher when she faced her new fourth grade class that year. Still she struggles as she begins the year with an especially difficult class, and she wondered whether they would ever be able to learn to choose or choose to learn. Kentucky's state testing requirements are rigorous, and schools are judged by the students' performance on a battery of performance and portfolio assessments. The fourth grade is a key year for these tests. If schools don't meet expectations, a series of punitive measures can be imposed up to and including the state taking over the schools' operation.

. . . *"I had never heard such a squabbling and bickering group of students. They got off the bus quarreling and left my room at the end of the day [the same way] and probably continued all the way home."*

The group wasn't able to make decisions at a level Judy had anticipated. Focusing on helping them become decision makers, rather than reverting to a more teacher-directed approach, seemed risky. But, with the stubbornness common to teachers like Judy, she chose to take the time to help the students learn to choose. The process required all of her patience and grit.

"We began with small decisions which grew larger almost every day. Once the students became confident that I truly valued their ideas; they tried even harder to come up with bigger and better plans."

Finally, the students were challenged to consider ways they might meet science requirements. They took up the challenge and decided to study a nearby old-growth forest. By the end of the year, students had completed an impressive array of learning experiences, all using the forest as a basis for study. They had met their science, social studies, and writing requirements. But the final evaluation of Judy's move to create a community of decision makers would come when her class faced the state tests.

"Our overall writing scores were up. . . . The proctor was impressed with the way the group of students attacked their group [performance] task, [how they] distributed jobs within their groups and worked together to find solutions. . . . Beyond all of the wonderful student-initiated learning, I believe the changes within the students themselves were the most remarkable."

Student attendance was up, there were few discipline issues, every student could find important and meaningful ways to contribute to the group while doing work appropriate to her or his own academic and social needs and strengths.

"At the end of the year I was as proud as a mother hen with her brood of chicks under her wings. This group had been, without a doubt, the most quarrelsome, most frustrating, hardest-working, and most productive class I'd ever had."[10]

Learners in all classrooms have always had the power to make the most basic choice about their learning: they may choose to engage in learning or to disengage. We cannot remove that choice. Our goal is to inspire students to choose to engage. When they do, we know they can and will make good choices about how they learn, how they use what they learn, and how they assess their learning. And we can help them exceed all expectations. In short, we want students to choose to learn and choose in order to learn.

Notes

1. Wilfred Aiken, *The Story of the Eight-Year Study with Conclusions and Recommendations* (New York: Harper & Row, 1942).

2. Alfie Kohn, "Choices for Children: Why and How to Let Students Decide," *Phi Delta Kappan,* September 1993, pp. 8–20.

3. Carol Coe, "Turning over Classroom Decision Making," *The Active Learner: A Foxfire Journal for Teachers,* August 1997, pp. 7–9.

4. John Dewey, *How We Think* (Lexington, Mass.: D.C. Heath, 1933), p. 218.

5. John Dewey, *Experience and Education* (New York: Simon & Schuster, 1938), p. 38.

6. Diane E. Sanna, "Waiting for Magical Moments," *The Active Learner: A Foxfire Journal for Teachers,* Winter 1998, pp. 18–19.

7. Ibid.

8. Dewey, *Experience and Education,* p. 67.

9. Alfred North Whitehead, *The Aims of Education and Other Essays* (New York: Macmillan, 1929), p. 10.

10. Condensed from Judy Bryson, "Learning in a Forest," *The Active Learner: A Foxfire Journal for Teachers,* August 1996, pp. 22–26.

BOBBY ANN STARNES is president of the Foxfire Fund, Mountain City, Ga. (foxfire@foxfire.org). **CYNTHIA PARIS** is an associate professor of education at Rider University, Lawrenceville, N.J. (parisc@rider.edu). © 2000, The Foxfire Fund, Inc.

Ten Big Effects of the No Child Left Behind Act on Public Schools

The Center on Education Policy has been carefully monitoring the implementation of NCLB for four years. Now Mr. Jennings and Ms. Rentner consider the comprehensive information that has been gathered and present their conclusions about the law's impact thus far.

JACK JENNINGS AND DIANE STARK RENTNER

Test-driven accountability is now the norm in public schools, a result of the No Child Left Behind (NCLB) Act, which is the culmination of 15 years of standards-based reform. Many state and local officials believe that this reliance on tests is too narrow a measure of educational achievement, but NCLB has directed greater attention to low-achieving students and intensified efforts to improve persistently low-performing schools.

For the past four years, the Center on Education Policy (CEP), an independent nonprofit research and advocacy organization, has been conducting a comprehensive and continuous review of NCLB, producing the annual reports contained in the series *From the Capital to the Classroom* as well as numerous papers on specific issues related to the law.[1] Each year, the CEP gathers information for this review by surveying officials in all the state departments of education, administering a questionnaire to a nationally representative sample of school districts, conducting case studies of individual school districts and schools, and generally monitoring the implementation of this important national policy.

Ten Effects

Ten major effects of NCLB on American education are evident from this multi-year review and analysis. We describe these effects broadly, because our purpose is to assess the overall influence of this policy on public schools. The effects on particular schools and districts may be different.

1. State and district officials report that student achievement on state tests is rising, which is a cause for optimism. It's not clear, however, that students are really gaining as much as rising percentages of proficient scores would suggest. Scores on state tests in reading and mathematics that are used for NCLB purposes are going up, according to nearly three-fourths of the states and school districts, and the achievement gaps on these same tests are generally narrowing or staying the same. States and districts mostly credit their own policies as important in attaining these results, although they acknowledge that the "adequate yearly progress" (AYP) requirements of NCLB have also contributed. However, under NCLB, student achievement is equated with the proportion of students who are scoring at the proficient level on state tests, and states have adopted various approaches in their testing programs, such as the use of confidence intervals, that result in more test scores being counted as proficient. In addition, some national studies support our survey findings of increased student achievement, while others do not.

2. Schools are spending more time on reading and math, sometimes at the expense of subjects not tested. To find additional time for reading and math, the two subjects that are required to be tested under NCLB and that matter for accountability purposes, 71% of districts are reducing time spent on other subjects in elementary schools—at least to some degree. The subject most affected is social studies, while physical education is least affected. In addition, 60% of districts require a specific amount of time for reading in elementary schools. Ninety-seven percent of high-poverty districts have this requirement, compared to 55%-59% of districts with lower levels of poverty.

3. Schools are paying much more attention to the alignment of curriculum and instruction and are analyzing test score data much more closely. Changes in teaching and learning are occurring in schools that have not made AYP for two years. The most common improvements are greater alignment of curriculum and instruction with standards and assessments, more use of test data to modify instruction, use of research to inform decisions about improvement strategies, improvement in the quality and quantity of professional development for teachers, and the provision of more intensive instruction to low-achieving students.

4. Low-performing schools are undergoing makeovers rather than the most radical kinds of restructuring. More intensive changes are taking place in schools that have not made AYP for five consecutive years and thus must be "restructured" under NCLB. Greater efforts to improve curriculum, staffing, and leadership are the most common changes, but very few of these restructured schools have been taken over by the states, dissolved, or made into charter schools. Though only about 3% of all schools were in restructuring during the 2005-06 school year, the number may increase in the current year. The longer the law is in effect, the more likely it is that some schools will not make AYP for five years.

5. Schools and teachers have made considerable progress in demonstrating that teachers meet the law's academic qualifications—but many educators are skeptical this will really improve the quality of teaching. With regard to teacher quality, 88% of school districts reported that by the end of the 2005-06 school year all their teachers of core academic subjects would have met the NCLB definition of "highly qualified." Problems persist, however, for special education teachers, high school math and science teachers, and teachers in rural areas who teach multiple subjects. Despite this general compliance with NCLB's provisions, most districts expressed skepticism that this requirement will improve the quality of teaching.

6. Students are taking a lot more tests. Students are taking many more tests as a result of NCLB. In 2002, 19 states had annual reading and mathematics tests in grades 3-8 and once in high school; by 2006, every state had such testing. In the 2007-08 school year, testing in science will be required under NCLB (although the results need not be used for NCLB's accountability requirements), leading to a further increase in the number of assessments.

7. Schools are paying much more attention to achievement gaps and the learning needs of particular groups of students. NCLB's requirement that districts and schools be responsible for improving not only the academic achievement of students as a whole but also the achievement of each subgroup of students is directing additional attention to traditionally underperforming groups of students, such as those who are from low-income families or ethnic and racial minorities, those who are learning English, or those who have a disability. States and school districts have consistently praised NCLB's requirement for the disaggregation of test data by subgroups of students, because it has shone a light on the poor performance of students who would have gone unnoticed if only general test data were considered.

For the past three years, though, states and districts have repeatedly identified as NCLB problem areas the law's testing and accountability provisions for students with disabilities and students learning English. State and district officials have voiced frustration with requirements to administer state exams to students with disabilities because, for disabled students with cognitive impairments, the state test may be inappropriate and serve no instructional purpose. Similarly, officials don't see the merit in administering an English/language arts test to students who speak little or no English. The U.S. Department of Education (ED) has made some administrative changes in those areas, but, in the view of state officials and local educators, these modifications have not been enough.

8. The percentage of schools on state "needs improvement" lists has been steady but is not growing. Schools so designated are subject to NCLB sanctions, such as being required to offer students public school choice or tutoring services. Over the past several years, there has been a leveling off in the number of schools not making AYP for at least two years. About 10% of all schools have been labeled as "in need of improvement" for not making AYP, though these are not always the same schools every year. Urban districts, however, report greater proportions of their schools in this category than do suburban and rural districts. Earlier predictions had been that by this time there would be a very large number of U.S. schools not making AYP. A major reason for the overall stabilization in numbers of such schools is that, as already noted, test scores are increasing. Another reason is that ED has permitted states to modify their NCLB accountability systems so that it is easier for schools and districts to make AYP.

In the last four years, about 2% of eligible students each year have moved from a school not making AYP for at least two years to another school, using the "public school choice" option. Approximately 20% of eligible students in each of the last two years have taken advantage of additional tutoring (called "supplemental educational services") that must be offered to students from low-income families in schools not making AYP for at least three consecutive years. Although student participation in tutoring has been stable, the number of providers of supplemental services has grown dramatically in the last two years, with more than half of the providers now being for-profit entities. Lower proportions of urban and suburban school districts report that they are providing these services than in the past. School districts are skeptical that the choice option and tutoring will lead to increases in academic achievement, though they are somewhat less skeptical about tutoring than they are about choice. (This month's *Kappan* includes a Special Section on Supplemental Educational Services, which begins on page 117.)

9. The federal government is playing a bigger role in education. Because of NCLB, the federal government is taking a much more active role in public elementary and secondary education than in the past. For example, ED must approve the testing programs states use to carry out NCLB as well as the accountability plans that determine the rules for how schools make AYP. In CEP surveys for the last three years, the states have judged ED's enforcement of many of the key features of the law as being strict or very strict, even while ED was granting some changes in state accountability plans. More states in 2005 than in 2004 reported that ED was strictly or very strictly enforcing the provisions for AYP, supplemental services, public school choice, and highly qualified teachers.

10. NCLB requirements have meant that state governments and school districts also have expanded roles in school operations, but often without adequate federal funds to carry out their duties. State governments are also taking a much more active role in public education, because they must carry out NCLB provisions that affect all their public schools. These state responsibilities include creating or expanding testing programs for grades 3-8 and one year of high school, setting minimum testing goals that all schools must achieve in general and also for their various groups of students, providing assistance to schools in need of improvement, certifying supplemental service providers and then evaluating the quality of their programs, and establishing criteria to determine whether current teachers meet NCLB's teacher-quality requirements. Most state departments of education do not have the capacity to carry out all these duties. Last year, 36 of the 50 states reported to CEP that they lacked sufficient staff to implement NCLB's requirements.

Local school districts must also assume more duties than before because of NCLB. More tests must be administered to students, more attention must be directed to schools in need of improvement, and judgments must be made about whether teachers of core academic subjects are highly qualified. In carrying out these responsibilities, 80% of districts have reported for two years in a row that they are absorbing costs that federal funds are not covering. Overall, federal funding for NCLB has stagnated for several years. Provisions of the law have resulted in a shift of funds so that, in school year 2005-06, two-thirds of school districts in the country received no increases or lost funds compared to the previous year.

NCLB's Future

NCLB is clearly having a major impact on American public education. There is more testing and more accountability. Greater attention is being paid to what is being taught and how it is being taught. Low-performing schools are also receiving greater attention. The qualifications of teachers are coming under greater scrutiny. Concurrently with NCLB, scores on state reading and mathematics tests have risen.

Yet some provisions of the act and of its administration are causing persistent problems. State and local officials have identified the testing and accountability requirements for students with disabilities and for students learning English as troublesome, and other requirements—such as the one to offer a choice of another public school to students in schools needing improvement—have caused administrative burdens with little evidence that they have raised student achievement.

The lack of capacity of state departments of education could undercut the effective administration of NCLB. ED cannot deal with all school districts in the country and so must rely on state agencies to assist in that task. Yet these agencies are under great strain, with little relief in sight. Local school districts must also carry out additional tasks, and they must dig into their own pockets to do so.

The U.S. Congress has begun hearings on the effects of NCLB to prepare for its reauthorization in the new Congress that will assemble in 2007. The key question is whether the strengths of this legislation can be retained while its weaknesses are addressed.

Note

1. For more information on NCLB, including the four annual reports and special papers, go to www.cep-dc.org, the Web site for the Center on Education Policy.

JACK JENNINGS is president of the Center on Education Policy, Washington, D.C., where DIANE STARK RENTNER is director of national programs.

StrengthsQuest in Application

The Power of Teaching Students Using Strengths

Gloria Henderson

Like Chip Anderson, I was initially taught to use the deficit-remediation model with my students. Even in that negative context, though, and with no exposure at all to strengths-based education, I unconsciously based my early teaching on four of my five Clifton StrengthsFinder signature themes: *Significance* (I wanted to be recognized for having made a difference to each student); *Achiever* (I focused on individual students and tried to energize them to establish and reach their goals); *Restorative* (I was confident that I would create success in even those students who had lost all hope); and *Futuristic* (I developed a vision for my students with the identified deficits reduced or eliminated).

As I learned about strengths-based education after I entered Azusa Pacific University's doctoral program, I came to realize the importance of systematic research and the application of research results in developing the most effective instructors possible. I became determined to use my own strengths consciously and deliberately.

Consciously Applying Strengths to Decide on a Job

I knew I had found my calling when I saw a position posting for a late-term-replacement teacher of at-risk kids in a program structured as a school-within-a-school. The school offers more Advanced Placement, International Baccalaureate, and honors classes than regular classes. The students I would teach composed the "school within." They had covered only a minimal amount of content and had not met the state standards.

Being Restorative, I found it natural to identify and take a constructive approach to the students' deficits in skills and the lack of decorum in the classroom. I looked at each student as an individual to determine areas in which performance was satisfactory and those in which it needed improvement. Being Futuristic, I dreamed big for my new students, and being an Achiever, I developed a plan to make my vision a reality. I conducted research to find lessons, discipline plans, and other resources to assist my students. I also sought advice from other teachers, who brought different strengths to bear. Although I endured many tests from those students, I became a much more effective teacher by consciously using my strengths and encouraging them to use theirs.

Consciously Applying Strengths to Develop Teaching Style

I now teach a sophomore English class for at-risk students at the same school. As an Achiever I set high expectations because I know that if I lower the bar and set expectations that are too easy to reach, the students will meet the expectations yet still not pass the required high school exit exam.

Although I fully intend that every student will pass the exit exam (Significance), I employ a Restorative teaching style that seems to fit my students particularly well. I tease them, cajole them, encourage them, tell them they are better than they think they are, and express my concerns and my hopes for them. I do not focus my efforts on content, but they seem to have a huge impact on how well the students learn the content.

So far the fit between my strengths and my job seems to be working well for the students. I have overheard students telling their friends, "Our English class is fun," "We didn't learn how to do that last year," "Can I take this class next semester?" and "I got a B on a test!" And although it is expected that my at-risk students will not perform as well as the others in the school, they did perform as well, if not better, on recent vocabulary benchmark tests.

After I initiated a video-technology program for the school, my at risk students successfully took on the challenge of learning theory and abstract application with very limited experiential learning. Even though the equipment arrived late, the students completed a number of well done projects—remakes, public service announcements, school- and community-focused films, music videos, instructional videos, independent films, and trailers—in only a few short weeks.

For years my students have been told that they are not the best—or worse than that. Evidently, though, many students simply did not understand what was expected of them or lacked the incentive to perform. By consciously using my own strengths, I have been able to address such specific needs. In return I have found it gratifying to make a real, measurable difference. By consciously matching the challenges I undertake with my strengths, I have been able to enjoy greater initial success than I would have otherwise. I have come to believe that although most people already use their strengths intuitively, any teacher will foster greater student achievement and success by clearly identifying and consciously applying strengths.

GLORIA HENDERSON teaches English, video technology, and psychology at Diamond Bar High School in Diamond Bar, California.

From *Educational Horizons,* Vol. 83, Spring 2005, pp. 202–204. Copyright © 2005 by Gloria Henderson. Educational Horizons is the quarterly journal of Pi Lambda Theta Inc., International Honor Society and Professional Association in Education. Reprinted with permission of the author.

The New First Grade: Too Much Too Soon?

Kids as young as 6 are tested, and tested again, to ensure they're making sufficient progress. Then there's homework, more workbooks and tutoring.

PEG TYRE

Brian and Tiffany Aske of Oakland, Calif., desperately want their daughter, Ashlyn, to succeed in first grade. That's why they're moving—to Washington state. When they started Ashlyn in kindergarten last year, they had no reason to worry. A bright child with twinkling eyes, Ashlyn was eager to learn, and the neighborhood school had a great reputation. But by November, Ashlyn, then 5, wasn't measuring up. No matter how many times she was tested, she couldn't read the 130-word list her teacher gave her: words like "our," "house" and "there." She became so exhausted and distraught over homework—including a weekly essay on "my favorite animal" or "my family vacation"—that she would put her head down on the dining-room table and sob. "She would tell me, 'I can't write a story, Mama. I just can't do it'," recalls Tiffany, a stay-at-home mom.

The teacher didn't seem to notice that Ashlyn was crumbling, but Tiffany became so concerned that she began to spend time in her daughter's classroom as a volunteer. There she was both disturbed and comforted to see that other kids were struggling, too. "I saw kids falling asleep at their desks at 11 a.m.," she says. At the end of the year, Tiffany asked the teacher what Ashlyn could expect when she moved on to the first grade. The requirements the teacher described, more words and more math at an even faster pace, "were overwhelming. It was just bizarre."

So Tiffany and Brian, a contractor, looked hard at their family finances to see if they could afford to send Ashlyn to private school. Eventually, they called a real-estate agent in a community where school was not as intense.

In the last decade, the earliest years of schooling have become less like a trip to "Mister Rogers' Neighborhood" and more like SAT prep. Thirty years ago first grade was for learning how to read. Now, reading lessons start in kindergarten and kids who don't crack the code by the middle of the first grade get extra help. Instead of story time, finger painting, tracing letters and snack, first graders are spending hours doing math work sheets and sounding out words in reading groups. In some places,

recess, music, art and even social studies are being replaced by writing exercises and spelling quizzes. Kids as young as 6 are tested, and tested again—some every 10 days or so—to ensure they're making sufficient progress. After school, there's homework, and for some, educational videos, more workbooks and tutoring, to help give them an edge.

Not every school, or every district, embraces this new work ethic, and in those that do, many kids are thriving. But some children are getting their first taste of failure before they learn to tie their shoes. Being held back a grade was once relatively rare: it makes kids feel singled out and, in some cases, humiliated. These days, the number of kids repeating a grade, especially in urban school districts, has jumped. In Buffalo, N.Y., the district sent a group of more than 600 low-performing first graders to mandatory summer school; even so, 42 percent of them have to repeat the grade. Among affluent families, the pressure to succeed at younger and younger ages is an inevitable byproduct of an increasingly competitive world. The same parents who played Mozart to their kids in utero are willing to spend big bucks to make sure their 5-year-olds don't stray off course.

> **'I worry that we are creating school environments that are less friendly to kids who just aren't ready . . . Around third grade, sometimes even the most precocious kids begin to burn out.'**
>
> —Holly Hultgren, Principal
> Lafayette Elementary School

Like many of his friends, Robert Cloud, a president of an engineering company in suburban Chicago, had the Ivy League in mind when he enrolled his sons, ages 5 and 8, in a weekly after-school tutoring program. "To get into a good school, you need to have good grades," he says. In Granville, Ohio, a city known for its overachieving high-school and middle-school students, an elementary-school principal has noticed a dramatic shift over the past 10 years. "Kindergarten, which was once very play-based," says William White, "has become the new first grade." This pendulum has been swinging for nearly a century: in some decades, educators have favored a rigid academic curriculum, in others, a more child-friendly classroom style. Lately, some experts have begun to question whether our current emphasis on early learning may be going too far. "There comes a time when prudent people begin to wonder just how high we can raise our expectations for our littlest schoolkids," says Walter Gilliam, a child-development expert at Yale University. Early education, he says, is not just about teaching letters but about turning curious kids into lifelong learners. It's critical that all kids know how to read, but that is only one aspect of a child's education. Are we pushing our children too far, too fast? Could all this pressure be bad for our kids?

Kindergarten and first grade have changed so much because we know so much more about how kids learn. Forty years ago school performance and intelligence were thought to be determined mainly by social conditions—poor kids came from chaotic families and attended badly run schools. If poor children, blacks and Hispanics lagged behind middle-class kids in school, policymakers dismissed the problem as an inevitable byproduct of poverty. Its roots were too deep and complex, and there wasn't the political will to fix it anyway. Since then, scientists have confirmed what some kindergarten teachers had been saying all along—that *all* young children are wired to learn from birth and an enriched environment, one with plenty of books, stories, rhyming and conversation, can help kids from all kinds of backgrounds achieve more. Politicians began taking aim at the achievement gap, pushing schools to reconceive the early years as an opportunity to make sure that all kids got the fundamentals of reading and math. At the same time, politicians began calling for tests that would measure how individual students were doing, and high-stakes testing quickly became the sole metric by which a school was measured.

President George W. Bush's No Child Left Behind Act, which required every principal in the country to make sure the kids in his or her school could read by the third grade, was signed into federal law in 2002. Its aim was both simple and breathtakingly grand: to level the academic playing field by holding schools accountable or risk being shut down.

So if the curriculum at Coronita Elementary School, 60 miles outside Los Angeles, is intense, that's because it has to be. Seventy percent of kids who go there live below the poverty line. Thirty percent don't speak English at home. Even so, No Child Left Behind mandates that Coronita principal Alma Backer and her staff get every student reading proficiently in time for the California state test in the spring of second grade or face stiff penalties: the school could lose its funding and the principal could lose her job. "Our challenges are great," she says. "From day one, our kids are playing catch-up." First grade is like literacy boot camp. Music, dance, art, phys ed—even social studies and science—take a back seat to reading and writing. Kids are tested every eight weeks to see if they are hitting school,

district and statewide benchmarks. If they aren't, they get remedial help, one-on-one tutoring and more instruction. The regular school day starts at 7:45 A.M. and ends at 2:05 P.M.; about a fifth of the students go to an after-school program until 5:30, where they get even more instruction: tutoring, reading group and homework help. Backer says most parents appreciate what the school is trying to do. "Many of them have a high-school diploma or less," says Backer, "but they're still ambitious for their children."

> 'If you push kids too hard, they get frustrated. Those are the kids who act out, and who can look like they have attention-span or behavior problems.'
>
> —Dominic Gullo, Professor
> Queens College, N.Y.

Parents whose kids attend Clemmons Elementary School near Winston-Salem, N.C., are ambitious for their children, too. But the scale of their expectations is different: the upper-middle-class, college-educated parents in this district don't just want their kids to get a good education, they want them to be academic stars. Principal Ron Montaquila says kids of all ages are affected. Last year, says Montaquila, one dad wanted to know how his son stacked up against his classmates. "I told him we didn't do class ranking in kindergarten," recalls Montaquila. But the father persisted. If they did do rankings, the dad asked, would the boy be in the top 10th? Like almost all elementary schools, kindergarten and first grade at Clemmons have become more academic—but not because of No Child Left Behind. Unlike poor schools, wealthy schools do not depend on federal money. The kids come to school knowing more than they used to. "Many of our kindergartners come in with four years of preschool on their résumé," says Montaquila. Last year nine children started kindergarten at Clemmons reading chapter books—including one who had already tackled "Little House on the Prairie."

In wealthier communities, where parents can afford an extra year of day care or preschool, they are holding their kids out of kindergarten a year—a practice known in sports circles as red-shirting—so their kids can get a jump on the competition. Clemmons parent Mary DeLucia did it. When her son, Austin, was 5, he was mature, capable, social and ready for school. But the word around the local Starbucks was that kindergarten was a killer. "Other parents said, 'Send him. He'll do just fine'," says DeLucia. "But we didn't want him to do fine, we wanted him to do great!" Austin, now in fourth grade, towers over his classmates, but he's hardly the only older kid in his grade. At Clemmons last year, 40 percent of the kindergartners started when they were 6 instead of 5. Other parents say they understand where the DeLucias are coming from but complain that red-shirting can make it hard for other kids to compete. "We're getting to the point," says Bill White, a Clemmons dad whose kids started on time, where "we're going to have boys who are shaving in elementary school."

Ten Ways to Prepare Your Child for School

For Kindergarten

1. **Read To Them**—Pull out the board books, get cozy and channel Mr. Rogers. Kids love repetition and there's no such thing as reading too much to your child.
2. **Talk To Them**—Sing songs, recite rhymes and narrate your activities as you go about the day. Ask questions and invite them to name objects and describe whatever they're seeing. At night, recap the day's events together out loud.
3. **Take Them On Trips**—No, not Europe. The supermarket, the post office, a museum or the zoo will do. Then, talk about what you see and ask questions.
4. **Write It Down**—Kids love to scribble. Give them paper and plenty of pencils, crayons, paints and markers. Finger paints are colorful and feel squishy, too.
5. **Socialize**—Whether it's a big birthday party or a one-on-one play date, kids benefit from hearing a range of words in a variety of voices. Story hour at the library or a puppet show can be especially good for encountering new sounds and ideas.
6. **Use Your Fingers**—Drawing, cutting and pasting can seem laborious but these activities will help them learn to write more legibly—and result in keepsakes.

For First Grade

7. **Read Some More**—Let them "read" to you, too, by flipping the pages—themselves, thank you very much—and retelling a favorite story in their own words.
8. **Teach Recognition**—Logos on food packages. Names and addresses on the mail. A stop sign. A "walk" signal. The letter B. Give them opportunities to demonstrate that they know what these things mean and then heap on praise.
9. **Do The Math**—Talk about numbers. Count everything out loud. How many grapes do you have on your plate? One more would make how many?
10. **Grow Their Attention Span**—Card games, board games, setting the table, picking photos out of a magazine. Set aside time to focus on a single activity or one task before moving on to active play.

Source: Dominic Gullo, Queens College, N.Y.

Parents are acutely aware of the pressure on their kids, but they're also creating it. Most kids learn to read sometime before the end of first grade. But many parents (and even some teachers and school administrators) believe—mistakenly—that the earlier the kids read independently, write legibly and do arithmetic, the more success they'll have all through school. Taking a cue from the success of the Baby Einstein line of videos and CDs, an entire industry has sprung up to help anxious parents give their kids a jump-start. Educate, Inc., the company that markets the learning-to-read workbooks and CDs called "Hooked on Phonics," just launched a new line of what it calls age-appropriate reading and writing workbooks aimed at 4-year-olds. In the last three years, centers that offer school-tutoring services such as Sylvan Learning Centers and Kumon have opened junior divisions. Gertie Tolentino of Darien, Ill., has been bringing her first grader, Kyle, for Kumon tutoring three times a week since he was 3 years old. "It's paying off," she says. "In kindergarten, he was the only one who could read a book at age 5." Two weeks ago Tiffani Chin, executive director of Edboost, a nonprofit tutoring center in Los Angeles, saw her first 3-year-old. His parents wanted to give him a head start, says Chin. "They had heard that kindergarten was brutal" and they wanted to give him a leg up.

All this single-minded focus on achievement leaves principals like Holly Hultgren, who runs Lafayette Elementary School in Boulder County, Colo., in a quandary. In this area of Colorado, parents can shop for schools, and most try to get their kids into the top-performing ones. Two years ago Hultgren moved to Lafayette from a more affluent school, in part to help raise the tests scores, improve the school's profile and raise attendance. Every day Hultgren has to help her staff strike a balance between the requirements of the state, the expectations of parents—and the very real, highly variable needs of all kinds of 5- and 6-year-olds. She is adamant that her staff won't "teach to the test." Yet, in keeping with her district's requirements, on the day before the first day of kindergarten, students come in for a reading assessment. Sitting one-on-one with her new teacher, a little girl named Jenna wrinkles her nose and in a whispery voice identifies most of the letters in the alphabet and makes their sounds. Naming words that start with each letter is harder for her. Asked to supply a word that starts with B, Jenna scrunches her face and shakes her head.

Hultgren is ambivalent about high-stakes testing. The district reading test, administered three times a year, helps parents see how the school measures up and helps teachers see "exactly what kind of instruction is working and what isn't." But the pressure to improve scores makes it hard for teachers to stay sensitive to the important qualities in children that tests can't measure—diligence, creativity and potential—or to nurture kids who develop more slowly. "I worry," she says, that "we are creating school environments that are less friendly to kids who just aren't ready."

Some scholars and policymakers see clear downsides to all this pressure. Around third grade, Hultgren says, some of the most highly pressured learners sometimes "burn out. They began to resist. They didn't want to go along with the program anymore." In Britain, which adopted high-stakes testing about six years before the United States did, parents and school boards are trying to dial back the pressure. In Wales, standardized testing of young children has been banned. Andrew Hargreaves, an expert on international education reform and professor at Boston College, says middle-class parents there saw that "too much testing too early was sucking the soul and spirit out of their children's early school experiences."

> 'When Austin was 5, he was ready for school. Other parents said, "Send him. He'll do just fine." But we didn't want him to do fine, we wanted him to do great!'
>
> —Mary DeLucia, Parent
> Clemmons Elementary School

While most American educators agree that No Child Left Behind is helping poor kids, school administrators say a bigger challenge remains: helping those same kids succeed later on. Until he resigned as Florida's school chancellor last year, Jim Warford says he scoured his budget, taking money from middle- and high-school programs in order to beef up academics in the earliest years. But then he began to notice a troubling trend: in Florida, about 70 percent of fourth graders read proficiently. By middle school, the rate of proficient readers began to drop. "We can't afford to focus on our earliest learners," says Warford, "and then ignore what happens to them later on."

What early-childhood experts know is that for children between the ages of 5 and 7, social and emotional development are every bit as important as learning the ABCs. Testing kids before third grade gives you a snapshot of what they know at that moment but is a poor predictor of how they will perform later on. Not all children learn the same way. Teachers need to

---

Interview: What Would Big Bird Do?

"Sesame Street" began in 1969 with a revolutionary idea: learning could be fun. The cast of furry Muppets and their inimitable songs became so popular among kids of all backgrounds—and not just the disadvantaged kids the show originally intended to help—that "Sesame Street" spawned an entire industry of DVDs, toys and computer games aimed at teaching ever-younger children. The show, meant for 2- to 4-year-olds, is watched today by kids as young as 9 months. NEWSWEEK's Julie Scelfo asked Rosemarie Truglio, "Sesame Street's" VP of education and research, whether she thinks this is a good idea. Excerpts:

SCELFO: Do You Think There's Too Much Pressure on Young Kids to Learn?

TRUGLIO: People want children to be ready to read in kindergarten, so that pressure is now being passed down to preschool and day-care centers. We're putting a lot of pressure on [teachers] and introducing children to some things that may or may not be age-appropriate. Stress is not conducive to learning. If you're put in a stressful environment, you're not going to learn.

What Should Preschoolers Be Learning?

The majority of kindergarten teachers want children to be able to function in a group setting. To be able to listen and take direction. Be able to get along. To be able to regulate their emotions. A lot of what I'm talking about is social-emotional development of children. If they can't function in a group setting, it will interfere with learning to read.

So Reading Is Important, but It's Not the Only Thing?

Every child learns at their own rate. During the preschool years, children's job is to explore and investigate, and adults need to assist learning and facilitate it. I'm not going to say a child can't read by the age of 5. But developmentally, most children in kindergarten are learning the precursors of

reading skills—they have sounds, they do the alphabet, they have rhyming—but they are not reading.

Then Why Do Parents Feel So Pressured?

One reason may be No Child Left Behind. I don't think the intention was for this kind of hysteria. The idea of accountability is great. But I think it's turned into this testing issue, and there's a lot of pressure about testing and performance which I think might be leading to anxiety.

Is That What Is Spurring Sales of All Those Videos for Infants?

What's happening now is, everything is getting pushed down to a younger and younger age. There's pressure even on babies to begin achieving, so parents are buying these videos to make their infants "smarter." But there's no research that shows exposure to videos increases learning.

But Aren't Kids Watching "Sesame Street" at Younger and Younger Ages?

Yes, and that's not something we can control. "Sesame Street" is a show for 2- to 4-year-olds. If you can get that word out, it would be great. Parents grew up on "Sesame Street" and they know it's a safe, educational viewing experience. They think, Why not have my little ones learn their letters and numbers at an accelerated pace? It makes parents feel proud. There's no harm, but the show's content isn't age-appropriate, so a lot of the learning is going over their heads. Also, they burn out. If you start watching it at 9 months, by the time you're 2 you want something else.

How Is This Affecting Children?

Learning should be fun. It shouldn't feel like they're learning, which is what "Sesame Street" is all about. A child's work is through play. I don't think preschoolers should be doing flashcards.

vary instruction and give kids opportunities to work in small groups and one on one. Children need hands-on experiences so that they can discover things on their own. "If you push kids too hard, they get frustrated," says Dominic Gullo, a professor of early education at Queens College in New York. "Those are the kids who are likely to act out, and who teachers can perceive as having attention-span or behavior problems."

There are signs that some parents and school boards are looking for a gentler, more kid-friendly way. In Chattanooga, Tenn., more than 100 parents camped out on the sidewalk last spring in hopes of getting their kids into one of the 16 coveted spots at the Chattanooga School for Arts and Sciences (CSAS), a K-12 magnet program that champions a sloweddown approach to education. The school, which admits kids from all socioeconomic backgrounds, offers students plenty of skills and drills but also stresses a "whole-child approach." The emphasis is not on passing tests but on hands-on learning. Two weeks ago newly minted kindergartners were spending the day learning about the color red. They wore red shirts, painted with bright red acrylic paint. During instructional time, they learned to spell RED. Every week each class meets for a seminar that encourages critical thinking. Two weeks ago the first graders had been read a book about a girl who was adopted. Then, the class discussed the pros and cons of adoption. One girl said she thought adoption was bad because "a kid isn't with her real mom and dad." A boy said it was good because the character "has a new mom and dad who love her." The children returned to their desks and drew pictures of different kinds of families. At CSAS, students are rarely held back, and in fourth grade— and in 12th grade—more than 90 percent of students passed the state's proficiency tests in reading last year.

Tiffany Aske says she wishes she could have found a school like CSAS in Oakland. Instead, they're pulling up stakes and moving to a suburban community in Washington where the school system seems more stable and has more outdoor space, and where the kids have more choices during the school day. In some ways, they feel as if they're swimming against the current. Most of their friends are scrambling, paying top dollar for houses in high-performing school districts. The Askes say they're looking for something more important than high test scores. "We want flexibility," says Tiffany. Ashlyn is a bright girl, says her mom, "but she's only a child." And childhood takes time.

With Matthew Philips, Julie Scelfo, Catharine Skipp, Nadine Joseph, Paul Tolme and Hilary Shenfeld.

UNIT 4

Development During Childhood: Family and Culture

Unit Selections

Key Points to Consider

- How can childrearing practices come to terms with genetic potentialities to maximize development?

- Why do American parents find it so difficult to say "no" to their children?

- Which is worse, a parent who torments, a parent who hovers, or an uninvolved parent, or are all behaving badly?

- Can bad behavior in children be blamed on bad parenting? Are good behaviors the result of good parenting? What roles do genetic factors play in behaviors?

- Are American schools equal? If not, why not? What is the future for school desegregation?

- Are we raising a generation of prosti-tots who idolize pop culture's bad girls?

- Do our young people have good ideas for reforming their academic and social cultures? Do we listen to them? If not, why not?

Student Web Site

www.mhcls.com/online

Internet References

Further information regarding these Web sites may be found in this book's preface or online.

Childhood Injury Prevention Interventions
http://depts.washington.edu/hiprc/
Families and Work Institute
http://www.familiesandwork.org/index.html
Parentsplace.com: Single Parenting
http://www.parentsplace.com/

Most people accept the proposition that families and cultures have substantial effects on child outcomes. How? New interpretations of behavioral genetic research suggest that genetically predetermined child behaviors may be having substantial effects on how families parent, how children react, and how cultures evolve. Nature and nurture are very interactive. Is it possible that there is a genetic predisposition towards more warlike, aggressive, and violent behaviors in some children? Do some childrearing practices suppress this genetic trait? Do others aggravate it? Are some children predisposed to care for others? The answers are not yet known.

If parents and societies have a significant impact on child outcomes, is there a set of cardinal family values? Does one culture have more correct answers than another culture? Laypersons often assume that children's behaviors and personalities have a direct correlation with the behaviors and personality of the person or persons who provided their socialization during infancy and childhood. Have Americans become paranoid about the extent of terrorist intentions? Do we try to justify our culture's flaws by claims that other cultures are worse? Do we teach our

children this fear? Conversely, do other cultures try to hide their atrocities and war-mongering behaviors behind the screen that Americans are worse, or that they must be stopped first?

Are you a mirror image of the person or persons who raised you? How many of their beliefs, preferences, and virtuous behaviors do you reflect? Did you learn their hatreds and vices as well? Do you model your family, your peers, your culture, all of them, or none of them? If you have a sibling, are you alike because the same person or persons raised you? What accounts for all the differences between people with similar genes, similar parenting, and the same cultural background? These and similar questions are fodder for future research.

During childhood, a person's family values get compared to and tested against the values of schools, community, and culture. Peers, schoolmates, teachers, neighbors, extracurricular activity leaders, religious leaders, and even shopkeepers play increasingly important roles. Culture influences children through holidays, styles of dress, music, television, world events, movies, slang, games played, parents' jobs, transportation, exposure to sex, drugs, and violence, and many other variables. The ecological theorist Urie Bronfenbrenner called these cultural variables exosystem and macrosystem influences. The developing personality of a child has multiple interwoven influences: from genetic potentialities through family values and socialization practices to community and cultural pressures for behaviors.

The first article in this unit, "The Blank Slate," suggests that family forces and cultural factors (e.g., fast foods full of fats and empty calories, Mozart CDs for babies) always interact with genetic potentialities. Parents and society cannot always be credited or blamed for every outcome in a developing child. Advice on how to raise happy, achieving children, and how to keep children healthy, physically fit, and well-nourished, is slavishly adhered to by many parents and caregivers. However, some children will simply not turn out as prescribed by the formulas. Our younglings cannot be molded like lumps of clay. Steven Pinker suggests that social progress proceeds with the inherent natures (both good and bad) of all humans. Blaming and/or crediting amounts to empty vocalizing. Working with our offsprings' genes makes more sense. Can we decipher what that is?

The second article continues to look at contemporary parents, but in a different light. Nancy Gibbs discusses the arena of parent-school interactions. Teachers want parent involvement in education. However, they sometimes get more than they require. Parents may hover like helicopters and volunteer too much. Other parents may torment them with criticisms and accusations. Teachers and parents need mutually supportive, not adversarial, relationships.

The third article cautions that parents are not the only force shaping behavior in children. Many behaviors are inherent in human nature, predetermined by genetic factors. They are found in peoples of every culture, regardless of parenting practices. Parents are important and good parenting is vital to a civilized society. Parents, however, should not be blamed or credited for

every action taken by normally behaving members of the human race in their childhoods.

Unit 4, subsection B (Culture), emphasizes our increasing population diversity. It is imperative that time and effort be spent to avoid life-threatening misunderstandings.

The first article in this subsection deals with the question of school desegregation in the United States. A Supreme Court decision ended segregated schools over 50 years ago. Other court decisions in the 1970's, 80's, and 90's weakened compliance with the 1954 *Brown v. Board of Education* ruling. Many inner-city schools are not only segregated, but also have fewer resources, more crowded conditions, and less teachers than schools in the affluent suburbs. Ellis Cose describes the historical changes in education since the Brown decision.

The second article, "Girls Gone Bad?" decries the influence of female sex symbols of pop culture who are adored by young teenagers. While parents denounce the behavior of these divas, adolescent girls are infatuated. They want to dress, talk, and act like their heroines. The author, Kathleen Deveny, reminds readers that parents also criticized the sex goddesses of the past (e.g., Marilyn Monroe, Liz Taylor, Madonna), and their daughters turned out well. The difference today is the power and pervasiveness of the media which reports on celebrity antics 24/7. This essay, and the next one, are effective together in portraying the paradox of social forces on our youth.

The last cultural commentary, "Disrespecting Childhood," presents evidence that America is not a child-loving nation. Our media overwhelmingly sputters about what is wrong with our juveniles (see "Girls Gone Bad?"). Our childrearing practices and educational policies are directed more at fixing what is wrong than with reinforcing what is right. The authors report on a project called What Kids Can Do, Inc., which respects and listens to the voices of young Americans and celebrates their strengths. It inspires hope for our future.

The Blank Slate

The long-accepted theory that parents can mold their children like clay has distorted choices faced by adults trying to balance their lives, multiplied the anguish of those whose children haven't turned out as hoped, and mangled the science of human behavior.

STEVEN PINKER

If you read the pundits in newspapers and magazines, you may have come across some remarkable claims about the malleability of the human psyche. Here are a few from my collection of clippings:

- Little boys quarrel and fight because they are encouraged to do so.
- Children enjoy sweets because their parents use them as rewards for eating vegetables.
- Teenagers get the idea to compete in looks and fashion from spelling bees and academic prizes.
- Men think the goal of sex is an orgasm because of the way they were socialized.

If you find these assertions dubious, your skepticism is certainly justified. In all cultures, little boys quarrel and fight, children like sweets, teens compete for status, and men pursue orgasms, without the slightest need of encouragement or socialization. In each case, the writers made their preposterous claims without a shred of evidence—without even a nod to the possibility that they were saying something common sense might call into question.

Intellectual life today is beset with a great divide. On one side is a militant denial of human nature, a conviction that the mind of a child is a blank slate that is subsequently inscribed by parents and society. For much of the past century, psychology has tried to explain all thought, feeling, and behavior with a few simple mechanisms of learning by association. Social scientists have tried to explain all customs and social arrangements as a product of the surrounding culture. A long list of concepts that would seem natural to the human way of thinking— emotions, kinship, the sexes—are said to have been "invented" or "socially constructed."

At the same time, there is a growing realization that human nature won't go away. Anyone who has had more than one child, or been in a heterosexual relationship, or noticed that children learn language but house pets don't, has recognized that people are born with certain talents and temperaments. An

acknowledgment that we humans are a species with a timeless and universal psychology pervades the writings of great political thinkers, and without it we cannot explain the recurring themes of literature, religion, and myth. Moreover, the modern sciences of mind, brain, genes, and evolution are showing that there is something to the commonsense idea of human nature. Although no scientist denies that learning and culture are crucial to every aspect of human life, these processes don't happen by magic. There must be complex innate mental faculties that enable human beings to create and learn culture.

Sometimes the contradictory attitudes toward human nature divide people into competing camps. The blank slate camp tends to have greater appeal among those in the social sciences and humanities than it does among biological scientists. And until recently, it was more popular on the political left than it was on the right.

But sometimes both attitudes coexist uneasily inside the mind of a single person. Many academics, for example, publicly deny the existence of intelligence. But privately, academics are *obsessed* with intelligence, discussing it endlessly in admissions, in hiring, and especially in their gossip about one another. And despite their protestations that it is a reactionary concept, they quickly invoke it to oppose executing a murderer with an IQ of 64 or to support laws requiring the removal of lead paint because it may lower a child's IQ by five points. Similarly, those who argue that gender differences are a reversible social construction do not treat them that way in their advice to their daughters, in their dealings with the opposite sex, or in their unguarded gossip, humor, and reflections on their lives.

No good can come from this hypocrisy. The dogma that human nature does not exist, in the face of growing evidence from science and common sense that it does, has led to contempt among many scholars in the humanities for the concepts of evidence and truth. Worse, the doctrine of the blank slate often distorts science itself by making an extreme position— that culture alone determines behavior—seem moderate, and by making the moderate position—that behavior comes from an interaction of biology and culture—seem extreme.

Although how parents treat their children can make a lot of difference in how happy they are, placing a stimulating mobile over a child's crib and playing Mozart CDs will not shape a child's intelligence.

For example, many policies on parenting come from research that finds a correlation between the behavior of parents and of their children. Loving parents have confident children, authoritative parents (neither too permissive nor too punitive) have well-behaved children, parents who talk to their children have children with better language skills, and so on. Thus everyone concludes that parents should be loving, authoritative, and talkative, and if children don't turn out well, it must be the parents' fault.

Those conclusions depend on the belief that children are blank slates. It ignores the fact that parents provide their children with genes, not just an environment. The correlations may be telling us only that the same genes that make adults loving, authoritative, and talkative make their children self-confident, well-behaved, and articulate. Until the studies are redone with adopted children (who get only their environment from their parents), the data are compatible with the possibility that genes make all the difference, that parenting makes all the difference, or anything in between. Yet the extreme position—that parents are everything—is the only one researchers entertain.

The denial of human nature has not just corrupted the world of intellectuals but has harmed ordinary people. The theory that parents can mold their children like clay has inflicted child-rearing regimes on parents that are unnatural and sometimes cruel. It has distorted the choices faced by mothers as they try to balance their lives, and it has multiplied the anguish of parents whose children haven't turned out as hoped. The belief that human tastes are reversible cultural preferences has led social planners to write off people's enjoyment of ornament, natural light, and human scale and forced millions of people to live in drab cement boxes. And the conviction that humanity could be reshaped by massive social engineering projects has led to some of the greatest atrocities in history.

The phrase "blank slate" is a loose translation of the medieval Latin term tabula rasa—scraped tablet. It is often attributed to the 17th-century English philosopher John Locke, who wrote that the mind is "white paper void of all characters." But it became the official doctrine among thinking people only in the first half of the 20th century, as part of a reaction to the widespread belief in the intellectual or moral inferiority of women, Jews, nonwhite races, and non-Western cultures.

Part of the reaction was a moral repulsion from discrimination, lynchings, forced sterilizations, segregation, and the Holocaust. And part of it came from empirical observations.

Waves of immigrants from southern and eastern Europe filled the cities of America and climbed the social ladder. African Americans took advantage of "Negro colleges" and migrated northward, beginning the Harlem Renaissance. The graduates of women's colleges launched the first wave of feminism. To say that women and minority groups were inferior contradicted what people could see with their own eyes.

Academics were swept along by the changing attitudes, but they also helped direct the tide. The prevailing theories of mind were refashioned to make racism and sexism as untenable as possible. The blank slate became sacred scripture. According to the doctrine, any differences we see among races, ethnic groups, sexes, and individuals come not from differences in their innate constitution but from differences in their experiences. Change the experiences—by reforming parenting, education, the media, and social rewards—and you can change the person. Also, if there is no such thing as human nature, society will not be saddled with such nasty traits as aggression, selfishness, and prejudice. In a reformed environment, people can be prevented from learning these habits.

In psychology, behaviorists like John B. Watson and B. F. Skinner simply banned notions of talent and temperament, together with all the other contents of the mind, such as beliefs, desires, and feelings. This set the stage for Watson's famous boast: "Give me a dozen healthy infants, well-formed, and my own specified world to bring them up in, and I'll guarantee to take any one at random and train him to become any type of specialist I might select—doctor, lawyer, artist, merchant-chief, and yes, even beggar-man and thief, regardless of his talents, penchants, tendencies, abilities, vocations, and race of his ancestors."

Watson also wrote an influential child-rearing manual recommending that parents give their children minimum attention and love. If you comfort a crying baby, he wrote, you will reward the baby for crying and thereby increase the frequency of crying behavior.

In anthropology, Franz Boas wrote that differences among human races and ethnic groups come not from their physical constitution but from their *culture*. Though Boas himself did not claim that people were blank slates—he only argued that all ethnic groups are endowed with the same mental abilities—his students, who came to dominate American social science, went further. They insisted not just that *differences* among ethnic groups must be explained in terms of culture (which is reasonable), but that *every aspect* of human existence must be explained in terms of culture (which is not). "Heredity cannot be allowed to have acted any part in history," wrote Alfred Kroeber. "With the exception of the instinctoid reactions in infants to sudden withdrawals of support and to sudden loud noises, the human being is entirely instinctless," wrote Ashley Montagu.

In the second half of the 20th century, the ideals of the social scientists of the first half enjoyed a well-deserved victory. Eugenics, social Darwinism, overt expressions of racism and sexism, and official discrimination against women and minorities were on the wane, or had been eliminated, from the political and intellectual mainstream in Western democracies.

At the same time, the doctrine of the blank slate, which had been blurred with ideals of equality and progress, began to show cracks. As new disciplines such as cognitive science, neuroscience, evolutionary psychology, and behavioral genetics flourished, it became clearer that thinking is a biological process, that the brain is not exempt from the laws of evolution, that the sexes differ above the neck as well as below it, and that people are not psychological clones. Here are some examples of the discoveries.

Hundreds of traits, from romantic love to humorous insults, can be found in every society ever documented.

Natural selection tends to homogenize a species into a standard design by concentrating the effective genes and winnowing out the ineffective ones. This suggests that the human mind evolved with a universal complex design. Beginning in the 1950s, linguist Noam Chomsky of the Massachusetts Institute of Technology argued that a language should be analyzed not in terms of the list of sentences people utter but in terms of the mental computations that enable them to handle an unlimited number of new sentences in the language. These computations have been found to conform to a universal grammar. And if this universal grammar is embodied in the circuitry that guides babies when they listen to speech, it could explain how children learn language so easily.

Similarly, some anthropologists have returned to an ethnographic record that used to trumpet differences among cultures and have found an astonishingly detailed set of aptitudes and tastes that all cultures have in common. This shared way of thinking, feeling, and living makes all of humanity look like a single tribe, which the anthropologist Donald Brown of the University of California at Santa Barbara has called the universal people. Hundreds of traits, from romantic love to humorous insults, from poetry to food taboos, from exchange of goods to mourning the dead, can be found in every society ever documented.

One example of a stubborn universal is the tangle of emotions surrounding the act of love. In all societies, sex is at least somewhat "dirty." It is conducted in private, pondered obsessively, regulated by custom and taboo, the subject of gossip and teasing, and a trigger for jealous rage. Yet sex is the most concentrated source of physical pleasure granted by the nervous system. Why is it so fraught with conflict? For a brief period in the 1960s and 1970s, people dreamed of an erotopia in which men and women could engage in sex without hang-ups and inhibitions. "If you can't be with the one you love, love the one you're with," sang Stephen Stills. "If you love somebody, set them free," sang Sting.

But Sting also sang, "Every move you make, I'll be watching you." Even in a time when, seemingly, anything goes, most people do not partake in sex as casually as they partake in food or conversation. The reasons are as deep as anything in biology. One of the hazards of sex is a baby, and a baby is not just any seven-pound object but, from an evolutionary point of view, our reason for being. Every time a woman has sex with a man, she is taking a chance at sentencing herself to years of motherhood, and she is forgoing the opportunity to use her finite reproductive output with some other man. The man, for his part, may be either implicitly committing his sweat and toil to the incipient child or deceiving his partner about such intentions.

On rational grounds, the volatility of sex is a puzzle, because in an era with reliable contraception, these archaic entanglements should have no claim on our feelings. We should be loving the one we're with, and sex should inspire no more gossip, music, fiction, raunchy humor, or strong emotions than eating or talking does. The fact that people are tormented by the Darwinian economics of babies they are no longer having is testimony to the long reach of human nature.

Although the minds of normal human beings work in pretty much the same way, they are not, of course, identical. Natural selection reduces genetic variability but never eliminates it. As a result, nearly every one of us is genetically unique. And these differences in genes make a difference in mind and behavior, at least quantitatively. The most dramatic demonstrations come from studies of the rare people who *are* genetically identical, identical twins.

Identical twins think and feel in such similar ways that they sometimes suspect they are linked by telepathy. They are similar in verbal and mathematical intelligence, in their degree of life satisfaction, and in personality traits such as introversion, agreeableness, neuroticism, conscientiousness, and openness to experience. They have similar attitudes toward controversial issues such as the death penalty, religion, and modern music. They resemble each other not just in paper-and-pencil tests but in consequential behavior such as gambling, divorcing, committing crimes, getting into accidents, and watching television. And they boast dozens of shared idiosyncrasies such as giggling incessantly, giving interminable answers to simple questions, dipping buttered toast in coffee, and, in the case of Abigail van Buren and the late Ann Landers, writing indistinguishable syndicated advice columns. The crags and valleys of their electroencephalograms (brain waves) are as alike as those of a single person recorded on two occasions, and the wrinkles of their brains and the distribution of gray matter across cortical areas are similar as well.

Identical twins (who share all their genes) are far more similar than fraternal twins (who share just half their genes). This is as true when the twins are separated at birth and raised apart as when they are raised in the same home by the same parents. Moreover, biological siblings, who also share half their genes, are far more similar than adoptive siblings, who share no more genes than strangers. Indeed, adoptive siblings are barely similar at all. These conclusions come from massive studies employing the best instruments known to psychology. Alternative explanations that try to push the effects of the genes to zero have by now been tested and rejected.

People sometimes fear that if the genes affect the mind at all they must determine it in every detail. That is wrong, for two reasons. The first is that most effects of genes are probabilistic. If one identical twin has a trait, there is often no more than an even chance that the other twin will have it, despite having a complete genome in common (and in the case of twins raised together, most of their environment in common as well).

The second reason is that the genes' effects can vary with the environment. Although Woody Allen's fame may depend on genes that enhance a sense of humor, he once pointed out that "we live in a society that puts a big value on jokes. If I had been an Apache Indian, those guys didn't need comedians, so I'd be out of work."

Studies of the brain also show that the mind is not a blank slate. The brain, of course, has a pervasive ability to change the strengths of its connections as the result of learning and experience—if it didn't, we would all be permanent amnesiacs. But that does not mean that the structure of the brain is mostly a product of experience. The study of the brains of twins has shown that much of the variation in the amount of gray matter in the prefrontal lobes is genetically caused. And these variations are not just random differences in anatomy like fingerprints; they correlate significantly with differences in intelligence.

People born with variations in the typical brain plan can vary in the way their minds work. A study of Einstein's brain showed that he had large, unusually shaped inferior parietal lobules, which participate in spatial reasoning and intuitions about numbers. Gay men are likely to have a relatively small nucleus in the anterior hypothalamus, a nucleus known to have a role in sex differences. Convicted murderers and other violent, antisocial people are likely to have a relatively small and inactive prefrontal cortex, the part of the brain that governs decision making and inhibits impulses. These gross features of the brain are almost certainly not sculpted by information coming in from the senses. That, in turn, implies that differences in intelligence, scientific genius, sexual orientation, and impulsive violence are not entirely learned.

The doctrine of the blank slate had been thought to undergird the ideals of equal rights and social improvement, so it is no surprise that the discoveries undermining it have often been met with fear and loathing. Scientists challenging the doctrine have been libeled, picketed, shouted down, and subjected to searing invective.

This is not the first time in history that people have tried to ground moral principles in dubious factual assumptions. People used to ground moral values in the doctrine that Earth lay at the center of the universe, and that God created mankind in his own image in a day. In both cases, informed people eventually reconciled their moral values with the facts, not just because they had to give a nod to reality, but also because the supposed connections between the facts and morals—such as the belief that the arrangement of rock and gas in space has something to do with right and wrong—were spurious to begin with.

We are now living, I think, through a similar transition. The blank slate has been widely embraced as a rationale for

morality, but it is under assault from science. Yet just as the supposed foundations of morality shifted in the centuries following Galileo and Darwin, our own moral sensibilities will come to terms with the scientific findings, not just because facts are facts but because the moral credentials of the blank slate are just as spurious. Once you think through the issues, the two greatest fears of an innate human endowment can be defused.

One is the fear of inequality. Blank is blank, so if we are all blank slates, the reasoning goes, we must all be equal. But if the slate of a newborn is not blank, different babies could have different things inscribed on their slates. Individuals, sexes, classes, and races might differ innately in their talents and inclinations. The fear is that if people do turn out to be different, it would open the door to discrimination, oppression, or eugenics.

But none of this follows. For one thing, in many cases the empirical basis of the fear may be misplaced. A universal human nature does not imply that *differences* among groups are innate. Confucius could have been right when he wrote, "Men's natures are alike; it is their habits that carry them far apart."

Regardless of IQ or physical strength, all human beings can be assumed to have certain traits in common.

More important, the case against bigotry is not a factual claim that people are biologically indistinguishable. It is a moral stance that condemns judging an *individual* according to the average traits of certain *groups* to which the individual belongs. Enlightened societies strive to ignore race, sex, and ethnicity in hiring, admissions, and criminal justice because the alternative is morally repugnant. Discriminating against people on the basis of race, sex, or ethnicity would be unfair, penalizing them for traits over which they have no control. It would perpetuate the injustices of the past and could rend society into hostile factions. None of these reasons depends on whether groups of people are or are not genetically indistinguishable.

Far from being conducive to discrimination, a conception of human nature is the reason we oppose it. Regardless of IQ or physical strength or any other trait that might vary among people, all human beings can be assumed to have certain traits in common. No one likes being enslaved. No one likes being humiliated. No one likes being treated unfairly. The revulsion we feel toward discrimination and slavery comes from a conviction that however much people vary on some traits, they do not vary on these.

Parents often discover that their children are immune to their rewards, punishments, and nagging. Over the long run, a child's personality and intellect are largely determined by genes, peer groups, and chance.

A second fear of human nature comes from a reluctance to give up the age-old dream of the perfectibility of man. If we are forever saddled with fatal flaws and deadly sins, according to this fear, social reform would be a waste of time. Why try to make the world a better place if people are rotten to the core and will just foul it up no matter what you do?

But this, too, does not follow. If the mind is a complex system with many faculties, an antisocial desire is just one component among others. Some faculties may endow us with greed or lust or malice, but others may endow us with sympathy, foresight, self-respect, a desire for respect from others, and an ability to learn from experience and history. Social progress can come from pitting some of these faculties against others.

For example, suppose we are endowed with a conscience that treats certain other beings as targets of sympathy and inhibits us from harming or exploiting them. The philosopher Peter Singer of Princeton University has shown that moral improvement has proceeded for millennia because people have expanded the mental dotted line that embraces the entities considered worthy of sympathy. The circle has been poked outward from the family and village to the clan, the tribe, the nation, the race, and most recently to all of humanity. This sweeping change in sensibilities did not require a blank slate. It could have arisen from a moral gadget with a single knob or slider that adjusts the size of the circle embracing the entities whose interests we treat as comparable to our own.

Some people worry that these arguments are too fancy for the dangerous world we live in. Since data in the social sciences are never perfect, shouldn't we err on the side of caution and stick with the null hypothesis that people are blank slates? Some people think that even if we were certain that people differed genetically, or harbored ignoble tendencies, we might still want to promulgate the fiction that they didn't.

This argument is based on the fallacy that the blank slate has nothing but good moral implications and a theory that admits a human nature has nothing but bad ones. In fact, the dangers go both ways. Take the most horrifying example of all, the abuse of biology by the Nazis, with its pseudoscientific nonsense about superior and inferior races. Historians agree that bitter memories of the Holocaust were the main reason that human nature became taboo in intellectual life after the Second World War.

But historians have also documented that Nazism was not the only ideologically inspired holocaust of the 20th century. Many atrocities were committed by Marxist regimes in the name of egalitarianism, targeting people whose success was taken as evidence of their avarice. The kulaks ("bourgeois peasants") were exterminated by Lenin and Stalin in the Soviet Union. Teachers, former landlords, and "rich peasants" were humiliated, tortured, and murdered during China's Cultural Revolution. City dwellers and literate professionals were worked to death or executed during the reign of the Khmer Rouge in Cambodia.

And here is a remarkable fact: Although both Nazi and Marxist ideologies led to industrial-scale killing, *their biological and psychological theories were opposites.* Marxists had no use for the concept of race, were averse to the notion of genetic inheritance, and were hostile to the very idea of a human nature rooted in biology. Marx did not explicitly embrace the blank slate, but he was adamant that human nature has no enduring properties: "All history is nothing but a continuous transformation of human nature," he wrote. Many of his followers did embrace it. "It is on a blank page that the most beautiful poems are written," said Mao. "Only the newborn baby is spotless," ran a Khmer Rouge slogan. This philosophy led to persecution of the successful and of those who produced more crops on their private family plots than on communal farms. And it made these regimes not just dictatorships but totalitarian dictatorships, which tried to control every aspect of life, from art and education to child rearing and sex. After all, if the mind is structureless at birth and shaped by its experience, a society that wants the right kind of minds must control the experience.

None of this is meant to impugn the blank slate as an evil doctrine, any more than a belief in human nature is an evil doctrine. Both are separated by many steps from the evil acts committed under their banners, and they must be evaluated on factual grounds. But the fact that tyranny and genocide can come from an anti-innatist belief system as readily as from an innatist one does upend the common misconception that biological approaches to behavior are uniquely sinister. And the reminder that human nature is the source of our interests and needs as well as our flaws encourages us to examine claims about the mind objectively, without putting a moral thumb on either side of the scale.

From the book *The Blank Slate* by Steven Pinker. Copyright © Steven Pinker, 2002. Printed by arrangement with Viking Penguin, a member of Penguin Putman Inc. Published in September 2002.

From *Discover*, October 2002, pp. 34–40. Copyright © 2002 by Steven Pinker. Reprinted by permission of the author.

Parents Behaving Badly

Inside the new classroom power struggle: what teachers say about pushy moms and dads who drive them crazy.

Nancy Gibbs

If you could walk past the teachers' lounge and listen in, what sorts of stories would you hear?

An Iowa high school counselor gets a call from a parent protesting the C her child received on an assignment. "The parent argued every point in the essay," recalls the counselor, who soon realized why the mother was so upset about the grade. "It became apparent that she'd written it."

A sixth-grade teacher in California tells a girl in her class that she needs to work on her reading at home, not just in school. "Her mom came in the next day," the teacher says, "and started yelling at me that I had emotionally upset her child."

A science teacher in Baltimore, Md., was offering lessons in anatomy when one of the boys in class declared, "There's one less rib in a man than in a woman." The teacher pulled out two skeletons—one male, the other female—and asked the student to count the ribs in each. "The next day," the teacher recalls, "the boy claimed he told his priest what happened and his priest said I was a heretic."

A teacher at a Tennessee elementary school slips on her kid gloves each morning as she contends with parents who insist, in writing, that their children are never to be reprimanded or even corrected. When she started teaching 31 years ago, she says, "I could make objective observations about my kids without parents getting offended. But now we handle parents a lot more delicately. We handle children a lot more delicately. They feel good about themselves for no reason. We've given them this cotton-candy sense of self with no basis in reality. We don't emphasize what's best for the greater good of society or even the classroom."

When our children are born, we study their every eyelash and marvel at the perfection of their toes, and in no time become experts in all that they do. But then the day comes when we are expected to hand them over to a stranger standing at the head of a room full of bright colors and small chairs. Well aware of the difference a great teacher can make—and the damage a bad teacher can do—parents turn over their kids and hope. Please handle with care. Please don't let my children get lost. They're breakable. And precious. Oh, but push them hard and don't let up, and make sure they get into Harvard.

But if parents are searching for the perfect teacher, teachers are looking for the ideal parent, a partner but not a pest, engaged but not obsessed, with a sense of perspective and patience. And somehow just at the moment when the experts all say the parent-teacher alliance is more important than ever, it is also becoming harder to manage. At a time when competition is rising and resources are strained, when battles over testing and accountability force schools to adjust their priorities, when cell phones and e-mail speed up the information flow and all kinds of private ghosts and public quarrels creep into the parent-teacher conference, it's harder for both sides to step back and breathe deeply and look at the goals they share.

> **"The parent doesn't know what you're giving and accepts what the child says. Parents are trusting children before they trust us. They have lost faith in teachers."**

Ask teachers about the best part of their job, and most will say how much they love working with kids. Ask them about the most demanding part, and they will say dealing with parents. In fact, a new study finds that of all the challenges they face, new teachers rank handling parents at the top. According to preliminary results from the MetLife Survey of the American Teacher, made available exclusively to TIME, parent management was a bigger struggle than finding enough funding or maintaining discipline or enduring the toils of testing. It's one reason, say the Consortium for Policy Research in Education and the Center for the Study of Teaching and Policy, that 40% to 50% of new teachers leave the profession within five years. Even master teachers who love their work, says Harvard education professor Sara Lawrence-Lightfoot, call this "the most treacherous part of their jobs."

"Everyone says the parent-teacher conference should be pleasant, civilized, a kind of dialogue where parents and teachers build alliances," Lawrence-Lightfoot observes. "But what most teachers feel, and certainly what all parents feel, is anxiety, panic and vulnerability." While teachers worry most about the parents they never see, the ones who show up faithfully pose a whole different set of challenges. Leaving aside the monster parents who seem to have been born to torment the teacher, even "good" parents can have bad days when their virtues exceed their boundaries: the eager parent who pushes too hard, the protective parent who defends the cheater, the homework helper who takes over, the tireless advocate who loses sight of the fact that there are other kids in the class too. "I could summarize in one sentence what teachers hate about parents," says the head of a private school. "We hate it when parents undermine the education and growth of their children. That's it, plain and simple." A taxonomy of parents behaving badly:

"You get so angry that you don't care what the school's perspective is. This is my child. And you did something that negatively impacted my child. I don't want to hear that you have 300 kids."

The Hovering Parent

It was a beautiful late morning last May when Richard Hawley, headmaster at University School in Cleveland, Ohio, saw the flock of mothers entering the building, eager and beaming. "I ask what brings them to our halls," he recalls. "They tell me that this is the last day the seniors will be eating lunch together at school and they have come to watch. To watch their boys eat lunch? I ask. Yes, they tell me emphatically. At that moment, a group of lounging seniors spot their mothers coming their way. One of them approaches his mother, his hands forming an approximation of a crucifix. 'No,' he says firmly to his mother. 'You can't do this. You've got to go home.' As his mother draws near, he hisses in embarrassment, 'Mother, you have no life!' His mother's smile broadens. 'You are my life, dear.'"

Parents are passionate, protective creatures when it comes to their children, as nature designed them to be. Teachers strive to be dispassionate, objective professionals, as their training requires them to be. Throw in all the suspicions born of class and race and personal experience, a culture that praises teachers freely but pays them poorly, a generation taught to question authority and a political climate that argues for holding schools ever more accountable for how kids perform, and it is a miracle that parents and teachers get along as well as they do. "There's more parent involvement that's good—and bad," notes Kirk Daddow, a 38-year veteran who teaches Advanced Placement history in Ames, Iowa. "The good kind is the 'Make yourself known to the teacher; ask what you could do.' The bad kind is the 'Wait until something happens, then complain about it and try to get a grade changed.'" Overall, he figures, "we're seeing more of the bad."

Long gone are the days when the school was a fortress, opened a couple of times a year for parents' night and graduation but generally off limits to parents unless their kids got into trouble. Now you can't walk into schools, public or private, without tripping over parents in the halls. They volunteer as library aides and reading coaches and Mentor Moms, supplement the physical-education offerings with yoga and kickboxing, sponsor faculty-appreciation lunches and fund-raising barbecues, supervise field trips and road games and father-daughter service projects. Even the heads of boarding schools report that some parents are moving to live closer to their child's school so that they can be on hand and go to all the games. As budgets shrink and educational demands grow, that extra army of helpers can be a godsend to strapped schools.

In a survey, 90% of new teachers agreed that involving parents in their children's education is a priority at their school, but only 25% described their experience working with parents as "very satisfying." When asked to choose the biggest challenge they face, 31% of them cited involving parents and communicating with them as their top choice. 73% of new teachers said too many parents treat schools and teachers as adversaries.

But parents, it turns out, have a learning curve of their own. Parents who are a welcome presence in elementary school as library helpers need to learn a different role for junior high and another for high school as their children's needs evolve. Teachers talk about "helicopter parents," who hover over the school at all times, waiting to drop in at the least sign of trouble. Given these unsettled times, if parents feel less in control of their own lives, they try to control what they can, which means everything from swooping down at the first bad grade to demanding a good 12 inches of squishy rubber under the jungle gym so that anyone who falls will bounce right back. "The parents are not the bad guys," says Nancy McGill, a teacher in Johnston, Iowa, who learned a lot about handling parents from being one herself. "They're mama grizzly bears. They're going to defend that cub no matter what, and they don't always think rationally. If I can remember that, it defuses the situation. It's not about me. It's not about attacking our system. It's about a parent trying to do the best for their child. That helps keep the personal junk out of the way. I don't get so emotional."

While it's in the nature of parents to want to smooth out the bumps in the road, it's in the nature of teachers to toss in a few more: sometimes kids have to fail in order to learn. As children get older, the parents may need to pull back. "I believe that the umbilical cord needs to be severed when children are at school," argues Eric Paul, a fourth- and fifth-grade teacher at Roosevelt Elementary School in Santa Monica, Calif. He goes to weekend ball games and piano recitals in an effort to bond with families but also tries to show parents that there is a line that shouldn't be crossed. "Kids need to operate on their own at school, advocate on their own and learn from each other. So in my class, parents' involvement is limited," he says.

High schools, meanwhile, find themselves fending off parents who expect instant responses to every e-mail; who request a change of teacher because of "poor chemistry" when the real issue is that the child is getting a poor grade; who seek out a doctor who will proclaim their child "exceptionally bright but with a learning difference" that requires extra time for testing; who insist that their child take five Advanced Placement classes, play three varsity sports, perform in the school orchestra and be in student government—and then complain that kids are stressed out because the school doesn't do enough to prevent scheduling conflicts. Teachers just shake their heads as they see parents so obsessed with getting their child into a good college that they don't ask whether it's the right one for the child's particular interests and needs.

> "They'll misbehave in front of you. You see very little of that 'I don't want to get in trouble' attitude because they know Mom or Dad will come to their defense."

And what if kids grow so accustomed to these interventions that they miss out on lessons in self-reliance? Mara Sapon-Shevin, an education professor at Syracuse University, has had college students tell her they were late for class because their mothers didn't call to wake them up that morning. She has had students call their parents from the classroom on a cell phone to complain about a low grade and then pass the phone over to her, in the middle of class, because the parent wanted to intervene. And she has had parents say they are paying a lot of money for their child's education and imply that anything but an A is an unacceptable return on their investment.

These parents are not serving their children well, Sapon-Shevin argues. "You want them to learn lessons that are powerful but benign. Your kid gets drunk, they throw up, feel like crap—that's a good lesson. They don't study for an exam, fail it and learn that next time they should study. Or not return the library book and have to pay the fine. But when you have a kid leave their bike out, it gets run over and rusty, and you say, 'O.K., honey, we'll buy you a new one,' they never learn to put their bike away."

The Aggressive Advocate

Marguerite Damata, a mother of two in Silver Spring, Md., wonders whether she is too involved in her 10-year-old son's school life. "Because he's not in the gifted and talented group, he's almost nowhere," she says. "If I stopped paying attention, where would he be?" Every week she spends two hours sitting in his math class, making sure she knows the assignments and the right vocabulary so that she can help him at home. And despite all she sees and all she does, she says, "I feel powerless there."

Parents understandably argue that there is a good reason to keep a close watch if their child is one of 500 kids in a grade

level. Teachers freely admit it's impossible to create individual teaching programs for 30 children in a class. "There aren't enough minutes in the day," says Tom Loveless, who taught in California for nine years and is now director of the Brown Center on Education Policy at the Brookings Institution. "You have to have kids tackling subject matter together as a group. That's a shoe that will pinch for someone." Since the passage of the No Child Left Behind Act, which requires schools to show progress in reading and math test scores in Grades 3 through 8 across all racial and demographic groups, parents are worried that teachers will naturally focus on getting as many students as possible over the base line and not have as much time to spur the strongest kids or save the weakest. Some educators argue that you can agree on the goals of accountability and achievement, but given the inequalities in the system, not all schools have the means to achieve them. "A really cynical person who didn't want to spend any more money on an educational system might get parents and teachers to blame each other and deflect attention away from other imperfect parts of the system," observes Jeannie Oakes, director of the Institute for Democracy, Education and Access at UCLA.

> "With the oldest, I think I micromanaged things. I had to come to a point where I said, These are his projects. They're not my projects. I'm not helping him."

Families feel they have to work the system. Attentive parents study the faculty like stock tables, looking for the best performer and then lobbying to get their kids into that teacher's class. "You have a lot of mothers who have been in the work force, supervising other people, who have a different sense of empowerment and professionalism about them," notes Amy Stuart Wells, professor of sociology and education at Columbia University's Teachers College. "When they drop out of the work force to raise their kids, they see being part of the school as part of their job." Monica Stutzman, a mother of two in Johnston, Iowa, believes her efforts helped ensure that her daughter wound up with the best teacher in each grade. "We know what's going on. We e-mail, volunteer on a weekly basis. I ask a lot of questions," she says. "I'm not there to push my children into things they're not ready for. The teachers are the experts. We've had such great experiences with the teacher because we create that experience, because we're involved. We don't just get something home and say, 'What's this?'"

> "Most teachers will do what they need to, but there are teachers who are uncomfortable, who turn their backs or close their eyes or ears because they do not want what they perceive might be a confrontation."

Parents seeking to stay on top of what's happening in class don't have to wait for the report card to arrive. "Now it's so easy for the parents through the Internet to get ahold of us, and they expect an immediate response," notes Michael Schaffer, a classroom veteran who teaches AP courses at Central Academy in Des Moines, Iowa. "This e-mail—'How's my kid doing?'—could fill my day. That's hyperbole. But it's a two-edged sword here, and unfortunately it's cutting to the other side, and parents are making demands on us that are unreasonable. Yeah, they're concerned about their kids. But I'm concerned about 150 kids. I don't have time during the day to let the parent know when the kid got the first B." As more districts make assignments and test scores available online, it may cut down on the "How's he doing" e-mails but increase the "Why did she get a B?" queries.

Beneath the ferocious jostling there is the brutal fact that outside of Lake Wobegon, not all children are above average. Teachers must choose their words carefully. They can't just say, "I'm sorry your child's not as smart as X," and no parent wants to hear that there are five other kids in the class who are a lot smarter than his or hers. Younger teachers especially can be overwhelmed by parents who announce on the first day of school that their child is going to be the smartest in the class and on the second day that he is already bored. Veteran teachers have learned to come back with data in hand to show parents who boast that their child scored in the 99th percentile on some aptitude test that 40 other students in the class did just as well.

It would be nice if parents and teachers could work together to improve the system for everyone, but human nature can get in the way. Both sides know that resources are limited, and all kinds of factors play into how they are allocated—including whose elbows are sharpest. Many schools, fearful of "bright flight," the mass departure of high-achieving kids, feel they have no choice but to appease the most outspoken parents. "I understand, having been a parent, the attitude that 'I don't have time to fix the whole system; I don't have time and energy to get rid of systemic injustice, racism, poverty and violence; I have to get what's right for my kid,'" says Syracuse's Sapon-Shevin. "But then the schools do educational triage. They basically attend to the most vocal, powerful people with more resources. They say, 'Don't get angry. We'll take care of this issue.' And they mean, 'We'll take care of it for your child. We'll get your kid out of the class with the bad teacher and leave the other kids in there.'"

At the deepest level, teachers fear that all this parental anxiety is not always aimed at the stuff that matters. Parents who instantly call about a grade or score seldom ask about what is being taught or how. When a teacher has spent the whole summer brightening and deepening the history curriculum for her ninth-graders, finding new ways to surprise and engage them, it is frustrating to encounter parents whose only focus is on test scores. "If these parents were pushing for richer, more meaningful instruction, you could almost forgive them their obnoxiousness and inattention to the interests of all the other children," says Alfie Kohn, a Boston-based education commentator and author of *Unconditional Parenting*. But "we have pushy parents pushing for the wrong thing." He argues that test scores often measure what matters least—and that even high test scores

should invite parents to wonder what was cut from the curriculum to make room for more test prep.

"It's a challenge to be a good parent of a high school student. You want to help our kids without putting too much pressure on."

Kohn knows a college counselor hired by parents to help "package" their child, who had perfect board scores and a wonderful grade-point average. When it was time to work on the college essay, the counselor said, "Let's start with a book you read outside of school that really made a difference in your life." There was a moment of silence. Then the child responded, "Why would I read a book if I didn't have to?" If parents focus only on the transcript—drive out of children their natural curiosity, discourage their trying anything at which they might fail—their definition of success will get a failing grade from any teacher watching.

The Public Defenders

By the time children turn 18, they have spent only 13% of their waking lives in the classroom. Their habits of mind, motivation and muscles have much more to do with that other 87%. But try telling that to an Ivy-educated mom and dad whose kids aren't doing well. It can't be the genes, Mom and Dad conclude, so it must be the school. "It's the bright children who aren't motivated who are most frustrating for parents and teachers," says Nancy McGill, a past president of the Iowa Talented and Gifted Association. "Parents don't know how to fix the kid, to get the kid going. They want us to do it, and discover we can't either." Sometimes bright kids intentionally work just hard enough to get a B because they are trying to make a point about what should be demanded of them, observes Jennifer Loh, a math teacher at Ursuline Academy in Dallas. "It's their way of saying to Mom and Dad, 'I'm not perfect.'" Though the best teachers work hard to inspire even the most alienated kids, they can't carry the full burden of the parents' expectations. In his dreams, admits Daddow, the Iowa history teacher, what he would like to say is "Your son or daughter is very, very lazy." Instead, he shows the parents the student's work and says, "I'm not sure I'm getting Jim's best effort."

When a teacher asks parents to be partners, he or she doesn't necessarily mean Mom or Dad should be camping in the classroom. Research shows that though students benefit modestly from having parents involved at school, what happens at home matters much more. According to research based on the National Education Longitudinal Study, a sample of nearly 25,000 eighth-graders, among four main areas of parental involvement (home discussion, home supervision, school communication and school participation), home discussion was the most strongly related to academic achievement.

Any partnership requires that both sides do their part. Teachers say that here again, parents can have double standards: Push hard, but not too hard; maintain discipline, but don't punish my child. When teachers tell a parent that a child needs to be reprimanded at home, teachers say they often get the response, "I don't reprimand, and don't tell me how to raise my child." Older teachers say they are seeing in children as young as 6 and 7 a level of disdain for adults that was once the reserve of adolescents. Some talk about the "dry-cleaner parents" who drop their rambunctious kids off in the morning and expect them to be returned at the end of the day all clean and proper and practically sealed in plastic.

At the most disturbing extreme are the parents who like to talk about values but routinely undermine them. "You get savvier children who know how to get out of things," says a second-grade teacher in Murfreesboro, Tenn. "Their parents actually teach them to lie to dodge their responsibilities." Didn't get your homework done? That's O.K. Mom will take the fall. Late for class? Blame it on Dad. Parents have sued schools that expelled kids for cheating, on the grounds that teachers had left the exams out on a desk and made them too easy to steal. "Cheating is rampant," says Steve Taylor, a history teacher at Beverly Hills High School in California. "If you're not cheating, then you're not trying. A C means you're a loser." Every principal can tell a story about some ambitious student, Ivy bound, who cheats on an exam. Teacher flunks her. Parents protest: She made a mistake, and you're going to ruin her life. Teachers try to explain that good kids can make bad decisions; the challenge is to make sure the kids learn from them. "I think some parents confuse advocating on behalf of their student with defending everything that the student does," says Scott Peoples, a history teacher at Skyview High School outside Denver.

> **"I called the parents on a discipline issue with their daughter. Her father called me a total jerk. Then he said, 'Well, do you want to meet someplace and take care of this man to man?'"**

Student-teacher disputes can quickly escalate into legal challenges or the threat of them. The fear of litigation that has given rise to the practice of defensive medicine prompts educators to practice defensive teaching. According to Forrest T. Jones Inc., a large insurer of teachers, the number of teachers buying liability insurance has jumped 25% in the past five years. "A lot of teachers are very fearful and don't want to deal with it," says Roxsana Jaber-Ansari, who teaches sixth grade at Hale Middle School in Woodland Hills, Calif. She has learned that everything must be documented. She does not dare accuse a student of cheating, for instance, without evidence, including eyewitness accounts or a paper trail. When a teacher meets with a student alone, the door always has to be open to avoid any suspicion of inappropriate behavior on the teacher's part. "If you become angry and let it get to you, you will quit your job," says Jaber-Ansari. "You will hate what you do and hate the kids."

Teacher's Pests
Some parents ask too much of the school or too little of their kids

Helicopter Parents
In order to grow, kids need room to fail; the always hovering parent gets in the way of self-reliance

Monster Parents
The lurking moms and dads always looking for reasons to disagree are a teacher's worst nightmare

Dry-cleaner Parents
They drop their rambunctious kids off and want them all cleaned up and proper by the end of the day

---

The Culture Warriors

Teachers in schools with economically and ethnically diverse populations face a different set of challenges in working with parents. In less affluent districts, many parents don't have computers at home, so schools go to some lengths to make contact easier. Even 20 minutes twice a year for a conference can be hard for families if parents are working long hours at multiple jobs or have to take three buses to get to the school. Some teachers visit a parent's workplace on a Saturday or help arrange language classes for parents to help with communication. Particularly since a great goal of education is to level the playing field, teachers are worried that the families that need the most support are least able to ask for it. "The standards about what makes a good parent are always changing," notes Annette Lareau, a professor of sociology at Temple University, who views all the demand for parent involvement as a relatively recent phenomenon. "And it's middle-class parents who keep pace."

Lareau also sees cultural barriers getting in the way of the strong parent-teacher alliance. When parents don't get involved at school, teachers may see it as a sign of indifference, of not valuing education—when it may signal the reverse. Some cultures believe strongly that school and home should be separate spheres; parents would no more interfere with the way a teacher teaches than with the way a surgeon operates. "Working-class and poor families don't have a college education," says Lareau. "They are looking up to teachers; they respect teachers as professionals. Middle-class parents are far less respectful. They're not a teacher, but they could have been a teacher, and often their profession has a higher status than teachers'. So they are much more likely to criticize teachers on professional grounds."

And while she views social class as a major factor in shaping the dynamic, Lareau finds that race continues to play a role. Middle-class black parents, especially those who attended segregated schools, often approach the teacher with caution. Roughly 90% of teachers are white and middle class, and, says Lareau, many black parents are "worried that teachers will have lowered expectations of black children, that black boys will be punished more than white boys. Since teachers want parents to be positive and supportive, when African-American parents express concerns about racial insensitivity, it can create problems in their relationship."

Finally, as church-state arguments boil over and principals agonize over what kids can sing at the Winter Concert, teachers need to be eternally sensitive to religious issues as well. This is an arena where parents are often as concerned about content as grades, as in the debate over creationism vs. evolution vs. intelligent design, for instance. Teachers say they have to become legal scholars to protect themselves in a climate where students have "rights." Jaber-Ansari was challenged for hanging Bible quotes on her classroom walls. But she had studied her legal standing, and when she was confronted, "the principal supported me 100%," she says.

Perhaps the most complicated part of the conversation—beyond all the issues of race and class and culture, the growing pressures to succeed and arguments over how success should be defined—is the problem of memory. When they meet in that conference, parent and teacher bring their own school experiences with them—what went right and wrong, what they missed. They are determined for it to be different for the child they both care about. They go into that first-grade room and sit in the small chairs and can easily be small again themselves. It is so tempting to use the child's prospects to address their own regrets. So teachers learn to choose their words with care and hope that they can build a partnership with parents that works to everyone's advantage and comes at no one's expense. And parents over time may realize that when it comes to their children, they still have much to learn. "I think that we love our children so much that they make us a little loony at times," says Arch Montgomery, head of the Asheville School in North Carolina. He winces at parents who treat their child as a cocktail-party trophy or a vanity sticker for the window of their SUV, but he also understands their behavior. "I think most parents desperately want to do what is right for their kids. This does not bring out the better angels of our natures, but it is understandable, and it is forgivable."

With reporting by Amanda Bower, New York, Melissa August, Washington, Anne Berryman, Athens, Cathy Booth Thomas, Dallas, Rita Healy, Denver, Elizabeth Kauffman, Nashville, Jeanne McDowell, Los Angeles and Betsy Rubiner, Des Moines

Where Personality Goes Awry

A multifaceted research approach is providing more clues to the origins of personality disorders.

CHARLOTTE HUFF

Over the years, few large-scale prospective studies have targeted the causes of personality disorders (PDs). But recently, a new body of research has begun to explore the potential influences of several factors, from genetics and parenting to peer influences, and even the randomness of life events.

Indeed, says Patricia Hoffman Judd, PhD, clinical professor of psychiatry at the University of California, San Diego, research into the origins of PDs is just beginning to take off. "I think for years people thought, 'It's just personality—you can't do anything about it,'" she explains. "There's also been moralism [that people with such disorders] are evil, that they are lazy," adds Judd, author of "A Developmental Model of Borderline Personality Disorder" (American Psychiatric Publishing, 2003).

But research is helping to turn such misconceptions around. Genetics researchers, for example, are closer to identifying some of the biological underpinnings that may influence PDs. Last year, for example, a team located—and described in *Molecular Psychiatry* (Vol, 8. No. 11)—a malfunctioning gene they believe may be a factor in obsessive-compulsive disorder. Other researchers are investigating genetic links to aggression, anxiety and fear—traits that could be influential in the later development of a personality disorder.

However, genetics don't work in a vacuum. Studies continue to indicate that abuse, even verbal abuse, can amplify the risk of developing a personality disorder.

For some disorders, such as antisocial PD, the evidence suggests that genetic factors play a significant role, while others, such as dependent personality disorder, appear to be more environmentally influenced, says longtime PD researcher Theodore Millon, PhD, DSc, editor of an ongoing book series, "Personality-guided Psychology" (APA).

But regardless of the specific disorder, researchers increasingly observe a back-and-forth interplay between genetic and environmental influences.

"We see a paradigm shift taking place in the field now toward a more interactionist perspective," says Jeffrey G. Johnson, PhD, associate professor of clinical psychology in Columbia University's psychiatry department. "I think the field is getting away from genetics versus environment—it's a major change."

The Genetic/Environmental Convergence

One of the largest efforts to look at PDs, the Collaborative Longitudinal Personality Disorders Study (CLPS), is attempting to gain insight into a cross-section of the disorders' characteristics, stability and progression. The multisite study, funded by the National Institute of Mental Health until 2005, has since 1996 enrolled 668 people with the diagnoses of avoidant, borderline, obsessive-compulsive or schizotypal personality disorders. A summary of the study's aims appeared in the *Journal of Personality Disorders* (Vol. 14. No. 4).

Although the study is not looking directly at causes, it's collecting historical information that may one day provide some insights, says Tracie Shea, PhD, associate professor in the department of psychiatry and human behavior at Brown Medical School and one of CLPS's principal investigators. "I like to think of it as generating hypotheses that can be tested," she says.

Shea co-authored a 2002 study in the *Journal of Nervous and Mental Disease* (Vol. 190, No. 8) that looked at CLPS data and found an association between the severity of specific PDs and the number and type of childhood traumas. In particular, people with borderline PDs reported particularly high rates of childhood sexual trauma—55 percent detailing physically forced, unwanted sexual contact. The researchers note, however, that the type of analysis couldn't determine if the personality adaptations occurred in response to the trauma or whether the individuals' underlying character pathology predisposed them.

Among those exploring the genetic and environmental influences linking normal and abnormal personality is Robert Krueger, PhD, associate professor of psychology at the University of Minnesota. In 2002, Krueger co-authored a study in the *Journal of Personality* (Vol. 70, No. 5) that looked at the personality traits of 128 twin pairs who had been raised apart. The study found that the identical twins were more similar in personality traits than the fraternal twins.

Thus, although both genetics and environment contributed to the association between normal and abnormal personality, genetics appeared to play the greater role overall, Krueger says. "The predominant reason normal and abnormal personality are linked to each other is because they are linked to the same underlying genetic mechanisms," he explains.

With borderline PD, for example, ongoing research indicates that there may be a genetic base for the problems with impulsivity and aggression, says the University of California's Judd. But environmental influences are significant and can extend deep into childhood, even infancy, Judd adds.

"There is a pretty high prevalence of maltreatment by caregivers across all personality disorders," she notes. "One of the key problems appears to be neglect. Probably more of an emotional neglect—more of a lack of attention to a child's emotional needs."

Judd points to several studies by Johnson, including one published in 1999 in the *Archives of General Psychiatry* (Vol. 56, No. 7) that followed 639 New York state families and their children for nearly two decades. Children with documented instances of childhood abuse or neglect were more than four times as likely to develop a PD in early adulthood, according to the research.

Another study, led by Johnson and published in 2001 in *Comprehensive Psychiatry* (Vol. 42, No. 1), came to a similar conclusion when examining maternal verbal abuse in the same New York group of families, involving this time 793 mothers and their children. The prospective study asked mothers a variety of questions, including whether they had screamed at their children in the previous month and whether they had told their child they didn't love them or would send them away. Offspring who experienced verbal abuse in childhood—compared with those who didn't—were more than three times as likely to be diagnosed as adults with borderline, narcissistic, obsessive-compulsive and paranoid PDs.

Shea cautions, though, that at this point research into childhood neglect and abuse, albeit intriguing, has largely been suggestive because prospective studies remain limited.

"It's likely that these childhood abuse factors do play an important role," he explains. "It's hard to say what and how big that role is, more specifically."

The Parent-Blame Problem

The role of abuse is particularly controversial among family members of people with a borderline disorder, who say they are being unfairly blamed—similar to what happened in the early days of schizophrenia research. Emphasizing maltreatment and abuse is misleading and has a devastating effect on families, says Valerie Porr, president of a New York-based nonprofit group, Treatment and Research Advancements National Association for Personality Disorder (www.tara4bpd.org/tara.html).

Porr doesn't deny that parental behavior can play a role in borderline PD. "But it's not like it's the evil mother beating her children," she says. Rather, she explains, the child's "behavior is so off the wall [that] the family's responses are off the wall."

Porr, who has a family member with borderline personality disorder, points to emerging research, including that of Harvard University-based psychologist Jerome Kagan, PhD, identifying the high sensitivity to outside stimuli of some children as significant. Family members of people with borderline PD report unusual responses even in the first months of life, Porr says, noting that, "They say, 'The light bothers them. They are sensitive to noise. Texture bothers them.'"

But Kagan, in a 2002 *Dialogues in Clinical Neuroscience* article (Vol. 4, No. 3), says that the role of high reactivity in infancy is far from clear-cut. It's true, he says, that highly reactive infants are more likely to develop shy, timid or anxious personalities. Still, there are puzzling questions, including the significant gap between the percentage of children—20 percent—who are highly reactive infants and the prevalence—less than 10 percent—of those who develop social phobias.

"This fact suggests that many high reactives find an adaptive niche in their society that allows them to titer unpredictable social encounters," Kagan writes.

In the end, says Johnson, the goal of research into environmental influences is not to blame, but to help parents. "We must understand what parenting behaviors are associated with greater risk to the child," he says. "When we identify those parenting behaviors, we can use them to design intervention."

The Role of Peers

Psychologists' findings also suggest that caregivers, teachers and even peers may play a role in PDs—both in positive as well as negative ways. Even a single strong positive relationship—say a close bond with a grandmother—can offset negative influences in a dysfunctional household.

"The child with a predisposition toward developing a personality disorder doesn't need the perfect teacher or the perfect friends to not develop the disorder," says Judith Beck, PhD, director of the Beck Institute for Cognitive Therapy and Research in suburban Philadelphia. "If the child is in an extreme environment, such as abuse or neglect, that may make the difference in terms of developing a personality disorder."

And life events can help tip the balance, Beck says. For example, a child with obsessive-compulsive tendencies who has alcoholic parents may assume the responsibility of caring for his younger siblings—a move that may amplify his propensities until he meets the diagnosis of a disorder. "It's the fit between your environment and your personality," Beck explains.

Over time, researchers will continue probing that fit and will likely identify more than a few causes even for a single personality disorder, says Millon, dean of the Florida-based Institute for Advanced Studies in Personology and Psychopathology. Narrowing down potential causes will help psychologists more quickly isolate what might be influencing a particular patient, he says.

Millon explains: "Once you identify the one cause that seems most probable and most significant, then you can design your therapy in order to unlearn what seemed most problematic for that individual."

CHARLOTTE HUFF is a freelance writer in Fort Worth, Texas.

Brown v. Board: A Dream Deferred

Fifty years ago, a landmark ruling seemed to break Jim Crow's back and usher in an era of hope for integrated education. But the reality has fallen short of the promise. The fight for decent schooling for black kids goes on.

ELLIS COSE

Sometimes history serves as a magnifying mirror—making momentous what actually was not. But *Brown v. Board of Education of Topeka, Kansas,* is the real thing: a Supreme Court decision that fundamentally and forever changed America. It jump-started the modern civil-rights movement and excised a cancer eating a hole in the heart of the Constitution.

So why is the celebration of its 50th anniversary so bittersweet? Why, as we raise our glasses, are there tears in our eyes? The answer is simple: *Brown,* for all its glory, is something of a bust.

Clearly *Brown* altered forever the political and social landscape of an insufficiently conscience-stricken nation. "*Brown* led to the sit-ins, the freedom marches . . . the Civil Rights Act of 1964 . . . If you look at *Brown* as . . . the icebreaker that broke up . . . that frozen sea, then you will see it was an unequivocal success," declared Jack Greenberg, former head of the NAACP Legal Defense & Educational Fund Inc. and one of the lawyers who litigated *Brown*. Still, measured purely by its effects on the poor schoolchildren of color at its center, *Brown* is a disappointment—in many respects a failure. So this commemoration is muted by the realization that *Brown* was not nearly enough.

Increasingly, black and Latino kids are likely to find themselves in classrooms with few, if any, nonminority faces. The shift is due in part to Supreme Court decisions that undermined *Brown*.

While most white and Hispanic Americans (59 percent for each group) think their community schools are doing a good or excellent job, only 45 percent of blacks feel that way, according to an exclusive *Newsweek* Poll. That is up considerably from the 31 percent who thought their schools were performing well in 1998, but it means a lot of people are still unhappy with the deck of skills being dealt to black kids.

Only 38 percent of blacks think those schools have the resources necessary to provide a quality education, according to the poll. And African-Americans are not alone in feeling that funding should increase. A majority of the members of all ethnic groups support the notion that schools attended by impoverished minority children ought to have equivalent resources to those attended by affluent whites. Indeed, most Americans go even further. They say schools should be funded at "whatever level it takes to raise minority-student achievement to an acceptable national standard." Sixty-one percent of whites, 81 percent of Hispanics and a whopping 93 percent of blacks agree with that statement—which is to say they agree with the proposition of funding schools at a level never seriously countenanced by the political establishment: a total transformation of public education in the United States.

Most white and Hispanic Americans (59% for each group) think their local schools do a good or excellent job. Only 45% of blacks feel that way.

So now, 50 years after the court case that changed America, another battle is upon us—and only at this moment becoming clear. It began at the intersection of conflicting good intentions, where the demands of politicians and policymakers for high educational standards collided with the demands of educators and children's advocates for resources. Throw in a host of initiatives spawned, at least in part, by frustration at low student achievement—vouchers, charter schools, privatization, curbs on social promotion, high-stakes testing (all issues now swirling around the presidential campaign)—and you have the making of an educational upheaval that may rival *Brown* in its ramifications. It may in some ways be the second phase of *Brown*: a continuation by other means of the battle for access to a decent education by those whom fortune left behind.

On May 17, 1954, the day the walls of segregation fell, the Supreme Court actually handed down two decisions, involving five separate cases—in South Carolina, Virginia, Delaware, Kansas and Washington, D.C.—all of which came collectively to be known as *Brown*. Instead of abolishing segregation straightaway, the justices sought advice on how—and when—desegregation was to come about. So *Brown* spawned what came to be known as *Brown* II—a decision in May 1955 that provided neither a timetable nor a plan. Instead it ordered the South to proceed with "all deliberate speed," which the South took as an invitation to stall. But something more was wrong.

The decision rested on an assumption that simply wasn't true: that once formal, state-mandated segregation ended, "equal educational opportunities" would be the result. A half century later, school segregation is far from dead and the goal of educational equality is as elusive as ever. Since the early 1990s, despite the continued growth of integration in other sectors of society, black and Latino children are increasingly likely to find themselves in classes with few, if any, non-minority faces.

The shift is due, at least in part, to Supreme Court decisions that essentially undermined *Brown*. In 1974 the court ruled that schools in white suburbs were not obliged to admit black kids from the inner city. And in 1992 the court decided that local school boards, even if not in full compliance with desegregation orders, should be released from court supervision as quickly as possible. "Racial balance is not to be achieved for its own sake," proclaimed the court.

For most black parents, of course, *Brown* was never about integration "for its own sake"—though blacks strongly support integration. Instead, it was about recognition of the fact that unless their children went to school with the children of the whites who controlled the purse strings, their children were likely to be shortchanged.

Most blacks are no longer convinced their kids necessarily do better in integrated settings. Some 57 percent of black parents say the schools' racial mixture makes no difference, significantly more than the 41 percent who said that in 1988. But they also know resource allocation is not colorblind. Hence, 59 percent of blacks, 52 percent of Hispanics and 49 percent of whites agree that it will be impossible to provide equal educational opportunities for all "as long as children of different races in this country basically go to different schools."

Today, by virtually any measure of academic achievement, blacks, Puerto Ricans and Mexican-Americans are, on average, far behind their white and Asian-American peers. A range of factors, from bad prenatal care to intellectually destructive neighborhood or home environments, have been implicated to explain the disparity. Certainly one reason for the difference is that blacks (and Puerto Ricans and Mexican-Americans) do not, for the most part, go to the same schools, or even the same types of schools, as do the majority of non-Hispanic whites. They

are more likely to go to schools such as those found in parts of rural South Carolina—schools that, were it not for the American flags proudly flying over the roofs, might have been plucked out of some impoverished country that sees education as a luxury it can barely afford.

Take a tour of Jasper County and you will find a middle school with a drainpipe in the corridor, which occasionally spills sewage into the hallway. You'll find labs where the equipment doesn't work, so children have to simulate, rather than perform, experiments. In nearby Clarendon County resources are also lacking. Were Thurgood Marshall to find himself in Clarendon County today, "he would think [*Brown*] had been reversed," state Sen. John Marshall told a visitor. So Clarendon County is again in court, refighting the battle for access to a decent education that Clarendon's children, and all the children of *Brown*, presumably won a long time ago.

In 1951, kids walked out to protest school conditions in Farmville, Va. Despite *Brown*, relief did not come. The schools were shuttered for five years. Today the dream of integration is thriving there.

The saga of Clarendon County began in 1947 with a simple request for a bus. The county's white schoolchildren already had 30 school buses at their disposal. Though black children outnumbered whites by a margin of nearly three to one, they had not a single bus. So a local pastor, J. A. DeLaine, went on a crusade. His request for transportation led angry whites to burn down his church and his home, to shoot at him and to literally run him out of town under cover of night. It also spawned a lawsuit known as *Briggs v. Elliot*, which challenged the doctrine of "separate but equal" and was later bundled into *Brown*.

Instead of integrating its school systems, as *Brown* had decreed, South Carolina maneuvered to keep segregation alive. It structured school districts in such a way that blacks were largely lumped together, and having clustered them together, the state "systematically neglected to adequately fund those districts," says Steve Morrison, a partner in the law firm that is currently suing the state for additional resources for Clarendon and more than 30 other counties.

Blacks (83%) and Hispanics (91%) are more likely than whites (73%) to feel it's important to use standardized tests to raise academic standards

It is a sign of how much, in some respects, attitudes have changed that the state's largest law firm—Nelson Mullins Riley & Scarborough—is on the side of the plaintiffs. During a conversation in the offices of the law firm that bears his name,

Richard Riley, former governor of South Carolina and former U.S. secretary of Education, remarked, "If *Brown* had been 100 percent successful, we wouldn't have this situation." In opening arguments Carl Epps, another Nelson Mullins attorney, compared the suit to Brown itself, calling it the kind of case that comes along only "every generation or two."

Certainly, when aggregated with a multitude of similar cases, the Clarendon case—known as *Abbeville County School District, et al. v. The State of South Carolina, et al.*—represents a major shift in tactics among those fighting for the educational rights of poor people. Once upon a time the emphasis was on "equity": on trying to ensure that the most economically deprived students were provided with resources equal to those lavished on the children of the rich. Now the cases are about whether states are providing sufficient resources to poor schools to allow the students who attend them to effectively compete in society. They are called "adequacy" cases, and they aspire to force states to produce graduates capable of functioning competently as citizens and as educated human beings.

The shift in strategy stems, in part, from the Supreme Court's making equity cases more difficult to win but leaving the door open to adequacy claims. In a seminal moment for this new movement, the Kentucky Supreme Court decided in 1989 that students in Kentucky had a right to a much better education than they were receiving. In response, the legislature totally overhauled the state's educational system.

Elsewhere, legislative reforms—so far—have been less dramatic as politicians have fought efforts to mandate spending increases. But in several states, including New York, judges are looking on adequacy suits with favor. Indeed, last week a group of high-profile businessmen called on New York politicians to heed the call for more and smarter education funding. The notion that schools ought to invest more in those whose need is greatest goes against American tradition, but it seems an idea whose time is coming. Conversely, the notion that integration ought to be an explicit goal driving policy seems to be an idea whose time (at least among most whites) has passed. While close to two thirds of blacks and Hispanics feel that "more should be done" to integrate schools, only one third of whites agree. And only 18 percent of whites think whites receive a better education if they are in a racially mixed environment.

This is not to say that the push for integration has been a total failure. Indeed, in Farmville, Va., a small town little more than an hour's drive southwest of Richmond, the state capital, the dream of school integration is thriving. In the early 1950s, black high-school students in Farmville were relegated to a tiny structure. Students who could not be accommodated in the main building were relegated to flimsy shacks covered with tar paper, each heated with a single wood-burning stove. As former student leader John Stokes recalls, "The buildings were so bad that the people sitting near the windows or the door had to wear an overcoat, and the person sitting near the stove burned up." In 1951 the students walked out and took their complaints to the NAACP. That led to a case called *Davis v. County School Board of Prince Edward County*, which was eventually made part of *Brown*.

After the Supreme Court declared the era of separate but equal over, Virginia's legislature prohibited expenditure of funds on integrated schools. And when delay was no longer an option, Prince Edward County closed its public schools altogether. From the fall of 1959 through much of 1964 the schools were shuttered. Those whites whose parents had a little money could go to Prince Edward Academy, the newly established "private" school. But most blacks, who were barred from the (state subsidized) segregation academies, saw their educational hopes wither.

On May 25, 1964, the Supreme Court finally brought Prince Edward County's resistance to an end. "The time for mere 'deliberate speed' has run out," wrote Justice Hugo Black. But it was only this year that the Virginia State Legislature (prodded by Viola Baskerville, a black delegate, and Ken Woodley, editor of The Farmville Herald) passed a bill to provide some belated scholarship assistance to those who had missed school so long ago.

For Farmville's current generation of high-school students, integration has become a way of life. The racial composition (60 percent black, 39 percent white, in a high school of nearly 3,000) is a source of delight: "I talk about being proud that we are diverse," says school superintendent Margaret Blackmon. And nearly three fourths of those who graduate from Prince Edward County High go to college.

One reason Prince Edward County was able to integrate successfully no doubt has to do with size. Once desegregation was forced on it, tiny Farmville didn't really have the option of carving out separate black and white districts. And once the region's racial madness ended and the segregation academy fell on hard times, the public school seemed a less objectionable alternative. There was, in other words, no real room for whites to flee and, as time wore on, increasingly less reason to do so. In much of the rest of America, there are plenty of places to run. Nonetheless, to visit a place like Farmville, with full knowledge of its wretched history, is to experience a certain wistfulness—to wonder about what might have been.

66% of blacks and 67% of Hispanics favor vouchers, as do 54% of whites. But they're unlikely to get vouchers to send kids to any school they want

If integration is not the answer (at least not now), what is? If the heat generated around the issue is any indication, there are two popular answers: testing and choice, considered either separately or in combination.

In one state after another, politicians have seized on tests as the solution. Without question, testing is popular with the public. And though it may come as a surprise to some, testing is particularly popular with the black and Latino public. Blacks (83 percent) and Hispanics (91 percent) are much more likely than whites (73 percent) to believe that it is important or very important to use "standardized tests to raise academic standards and student achievement." Some 74 percent of blacks and 64 percent of Hispanics think "most" or "some" minority students would show academic improvement if required to pass standardized tests before being promoted from one grade to another.

My guess is that the numbers measure support more for the idea of testing than for the reality of what testing has become. The idea—that ability can be recognized and developed, that deficiencies can be diagnosed and remedied—is impossible to argue with. It is far from clear at this juncture that that is what is happening.

When it comes to children of color, we ask the wrong question. We ask, 'Why are you such a problem?' when we should ask, 'What have we not given you that we routinely give to upper-middle-class white kids?'

In a report assessing the first-year results of the No Child Left Behind Act in 11 urban districts, researchers from the Civil Rights Project at Harvard concluded: "In each of the districts we studied, fewer than 16% of eligible students requested and received supplemental educational services. In most of these districts it was less than 5% of the eligible students, and in some it was less than 1%."

The use of choice as a tool of educational reform has also been controversial, particularly when it comes to the issue of vouchers. On one side are those who claim that poor kids in ghettos and barrios have the right (and ought to receive public money) to leave crummy schools and seek a quality education elsewhere. On the other side are those who say that vouchers will not appreciably increase the options of children attending wretched schools but will instead deprive public schools of resources they can ill afford to lose.

In the last several years, voucher programs have sprouted in a number of states. Florida's program—actually three different programs—is the most ambitious. In December 2003 an audit of those programs by the state's chief financial officer led to several probes for criminal irregularities. In a blistering editorial in February, *The Palm Beach Post,* which had written several critical investigative pieces on the programs, concluded that "as the state is running it, the entire voucher program is a fraud." Even the Florida Catholic Conference, a presumptive beneficiary of the programs, appealed for reforms.

At the very least the conference wanted schools to be accredited, to have some kind of track record and to give standardized tests so parents would know how the schools were performing relative to others.

Certainly there is evidence that voucher programs can help some students. And most people view vouchers in a positive light. Some 66 percent of blacks and 67 percent of Hispanics favor vouchers, as do 54 percent of whites. But most people understand quite clearly that in the real world they are not likely to get a voucher that will allow them to send a child to any school of their dreams. So it is not inconsistent that a majority of Americans favor increasing funding for public education over providing parents with vouchers. Nor it is surprising that blacks, even more than whites, strongly support funding for public schools.

The voucher debate is bound to rage for years to come. With the backing of the Bush administration, Washington, D.C., is launching an ambitious new voucher experiment. Indeed, George W. Bush is running for re-election as the education president, as the leader who championed No Child Left Behind and who is making schools accountable with testing regimes and more demanding curricula. Not to be outdone, John Kerry has come up with his own education proposals, which include programs to keep young people, particularly people of color, in school and more funding for NCLB and special education.

The national dialogue on education that is emerging from the rhetoric of warring politicians—and from all these suits, all this testing and all these experiments with choice—must ultimately get beyond what happens in the school to what is happening in the larger society, and in the larger environment in which children exist.

In too many ways, when it comes to children of color, we continue to ask the wrong questions. We poke and probe and test those kids as we wrinkle our brows and ask, with requisite concern, "Why are you such a problem? What special programs do you need?" when we should be asking, "What have we not given to you that we routinely give to upper-middle-class white kids? What do they have that you don't?"

The answer is simple. They have a society that grants them the presumption of competence and the expectation of success; they have an environment that nurtures aspiration, peers who provide support and guardians who provide direction. If we are serious about realizing the promise of *Brown,* about decently educating those who begin with the least, we will have to ponder deeply how to deliver those things where they are desperately needed.

In the end, it may be that the true and lasting legacy of *Brown* has little to do with desegregation as such. It may instead be that *Brown* put us on a path that will, ideally, let us see children of color—and therefore our entire country—in a wholly new and beautiful light.

From *Newsweek,* May 17, 2004, pp. 52+. Copyright © 2004 by Newsweek. Reprinted by permission via PARS International Corp., phone 212–221–9595.

Girls Gone Bad?

Paris, Britney, Lindsay & Nicole: They seem to be everywhere and they may not be wearing underwear. Tweens adore them and teens envy them. But are we raising a generation of 'prosti-tots'?

KATHLEEN DEVENY WITH RAINA KELLEY

My 6-year-old daughter loves Lindsay Lohan. Loves, loves, *loves* her. She loves Lindsay's hair; she loves Lindsay's freckles. She's seen "The Parent Trap" at least 10 times. I sometimes catch her humming the movie's theme song, Nat King Cole's "Love." She likes "Herbie Fully Loaded" and now we're cycling through "Freaky Friday." So when my daughter spotted a photo of Lindsay in the New York Post at the breakfast table not long ago, she was psyched. "That's Lindsay Lohan," she said proudly. "What's she doing?"

I couldn't tell her, of course. I didn't want to explain that Lindsay, who, like Paris Hilton and Britney Spears, sometimes parties pantyless, was taking pole-dancing lessons to prepare for a movie role. Or that her two hours of research left her bruised "everywhere." Then again, Lindsay's professional trials are easy to explain compared with Nicole Richie's recent decision to stop her car in the car-pool lane of an L.A. freeway. Or Britney Spears's "collapse" during a New Year's Eve party in Las Vegas. Or the more recent report that Lindsay had checked into rehab after passing out in a hotel hallway, an item that ran on the Post's Page Six opposite a photo of Kate Moss falling down a stairway while dressed in little more than a fur jacket and a pack of cigarettes.

Something's in the air, and I wouldn't call it love. Like never before, our kids are being bombarded by images of oversexed, underdressed celebrities who can't seem to step out of a car without displaying their well-waxed private parts to photographers. Videos like "Girls Gone Wild on Campus Uncensored" bring in an estimated $40 million a year. And if US magazine, which changed the rules of mainstream celebrity journalism, is too slow with the latest dish on "Brit's New Man," kids can catch up 24/7 with hugely popular gossip blogs like perezhilton.com, tmz.com or defamer.com.

Allow us to confirm what every parent knows: kids, born in the new-media petri dish, are well aware of celebrity antics. But while boys are willing to take a peek at anyone showing skin, they're baffled by the feuds, the fashions and faux pas of the Brit Pack. Girls, on the other hand, are their biggest fans. A recent NEWSWEEK Poll found that 77 percent of Americans believe that Britney, Paris and Lindsay have too much influence on young girls. Hardly a day passes when one of them isn't making news. Paris Hilton "was always somewhere, doing something," says Melissa Monaco, an 18-year-old senior at Oldfield's boarding school for girls in Maryland, who describes herself as a recovered Paris Hilton addict. "I loved everything from her outfits to her attitude," she says. And it's not just teenagers. Julie Seborowski, a first-grade teacher at Kumeyaay Elementary School in San Diego, says she sees it in her 7-year-old students: girls using words like "sexy," singing pop songs with suggestive lyrics and flirting with boys.

That's enough to make any parent cringe. But are there really harmful long-term effects of overexposure to Paris Hilton? Are we raising a generation of what one L.A. mom calls "prosti-tots," young girls who dress like tarts, live for Dolce & Gabbana purses and can neither spell nor define such words as "adequate"? Or does the rise of the bad girl signal something more profound, a coarsening of the culture and a devaluation of sex, love and lasting commitment? We're certainly not the first generation of parents to worry about such things, nor will we be the last. Many conservative thinkers view our sex-drenched culture as dangerous; liberals are more prone to wave off fears about the chastity of our daughters as reactionary. One thing is not in doubt: a lot of parents are wondering about the effect our racy popular culture may have on their kids and the women they would like their girls to become. The answers are likely to lie in yet another question: where do our children learn values?

Here's a radical idea—at home, where they always have. Experts say attentive parents, strong teachers and nice friends are an excellent counterbalance to our increasingly sleazy culture. Statistical evidence indicates that our girls are actually doing pretty well, in spite of Paris Hilton and those like her: teen pregnancy, drinking and drug use are all down, and there is no evidence that girls are having intercourse at a younger age. And in many ways it's a great time to be a girl: women are excelling in sports, academics and the job market. It's just that the struggle to impart the right values to our kids is a 24/7 proposition. It can be done, but an ancient rule of warfare applies: first, know thy enemy.

"I didn't want to explain to my 6-year-old that Lindsay was taking pole dancing to prepare for a movie role."

"It takes a very strong adolescent to know what's right and what's wrong and not get sucked into all this stuff," says Emily Waring, 40, a paralegal from San Diego and mother of two girls, ages 9 and 2. Waring says her "mom radar" is always on because she believes negative influences, including entertainers like Britney Spears, are everywhere. "Kids can so easily stray," she says.

Nobody wants her bright, innocent girls to grow up believing "hard-partying heiress" is a job title to which they can aspire. But does dressing like Paris or slavishly following the details of Britney's love life make kids more likely to stray? Educators say they don't believe most girls in middle school wear short skirts or midriff shirts to attract the attention of older men, or even boys. (High school is, granted, a different story.) Sixth graders dress to fit in with other girls and for acceptance in social groups. "They dress that way because that's what they see in the media," says Nancy T. Mugele, who works in communications at Roland Park Country School in Baltimore. "They don't want to be different."

Which is not to say that hearing about Lindsay Lohan's, um, "fire crotch" doesn't affect the way kids think about sex. A study published last year in the journal Pediatrics concluded that for white teens, repeated exposure to sexual content in television, movies and music increases the likelihood of becoming sexually active at an earlier age. (Black teens appear less influenced by media, and more by their parents' expectations and their friends' sexual behavior; those who had the least exposure to sexual content were also less likely to have intercourse.) Specifically, the study found that 55 percent of teens who were exposed to a lot of sexual material had intercourse by 16, compared with only 6 percent of teens who rarely saw sexual imagery in the media. That jibes with what many Americans fear: 84 percent of adults in the NEWSWEEK Poll said sex plays a bigger role in popular culture than it did 20 or 30 years ago, and 70 percent said that was a bad influence on young people.

Many factors affect kids' sexual behavior, and it may be that kids who are already considering sex are more likely to seek out sexy shows and music. But researchers say one of the strongest predictors of early intercourse is the impression—real or imagined—that everybody else is doing it. For some teens, especially those who aren't getting strong messages about abstinence from their parents, the media can become a sort of "sexual superpeer," according to Jane D. Brown, a journalism professor at UNC Chapel Hill, and an author of the Pediatrics study. The message, says Brown, is that "you can walk around with no clothes on, you can have sex with whoever shows up, you can have a baby and not be married."

Some observers think the real effect of the Brit Pack on our culture is more subtle, but no less negative. Rather than instantly inspiring kids to rush and have sex, out-of-control celebs create a sense of normalcy about behavior—drinking, smoking, casual sex—that is dangerous for teens. Britney, Paris and Lindsay have no shortage of "boyfriends" but seem to have few real relationships. "It creates a general sense that life is about being crazy, being kooky, having fun and not carrying on serious relationships," says Christian Smith, professor of sociology at Notre Dame. But the really insidious consequence is that teenagers often consider themselves immune to these influences. "They don't have enough perspective on how they are being formed by the world around them—and when they don't realize it, it can be more powerful," he says.

"Eighty-four percent of adults say sex plays a bigger role in popular culture than it did 20 or 30 years ago."

Still, this seems like a lot to place on the slender shoulders of Nicole Richie and her frenemies. That some girls dress like Paris/Britney/Lindsay is empirically true. But it's difficult to draw a straight line between the behavior of celebrities and the behavior of real girls. "We certainly don't see our girls clamoring to get to downtown Chicago to the clubs," says Mark Kuzniewski, principal of Aptakisic Junior High in Buffalo Grove, Ill. And while girls may admire Britney's clothes and dance moves, her students "can't understand why Britney would wear no underwear," says Michelle Freitag, fifth-grade teacher in suburban Chicago. Their verdict: Britney is a "hootch," which is a polite way of saying "slut."

Our anxiety about girls and sex is growing just as the statistics seem to be telling as different story. Sex surveys are notoriously unreliable, but the best available data show that the average age of first sexual intercourse for girls is 17, according to the Guttmacher Institute, and hasn't changed by more than a few months in 20 years. The overall teenage pregnancy rate in 2002, the most recent available, was down 35 percent from 1990, according to the Centers for Disease Control. And while celebrity idols stumble in and out of rehab, the rates of drinking, smoking and overall drug use among teenage girls have declined in recent years, says the Institute for Social Research at the University of Michigan.

Girls born after 1990 live in a world where they have ready access to organized sports, safe contraception and Ivy League colleges. Yale didn't admit women until 1969; its freshman class is currently half female. In the 2004-2005 school year, women earned 57 percent of all bachelor's degrees awarded and 59 percent of master's degrees. The Congress now has 90 female members—the highest in history—with 16 in the Senate and 74 in the House, including Speaker Nancy Pelosi. Hillary Clinton, our first viable female presidential candidate, has thrown her hat into the ring.

Dan Kindlon, a professor of child psychology at Harvard and author of "Alpha Girls," calls these girls the daughters of the revolution, the first generation that is reaping the full benefit of the women's movement. "Sure, there are plenty of girls with big problems out there," he says. "Like the 'Girls Gone Wild' videos. But what percentage of the college population is that?" There is still plenty of pressure to be beautiful and thin, he adds, but now there are more options. Girls can define themselves as athletes or good students. For better or for worse, it may also be that they now feel entitled to dress as crassly as they choose, date unwisely and fall down drunk, the way men have since the dawn of time.

"Plenty of high-school bad girls (us, for instance!) grow up to be successful people with happy home lives."

That's at least how long parents have worried about how their children would turn out. The text on a Sumerian tablet from the village of Ur (located in modern-day Iraq) says: "If the unheard-of actions of today's youth are allowed to continue, then we are doomed." Certainly, queens and noblewomen have long gotten away with behaving badly: in the early 16th century, Anne Boleyn not only had an affair with the King of England, Henry VIII, but helped persuade him to throw the Roman Catholic Church out of the country (although we all know how that ended). Their daughter, Elizabeth I, was the "virgin queen" who slept around.

But for most of history, average women who had sex outside the vows of marriage were subject to banishment, beating or death. When Jesus said, "If any of you is without sin, let him be the first to throw a stone at her," he was protecting a woman caught in adultery. In her book "Promiscuities," Naomi Wolf recalls a searing image she came across in her research: a photo of the mummified remains of a 14-year-old German girl from the first century A.D.: "Her right arm still clutched the garrote that had been used to twist the rope around her neck. Her lips were open in an 'O' of surprise or pain . . ." Historians had concluded that the girl had been blindfolded, strangled and drowned, most likely as retribution for "adultery," or what we would now call premarital sex.

Until after the Civil War, women didn't have enough freedom to create much of a public scandal. By the turn of the century, however, the Industrial Revolution had transformed the lives of adolescent daughters of working-class families. Once confined to home, young white women could now work in offices, stores and factories, where they enjoyed unprecedented social freedoms—much to the chagrin of their parents and social critics. Young African-American women didn't have the same economic opportunities, but did gain new autonomy as they fled farms in the South to live and work in Northern cities.

Meanwhile, improved literacy along with technological advances like the wireless telegraph and radio gave rise to a national media. By 1900, there were more than 16,000 newspapers in the United States; circulation numbers at the biggest topped 1 million. Keeping a dirty little secret had become much, much harder. By the time the 1920s rolled around, bad girls could grow up to become not just the destroyers of men (in the tradition of Salome and Delilah), but also to be rich and famous.

Mae West, best remembered for one-liners like "If you don't like my peaches, why do you shake my tree," may have been the original bad girl of the 20th century. Born in Brooklyn in 1893, she wrote and starred in bawdy theatrical productions, delighting and scandalizing audiences. She went too far, however, when she wrote a play called "Sex," about waterfront hookers and pimps, which became a national hit. In 1927, the New York production was raided and she was arrested, convicted of a performance that "tended to corrupt the morals of youth and others," and sentenced to 10 days in jail, according to The New York Times. Seven years later she was featured on the cover of NEWSWEEK for a story titled "The Churches Protest," which called her the "personification of Hollywood's sins."

Gypsy Rose Lee, born In 1914, followed closely on Mae West's spike heels. A burlesque superstar, Lee's shows at Minsky's Winter Garden in New York in the 1930s were a sensation. Before a congressional committee in 1937, Herbert Minsky, who co-owned the theater, called Lee "one of the most highly publicized stars in the country." According to a Washington Post account, "A momentary hush fell on the hearings . . . The name of Gypsy Rose Lee had been mentioned." Despite her fame—and $2,000-a-week salary—Lee was arrested numerous times by the NYPD for public indecency, once allegedly protesting, "I wasn't naked. I was completely covered by a blue spotlight."

By the '50s, both Hollywood and the public took a harsh view of female stars' off-screen indiscretions. In 1950, Ingrid Bergman was America's sweetheart, having starred in "The Bells of St. Mary's" and "Notorious." But when Bergman, then married, had an affair with director Roberto Rossellini, who was also married, and gave birth to their child, she was shunned by Hollywood and called "a powerful influence for evil" on the floor of the Senate. (Hollywood "forgave" Bergman a few years later by giving her an Oscar for "Anastasia.") After news broke that Marilyn Monroe would be featured in a nude calendar, Hollywood proclaimed her career DOA. (She was on the cover of Life magazine a month later, and went on to the biggest roles of her career.)

America was scandalized in 1962 when Elizabeth Taylor cheated on Eddie Fisher with Richard Burton during the filming of "Cleopatra." The Vatican denounced her as "a woman of loose morals." When "Dickenliz," as they were known, checked into a Toronto hotel, protesters marched outside with signs that read DRINK NOT THE WINE OF ADULTERY, according to a 1964 NEWSWEEK article. But soon America's priorities shifted. The Vietnam War was on television; the civil-rights movement was in the streets, and the national mood had been sobered by the assassinations of John F. Kennedy, Martin Luther King Jr. and Robert Kennedy. The '60s also brought reliable contraception in the form of the birth-control pill and ushered in the sexual revolution. We no longer needed to look to Hollywood for bad influences; the girl next door, the one with birth-control pills and a couple of joints tucked into her fringed purse, became the new object of our anxiety.

America had become harder to shock—until 1984, that is, when Madonna showed up in a wedding dress at the first MTV Video Music Awards and sang "Like a Virgin" while writhing on the floor. When her "Virgin" tour opened a year later, parents fretted over the hordes of Madonna wannabes who thronged her concerts dressed in tatty lace, spandex and armfuls of black rubber bracelets. The Material Girl went on to outrage both Planned Parenthood and the Catholic Church in 1986 with her single "Papa Don't Preach," about a pregnant teenager. The 1992 coffee-table book called "Sex," which glorified nearly every sexual fetish you can think of, cemented her title as the Queen of Bad Girls. Eleven years later she passed on her crown to Britney with a lingering French kiss on the stage of yet another MTV Video Music Awards ceremony.

And Brit, as we know, has run with it. One-day marriages aside, why wouldn't girls be fascinated by her and her celebrity pals? These 21st-century "bad influences" are young, beautiful and rich, unencumbered by school, curfews or parents. "They've got great clothes and boyfriends. They seem to have a lot of fun," explains Emma Boyce, a 17-year-old junior at Louise S. McGehee School in New Orleans. But fascination and admiration are two very different things. As they get arrested for driving drunk and feuding with their former BFFs, the Brit Pack makes it easy for young women like Boyce, a top student and accomplished equestrian, to feel superior to them. "My friends and I look at them to laugh at them," adds Boyce. "Our lives seem pretty good by comparison. We're not going to rehab like Lindsay."

Boyce says she and her friends have simply outgrown their devotion to celebrities. Twelve- to 14-year-olds are probably the most vulnerable to stars' influence. "Clearly it is at this age for girls that they are trying to find an identity to associate with," says Kuzniewski, the junior-high principal from Buffalo Grove, Ill. "It seems desirable to be Lindsay Lohan." Now that's a legitimate cause for parental concern. But it may very well be fleeting. After all, have you read your junior-high journals lately? Like us, you were probably obsessed with trivial things that had little bearing on the person you became at 24 or 34. Even if your daughter does dress like Paris or behave like Lindsay, that doesn't mean she's doomed to a life on the pole. Plenty of high-school bad girls (us, for instance!) grow up to be successful professionals with happy home lives.

And as much as we hate to admit it, we grown-ups are complicit. We're uncomfortable when kids worship these girls, yet we also love US magazine; we can't get enough of YouTube videos or "E! True Hollywood Stories." So rather than wring our hands over an increase in 17-year-olds getting breast implants,

what if we just said no? They're minors, right? And while we worry that middle-schoolers are dressing like hookers, there are very few 11-year-olds with enough disposable income to keep Forever 21 afloat. The greatest threat posed by these celebrity bad girls may be that they're advertising avatars, dressed by stylists and designers, who seem to live only to consume: clothes, cell phones, dogs and men. But there's good news: that problem is largely under the control of we who hold the purse strings.

And even if our adolescents pick up a few tricks from the Brit Pack, we have a big head start on them. We begin to teach our kids values while they're still in diapers. "Kids learn good morals and values by copying role models who are close to them," says Michele Borba, author of "Teaching Moral Intelligence."

Good Times, Bad Apples

By the 20th century, women had freedom enough to cause public scandals. Social critics have been wringing their hands ever since.

1. Ingrid Bergman — The married star had an affair in 1950 with Roberto Possellini, who was also married, and Bergman gave birth to their child. She was denounced on the floor of the Senate.

2. Mae West — The vaudeville performer spent 10 days in jail for the 1927 play 'Sex.'

3. Marilyn Monroe — Long before she purred 'Happy Birthday' to JFK, she appeared in a calendar in her birthday suit. Hollywood called her career DOA.

4. Monica Lewinsky — The former intern helped create myriad teaching moments about oral sex after her liaison with President Clinton.

5. Madonna — Parents flipped in '85 when girls showed up at her concerts dressed in spandex and black rubber bracelets.

6. Kate Moss — Photos of her apparently using coke showed up in a British tab in 2005. She went to rehab, and has regained her status as a fashion icon.

7. Liz Taylor — She had an affair with Richard Burton in 1962 during the filming of 'Cloepatra'; the Vatican called her 'a woman of loose morals.'

8. Gypsy Rose Lee — A burlesque superstar in the '30s, she was arrested numerous times for taking it almost all off.

9. Nicole Richie — She was arrested last fall for parking on an L.A. freeway.

Experts say that even the most withdrawn teens scrutinize their parents for cues on how to act. So watch your behavior; don't gossip with your friends in front of the kids and downplay popularity as a lifetime goal. Parents need to understand and talk about the things that interest their kids—even if it's what Paris is wearing—without being judgmental. That makes it easier for kids to open up. "The really subtle thing you have to do is hear where they are coming from, and gently direct them into thinking about it," says Borba. That means these celebrities gone wild and all their tabloid antics can be teachable moments. Lesson No. 1: wear underwear.

With Jamie Reno, in San Diego; Karen Springen in Chicago and Susannah Meadows, Anne Underwood and Julie Scelfo in New York.

Disrespecting Childhood

Although Americans see ours as a child-loving nation, the authors present evidence of policies and practices that are not respectful of children or childhood. They call on us to question the assumptions about our young people that form the basis for our teaching, research, and policies.

CURT DUDLEY-MARLING, JANICE JACKSON, AND LISA PATEL STEVENS

What I discovered in Spain was a culture that held children to be its meringues and eclairs. My own culture . . . tended to regard children as a sort of toxic waste.[1]

I n the popular imagination, Americans are a child-loving people. Across the land, selfless parents take classes, read books, create playgroups, and exchange the latest information about how to ensure safe, contented, and productive childhoods. Thousands of contemporary American families indulge their children materially to a degree that may be unparalleled in the world and in our own history. As a society, we have enacted a range of laws designed to protect children from physical and psychological abuse and economic and sexual exploitation. We have legions of pediatricians specially trained to attend to the physical and mental well-being of our children. Even the presence of metal detectors at the entrances of our schools can be taken as emblematic of our collective desire to protect the nation's children.

The range of public programs and policies benefiting children, directly or indirectly, offers further evidence of the high regard Americans have for their children. Tax credits for children and child care, child nutrition and health-care programs, preschool programs like Head Start, and billions of dollars spent each year to support elementary, secondary, and postsecondary education all demonstrate the desire of federal, state, and local governments to look after the physical, emotional, and intellectual well-being of the young. The prominence we give to educational issues in local, state, and federal elections further supports the assertion that children are indeed a high priority for Americans.

More than 133,000 children are in juvenile or adult correctional facilities on any given day.

While these commonly held beliefs communicate a consistent and shared regard for children, when we dig beneath the platitudes,

we find a far messier and more complex set of assumptions, beliefs, and challenges to this inspiring image of the United States as a child-loving society. Writing over 20 years ago, Letty Pogrebin argued that "America is a nation fundamentally ambivalent about its children, often afraid of its children, and frequently punitive towards its children."[2] Pogrebin cited attacks on the cost of public education and child health and nutrition programs, along with an inclination to pathologize an entire period in children's lives—that is, adolescence—to support her contention that the country was afflicted by what she called "an epidemic of pedophobia."[3]

Novelist Barbara Kingsolver has observed that children have come to hold an increasingly negative position in the economy.[4] Children are spoken of as a responsibility, a legal liability, and an encumbrance[5]—or they are seen in terms of potential profits. Today's children and adolescents, weaned on images of McDonald's and toy companies, are targeted as a ripe segment of the market for building powerful brand loyalty for everything from video games to prescriptions for drugs to treat attention deficit disorders.[6] And, if Pogrebin, writing in the early Reagan years, saw child-focused government programs under attack, then Kingsolver, writing 14 years later, had seen many of these same programs ravaged. Funding for virtually every program that benefits children in this country, Kingsolver writes—from "Sesame Street" to free school lunches—has been cut back in the past decade, in many cases cut to nothing.[7] Indeed, programs that support children in the U.S. are, in Kingsolver's words, the hands-down worst in the industrialized world.[8]

The Kingsolver quote that serves as epigraph to this article is disturbing. After all, it is a rare parent who does not put the needs of his or her children first, and Americans generally do care about *their own* children. But the evidence suggests that Americans are not consistent in caring for other people's children, especially children from marginalized populations. Nearly one in six children in the U.S. lives in poverty, a rate as much as two to three times higher than that in other industrialized nations.[9] The data for children of color are even more distressing, as black (32%) and Hispanic (29%) children are far more likely than white children (14%) to live in poverty. And many of these same children attend deteriorating, underfunded schools.[10] Here are some additional statistics from

The State of America's Children: more than 133,000 children are in juvenile or adult correctional facilities on any given day; children under 18 are increasingly incarcerated in adult facilities (more than 21,000 youths under 18 are being held in adult correctional facilities); in 2003, youth jobless rates for ages 16–19 reached nearly 60%, as compared to the 6% unemployment rate for all ages; in 2002, nearly 9.3 million American children were not covered by health insurance; also in 2003, 2,911 children and teens were killed by gunfire; and in 2002, an estimated three million children in the U.S. were reported as suspected cases of child abuse or neglect.[11] While these statistics arise from a complex set of social and economic circumstances, taken together, they challenge the image of America as a child-loving society.

Additional evidence of America's antipathy toward its youths comes from a Public Agenda survey of the attitudes of adult Americans toward the next generation.[12] Only 23% of the respondents had anything positive to say about children and adolescents, while just 37% of the adults surveyed thought that today's children would grow up to make the world a better place; 61% believed that many young people were failing to learn such values as honesty, respect, and responsibility; and just 12% thought it was common for children and adolescents to treat people with respect. Writing in *The Nation,* Annette Fuentes observed that policies like zero tolerance really mean that "to be young is to be suspect,"[13] and a 1995 U.S. Supreme Court ruling supports the notion that simply being an adolescent is reasonable cause for authorities to suspect drug abuse and demand urine samples.[14] Massachusetts is one of a number of jurisdictions proposing widespread "voluntary" drug testing of high school students.[15] This negative assessment of the nation's youths undoubtedly lies behind the willingness of the American public to support a range of "get tough on kids" policies.

America's ambivalence toward young people manifests itself in the suspicion and fear of adolescents. Although we see children largely as burdens of responsibility, we nonetheless romanticize younger children as pliable potential citizens in need of close adult guidance and care. Various public policies seek to preserve their perceived innocence. Indeed, some have argued that an overly myopic focus on children is an attempt to defer—and potentially avoid—"dealing with" the miscreant tendencies of adolescence.[16]

Children under 18 are increasingly incarcerated in adult facilities (more than 21,000 youths under 18 are being held in adult correctional facilities).

The nation's low opinion of its youths is also apparent in the frequent media campaigns that link young people to a host of social "crises," including youth violence, teen pregnancy, violent and sexually explicit movies and video games, offensive lyrics in popular music, drug and alcohol abuse, smoking, and suicide. Underlying the critiques of the American Decency Association and others who blame popular culture for many of the problems of adolescence are two sets of assumptions. First, young people are assumed to mediate their senses of self through the popular culture of music and films. (Arguably, anyone living in this Information Age engages in that kind of identity work, finding and creating images, sounds, and messages that resonate with a sense of self.) However, the association between young people and the texts of popular culture all but equates the two. This is a misuse and confusion of the terms and concepts of popular culture, youth subculture, and mass-mediated culture. In truth, the variety, breadth, and seemingly endless choices of mass-mediated texts are pervasive throughout the lives of citizens today.

The second assumption underlying the critiques of popular culture's impact on youths is that young people are so impressionable and shallow that a movie scene, rock lyric, or T-shirt slogan will lead them to violence, promiscuity, or drug addiction. While it is not our purpose here to explore the hotly debated relationships between images, beliefs, and behaviors, we simply note that it is taken for granted that youths in general cannot discriminate, be critical, or add perspectives to these media-based practices. In fact, the disregard of young people has begun to affect even those youths who are largely considered to be fortunate, supported, and well loved: the middle class. As sociologist and journalist Elliott Currie argues, the very culture of middle-class materialism and individualism has all but ensured a context of disconnection and stripped-down communities for young people.[17]

Fear, suspicion, and resentment toward the nation's young have led to the appearance of groups of child-free adults, such as No Kidding!, that challenge "family-friendly" public policies seen to (unfairly) favor people with children.[18] Advocacy groups for childless adults seek the creation of child-free zones in such public spaces as restaurants, supermarkets, and health clubs.[19] If it takes a village to raise a child, many villagers are abdicating their responsibilities.

In the face of such examples, we would do well to reconsider our sense of ourselves as a child-loving people. Examining the policies, discourses, and practices that surround children and adolescents sheds light on our ambivalence toward them, at best, and a profound mistrust and disrespect of our youngest charges, at worst. As educators, we have the responsibility to care for and guide our nation's young people, and so we must be prepared to challenge the policies that frame our work with them. Just as the kind of marketing directed toward adolescents tells us something about how certain economic sectors see them, so does the language of our education policies reveal our societal attitudes. Underlying education reform proposals are sets of assumptions about children and adolescents and about childhood and adolescence as stages of life. Underpinning child-centered and back-to-basics reforms, for example, are fundamentally different beliefs about how children learn and about the nature of childhood. Below, we examine some of the dominant themes underlying two strands of education reform—standards and accountability and safe schools—to see what we can learn about the nation's respect for its young people and for childhood and adolescence as special times of life. Then we briefly discuss an alternative and, we believe, more respectful vision of school reform that seeks to engage students in the process.

Standards and Accountability

Former *New York Times* education columnist Richard Rothstein distinguishes two meanings for standards-based reform:

> Standards-based reform has two contradictory meanings. Some policy makers want minimum standards representing what all students must know for promotion or graduation. Others want high standards as goals toward which all

students should strive but not all may achieve. Schools need both, but one standard cannot do both jobs.[20]

The first of these two strands of standards-based reform, which emphasizes high expectations for all students regardless of who they are or where they live, demonstrates respect for students by assuming that all children can (and should) learn. The second, as Rothstein observes, sets up high expectations by requiring that all students achieve the highest standards in all subjects. We argue below that this version of standards-based reform, which has come to dominate today's landscape of reform, is not respectful of children or of childhood and adolescence.

High stakes. Many education reformers assume that the failures of American education alleged in *A Nation at Risk* can be remedied only by high standards tied to sanctions. Presumably, because they lack the intrinsic motivation to excel in school, students can be motivated by the desire to avoid such sanctions as grade retention, the threat of failing courses, and the withholding of high school diplomas. But the desire to get tough on kids through high-stakes decisions is not supported by research. Neither grade retention nor course failure, for example, appears to be related to improved academic performance; grade retention does, however, increase the chances students will drop out of school.[21] Increased dropout rates may also be one of the principal effects of linking high school diplomas to the results of high-stakes tests.[22]

In 2003, youth jobless rates for ages 16–19 reached nearly 60%, as compared to the 6% unemployment rate for all ages.

Education reformers who demand that *all students* be held accountable to the highest standards often argue that they are motivated by faith in the ability of all children to learn challenging academic material. This logic sits uncomfortably beside the underlying assumption that extrinsic retribution is needed to motivate learning. Furthermore, the evidence indicates that *high standards* enforced through grade retention, failing grades, and high school exit exams are diminishing the life chances of significant numbers of students, especially poor and minority students, who are more likely to be retained or drop out of school.[23]

Intensification of schooling. Working from assumptions about needing extrinsic goals to motivate learners, the education reform of "getting tough on kids" has led to an intensification of schooling. Political platforms of more homework, longer school days, and longer school years imply that children need to be pushed to do more of what they've been asked to do in the past. Former Republican leader of the U.S. House of Representatives Newt Gingrich asserted that "every child . . . should be required to do at least two hours of homework a night, or they're being cheated for the rest of their lives."[24]

School districts across the country have taken up this challenge as elementary and secondary students in the U.S. are doing more homework than ever.[25] In some school districts, even kindergartners are doing up to 30 minutes of homework each night and working toward academic report cards.[26] But using intensified homework as a means of increasing academic achievement, especially for elementary students, is unsupported by research.[27] Nonetheless, for many children the increased homework demands, by extending the reach of schooling into children's homes, have

significantly reduced the time available for leisure and recreational opportunities.[28]

Schooling is also being intensified by cutting back on recess for elementary students, as up to 40% of the nation's school districts have either curtailed or eliminated recess.[29] A former superintendent of the Atlanta Public Schools defended the elimination of recess in his district by arguing that academic performance cannot be improved by having kids hanging on the monkey bars.[30] Similar reasoning has been used to justify cutting such educational "frills" as art and music. Of course, recess, art, and music are far more likely to be cut in urban schools—populated disproportionately by children of color and children living in poverty—than in suburban schools, suggesting that, as a nation, we believe that art, music, and play time are more important for some children than for others.

In 2002, nearly 9.3 million American children were not covered by health insurance.

Standardization. Enforcing standards through high-stakes testing demands standards that are specific, measurable, and uniform across jurisdictions.[31] Arguably, such uniform standards lead to a focus on those aspects of learning that can most easily be standardized and, inevitably, create a one-size-fits-all curriculum in which students are processed like so many widgets. Put in raw material at one end, treat it all in exactly the same way, and there will emerge at the other end a predictable and standardized product.[32]

Relegating students to such a passive role—treating them as objects—reveals a fundamental lack of respect for children and adolescents as rational, thoughtful, varied, and interesting people.[33] The expectation that standardized approaches to education can lead to "predictable and standardized" products assumes that, at some level, children (the raw material) are, essentially, all the same. This view of learning, which renders differences in students' learning opportunities, abilities, development levels, background knowledge, and experience irrelevant and even problematic, respects neither children and adolescents nor the homes, neighborhoods, and cultures from which they come.

Focusing relentlessly on academic achievement, as determined by high-stakes tests,[34] has turned many American classrooms into dreary workplaces where the basics are translated into worksheets while art, music, and recess games are seen as unnecessary distractions. High standards and high stakes are creating high-stress environments that leave little room for the playful and aesthetic pursuits of children—in or out of school. David Elkind's words echo across the decades:

> The concept of childhood, so vital to the traditional American way of life, is threatened with extinction in the society we have created. Today's child has become the unwilling, unintended victim of overwhelming stress—the stress born of rapid, bewildering social change and constantly rising expectations.[35]

Safe Schools

As a society, we love children—when they are under control. We hate children who defy us, children who are independent, quirky, free-thinking, nonconforming, idiosyncratic, precocious, or critical of adults.[36]

Despite evidence of a slight decline in violence in our schools,[37] Americans continue to identify lack of discipline, fighting, violence, and substance abuse as serious problems in our schools.[38] Certainly, official data on the decreasing incidence of violence in schools have not been as readily available to the public as media reports on school shootings, infighting among adolescent females, or violent plots in New Bedford, Massachusetts. Influenced by sensational reports in the media, most Americans would probably agree that the gravity of youth violence has increased dramatically in recent years.[39] Conflicts that used to result in fist fights and end with bloody noses, black eyes, and the occasional chipped tooth are now said to result in the drawing of weapons and to end with life-threatening lacerations and occasional gunshot wounds.

Whatever the actual rate of violence in our schools, no one would dispute that all students are entitled to safe, secure learning environments. There is, however, strong disagreement over the means by which safe schools might be best achieved. Social scientists and professional educators tend to prefer approaches to safe schools that focus on improving the school climate through expanded curricular offerings, decreased school and class size, increased staffing, and teaching the skills of conflict resolution.[40] Underlying these initiatives is an assumption that, given an environment that is respectful of their social, emotional, and intellectual needs, children and adolescents will be generally respectful of the needs of teachers and other students. From this perspective, respect begets respect.

Legislators, media pundits, and some segments of the public, on the other hand, are disposed to embrace politically expedient, get-tough-on-kids policies that play on the nation's generally low opinion and fear of its youths. The surveillance cameras, random locker searches, drug testing, and zero tolerance policies that characterize safe school efforts in many states reinforce the impression of youths as "savage beasts," a provocative phrase used by Lilia Bartolome in 1994 and a sentiment that is still common in contemporary circles.[41] The phrase invokes the image of young people who require nearly constant surveillance and control and justifies denying students any right to privacy or due process.

In the absence of data on the efficacy of various get-tough-on-youth policies, it could easily be concluded that the desire to enact these policies is motivated by a general loathing of youths, especially minority youths. The degree to which such policies predominate in urban schools, which are disproportionately populated by students of color, signals a national fear of minority youths out of control. The desire to control children of color may also underlie the proliferation of heavily scripted learning programs that effectively control the bodies and minds of students in urban schools.[42] Whatever the means, control is a quintessentially disrespectful act.

All children and adolescents are entitled to safe schools and challenging curricula. All too often, however, the impulse to create safe and challenging schools is underpinned by an antipathy toward children and adolescents that has resulted in policies and practices that are fundamentally disrespectful of American youths. While the effectiveness of these policies is debatable, they are rarely evaluated at all on the basis of their underlying regard for children and young people. Indeed, a recent book by two fellows at the conservative American Enterprise Institute ridicules school-based practices that attend to students' emotional well-being because they have no demonstrable link to academic achievement[43]—as if

students' psychological and emotional health are beyond the purview of schooling. Other conservative scholars have challenged the efficacy of health and dental care and hot lunch programs because they don't affect measures of academic achievement.[44] Examining the assumptions about our young people that pervade schooling is one way of taking an important step back to consider matters that are often drowned out by the cacophony of agendas, reforms, and platforms.

Including Student Voices: A Demonstration of Respect

I'm not adult enough to get a job and have my own apartment, but I'm adult enough to make decisions on my own, know right from wrong, have ideas about the world. That's why it's hard to be a teenager—it's like a middle stage. . . . To a certain extent [teachers] have to have a personality that students respond to. But that doesn't mean you have to be our best friend, because that will cause our education to suffer. I hate to admit it, but respect and authority are a part of the job. Kids expect adults to give us directions and boundaries, but it's a balance.[45]

The debate about reforming schools to make them better places to prepare young people to participate fully in the life of the community has been raging at least since the 1996 *Breaking Ranks* report from the National Association of Secondary School Principals. In particular, there has been great attention given to redesigning high schools into places that will improve student learning. There have been two main approaches: a policy-oriented, managerial approach and a student-centered approach.[46] The former advocates the alignment of standards, curriculum, and assessment. The latter advocates a cultural change in schools that creates an environment supportive of students' academic and social/emotional development.

Though there is much conversation about improving the relationships between adults and students, neither approach has advocated for including students' ideas as an essential element in a successful reform strategy. Many policy makers and school personnel believe that students lack the ability to be thoughtful about their own circumstances; therefore, little attention is paid to the knowledge and perspectives that students bring with them to the classroom. The students of What Kids Can Do, Inc. (WKCD) call the adults' mistrust into question. Vance, quoted above, was a member of a project to listen to students' thoughts about high school. Their work culminated in the book *Fires in the Bathroom: Advice for Teachers from High School Students,* from which Vance's words are taken. As this work demonstrates, young people are quite articulate about their experience of schooling, and they could make meaningful contributions to conversations regarding the reform of school culture, school governance, curriculum, and pedagogy.

The inclusion of the student voice could provide insights that would help policy makers and school personnel understand students' disengagement from school and how it leads to an increase in the dropout rate. It could provide adults with better insights into the various youth subcultures and young peoples' varied responses to them. "Meaningful and sustained school reform has at its core the involvement and engagement of students. Student voice can be a powerful mechanism for building school morale, improving school climate, and creating demand for high quality instruction," according to students in the Boston project Student Researchers for High School Renewal.[47]

Another WKCD project was the Students-as-Allies Initiative, which was designed to help students and teachers become allies in solving the problems arising in their school communities. In collaboration with the MetLife Foundation, WKCD selected five cities to participate in the project: Chicago, Houston, Oakland, Philadelphia, and St. Louis. WKCD identified local nonprofit organizations in each city to guide the process. The goals of the initiative were to support student voice, to strengthen the relationships between students and teachers in order to bolster school improvement efforts, to provide opportunities for students to serve as resources to their schools and communities, and to model relationship building. The nonprofit partners set the criteria for the development of teams made up of students and teachers to conduct research about their particular schools, to analyze the data, to engage in dialogue, to make recommendations for action, and, finally, to take action.[48]

One objective was to enlist students who were not usually recognized in their schools as leaders. In Houston, teachers wove the project into their writing classes so that all the students they taught could participate. In St. Louis, teachers recruited students in order to build a team that was representative of the many cliques in the school. In Oakland, students were enrolled in a special class designed to cultivate nontraditional leaders.

The participants decided that surveys would be the best tools for gathering information, and each team designed its own survey after looking at a common core of questions derived from a review of teacher and student surveys that had been conducted by MetLife. The focus was on "areas where knowing the thoughts of students and teachers would help students become actors in improving their schools." The teams were taught principles of survey research and guided through an analysis of the data. They learned to present the data and to host dialogues in their schools and communities.

The final phase of the project is to engage students in making recommendations for solutions and in taking appropriate actions. Each of the partnerships is in the early stages of taking action. Detailed information about the initiative can be found on the website of What Kids Can Do, Inc. (www.whatkidscando.org/index.asp).

The work of this group of students demonstrates that many young people care deeply about their own education and are capable of contributing to the reform of high schools in ways that could make deep and long-lasting changes for themselves and their teachers. These examples are not intended to serve as simplistic recommendations of actions to be taken at all levels and in all contexts. Rather, we offer them as examples of the kinds of initiatives that can be entertained when children and adolescents are treated as thoughtful participants in the enterprise of American education and not as problems to be overcome—in short, if they are treated with respect.

When we look past the naive belief that we treat our children with undying care, we find a disconcerting mix of policies and practices that are not respectful of children or of childhood. Examining these platforms and actions is far from a simple matter. We must move beyond simple quantitative tally sheets of how much money is devoted to education and the care of our young. We must also ask what kind of institutional spaces are created for children, what we expect from them, and what we have assumed about them that may in fact restrict their abilities to thrive.

In reform after reform, the lens has not been widened enough to consider underlying assumptions about children. In the application of NCLB to students, younger and older, a consistent set of mistakes marks the policy territory: a fundamental lack of explicit, evidence-based knowledge and respect for students coupled with an overwhelming emphasis on control and singular measurements. We must learn to question what forms the basis for our teaching, research, and policy. And in reviewing our practices, necessarily a discursive and recursive process, we must also consider the ways in which we represent, understand, and listen to our children and young people.

How then do we begin the considerable work of truly valuing and respecting our nation's young? Education is just one institutional site for the enactment, performance, and mediation of values, but it is a multifaceted one. Thus the efforts to reconfigure our beliefs and practices must affect the daily lives of students, teachers, researchers, and policy makers. All of these groups can take the same first step: examining the assumptions we hold about our young.

Notes

1. Barbara Kingsolver, *High Tide in Tucson: Essays from Now or Never* (New York: HarperPerennial, 1996), p. 100.

2. Letty Cottin Pogrebin, *Family Politics: Love and Power on an Intimate Frontier* (New York: McGraw-Hill, 1983), p. 42.

3. Ibid., p. 46.

4. Kingsolver, p. 102.

5. Ibid.

6. Alissa Quart, *Branded: The Buying and Selling of Teenagers* (Cambridge, Mass.: Perseus, 2003).

7. Kingsolver, p. 102.

8. Kingsolver, p. 101.

9. *The State of America's Children, 2004* (Washington, D.C.: Children's Defense Fund, 2004), p. 3; and "Young Children in Poverty Fact Sheet," National Center for Children in Poverty, 1999, available at www.nccp.org, click on Fact Sheets.

10. Jonathan Kozol, *Savage Inequalities: Children in America's Schools* (New York: Crown, 1991).

11. *The State of America's Children, 2004.*

12. Ann Duffet, Jean Johnson, and Steve Farkas, *Kids These Days: What Americans Really Think About the Next Generation* (Washington, D.C.: Public Agenda, 1999).

13. Annette Fuentes, "The Crackdown on Kids," *The Nation,* 15/22 June 1998, pp. 20–22.

14. Mike A. Males, *The Scapegoat Generation: America's War on Adolescents* (Monroe, Me.: Common Courage Press, 1996).

15. John R. Knight, "An F for School Drug Tests," *Boston Globe,* 13 June 2005, p. 15.

16. Allan Luke and Carmen Luke, "Adolescence Lost and Childhood Regained," *Australian Journal of Language and Literacy,* July 2001, pp. 91–120.

17. Elliott Curie, *The Road to Whatever: Middle-Class Culture and the Crisis of Adolescence* (New York: Henry Holt, 2005).

18. Scott Lehigh, "No Kidding," *Boston Globe,* 21 May 2000, pp. E-1, E-5.

19. Elinor Burkett, *The Baby Boon: How Family-Friendly America Cheats the Childless* (New York: Free Press, 2000).

20. Richard Rothstein, "In Judging Schools, One Standard Doesn't Fit All," *New York Times,* 8 December 1999, p. A-20.

21. See, for example, Eugene R. Johnson et al., "The Effects of Early Grade Retention on the Academic Achievement of Fourth-Grade Students," *Psychology in the Schools,* October 1990, pp. 333–38; William A. Owings and Susan Magliaro, "Grade Retention: A History of Failure," *Educational Leadership,* September 1998, pp. 86–88; Melissa Roderick, "Grade Retention and School Dropout: Investigating the Association," *American Educational Research Journal,* Winter 1994, pp. 729–59; Melissa Roderick and Eric Camburn, "Risk and Recovery from Course Failure in the Early Years of High School," *American Educational Research Journal,* Summer 1999, pp. 303–43; Lorrie A. Shepard and Mary L. Smith, "Synthesis of Research on Grade Retention," *Educational Leadership,* May 1999, pp. 84–88; and C. Kenneth Tanner and F. Edward Combs, "Student Retention Policy: The Gap Between Research and Practice," *Journal of Research in Childhood Education,* Fall/Winter 1993, pp. 69–77.

22. Walt Haney, "The Myth of the Texas Miracle in Education," *Education Policy Analysis Archives,* August 2000, available at http://epaa.asu.edu/epaa/v8n41.

23. Ibid.

24. Joel H. Spring, *Political Agendas for Education: From the Christian Coalition to the Green Party* (Mahwah, N.J.: Erlbaum, 1997), p. 16.

25. Sandra Hofferth, "Healthy Environments, Healthy Children: Children in Families," University of Michigan Institute for Social Research, ERIC ED 426779, 1998.

26. Diane Loupe, "Value of Homework Comes Under Question," *Atlanta Constitution,* 22 April 1999, p. 5JA.

27. Harris Cooper, *Homework* (New York: Longman, 1989).

28. Etta Kralovec and John Buell, *The End of Homework: How Homework Disrupts Families, Overburdens Children, and Limits Learning* (Boston, Mass.: Beacon Press, 2000).

29. Donald B. Gratz, "High Standards for Whom?," *Phi Delta Kappan,* May 2000, pp. 681–87; and Anthony D. Pellegrini and Catherine M. Bohn, "The Role of Recess in Children's Cognitive Performance and School Adjustment," *Educational Researcher,* January/February 2005, pp. 13–19.

30. Susan Ohanian, *One Size Fits Few: The Folly of Educational Standards* (Portsmouth, N.H.: Heinemann, 2000), pp. 13–14.

31. Anne T. Lockwood, *Standards: From Policy to Practice* (Thousand Oaks, Calif.: Corwin, 2000).

32. Frank Smith, *The Book of Learning and Forgetting* (New York: Teachers College Press, 1998).

33. Alfie Kohn, *The Schools Our Children Deserve: Moving Beyond Traditional Classrooms and "Tougher Standards"* (Boston: Houghton Mifflin, 1999).

34. Marc S. Tucker and Judy B. Codding, *Standards for Our Schools: How to Set Them, Measure Them, and Reach Them* (San Francisco, Calif.: Jossey-Bass, 1998).

35. David Elkind, *The Hurried Child: Growing Up Too Fast, Too Soon,* rev. ed. (Reading, Mass.: Addison-Wesley, 1988), p. 3.

36. Pogrebin, op. cit.

37. Michael F. Heaney and Robert J. Michela, "Safe Schools: Hearing Past the Hype," *High School Magazine,* May/June 1999, pp. 14–17.

38. Lowell C. Rose and Alec M. Gallup, "The 37th Annual Phi Delta Kappa/ Gallup Poll of the Public's Attitudes Toward the Public Schools," *Phi Delta Kappan,* September 2005, p. 44.

39. Paul M. Kingery, Mark B. Coggeshall, and Aaron A. Alford, "Weapon Carrying by Youth: Risk Factors and Prevention," *Education and Urban Society,* May 1999, pp. 309–33.

40. James A. Fox and Jack Levin, "The Hard (but Doable) Job of Making Schools Safe," *Boston Globe,* 22 August 1999, pp. F-1, F-3.

41. Lilia I. Bartolome, "Beyond the Methods Fetish: Toward a Humanizing Pedagogy," *Harvard Educational Review,* Summer 1994, pp. 173–94; and Nancy Lesko, *Act Your Age! A Cultural Construction of Adolescence* (New York: Routledge, 2001).

42. Jonathan Kozol, "Confections of Apartheid: A Stick-and-Carrot Pedagogy for the Children of Our Inner-City Poor," *Phi Delta Kappan,* December 2005, pp. 264–75.

43. Christina Hoff Sommers and Sally Satel, *One Nation Under Therapy: How the Helping Culture Is Eroding Self-Reliance* (New York: St. Martin's Press, 2005).

44. Gary L. Adams and Siegfried Engelmann, *Research on Direct Instruction: 25 Years Beyond DISTAR* (Seattle: Educational Achievement Systems, 1996).

45. Kathleen Cushman, *Fires in the Bathroom: Advice for Teachers from High School Students* (New York: New Press, 2003).

46. Lynn Olson, "Report Points Out Lack of Clarity for High School Reforms," *Education Week,* 19 May 2004.

47. *School Climate in Boston's High Schools: What Students Say* (Boston, Mass.: Boston Plan for Excellence, 2004).

48. Students as Allies, *Breaking Ranks: Changing an American Institution* (Reston, Va.: National Association of Secondary School Principals, 1996).

CURT DUDLEY-MARLING is a professor of education at the Lynch School of Education, Boston College, Chestnut Hill, Mass., where **JANICE JACKSON** and **LISA PATEL STEVENS** are assistant professors.

UNIT 5

Development During Adolescence and Young Adulthood

Unit Selections

Key Points to Consider

- What evidence do you see of pop culture's influence of those you contact daily?

- What brain changes occur during adolescence? How do these changes affect behavior?

- What parental behaviors help ensure a peaceful adolescence?

- What leads young people to the life of the streets? How can they avoid that life, or once in it, get out of it?

- Should incarcerated adolescents continue their education in jail? What would a jail school teach?

- Why are college students so stressed-out? What can be done to reduce campus pressures?

- How do spiritual values impact the American psyche?

- Can brain power be boosted with drugs? If so, should it be?

- How can young adults who take "off-ramps" to care for children find appropriate new "on-ramps" to resume their careers?

Student Web Site

www.mhcls.com/online

Internet References

Further information regarding these Web sites may be found in this book's preface or online.

ADOL: Adolescent Directory On-Line
http://education.indiana.edu/cas/adol/adol.html

AMA—Adolescent Health On-Line
http://www.ama-assn.org/ama/pub/category/1947.html

American Academy of Child and Adolescent Psychiatry
http://www.aacap.org/

The term "adolescence" was coined in 1904 by G. Stanley Hall, one of the world's first psychologists. He saw adolescence as a discrete stage of life bridging the gap between sexual maturity (puberty) and socioemotional and cognitive maturity. He believed it to be characterized by "storm and stress." At the beginning of the twentieth century, it was typical for young men to begin working in middle childhood (there were no child labor laws), and for young women to become wives and mothers as soon as they were fertile and/or spoken for. At the turn of the twenty-first century, the beginning of adolescence is marked by the desire to be independent of parental control. The end of adolescence, which once coincided with the age of legal maturity (usually 16 or 18, depending on local laws), has now been extended upwards. Although legal maturity is now 18 (voting, enlisting in the armed services, owning property, marrying without permission), the social norm is to consider persons in their late teens as adolescents, not adults. The years between 18 and 21 are often problematic for youth tethered between adult and not-adult status. They can be married, with children, living in homes of their own, running their own businesses, yet not be able to drive their cars in certain places or at certain times. They can go to college and participate in social activities, but they cannot legally drink. Often the twenty-first birthday is viewed as a rite of passage into adulthood in the United States because it signals the legal right to buy and drink alcoholic beverages. "Maturity" is usually reserved for those who have achieved full economic as well as socioemotional independence as adults.

Erik Erikson, the personality theorist, marked the passage from adolescence to young adulthood by a change in the nuclear conflicts of two life stages: identity versus role confusion and intimacy versus isolation. Adolescents struggle to answer the question, "Who am I?" Young adults struggle to find a place within the existing social order where they can feel intimacy rather than isolation. In the 1960s, Erikson wrote that females resolve both their conflicts of identity and intimacy by living vicariously through their husbands, an unacceptable idea to many females today.

As adolescence has been extended, so too has young adulthood. One hundred years ago, life expectancy did not extend too far beyond menopause for women and retirement for men. Young adulthood began when adolescents finished puberty. Parents of teenagers were middle-aged, between 35 and 55. Later marriages and delayed childbearing have redefined the line between young adulthood and middle age. Many people today consider themselves young adults well into their 40s.

Jean Piaget, the cognitive theorist, marked the end of the development of mental processes with the end of adolescence. Once full physical maturity, including brain maturity, was achieved, one reached the acme of his or her abilities to assimilate, accommodate, organize, and adapt to sensations, perceptions, associations, and discriminations. Piaget did not feel cognitive processing of information ceased with adulthood. He believed, however, that cognitive judgments would not reach a stage higher than the abstract, hypothetical, logical reasoning of formal operations. Today many cognitive theorists believe postformal operations are possible.

The first article, "Parents or Pop Culture?," explores how parents, families, and minorities are portrayed in the popular culture and how those portrayals affect behaviors.

The second article, "A Peaceful Adolescence," addresses the G. Stanley Hall belief that adolescence was a stage of life marked by "storm and stress." While some teenagers do have conflicts with their parents, new research documents that many teenagers have peaceful passages through adolescence. The authors of this article, Barbara Kantrowitz and Karen Springen, report on what adults do to nurture successful teen years.

The third article, "Understanding Street Culture," examines conditions that lead youth to life on the street.

The fourth selection, "Jail Time Is Learning Time," describes efforts to help jailed youth acquire GED instruction and earn high school equivalency diplomas. The program described also teaches anger management and vocational/job skills. Many adolescents are incarcerated in the Unites States every year. They should not be forgotten.

The first article in the Young Adulthood portion of this unit, "How Spirit Blooms," describes the mid-20's faith journey of a woman raised in the Roman Catholic religion. It gives factual information about many contemporary spiritual belief systems, without being preachy. Readers will be stimulated to discuss many of Suzanne Clores' travel discoveries.

The second article of this unit reviews some of the ways in which neuroscientific discoveries may boost our brain power in the years to come. "The Battle for Your Brain" discusses the pros and cons of doing so. Bioethicists weigh in with their opinions about changing the human brain in order to improve mood, memory, intelligence, and perhaps more.

This unit ends with "Getting Back on Track," an exposition about adults who take time off from their career tracks to care for family. The "off-ramps" are not difficult. However, finding an appropriate "on-ramp" leading to a fulfilling job which utilizes the young adult's talents and education may be very troublesome. Daniel McGinn reports that some business schools are providing assistance. They are offering, or planning to offer, courses that teach about how to job hunt and/or jump-start a second career.

Parents or Pop Culture? Children's Heroes and Role Models

What kind of heroes a culture promotes reveals a great deal about that culture's values and desires.

KRISTIN J. ANDERSON AND DONNA CAVALLARO

One of the most important features of childhood and adolescence is the development of an identity. As children shape their behavior and values, they may look to heroes and role models for guidance. They may identify the role models they wish to emulate based on possession of certain skills or attributes. While the child may not want to be exactly like the person, he or she may see *possibilities* in that person. For instance, while Supreme Court Justice Ruth Bader Ginsberg may not necessarily directly influence girls and young women to become lawyers, her presence on the Supreme Court may alter beliefs about who is capable of being a lawyer or judge (Gibson & Cordova, 1999).

Parents and other family members are important role models for children, particularly early on. Other influences may be institutional, such as schools, or cultural, such as the mass media. What kind of heroes a culture promotes reveals a great deal about the culture's values and desires. Educators not only can model important behaviors themselves, but also can teach about values, events, and people that a culture holds dear.

Television, movies, computer games, and other forms of media expose children to an endless variety of cultural messages. Which ones do children heed the most? Whom do children want to be like? Do their role models vary according to children's ethnicity and gender? Finally, what role can educators play in teaching children about role models they may never have considered?

This article examines the impact of the mass media on children's choices of heroes and role models. The authors address the questions posed above in light of results from a survey and focus groups conducted with children ages 8 to 13.

The Menu of Pop Culture Choices
Television and Film for Children

Male characters—cartoon or otherwise—continue to be more prevalent in children's television and film than female characters. Gender-stereotyped behaviors continue to be the norm. For instance, male characters are more commonly portrayed as independent, assertive, athletic, important, attractive, technical, and responsible than female characters. They show more ingenuity, anger, leadership, bravery, and aggression, and they brag, interrupt, make threats, and even laugh more than female characters do. In fact, since male characters appear so much more frequently than female characters, they do more of almost *everything* than female characters. Also, while the behavior of female characters is somewhat less stereotypical than it was 20 years ago, in some ways male characters behave *more* stereotypically than 20 years ago (for instance, males are now in more leadership roles, are more bossy, and are more intelligent) (Thompson & Zerbinos, 1995). These gender-stereotyped images, and the inflexibility of male characters' roles, make for a restricted range of role models.

Parents, educators, and policymakers are also concerned about the aggressive and violent content in children's programs. Gerbner (1993) studied the violent content of children's programs and observed that "despite all the mayhem, only 3.2% of Saturday morning characters suffer any injury"; thus, children do not learn about the likely consequences of aggressive action. In children's shows, bad characters are punished 59 percent of the time. Even more telling, good characters who engage in violence are punished only 18 percent of the time. The characters that might be the most appealing to kids—the heroes and protagonists—rarely feel remorse, nor are they reprimanded or impeded when they engage in violence (National Television Violence Study, 1998). The authors found that 77 percent of the children surveyed watch television every day. Thus, many children may be learning to use violence as a problem-solving tool.

Characters in animated films also tend to follow stereotypes. While some positive changes in the portrayal of ethnic minority and female characters can be noted, both groups often remain narrowly defined in children's animated films. In his discussion of Disney films, Henry Giroux (1997) notes how the villains in the film *Aladdin* are racially stereotyped. The main character, Aladdin, the hero of the film, is drawn with very light skin, European features, and no accent. Yet the villains in the story appear as Middle Eastern caricatures: they have beards, large noses, sinister eyes, heavy accents, and swords. *Pocahontas,* who in real life was a young Native American girl, was portrayed by Disney as a brown-skinned, Barbie-like supermodel with an hourglass figure (Giroux, 1997). Consequently, animated characters, even those based on historical record, are either stereotyped or stripped of any meaningful sign of ethnicity. Fortunately, educators have the power to counter such unrealistic images with more accurate representations of historical characters.

Real-Life Television Characters

While some progress can be seen in the representation of ethnic minorities on television, the late 1990s actually brought a decrease in the number of people of color on prime time programming. In 1998, only 19 percent of Screen Actors Guild roles went to people of color. Roles for African American, Latinos, and Native Americans decreased from 1997 to 1998 (Screen Actors Guild [SAG], 1999). Women make up fewer than 40 percent of the characters in prime time. Female characters tend to be younger than male characters, conveying the message to viewers that women's youthfulness is more highly valued than other qualities. In terms of work roles, however, female characters' occupations are now less stereotyped, while male characters' occupations continue to be stereotyped (Signorielli & Bacue, 1999). This research

suggests that girls' potential role models are somewhat less gender-stereotyped than before, while boy's potential role models are as narrowly defined as ever.

From Comic Book to Playground

Superheroes are the larger-than-life symbols of American values and "maleness." Perhaps the medium in which superheroes are most classically represented is comic books, which date back to the 1930s. The role of the hero is central to the traditional comic book. While female superheroes can be found in comics today (e.g., Marvel Girl, Phoenix, Shadow Cat, Psylocke), they represent only a small proportion—about 24 percent of Marvel Universe superhero trading cards (Young, 1993). Moreover, women and people of color do not fare well in superhero comics. To the extent that female characters exist, they often appear as victims and nuisances. People of color are marginalized as well. African American and Native American characters are more likely to be portrayed as villains, victims, or simply incompetent than as powerful and intelligent (Pecora, 1992).

One indirect way to gauge the impact of role models on children is to examine the nature of superhero play. Superhero play involving imitation of media characters with superhuman powers is more prevalent among boys than girls (Bell & Crosbie, 1996). This might be a function of the mostly male presence of superhero characters in comics and on television, or it may be due to girls receiving more sanctions from parents and teachers against playing aggressively. Children's imitations of superheroes in play concerns many classroom teachers, because it usually involves chasing, wrestling, kicking, and mock battles. Some researchers argue that superhero play may serve an important developmental function by offering children a sense of power in a world dominated by adults, thus giving children a means of coping with their frustrations. Superhero play also may allow children to grapple with ideas of good and evil and encourage them to work through their own anxieties about safety. Such play also may help children safely express anger and aggression (Boyd, 1997).

Other researchers and educators express concern that superhero play may legitimize aggression, endanger participants, and encourage stereotypical male dominance (Bell & Crosbie, 1996). One researcher observed children's superhero play in a school setting and found that boys created more superhero stories than girls did, and that girls often were excluded from such play. When girls were included they were given stereotypical parts, such as helpers or victims waiting to be saved. Even powerful female X-Men characters were made powerless in the boys' adaptations (Dyson, 1994). Thus, without teacher intervention or an abundance of female superheroes, superhero play may only serve to reinforce gender stereotypes.

One way to gauge popular culture's influence on superhero play is to compare the kind of play children engaged in before and after the arrival of television. In one retrospective study (French & Pena, 1991), adults between the ages of 17 and 83 provided information about their favorite childhood play themes, their heroes, and the qualities of those heroes. While certain methodological pitfalls common to retrospective studies were unavoidable, the findings are nevertheless intriguing. People who grew up before television reported engaging in less fantasy hero play and playing more realistically than kids who grew up with television. While media was the main source of heroes for kids who grew up with television, the previous generations found their heroes not only from the media, but also from direct experience, friends/siblings, and parents' occupations (French & Pena, 1991).

Recent Media Forms: Music Television and Video Games

Video games and music television videos are relatively recent forms of media. In a recent poll, girls and boys from various ethnic backgrounds reported that television and music were their favorite forms of media (Children Now, 1999). What messages about race/ethnicity and gender emerge from music videos—the seemingly perfect merger of children's favorite two media? Seidman (1999) found that the majority of characters were white (63 percent) and a majority were male (63 percent). When people of color, especially women of color, appeared in a video, their characters were much less likely to hold white collar jobs. In fact, their occupations were more gender-stereotyped than in real life. Gender role behavior overall was stereotypical. Thus, music television is yet another domain that perpetuates racial and gender stereotypes.

In the survey described below, the authors found that nearly half (48 percent) of the children surveyed played video and computer games every day or almost every day. Boys, however, were much more likely than girls to play these games. Of those who play computer/video games every day or almost every day, 76 percent are boys and only 24 percent are girls. Consequently, girls and boys might be differentially influenced by the images represented in video and computer games.

What *are* the images presented in video and computer games? Dietz's (1998) content analysis of popular video and computer games found that 79 percent of the games included aggression or violence. Only 15 percent of the games showed women as heroes or action characters. Indeed, girls and women generally were *not* portrayed—30 percent of the videos did not include girls or women at all. When female characters were included, 21 percent of the time they were the damsel in distress. Other female characters were portrayed as evil or as obstacles. This research points to at least two implications of these games. First, girls may not be interested in playing these video and computer games, because the implicit message is that girls are not welcome as players, and that girls and women can only hope to be saved, destroyed, or pushed aside (see also Signorielli, 2001). Second, these images of girls and women found in video and computer games may influence boys' perceptions of gender.

In the past few years, a growing number of computer and video games geared toward girls have been made available by companies such as Purple Moon and Girl Games. These games have adventurous content without the violence typical of games geared toward boys. Two of the best-selling computer games for girls, however, have been *Cosmopolitan Virtual Makeover* and *Barbie Fashion Designer*. While these games may encourage creativity, ultimately their focus is on beauty. One columnist addresses the dilemma of creating games that will appeal to girls while fostering creativity and ingenuity:

> A girl given a doll is being told, "Girls play with dolls just like mommies take care of babies." A boy given a computer game is being told, "Boys play with computers just like daddies use them for work." A girl given *Barbie Fashion Designer* is being told, "Girls play with computers just like girls play with dolls." A lucky few might get the message that, as some girls exchange dolls for real babies, others might progress from *Barbie Fashion Designer* to real-life fashion designer, or engineering systems designer, or software designer. But there's a good chance that many will not. (Ivinski, 1997, p. 28)

As more and more educators begin using the Internet, CD-ROMS, and videos as teaching tools (Risko, 1999), they will be faced with the challenge of finding materials that fairly represent a wide range of characters, people, and behavior. Paradoxically, the use of "new" technology, such as CD-ROMs and computer games, implies that a student is going to enjoy a progressive, cutting-edge experience. However, educators must be vigilant about the content, as they should be with any textbook or film. The cutting-edge format of these new technologies does not guarantee nonstereotyped material.

A Survey of Children's Role Models and Heroes

Whom do children actually choose as role models, and why? The authors surveyed children about their heroes and role models, both people they know and famous people or imaginary characters. Survey questions also addressed children's interaction with television, film, computer/video games, books, and comic books. The children talked about their answers in small groups. One hundred and seventy-nine children, ages 8 to 13, were surveyed from five day camp sites in central and southern California. The ethnic breakdown of the survey sample was as follows: 24 African Americans, 31 Asian Americans, 74 Latinos, 1 Middle Eastern American, 2 Native Americans, 45 whites, and 2 "other." Ninety-five girls and 84 boys participated. The samples of ethnic and gender categories were then weighted so that each of these demographic groups, when analyzed, reflects their actual contribution to the total population of children in the United States.

Do Children Admire People They Know or Famous People?

The survey began with the following: "We would like to know whom you look up to and admire. These might be people you know, or they might be famous people or characters. You may want to be like them or you might just think they are cool." More respondents described a person they knew (65 percent) rather than a person they did not know, such as a person or character in the media (35 percent). When asked in focus groups why they picked people they knew instead of famous people, one 10-year-old white girl said, "I didn't put down people I don't know because when nobody's paying attention, they do something bad." Another student said, "Some [media figures] are just not nice. Some famous people act good on TV but they're really horrible." Thus, some children employed a level of skepticism when judging the worthiness of a role model.

Figure 1 represents the percentages of role models the children knew versus media heroes they identified. Similar to the overall sample, 70 percent of the African American and 64 percent of the White children chose people they knew as heroes. In contrast, only 35 percent of the Asian American kids and 49 percent of the Latino kids named people they knew. This latter finding seems paradoxical; Asian American and Latino children

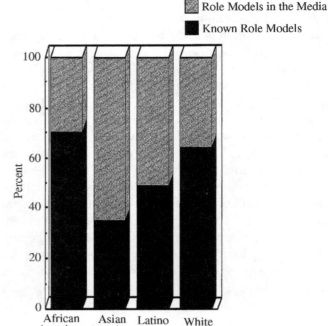

Figure 1 **Percentages of Known Role Models and Media Role Models**

would seem more likely to choose people they know as role models because their ethnic groups are represented less frequently in mass media than are African Americans and whites. Perhaps Asian American and Latino children have internalized a message that they should not look up to fellow Asian Americans or Latinos as role models, or it may be a byproduct of assimilation. Obviously, further work in this area is needed.

On average, responses from girls and boys differed. While both girls and boys named people they knew as their heroes, 67 percent of the girls did so as compared with only 58 percent of the boys. Since boys and men are seen more frequently as sports stars, actors, and musicians, girls may have a smaller pool of potential role models from which to choose. Another factor might be that the girls in this study reported watching less television than the boys did, and so they may have known fewer characters. Sixty-seven percent of the girls reported watching television one hour a day or more, while 87 percent of the boys reported watching television this amount.

Do Children Choose Role Models Who Are Similar to Themselves?

One feature of role modeling is that children tend to choose role models whom they find relevant and with whom they can compare themselves (Lockwood & Kunda, 2000).

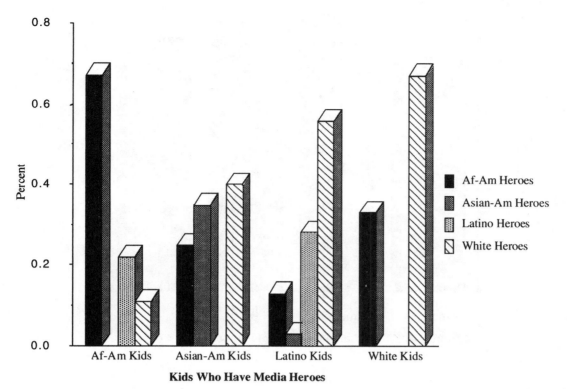

Figure 2   Ethnicity of Media Heroes

Children who do not "see themselves" in the media may have fewer opportunities to select realistic role models. Two ways to assess similarity is to consider the ethnicity and gender of children's chosen role models. Do children tend to select heroes who are of their same ethnic background? Because data was not available on the ethnic background of the reported role models whom the children knew personally, the authors examined only the heroes from the media, whose backgrounds were known, to explore this question (see Figure 2). African American and white children were more likely to have media heroes of their same ethnicity (67 percent for each). In contrast, Asian American and Latino children chose more white media heroes than other categories (40 percent and 56 percent, respectively). Only 35 percent of the Asian Americans respondents, and 28 percent of the Latino respondents, chose media heroes of their own ethnicity.

How can we explain the fact that African American and white children are more likely to have media heroes of their same ethnicity, compared to Asian American and Latino children? There is no shortage of white characters for white children to identify with in television and film, and African Americans now make up about 14 percent of television and theatrical characters (SAG, 2000). While African American characters are represented less frequently than white characters, their representation on television, film, and music television is much higher than for Asian American and Latino characters (e.g., Asians represent 2.2 percent, and Latinos represent 4.4 percent, of television and film characters) (SAG, 2000). Also, fewer famous athletes are Asian American or Latino, compared to African American or white.

Also of interest was whether children choose role models of the same, or other, gender. Overall, children in this study more often chose a same-gender person as someone they look up to and admire. This pattern is consistent across all four ethnic groups, and stronger for boys than girls. Only 6 percent of the boys chose a girl or woman, while 24 percent of the girls named a boy or man. Asian American boys actually picked male heroes exclusively. Asian American girls chose the fewest female role models (55 percent) compared to the other girls (see Figure 3). These findings associated with Asian American children present a particular challenge for educators. Asian Americans, and particularly Asian American women, are seldom presented as heroes in textbooks. This is all the more reason for schools to provide a broader and more diverse range of potential role models.

At the same time, it has been reported that boys will tend to imitate those who are powerful (Gibson & Cordova, 1999). Thus, while boys tend to emulate same-gender models more than girls do, boys may emulate a woman if

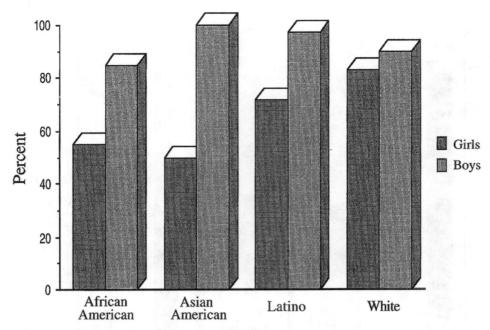

Figure 3   Children Who Have Same-Gender Role Models

she is high in social power. Therefore, boys may be especially likely to have boys and men as role models because they are more likely to be portrayed in positions of power. It also has been noted that college-age women select men *and* women role models with the same frequency, whereas college-age men still tend to avoid women role models. The fact that young women choose both genders as role models might be a result of the relative scarcity of women in powerful positions to serve as role models (Gibson & Cordova, 1999).

Who Are Children's Role Models and Heroes?

Overall, children most frequently (34 percent) named their parents as role models and heroes. The next highest category (20 percent) was entertainers; in descending order, the other categories were friends (14 percent), professional athletes (11 percent), and acquaintances (8 percent). Authors and historical figures were each chosen by only 1 percent of the children.

Patterns were somewhat different when ethnicity was taken into account. African American and white children chose a parent more frequently (30 percent and 33 percent, respectively). In contrast, Asian Americans and Latinos chose entertainers (musicians, actors, and television personalities) most frequently (39 percent for Asian Americans and 47 percent for Latinos), with parents coming in

second place. When gender was taken into account, both girls and boys most frequently mentioned a parent (girls 29 percent, boys 34 percent), while entertainers came in second place. Figure 4 illustrates these patterns.

When taking both ethnicity and gender into account, the researchers found that Asian American and Latina girls most frequently picked entertainers (50 percent of the Asian American girls and 41 percent of the Latinas), while African American and white girls chose parents (33 percent and 29 percent, respectively). Asian American boys most frequently named a professional athlete (36 percent), African American boys most frequently picked a parent (30 percent), Latino boys most frequently chose entertainers (54 percent), and white boys picked parents (38 percent).

What Qualities About Their Role Models and Heroes Do Children Admire?

When asked why they admired their heroes and role models, the children most commonly replied that the person was nice, helpful, and understanding (38 percent). Parents were appreciated for their generosity, their understanding, and for "being there." For instance, an 11-year-old African American girl who named her mother as her hero told us, "I like that she helps people when they're in a time of need." Parents were also praised for the lessons they teach

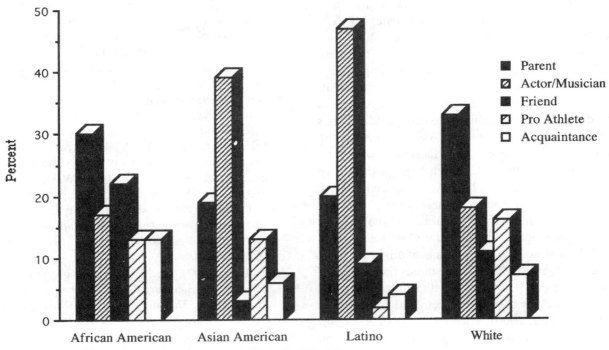

Figure 4 **Most Frequently Chosen Role Models By Ethnicity**

their kids. A 9-year-old Asian American boy told us, "I like my dad because he is always nice and he teaches me."

The second most admired feature of kids' role models was skill (27 percent). The skills of athletes and entertainers were most often mentioned. One 12-year-old white boy said he admires Kobe Bryant because "he's a good basketball player and because he makes a good amount of money." A 10-year-old Asian American girl chose Tara Lipinski because "she has a lot of courage and is a great skater." A 9-year-old Latino boy picked Captain America and said, "What I like about Captain America is his cool shield and how he fights the evil red skull." The third most frequently mentioned characteristic was a sense of humor (9 percent), which was most often attributed to entertainers. For instance, a 10-year-old Latino boy picked Will Smith "because he's funny. He makes jokes and he dances funny."

These findings held true for children in all four ethnic groups and across the genders, with two exceptions: boys were more likely than girls to name athletes for their skill, and entertainers for their humor. Given the media attention to the U.S. women's soccer team victory in the World Cup in 1999, and the success of the WNBA (the women's professional basketball league), the researchers expected girls to name women professional athletes as their heroes. However, only four girls in the study did so. Despite recent strides in the visibility of women's sports,

the media continue to construct men's sports as the norm and women's sports as marginal (e.g., references to men's athletics as "sports" and women's athletics as "women's sports").

When children's heroes were media characters, African American and white children were more likely to name media heroes of their same ethnicity. In contrast, Asian American and Latino children tended to name media heroes who were not of their same ethnicity.

Summary and Implications

Whether the children in this study had heroes they knew in real life, or whether they chose famous people or fictional characters, depended, to some extent, on the respondents' ethnicity and gender. Overall, however, the most frequently named role model for kids was a parent. This is good news for parents, who must wonder, given the omnipresence of the media, whether they have any impact at all on their children. Popular culture was a significant source of heroes for children as well. Entertainers were the second most frequently named role models for the children, and the number increases significantly if you add professional athletes to that category. The attributes that children valued depended on whom they chose. For instance, children who named parents named them because they are helpful and understanding. Media characters were chosen because of their skills. When children's heroes were media characters, African American and white children were more likely to name media heroes of their same ethnicity. In contrast, Asian American and Latino children tended to name media heroes who were not of their same ethnicity. Children kept to their own gender when choosing a hero; boys were especially reluctant to choose girls and women as their heroes.

The frequency with which boys in this study named athletes as their role models is noteworthy. Only four girls in the study did the same. The implications of this gender difference are important, because many studies find that girls' participation in sports is associated with a number of positive attributes, such as high self-esteem and self-efficacy (Richman & Shaffer, 2000). Therefore, school and community support of girls' athletic programs and recognition of professional women athletes would go a long way to encourage girls' participation in sports, as well as boys' appreciation of women athletes as potential role models.

The mass media are hindered by a narrow view of gender, and by limited, stereotyped representations of ethnic minorities. Parents and educators must take pains to expose children to a wider variety of potential role models than popular culture does. Historical figures and authors constituted a tiny minority of heroes named by the children surveyed. Educators can play a significant role by exposing students to a wide range of such historical heroes, including people from various professions, people of color, and women of all races.

Finally, educators could capitalize on children's need for guidance to expose them to a greater variety of role models. Doing so affirms for the children that their race and gender are worthy of representation. A variety of potential heroes and role models allows children to appreciate themselves and the diversity in others.

References

Bell, R., & Crosbie, C. (1996, November 13). Superhero play of 3-to 5-year-old children. Available: http://labyrinth.net.au/~cccav/ sept97/superhero.html.

Boyd, B. J. (1997). Teacher response to superhero play: To ban or not to ban. *Childhood Education, 74,* 23–28.

Children Now. (1999, September). *Boys to men: Messages about masculinity.* Oakland, CA: Author.

Dietz, T. L. (1998). An examination of violence and gender role portrayals in video games: Implications for gender socialization. *Sex Roles, 38,* 425–433.

Dyson, A. H. (1994). The ninjas, the X-men, and the ladies: Playing with power and identity in an urban primary school. *Teachers College Record, 96,* 219–239.

French, J., & Pena, S. (1991). Children's hero play of the 20th century: Changes resulting from television's influence. *Child Study Journal, 21,* 79–94.

Gerbner, G. (1993). *Women and minorities on television: A study in casting and fate.* A report to the Screen Actors Guild and the American Federation of Radio and Television Artists, Philadelphia: The Annenberg School of Communication, University of Pennsylvania.

Gibson, D. E., & Cordova, D. I. (1999). Women's and men's role models: The importance of exemplars. In A. J. Murrell, F. J. Crosby, & R. J. Ely (Eds.), *Mentoring dilemmas: Developmental relationships within multicultural organizations* (pp. 121–141). Mahwah, NJ: Lawrence Erlbaum Associates.

Giroux, H. A. (1997). Are Disney movies good for your kids? In S. R. Steinberg & J. L. Kincheloe (Eds.), *Kinderculture: The corporate construction of childhood* (pp. 53–67). Boulder, CO: Westview Press.

Ivinski, P. (1997). Game girls: Girl market in computer games and educational software. *Print, 51,* 24–29.

Lockwood, P., & Kunda, Z. (2000). Outstanding role models: Do they inspire or demoralize us? In A. Tesser, R. B. Felson, et al. (Eds.), *Psychological perspectives on self and identity* (pp. 147–171). Washington, DC: American Psychological Association.

National Television Violence Study. Vol. 3. (1998). Thousand Oaks, CA: Sage.

Pecora, N. (1992). Superman/superboys/supermen: The comic book hero as socializing agent. In S. Craig (Ed.), *Men, masculinity, and the media* (pp. 61–77). Newbury Park, CA: Sage.

Richman, E. L., & Shaffer, D. R. (2000). "If you let me play sports": How might sport participation influence the self-esteem of adolescent females? *Psychology of Women Quarterly, 24,* 189–199.

Risko, V. J. (1999). The power and possibilities of video technology and intermediality. In L. Semali & A. Watts Pailliotet (Eds.), *Intermediality: The teachers' handbook of critical media literacy* (pp. 129–140). Boulder, CO: Westview Press.

Screen Actors Guild. (1999, May 3). *New Screen Actors Guild employment figures reveal a decline in roles for Latinos, African American and Native American Indian performers.* Press Release. Available: www.sag.org.

Screen Actors Guild. (2000, December 20). *Screen Actors Guild employment statistics reveal percentage increases in available roles for African Americans and Latinos, but total number of roles to minorities decrease in 1999.* Press Release. Available: www.sag.org.

Seidman, S. A. (1999). Revisiting sex-role stereotyping in MTV videos. *International Journal of Instructional Media, 26,* 11.

Signorielli, N. (2001). Television's gender role images and contribution to stereotyping: Past, present, future. In D. G. Singer & J. L. Singer (Eds.), *Handbook of children and the media* (pp. 341–358). Thousand Oaks, CA: Sage.

Signorielli, N., & Bacue, A. (1999). Recognition and respect: A content analysis of prime-time television characters across three decades. *Sex Roles, 40,* 527–544.

Thompson, T. L., & Zerbinos, E. (1995). Gender roles in animated cartoons: Has the picture changed in 20 years? *Sex Roles, 32,* 651–673.

Young, T. J. (1993). Women as comic book superheroes: The "weaker sex" in the Marvel universe. *Psychology: A Journal of Human Behavior, 30,* 49–50.

KRISTIN J. ANDERSON is Assistant Professor, Psychology and Women's Studies, Antioch College, Yellow Springs, Ohio. **DONNA CAVALLARO** is graduate student, counseling psychology, Santa Clara University, Santa Clara, California.

Authors' Notes—This project was conducted in conjunction with Mediascope, a not-for-profit media education organization. The terms "hero" and "role model" tend to be used interchangeably in the literature. When a distinction between the terms is made, role models are defined as known persons (e.g., parents, teachers) and heroes are defined as figures who may be less attainable, or larger than life. Both kinds of persons and figures are of interest here; therefore, the terms are used interchangeably, and we specify whether known people or famous figures are being discussed.

A Peaceful Adolescence

The teen years don't have to be a time of family storm and stress. Most kids do just fine and now psychologists are finding out why that is.

BARBARA KANTROWITZ AND KAREN SPRINGEN

At 17, Amanda Hund is a straight-A student who loves competing in horse shows. The high school junior from Willmar, Minn., belongs to her school's band, orchestra and choir. She regularly volunteers through her church and recently spent a week working in an orphanage in Jamaica. Usually, however, she's closer to home, where her family eats dinner together every night. She also has a weekly breakfast date with her father, a doctor, at a local coffee shop. Amanda credits her parents for her relatively easy ride through adolescence. "My parents didn't sweat the small stuff," she says. "They were always very open. You could ask any question."

Is the Hund family for real? Didn't they get the memo that says teens and their parents are supposed to be at odds until . . . well, until forever? Actually, they're very much for real, and according to scientists who study the transition to adulthood, they represent the average family's experience more accurately than all those scary TV movies about out-of-control teens. "Research shows that most young people go through adolescence having good relationships with their parents, adopting attitudes and values consistent with their parents' and end up getting out of the adolescent period and becoming good citizens," says Richard Lerner, Bergstrom chair of applied developmental science at Tufts University. This shouldn't be news—but it is, largely because of widespread misunderstanding of what happens during the teen years. It's a time of transition, just like the first year of parenthood or menopause. And although there are dramatic hormonal and physical changes during this period, catastrophe is certainly not preordained. A lot depends on youngsters' innate natures combined with the emotional and social support they get from the adults around them. In other words, parents do matter.

The roots of misconceptions about teenagers go back to the way psychologists framed the field of adolescent development a century ago. They were primarily looking for explanations of why things went wrong. Before long, the idea that this phase was a period of storm and stress made its way into the popular consciousness. But in the last 15 years, developmental scientists have begun to re-examine these assumptions. Instead of focusing on kids who battle their way through the teen years, they're studying the dynamics of success.

At the head of the pack are Lerner and his colleagues, who are in the midst of a major project that many other researchers are following closely. It's a six-year longitudinal study of exactly what it takes to turn out OK and what adults can do to nurture those behaviors. "Parents and sometimes kids themselves often talk about positive development as the absence of bad," says Lerner. "What we're trying to do is present a different vision and a different vocabulary for young people and parents."

The first conclusions from the 4-H Study of Positive Youth Development, published in the February issue of The Journal of Early Adolescence, show that there are quantifiable personality traits possessed by all adolescents who manage to get to adulthood without major problems. Psychologists have labeled these traits "the 5 Cs": competence, confidence, connection, character and caring. These characteristics theoretically lead to a sixth C, contribution (similar to civic engagement). The nomenclature grows out of observations in recent years by a number of clinicians, Lerner says, but his study is the first time researchers have measured how these characteristics influence successful growth.

The 5 Cs are interconnected, not isolated traits, Lerner says. For example, competence refers not just to academic ability but also to social and vocational skills. Confidence includes self-esteem as well as the belief that you can make a difference in the world. The value of the study, Lerner says, is that when it is completed next year, researchers will have a way to quantify these characteristics and eventually determine what specific social and educational programs foster them.

During these years, parents should stay involved as they help kids move on.

In the meantime, parents can learn a lot from this rethinking of the teen years. Don't automatically assume that your kids become alien beings when they leave middle school. They still care what their parents think and they still need love and guidance—although in a different form. Temple University psychology professor Laurence Steinberg, author of "The Ten Basic Principles of Good Parenting," compares raising kids to building a boat that you eventually launch. Parents have to build a strong underpinning so their kids are equipped to face whatever's ahead. In the teen years, that means staying involved as you slowly let go. "One of the things that's natural in adolescence is that kids are going to pull away from their parents as they become increasingly interested in peers," says Steinberg. "It's important for parents to hang in there, for them not to pull back in response to that."

Communication is critical. "Stay in touch with your kids and make sure they feel valued and appreciated," advises Suniya Luthar, professor of clinical and developmental psychology at Columbia University. Even if they roll their eyes when you try to hug them, they still need direct displays of affection, she says. They also need help figuring out goals and limits. Parents should monitor their kids' activities and get to know their friends. Luthar says parents should still be disciplinarians and set standards such as curfews. Then teens need to know that infractions will be met with consistent consequences.

Adolescents are often critical of their parents but they're also watching them closely for clues on how to function in the outside world. Daniel Perkins, associate professor of family and youth resiliency at Penn State, says he and his wife take their twins to the local Ronald McDonald House and serve dinner to say thank you for time the family spent there when the children had health problems after birth. "What we've done already is set up the notion that we were blessed and need to give back, even if it's in a small way." That kind of example sets a standard youngsters remember, even if it seems like they're not paying attention.

Parents should provide opportunities for kids to explore the world and even find a calling. Teens who have a passion for something are more likely to thrive. "They have a sense of purpose beyond day-to-day teenage life," says David Marcus, author of "What It Takes to Pull Me Through." Often, he says,

kids who were enthusiastic about something in middle school lose enthusiasm in high school because the competition gets tougher and they're not as confident. Parents need to step in and help young people find other outlets. The best way to do that is to regularly spend uninterrupted time with teens (no cell phones). Kids also need to feel connected to other adults they trust and to their communities. Teens who get into trouble are "drifting," he says. "They don't have a web of people watching out for them."

Teens should build support webs of friends and adults.

At some point during these years, teen-agers should also be learning to build their own support networks—a skill that will be even more important when they're on their own. Connie Flanagan, a professor of youth civic development at Penn State, examines how kids look out for one another. "What we're interested in is how they help one another avoid harm," she says. In one of her focus groups, some teenage girls mentioned that they decided none would drink from an open can at a party because they wouldn't know for sure what they were drinking. "Even though you are experimenting, you're essentially doing it in a way that you protect one another," Flanagan says. Kids who don't make those kinds of connections are more likely to get in trouble because there's no one their own age or older to stop them from going too far. Like any other stage of life, adolescence can be tough. But teens and families can get through it—as long as they stick together.

With Julie Scelfo

Understanding Street Culture
A Prevention Perspective

JERRY FEST

Perhaps the greatest challenge we've faced as a nation in dealing with youth homelessness is recognizing the nature of the work that we are doing. In our efforts to secure funding and come to terms with the complexity of issues we often are led by our terminology. Labels such as "homeless" and "at-risk" youth guide our interventions through socio-economic or environmental filters. If the problem is that they are homeless, then the solution is to find them a home. If they are at-risk, then we alter their environment to remove or minimize the risk.

The problem is that being "on the streets" is not a socioeconomic condition or environmental circumstance. It is a way of thinking about yourself and your relationship to the world. It is identification with a defined culture that is separate and distinct from the dominant culture of adults. Recognizing the cultural environment in which homeless youth live is the key to successful interventions with this population. Understanding that you are doing cross-cultural work when reaching out to homeless youth is the most important prerequisite for successful outcomes.

The Culture of the Streets

In my work with homeless youth I have received quite an education on the culture of the streets. "Street Culture" is not a catch-phrase or an interesting way of looking at street-related issues. Rather, it is a definable culture that is every bit as real as any other culture you'll encounter. What is it that defines a culture? A culture will have beliefs, values, and principles that are shared by the culture's members. It will have defined patterns of behaviors and mores, a "code of conduct" that governs how things are done with distinct taboos and political do's and don'ts. There will be a sense of history with often-told stories, traditions, and ethical standards. All of these things exist for young people on the streets in such an identifiable form that I have been able to compile a description for use by youth workers in a manual titled *Street Culture: An epistemology of street-dependent youth.*

When the culture of the streets is defined and programs realize that the nature of their work is cross-cultural, it changes the focus of the services we offer. The most important factor in helping youth transition out of street life lies not in meeting basic physical needs (food, clothing, shelter, etc.), it lies in addressing conceptual needs. The "streets" aren't under a youth's feet, they're under a youth's scalp. Unless we reach out with a cross-cultural awareness and address conceptual needs, we can provide all the food, clothing, and shelter money can buy, but we are unlikely to see any significant behavioral changes.

The culture of the streets is a factor in youth homelessness that is so defined as to be universal. While regional differences exist, programs across the United States, as well as programs in other parts of the world such as Norway, Guam, Australia, Israel, Turkey, and South Korea find the information in *Street Culture* applicable to the homeless youth they serve. The reason is that while national cultures may be vastly different, the life experiences of youth on the streets are strikingly similar. Take for example the following quotes from an article in a Portland, Oregon newspaper, written about a shelter for runaway girls:

- "Girls fleeing brutal homes find a haven that helps them avoid lives of drugs, crime and prostitution."
- "For years, (we) chose to ignore the problem of . . . runaway youth. But as more and more children have taken to the streets—and fallen prey to prostitution, crime and addiction to cheap and plentiful heroin—(we've) had no choice but to act."
- "Divorce, addiction, poverty and the bizarre demands of parents are the main causes of runaways," said the 30-year-old manager of . . . the shelter . . . "There are parents who force their children to steal money for their heroin addiction. There are parents who brutally beat their children."
- "We don't want to leave them on the streets because they'll end up as prostitutes . . . We are making a long-term investment (in) these girls."

These quotes could come from a description of any shelter anywhere in the United States. The title of the article, however, was "Shelter Serves as Lone Escape for Abused Iranian Runaways." The shelter is located in Tehran, Iran.

Understanding that you are doing cross-cultural work when reaching out to homeless youth is the most important prerequisite for successful outcomes.

While recognizing the dynamics of street culture has important application to intervention efforts, it also gives us valuable insight into prevention efforts. This prevention element may even be more important since the problem with intervention is that it's not useful until youth are already on the streets. The question becomes what can street culture teach us that will help us prevent youth from ending up on the streets in the first place? The first lesson may be a somewhat controversial assertion.

There Are Elements of Choice in Street Involvement

It is far easier for adult helpers to see youth on the streets as victims of circumstances beyond their control. To a great extent that may be true. The childhood abuse and neglect that most have experienced was neither under their control, nor are they in any way responsible for it. But while we often have neither control over—nor choices about—the circumstances of our lives, we do have control over how we respond to those circumstances.

Psychologist Nathanial Brandon tells the story of two sons of an alcoholic father—one who became an alcoholic himself, the other who did not. When asked separately why they did or did not drink, both sons gave the same response—"that's easy, I grew up watching my father." While they both had the same childhood circumstances, they responded to those circumstances in dramatically different ways.

This helps to explain why "cause and effect" research statistics have not been very helpful in prevention efforts. Most programs will support statistics that show 80% or more of juveniles involved in prostitution were sexually abused as children. What these statistics don't tell us is why the other 20% are out there, and why there are vastly greater numbers of sexually abused children who do not become involved in street prostitution. Yes, we are products of our environments, but we are conscious products of these environments and we make choices. Our choices will naturally be strongly impacted by our life experience and the options we perceive as available to us, but they will be choices nonetheless.

We do street youth a disservice when we see them as hapless victims. They have been and continue to be victimized in their lives, but a "victim" does not survive on the streets. If we fail to recognize the role that choice plays in their street involvement, then we will fail to utilize their ability to make different choices, and fail to come up with viable alternatives to the choices they are making. Even more important, we will continue to fail in our efforts to prevent young people from making the choice to become street-involved in the first place.

Why Youth Choose the Streets

If we accept that becoming street-involved involves a level of choice, then the question becomes what is the attraction of that choice? The reality of life on the streets is not a pleasant one. It is a violent and unglamorous world of drugs and prostitution. It is a daily struggle for survival—often survival in a literal sense—where you are cold and hungry far more often than you are comfortable. You are living outside of society and the law with little future and a present filled with fear. It is a lifestyle that I once heard described as endless hours of excruciating boredom punctuated by moments of extreme terror. Why would anyone choose this?

Help from others was a critical factor in being able to resolve problems they faced.

The answer can be found in what the culture of the streets offers in a developmental sense. All young people experience a natural process of development where they are seeking ways to meet their basic physical and social needs. These needs include developing a sense of connection and commitment to others, a sense of belonging, and a perception that one has some control over their life. Youth who have had the benefit of a healthy childhood and the support of a stable and loving family are able

Case Study—Robbie

Robbie was 17 when he decided to drop out of school and get a job. His father agreed to let him go on living at home for $80 a week. But when Robbie decided to re-enroll in school and couldn't keep up the payments anymore, his father kicked him out. In October he pulled into the driveway of a local social service agency, in the beat-up car where he had been living for two months. Though he was enrolled in school full-time, he didn't have an alarm clock to help him get up in the morning, and he was often late. He had a small income from his part-time job, but he could hardly feed himself. If he was going to continue in school, he clearly needed the basics: housing, food, clothes and regular access to a shower. The agency helped him find a cheap apartment, bought him shampoo, toothpaste, school supplies and other necessities, helped him sign up for free breakfast and lunch at school, and directed him to the local soup kitchen. It negotiated with the school to reduce his class schedule so that he could continue to work, and provided him with tutoring, a particularly urgent need because Robbie had been diagnosed with learning disabilities and was considered academically limited.

From M. Wilson & A. Houghton. (1999). *A Different Kind of Smart: A Study of the Educational Obstacles Confronting Homeless Youth in New England.* New England Network for Child, Youth & Family Services. Reprinted with permission.

to meet these developmental needs through traditional structures and outlets. Young people with histories such as those experienced by most street youth, however, find that traditional structures often fail in meeting these developmental needs. They have not been able to develop healthy bonds within their family systems, and their life experience has often distanced them from their peers, and created issues and behaviors that label them within traditional structures. The attraction that street culture offers in an environment where they can succeed, where they are accepted, and where they can feel some measure of control over their lives.

Prevention Implications

Youth choose life on the streets because they perceive it as their best option for pursuing developmental needs. To prevent that choice we need to examine why traditional structures such as family and school fail to be viewed as a more viable option. When we look at the histories of abuse and neglect that most street-dependent youth have endured it is often easy to see where the family fails in this respect. What is more difficult to understand is how other systems are failing to meet these needs. We should examine the effect that traditional systems may have on the choices young people make by taking a look at two other "Effects."

The Hawthorne Effect

From 1927 to 1932, Harvard Business School professor Elton Mayo conducted studies intended to compare productivity and work conditions. Six women were selected from an assembly line to participate in the study, which involved frequent changes in their working conditions. Rest breaks were lengthened and shortened, added and dropped. Work hours were extended and reduced, and various other changes were tried. The confusing result of the study was that throughout all of these changes productivity steadily increased. There was no correlation to positive or negative changes, only a steady increase in productivity.

As it turned out there was a factor entirely different from working condition changes that was responsible for the increase in productivity. The six women who were selected for the experiment were participating of their own free will and were dealt with as cooperative partners in the study. They became a team with a shared sense of responsibility for the outcome. It was this sense of involvement and participation in the study that increased productivity, not the arbitrary changes in working conditions. Even when working conditions were made worse than what they were used to, such as working a full day without any breaks, medical checks showed no signs of cumulative fatigue and absence from work declined by 80 percent.

This has become known as the Hawthorne Effect. People are happier and function better in environments where they are active participants in the decisions that impact their lives, even if other environments may be "better."

Case Study—Tasha

An emancipated minor who was homeless before eventually moving into her own apartment, Tasha hated going to school with students who led the kind of middle-class, sheltered life she never had. "We're a different kind of smart," she said, glancing around the group of teenagers camped out on the floor and on sofas in an upstairs room of an agency's outreach center. "There's street-smart, and there's common sense smart, and a lot of people in school, they just don't have it. They may get it when they're older, but you can tell by listening to them flap their gums that they don't have it now. And it just burns me I had to be with them." It also made her angry that school officials didn't trust her enough to let her call herself in sick, even though the state considered her an adult. Like many homeless youth, she says her school was unwilling to recognize her problems as fundamentally more serious than the problems of most high school kids. "They want to know why I'm late to school and I'm like, 'Okay, the toilet in my apartment was overflowing, alright?' And they just look at you."

From M. Wilson & A. Houghton, (1999). *A Different Kind of Smart: A Study of the Educational Obstacles Confronting Homeless Youth in New England.* New England Network for Child, Youth & Family Services. Reprinted with permission.

Educational Needs of Middle School Homeless Students
The Pygmalion Effect

Many teachers are already familiar with the Pygmalion Effect from the book by Robert Rosenthal and Lenore Jacobson, *Pygmalion in the Classroom* (Holt, Rinehart and Winston, 1968). In a classic experiment, Rosenthal and Jacobson randomly picked 20% of the children in 18 elementary school classrooms. The teachers were told that these children were "intellectual bloomers" who could be expected to show remarkable progress during the year. The result was that in the three measured areas of verbal ability, reasoning, and overall IQ, these randomly selected youth all showed gains greater than the rest of the class. Why? Because that's what the teachers believed and expected.

The Pygmalion Effect is that people tend to conform to our beliefs and expectations of them. If we expect young people to be achievers and contributors, we work with achievers and contributors. If we expect young people to be troublemakers and problems, we work with troublemakers and problems.

Resiliency Research and Protective Factors

Research into human resiliency has found that overcoming challenges and difficult circumstances is an innate human quality that can be nurtured through specific methods of interaction. These methods, identified as "Protective Factors" by researchers, can be summarized as three broad approaches:

1. Caring and supportive relationships
2. High expectations
3. Opportunities for participation

Resiliency research correlates with the two "Effects" described in this article. The Hawthorne Effect demonstrates that opportunity for participation increases satisfaction and functioning. The Pygmalion Effect demonstrates that people respond to high expectations. Both of these "Effects" are best nurtured within the context of caring and supportive relationships. But it is precisely these three protective factors that are often missing in a young person's life as they make choices that lead them to the streets. Rather than being involved in choices and decisions that concern them, they are more often mandated to various treatments and interventions as systems attempt to correct their "problems." their behaviors are often disruptive and difficult for adults to deal with, lowering our expectations of them and leading us to see them through negative labels (manipulative, aggressive, etc.). Caring and supportive relationships become the exception in their lives, replaced by authoritarian and frustrated responses from the adults they know. Our responses become part of a self-fulfilling prophecy about their potential, and the culture of the streets begins to be perceived as a more attractive option to them. If we want to intervene and successfully prevent youth from becoming involved in the culture of the streets, we must focus on our behavior at least as much as we focus on the behavior of young people. It is the youth who challenge us who are on their way to street involvement. Do we respond by attempting to control their behavior, or do we reach out and include them in the solutions we seek? Do we see them as "problems" and lower our expectations of them, or do we see them as resources and expect that they can be successful? Prevention may truly be as simple—and as difficult—as what we believe about young people, and how far we are willing to go to work "with" them, rather than "at" them.

It is said that young people are our future. I don't think that's entirely accurate. Young people are a mirror of our present. If we don't like what we see, the change needs to begin with us.

JERRY FEST is the author of Street Culture: an Epistemology of Street-dependent Youth. He has been advocating for street-dependent young people since 1970. He is the founder and worked 12 years as the director of Janus Youth Program's Willamette Bridge. Mr. Fest can be reached at jtfest@in4y.com or (503) 231–3947.

From *The Prevention Researcher*, 8 (3), September 2001, pp. 8–10. Copyright © 2001 by Integrated Research Services, Inc. Reprinted by permission. www.tpronline.org

Article 29

Jail Time Is Learning Time

SIGNE NELSON AND LYNN OLCOTT

T here is excitement in the large, well-lit classroom. Student work, including history posters and artwork, adorn the walls. A polite shuffling of feet can be heard, as names are called and certificates presented. It is the graduation ceremony at the Onondaga County Justice Center in Syracuse, N.Y. The ceremony is held several times a year, recognizing inmates in the Incarcerated Education Program who have passed the GED exam or completed a 108-hour vocational program. The courses in the Incarcerated Education Program are geared to prepare inmates to transition successfully to several different settings.

The Incarcerated Education Program is a joint effort by the Syracuse City School District and the Onondaga County Sheriff's Office, and is housed inside the nine-story Onondaga County Justice Center in downtown Syracuse. The Justice Center is a 250,000 square-foot maximum-security, nonsentenced facility, completed and opened in 1995. The facility was built to contain 616 beds, but currently houses 745 inmates. Between 13,000 and 14,000 inmates passed through booking during 2004. About 2,500 of them were minors.

The Justice Center

The Justice Center is a state-of-the-art facility, designed for and operating on the direct supervision model. Direct supervision is a method of inmate management developed by the federal government in 1974 for presentenced inmates in the Federal Bureau of Prisons. There are about 140 such facilities operating throughout the United States and a few hundred currently under construction. Direct supervision places a single deputy directly in a "housing pod" with between 32 and 64 inmates. Maximum pod capacity in the Onondaga County Justice Center is 56 inmates. Inmates are given either relative freedom of movement within the pod or confined to their cells based on their behavior.

The program has been providing courses and classes at the Justice Center for 10 years, but this partnership between the school district and the sheriff's office began almost 30 years ago with the provision of GED instruction. The Incarcerated Education Program was originally conceived to ensure education for inmates who are minors. The program has grown tremendously and now has more than 20 offerings in academic, vocational and life management areas.

The Syracuse City School District professional staff includes six full-time and 18 part-time teachers and staff members. The program is unique in that there are three Onondaga County Sheriff's sergeants who hold New York State Adult Education certification and who teach classes in the vocational component. An average of 250 inmates, or about one-third of the Justice Center's incarcerated population, are enrolled in day and/or evening classes. There are about 250 hours of class time in the facility per week.

Varied Educational and Training Opportunities

As in the public education sector, vocational programs have evolved with the times. The Basic Office Skills class now offers two sections, and includes computer repair and office production skills. A course in building maintenance can be complemented by a course in pre-application to pre-apprenticeship plumbing, or in painting and surface preparation, a class that includes furniture refinishing. A baking class and nail technology have been added in the past few years. All vocational courses, before implementation, are approved by the New York State Education Department and are designed to be consistent with New York State Department of Labor employment projections for Onondaga County. No vocational programming is implemented without first identifying whether the occupation is an area of growth in the community.

Additionally, a broadly inclusive advisory board, made up of community representatives who are stakeholders in the local economy and in the quality of life in the Syracuse metropolitan area has been established. The Incarcerated Education Advisory Board meets approximately three times a year to discuss the perceived needs of the community and to address strategies for transitioning students into employment. Ongoing topics of study are issues surrounding employment, continuing education and housing.

Incarcerated Education Program planners are very aware that job skills are ineffective without proper work attitudes. Job Readiness Training addresses work ethic, proper work behavior, communication and critical behavior skills. Vocational classes are voluntary for the nonsentenced population. However, because of their popularity, a waiting list is maintained for several courses. Among these popular courses are Basic Office

Skills and Small Engine Repair. An additional section of Small Engine Repair has been added for female inmates in the class to ensure gender equity in this training opportunity.

New York State law requires that incarcerated minors continue their education while incarcerated. The Incarcerated Education Program enrolls inmates, ages 16 to 21, in Adult Basic Education/GED classes and addresses students with special needs. Other adult inmates attend on a voluntary basis. Inmates are given an initial placement test to determine math and reading skill levels. Because inmates work at a wide range of ability levels, instruction is individualized and materials are geared to independent work. English as a second Language and English Literacy/Civics are complementary offerings for inmates who are in need of assistance in English language proficiency and knowledge of American culture and history.

The GED exam is given at the Justice Center every 60 days or more often as needed. In the past three years, 225 students have taken the exam. Passing rates fluctuate between 63 percent and 72 percent. The average passing rate for correctional institutions in New York is about 51 percent. The state average passing rate for the general public in community-based courses is fairly stable at 50 percent.[1]

Of course, not everyone will take the GED. Student turnover is high, as inmates are released, bailed out, sent to treatment centers, or sentenced to county, state and federal correctional facilities. Judy Fiorini is a GED teacher who has been with the program for more than 10 years. "Many go back out into our community. We try to teach them something useful for their lives," Fiorini explains.

Transition services form an integral part of the program. The focus is on minors, but help is available for everyone. Two fulltime staff members assist people upon release, with such important tasks as acquiring a driver's license, seeking housing, reenrolling in high school or preparing for job interviews. A very important part of transition services is helping people acquire birth certificates, social security cards and other documents crucial for identification.

Tackling Cognitive Issues

Corrections professionals and educators are aware that it is not enough to improve the skill base of an inmate. There must be cognitive changes as well. The justice center is not a treatment facility, but it has been evolving into a therapeutic community. As the Incarcerated Education Program has grown, there has been the flexibility to add several important courses dealing with life issues, attitude and decision-making. According to data provided by the justice center, about 80 percent of inmates have substance abuse-related issues at the time of their arrest. To support desired cognitive changes, the justice center began establishing "clean and sober" pods in 2002. Currently, there are several clean and sober pods, including pods for adult men, women and youths. There are waiting lists for placement in the clean and sober pods.

The Incarcerated Education Program has been offering anger management groups for several years. Anger management helps group members deal with compulsive behavior and focus on

long-term goals. Other life management offerings include family education, action for personal choice and a course called Parent and Child Together. Most courses of study are developed inhouse by experienced professional faculty. Additionally, the program established gender-specific courses, Men's Issues and Women's Issues, to help inmates become more directly aware of their own responsibilities, separate from the role of a partner or significant other in their lives. The Men's Issues class is led by certified professionals and focuses on actions and their consequences. As in most jails, male inmates significantly outnumber female inmates. Courses and groups continue to be added, though it is sometimes difficult to find space for the abundance of activity in the program.

The program is financially supported, using state and federal funds, via nine carefully coordinated grants. Also significant for the success of the program has been ongoing encouragement and technical assistance from the New York State Education Department, the New York State Association of Incarcerated Education Programs and support from the New York State Sheriffs' Association.[2]

The Incarcerated Education Program continues to encounter challenges. It takes energy and dedication to keep the varied curricula substantial and cohesive, despite high student turnover and complex student needs. With a large civilian staff, the program requires close coordination between security and civilian concerns to help civilian staff work most effectively within the safety and security priorities of the facility. Biweekly meetings facilitate ongoing communication.

Making the Most of Time

Every available square inch of classroom space is in constant use. Classes have exceeded available space and some classes meet in core areas of the justice center as well. Several classes are held in the residence pods, where heavy, white tables are pulled together and portable white-boards are erected to create nomadic classrooms. Overall, the program is succeeding in several ways. Incarcerated minors are directly and meaningfully involved in high school equivalency classes, and inmates older than 21 receive academic and vocational services on a voluntary basis. All inmates are offered the opportunity for life-skills classes and for transitional services upon release. Time served at the Onondaga County Justice Center can also be time used for valuable academic, vocational and life management achievements.

Notes

1. New York State Department of Education maintains statistics for educational activities at correctional facilities in New York state. Patricia Mooney directs the GED Program for the state through the GED Testing Office in the State Department of Education. Greg Bayduss is the State Department of Education coordinator in charge of Incarcerated Education Programs throughout New York state.

2. State Professional Organizations: The New York State Association of Incarcerated Education Programs Inc. is a professional organization for teachers, administrators and security personnel (www.nysaiep.org). Its mission is to

promote excellence in incarcerated education programs in the state, support research in this field and advocate for incarcerated education initiatives through collaboration with other professional organizations. The authors must mention the valuable assistance of the New York State Sheriffs' Association, supporting each county sheriff, as the chief law enforcement officer in his or her county (www.nyssheriffs.org). The association provides valuable information and technical assistance to county sheriffs to help implement programs in their jails.

SIGNE NELSON is the coordinator of the Incarcerated Education Program, and **LYNN OLCOTT** is a teacher at Auburn Correctional Facility in New York, formerly with the Incarcerated Education Program. The program could not have attained its present strength without the vision and support of law enforcement officials Sheriff Kevin Walsh, Chief Anthony Callisto, and Syracuse City School District administrator Al Wolf. Special thanks to Capt. John Woloszyn, commander of Support Services; Sgt. Joseph Powlina, administrative compliance supervisor; and Deputy Joseph Caruso, photographer. Their assistance in the production of this article was crucial and much appreciated.

How Spirit Blooms

Most people long for spirituality, but what path do you take, and what are its milestones? A writer who tried everything from Buddhism to voodoo describes the four steps to finding a spiritual connection.

SUZANNE CLORES

Occasionally, a strange feeling comes over you. You hear a call from inside your heart. A faint, faraway sound you can barely hear amid the office phones, the people who need you, the list of plans for the week, the month, the rest of your life. But when you breathe deeply, the sound is louder and you relax. Finally, one afternoon during your commute home, you hear yourself. You say you need to nurture your soul. But now that you have voiced this need, how do you respond?

I reluctantly began a spiritual search when I was 25. I hated my job—my entire direction—and entered an early midlife panic. Many told me it was just "the age," but I knew it was more. These were the symptoms: A dull sense of separation from my own heart. An uncertainty about what I loved. A feeling that even my family didn't really know me. Doubt that a career path was the only thing worth striving for. Everyone feels that way, said the people I knew. But I felt excluded, apart, even more than usual. I wished I could join the party everyone seemed to be having and wondered how I had become an outsider.

The fact that a recent Gallup poll found that some 84 percent of Americans long for spirituality suggests that many people feel like I did—dissatisfied.

But it's not so easy to suddenly have a relationship with God. There is cynicism, past experiences with organized religion, and the general unhipness of being "religious." There is also our very stressful culture. When the body is confronted by stress, as mine was, it enters a state of fight or flight that drains oxygen from the higher functions of the mind. This makes it difficult to sit still, let alone consider your concerns with God. At the time of my spiritual crisis I was often so stressed about my love life and urban living that spirituality for me was in the same category as TV—something that ate your time and turned your brain to mush. Of course now—like everyone with a meditation or yoga practice—I know better. God is accessible by getting quiet and turning inside. But hindsight is 20/20. And it doesn't account for the pain and suffering that is crucial to acknowledge when stepping onto the spiritual path.

Wicca

Roots: Derived from pre-Christian Celtic religion.

Philosophy/practice: Although many call themselves witches, Wiccans do not practice the evil spells or acts of sorcery commonly associated with the word. They believe in a ubiquitous force, which they refer to as the All or the One, and are guided by the cycles of nature, symbols, and deities of ancient Celtic society.

Modern take: Wicca has grown in popularity since its revival in the United Kingdom in the 1940s. It remains an earth-based religion, with an emphasis on preserving nature and working with natural forces to create harmony and healing.

Yet in the last several years numerous medical studies have linked the benefits of a spiritual practice to improved mental health, particularly coping with depression, anxiety, and long-term illness. Fifty-eight percent of female trauma survivors found that a relationship with God gave them strength to create positive relationships with others. But it takes time, trust, and self-inquiry to have a real spiritual practice. You have to want it. You have to make it happen, and often that means finding support in a strange new world all by yourself.

My trepidation, it turns out, is common. Studies have shown people in physical or psychological crisis often feel left out of their religious or spiritual traditions, even when faith is a priority in their lives. Why is it so hard to believe we belong? Plenty of scientific studies prove that spirituality is inherently part of us. Books like *The God Gene* by Dean Hamer and *The "God" Part of the Brain* by Matthew Alper propose that, like other cognitive functions, our spiritual instincts, cognitions, sensations, and behaviors are generated from a particular cluster of neurons in the brain. We are wired to believe in something larger. Then why do we have so many lapses in faith? Because in the face of extreme distress, we are also wired to forget.

While I could not walk the path of St. Catherine of Siena or St. Francis of Assisi and shun material items, social life, and other worldly things holy people relinquish, I still craved spiritual depth. Six years later, I am finally onto something. It took a three-year search before I finally found yoga, another year before I felt comfortable with meditation, and another two years before landing in a real community. In that time my whole life changed. I moved from New York City to Tucson, Arizona, traded the city for the desert, and became part of a yoga-based spiritual practice called Yoga Oasis, a group of Anusara yogis and meditators who create what senior yoga teacher John Friend calls a "kula," or community of the heart. We devote several hours a week to practicing at the yoga center, creating a safe environment where spiritual exploration is welcome. Finally, I know contentment is possible.

But there was a long time of discontent. And guilt about the discontent. (Why can't I just be happy like other people? Why can't I just be a good Catholic or a resigned atheist?) I doggedly moved from tradition to tradition. Each time I met with joy and astonishment and chaos. My life filled with elation. Then my life fell apart. It sounds dramatic, but I can tell you this: With effort and vigilance, you are safe on the spiritual path though it may mean that your life changes entirely.

From my journey I've distilled four steps. They may help your spirituality blossom.

1. Imagine What You Want

What do I want? It seems like an obvious question. But for a long time, I didn't know what I wanted. It is natural—and easier—to continue feeling dissatisfied with situations before actually articulating to yourself "I want something more." Like everyone, I needed the security of faith, a promise of survival. Think of spring flowers that wait to bloom until the summer sun is warm enough. Or underpaid employees who wait until they have another job before leaving the one they have. Spiritual

seekers are similar. We seek not just the right spiritual perspective but a safe environment in which to explore it.

The overwhelming but wonderful news is that help is available. The quest for calm has made it into our consumer culture, for better or worse. I soon found many organizations, groups, chat sites, books, magazines, and products available to a practitioner of anything. I know what you're thinking; it sounds like a trend seeker on a shopping spree. But not all investments in mala beads and yoga mats lead to materialism. As seekers we use these tools to respond to that inner voice, that inner calling. Once responding to that voice, you will soon meet others doing the same.

I found others at classes offered by spiritual spas and resorts like Omega, Esalen, and Kripalu. On the cliffs of Big Sur, Esalen had been exploring America's consciousness movement since the 1960s. Omega had intoxicating-looking psychospiritual programs for the New York intellectual, and Kripalu welcomed all seekers with restorative weekends in the bosom of the Berkshires in Massachusetts. Eventually I attended all of these centers and learned various teachings that helped create more peace in my life. But at the beginning of my search, even these resorts were too organized—I wanted raw experience.

I went to the right place. Something about the secrecy and female-centrism of paganism (specifically Wicca), called to me. I stepped into this rich, earth-based religion and found tools for acquiring security: The four elements—water, earth, air, and fire—were frequently invoked in bonfire chants and used in ceremonies to unify all life. How did I stave off my Catholic guilt while on a Wicca retreat? Don't laugh, but on some level I believed chanting around a fire at midnight and Drawing Down the Moon (when the Goddess is invoked in the priestess) was similar to drinking the wine and taking Communion. On a bus ride back to Manhattan from an outdoor pagan festival, I marveled at the idea that through nature, I was connected to the divine.

I arrived back in the concrete jungle knowing what I wanted: security; community; philosophical consistency; but not dogma; a connection with the divine that felt rooted and physical, not magical. I also knew that I didn't need ceremonies in the woods

---

Yoga

Roots: India, 4th century B.C.

Philosophy/practice: Yoga, which in Sanskrit means "union," is a practice of unifying with the divine Self, that exists beyond the ego, or small self. Yogis maintain that through physical, psychological, and spiritual practice, we can transcend the small, ego-driven chatter of our minds and enter into a higher consciousness.

Modern take: The physical aspect of yoga has attained an unparalleled following in the United States. A meditative, relaxing practice that also strengthens and tones the body, it appeals to people looking to stretch their spiritual frontiers—and their legs.

Sufism

Roots: First brought to America by Hazrat Inayat Khan in 1910.

Philosophy/practice: Sufism is best known as the mystical movement within the Islamic religion, emphasizing personal union with the divine. Ritual song and dance also play a role in Sufi tradition.

Modern take: *Adab*, a long-standing Sufi tradition that is still practiced, is defined as a "profound courtesy of heart that arises from the deep relationship with the Divine and expresses itself in refined behavior of all kinds with other beings." Today a small yet devoted group of about 500 to 600 Americans are actively associated with Sufi spiritual practice.

to find those things. In quiet moments I consulted with my level of self-connection: Do I feel secure now? When do I feel secure? How can I cultivate more security? I didn't know it at the time, but creating those quiet moments was the first step to creating a space for spiritual experience to exist.

2. Walk Around the Temple

Once I began my search, I kept my interests under wraps at first. I said nothing to my family. Not because they were Catholic, and not because they worried about me, but because my trust was brittle. I needed support, not reactions like, "What the heck are you doing?" or "That sounds weird; what's wrong with you?" If you ask around generally, most people claim openness to religious and spiritual freedom. Still, ours is a culture where most people consider non-Christian religion to be outside of the norm.

My whole life I had tried to understand how to be a good Catholic. I was exhausted and badly needed a fresh take on spirituality. Any outside doubts would have fanned the flames of my own doubts. And since doubt and cynicism were default attitudes among my peers, I felt it best to keep quiet.

But that may have been a mistake. It wasn't until my cousin Mary confided to me that she had been part of a Sufi community for 25 years—a secret she had held from the family for just as long—that I could see it was really possible to change my life. My cousin Mary remembers the loneliness in the first few years of her search. "When I first started looking for spiritual solace, I went to churches, synagogues, even Quaker meetings, and found nice people, but not what I was looking for. Eventually I found a spiritual teacher who called that part of the investigative process 'walking around the temple.' It was the time of seeking before I was ready to go inside."

People in crisis often feel left out of their religious or spiritual traditions, even when faith is a priority in their lives.

Carefully, I began talking to people. I mentioned to a friend's mother that I sought a kind of personal spirituality, and she gladly loaned me her dusty Kabbalah books. My Aunt Maureen invited me to a psychic fair featuring Sylvia Browne and John Edward. (She was hoping my grandfather would play one of his famous practical jokes from the beyond. He didn't.) I didn't know whether or how these spiritual events would fulfill my yearning, but I accepted everything people gave me. I regarded them as gifts, tokens from worlds that promised me something fantastic. But what?

It helps to see all spiritual offerings as gifts, even if not exactly fashioned for you. Also, try giving a little yourself. If you know people who are interested in making the world a safer, more sensitive place, talk with them. Sharing spiritual interests with open minds and hearts gives permission to others to do the same. My yoga community grows because people

---

Shamanism

Roots: Origins date back more than 30,000 years.
Philosophy/practice: Based on the belief that medicine men (shamans) in ancient hunter-gatherer societies possessed special healing powers that allowed them to act as mediums between the earth and spirit worlds. With these gifts, they were capable of everything from curing diseases to reviving weak crops.
Modern take: Modern-day medicine people continue to cultivate this subtle relationship. They are mostly found in Native American communities and come to their vocation in various ways. Some receive a calling in a dream state, others embark upon a "vision quest," and others apprentice with a skilled shaman.

---

share their experiences. We commemorate every life event—a war, a marriage, a birth, a death, a holy day—with a special yoga or meditation practice. Plus, there is a danger to keeping it all inside. If you don't share your needs, desires, or experiences with anyone, there is a chance the stress and alienation will cause psychic and bodily harm.

3. Conquer the Fear

So many of us spend time walking around the temple that it almost becomes a spiritual path in and of itself. Though my cousin Mary is now a devoted student of Indian teacher Meher Baba, she maintains that spiritual searching was an important part of finding her true teacher. I took her advice and for many months—years, actually—slowly confronted my spiritual longings. I didn't know what I wanted. So I tried this and that. With as much of my heart as I could, I took shamanic journeys. I attended pagan ceremonies. I sought out voodoo rituals. And while most of the time I had powerful spiritual experiences, there was a major problem: I was scared.

All heroic myths, fairy tales, and spiritual heroes encounter what is called "the dark night of the soul." It is a time when seekers are deeply frightened, lonely, and uncertain about going forward. Yet they are aware that they cannot turn back. Sometimes, I found, it lasts longer than a night. Even after I attended deeply meaningful ceremonies and found a yoga teacher I liked, I kept asking myself, Is this really necessary? Is it sacrilegious? Will I be punished somehow for leaving my old religion and trying to find something as abstract as spirituality? Despite my frustration at not having answers, asking questions was one of the most productive and helpful steps I could take to relieve myself of fear. Asking honest questions leads to hearing honest answers, and honest answers led me to the truth that I needed to surrender to the paths that felt right.

One man I met on the spiritual path encountered his darkest night after he had already been studying with a teacher. It came right after his teacher asked that he make a greater commitment. "I tried everything to bring about a transformation in myself," the man told me. "All of the deep experiences I'd had, all of my

Buddhism

Roots: India, 525 B.C., where Prince Siddhartha received enlightenment under the bodhi tree at the river Neranjara. Thereafter he was known as the Buddha, or Awakened One.

Philosophy/practice: Buddhist religion is based on the theory that life is a continual cycle of birth, death, and rebirth, and that we live in constant suffering. Meditation, persistent self-inquiry, and observance of moral precepts are the way to liberation and freedom from suffering.

Modern take: Buddhism thrives today as the fourth largest religion in the world. Buddhists practicing in the West are drawn to varying sects, including Theravada, Tibetan, Mahayana, and Zen.

Voodoo

Roots: The exact origins of voodoo are unknown, but it's generally believed to have begun in the West African nation of Benin during the slave trade. It's also practiced in Haiti, South America, and New Orleans.

Philosophy/practice: Voodoo practitioners believe in one god, but call upon spirits, the Loa, to heal the sick, help the needy and provide practical solutions to life's problems.

Modern take: Voodoo is a guiding force in communities where it's practiced, and voodoo priests are prominent, respected figures who perform many sacred functions.

understanding of dharma, even my will and perseverance had nothing to do with the kind of radical transformation that lay ahead. I began to experience intense confusion and fear, which grew into even more intense paranoia. I didn't know what to trust."

It took a year for this pilgrim to realize the transformation he needed to make, but he eventually did as a result of staying with it. "Transformation," he told me, "is a process of active surrender. You cannot will your own transformation at the soul level; you can only allow transformation to be enacted by forces greater than yourself."

4. Cross to Safety

There is no guarantee that stepping more deeply onto a spiritual path will solve all your problems. Rather, it demands more empathy and honesty from yourself than a lot of other relationships demand.

I found this can be more complex than comfortable. About two years into my exploration of various spiritual paths, my life had changed dramatically: I had left my long-term relationship, moved in with others on a spiritual path, changed my line of work to do freelance projects with various people. Very little in my life was stable. And yet the space gave my passion room to burn. I felt clear. My resolve was strong that I had made the right choices and let my spiritual vision guide me.

And then everything started collapsing. The couple I lived with were ending their marriage. The people I worked with were terminating our agreement prematurely. I was losing my home and job, and I was angry. What had I done wrong?

I phoned a shamanic practitioner I trusted. After consulting with her own spirit guides, she gave me news I had difficulty swallowing. She said, "The structures you have created for yourself are dissolving of your own doing. You must manifest a new structure for yourself."

I had expected her to say, "You are doing everything right, none of this is your fault. The universe will save you," I answered, with an edge to my voice, "How do I manifest a new life?"

She said seriously; "Get really clear in your mind. Meditate, chant, do whatever you have to do to clear the anxiety. Then dream what you want and need. Write it down very clearly and keep it somewhere."

"Dream?" I asked.

"Yes."

"And write it on a piece of paper?" I asked.

"Yes," she said.

I hung up, annoyed. This advice did not sound concrete. I was losing my home, and she wanted me to dream. But I had spent a year cultivating spiritual awareness and trust. So I sat down and did it. I dreamed a house in a different city than where I lived, with work and people whom I had never met. And within three months I had moved out of town unexpectedly, found the house, community, and work situation I had written on the page, almost exactly.

The spiritual path is not linear. This makes it hard to clear a weekend in October for a "spiritually deep" day. Like love, spiritual life does not work like that. And yet every moment provides an opportunity to begin. Perhaps on the radio, or on the news, a report mentions the word "spirituality," and your heart softens. Or perhaps when you hear somewhere that, post 9/11, attendance at spiritual retreats has increased, and that lay members of churches, synagogues, and mosques have begun to organize nationally, you somehow feel included. You know you are part of this group, these new pilgrims—maybe even the old ones—but how do you respond?

The truth is, to think about it is to begin. You have taken a crucial step. And you are not alone. I can tell you, the most important thing to remember is that you are not alone.

From *Body + Soul*, September 2004, pp. 76, 78–79, 108–110, 113. Copyright © 2004 by Body + Soul Magazine. Reprinted by permission.

The Battle for Your Brain

Science is developing ways to boost intelligence, expand memory, and more. But will you be allowed to change your own mind?

RONALD BAILEY

"We're on the verge of profound changes in our ability to manipulate the brain," says Paul Root Wolpe, a bioethicist at the University of Pennsylvania. He isn't kidding. The dawning age of neuroscience promises not just new treatments for Alzheimer's and other brain diseases but enhancements to improve memory, boost intellectual acumen, and fine-tune our emotional responses. "The next two decades will be the golden age of neuroscience," declares Jonathan Moreno, a bioethicist at the University of Virginia. "We're on the threshold of the kind of rapid growth of information in neuroscience that was true of genetics 15 years ago."

One man's golden age is another man's dystopia. One of the more vociferous critics of such research is Francis Fukuyama, who warns in his book *Our Posthuman Future* that "we are already in the midst of this revolution" and *"we should use the power of the state to regulate it"* (emphasis his). In May a cover story in the usually pro-technology *Economist* worried that "neuroscientists may soon be able to screen people's brains to assess their mental health, to distribute that information, possibly accidentally, to employers or insurers, and to 'fix' faulty personality traits with drugs or implants on demand."

There are good reasons to consider the ethics of tinkering directly with the organ from which all ethical reflection arises. Most of those reasons boil down to the need to respect the rights of the people who would use the new technologies. Some of the field's moral issues are common to all biomedical research: how to design clinical trials ethically, how to ensure subjects' privacy, and so on. Others are peculiar to neurology. It's not clear, for example, whether people suffering from neurodegenerative disease can give informed consent to be experimented on.

Last May the Dana Foundation sponsored an entire conference at Stanford on "neuroethics." Conferees deliberated over issues like the moral questions raised by new brain scanning techniques, which some believe will lead to the creation of truly effective lie detectors. Participants noted that scanners might also be able to pinpoint brain abnormalities in those accused of breaking the law, thus changing our perceptions of guilt and innocence. Most nightmarishly, some worried that governments could one day use brain implants to monitor and perhaps even control citizens' behavior.

But most of the debate over neuroethics has not centered around patients' or citizens' autonomy, perhaps because so many of the field's critics themselves hope to restrict that autonomy in various ways. The issue that most vexes *them* is the possibility that neuroscience might enhance previously "normal" human brains.

The tidiest summation of their complaint comes from the conservative columnist William Satire. "Just as we have antidepressants today to elevate mood," he wrote after the Dana conference, "tomorrow we can expect a kind of Botox for the brain to smooth out wrinkled temperaments, to turn shy people into extroverts, or to bestow a sense of humor on a born grouch. But what price will human nature pay for these nonhuman artifices?"

Truly effective neuropharmaceuticals that improve moods and sharpen mental focus are already widely available and taken by millions. While there is some controversy about the effectiveness of Prozac, Paxil, and Zoloft, nearly 30 million Americans have taken them, with mostly positive results. In his famous 1993 book *Listening to Prozac*, the psychiatrist Peter Kramer describes patients taking the drug as feeling "better than well." One Prozac user, called Tess, told him that when she isn't taking the medication, "I am not myself."

One Pill Makes You Smarter . . .

That's exactly what worries Fukuyama, who thinks Prozac looks a lot like *Brave New World*'s soma. The pharmaceutical industry, he declares, is producing drugs that "provide self-esteem in the bottle by elevating serotonin in the brain." If you need a drug to be your "self," these critics ask, do you really have a self at all?

Another popular neuropharmaceutical is Ritalin, a drug widely prescribed to remedy attention deficit hyperactivity disorder (ADHD), which is characterized by agitated behavior and an inability to focus on tasks. Around 1.5 million schoolchildren take Ritalin, which recent research suggests boosts the activity of the neurotransmitter dopamine in the brain. Like all psycho-active drugs, it is not without controversy. Perennial psychiatric critic Peter Breggin argues that millions of children are being "drugged into more compliant or submissive state[s]" to satisfy the needs of harried parents and school officials. For Fukuyama, Ritalin is prescribed to control rambunctious children because "parents and teachers . . . do not want to spend the time and energy necessary to discipline, divert, entertain, or train difficult children the old-fashioned way."

Unlike the more radical Breggin, Fukuyama acknowledges that drugs such as Prozac and Ritalin have helped millions when other treatments have failed. Still, he worries about their larger social consequences. "There is a disconcerting symmetry between Prozac and Ritalin," he writes. "The former is prescribed heavily for depressed women lacking in self-esteem; it gives them more the alpha-male feeling that comes with high serotonin levels. Ritalin, on the other hand, is prescribed largely for young boys who do not want to sit still in class because nature never designed them to behave that way. Together, the two sexes are gently nudged toward that androgynous median personality, self-satisfied and socially compliant, that is the current politically correct outcome in American society."

What really worries critics is that Prozac and Ritalin may be the pharmacological equivalent of bearskins and stone axes compared to the new drugs that are coming.

Although there are legitimate questions here, they're related not to the chemicals themselves but to who makes the decision to use them. Even if Prozac and Ritalin can help millions of people, that doesn't mean schools should be able to force them on any student who is unruly or bored. But by the same token, even if you accept the most radical critique of the drug—that ADHD is not a real disorder to begin with—that doesn't mean Americans who exhibit the symptoms that add up to an ADHD diagnosis should not be allowed to alter their mental state chemically, if that's an outcome they want and a path to it they're willing to take.

Consider Nick Megibow, a senior majoring in philosophy at Gettysburg College. "Ritalin made my life a lot better," he reports. "Before I started taking Ritalin as a high school freshman, I was doing really badly in my classes. I had really bad grades, Cs and Ds mostly. By sophomore year, I started taking Ritalin, and it really worked amazingly. My grades improved dramatically to mostly As and Bs. It allows me to focus and get things done rather than take three times the amount of time that it should take to finish something." If people like Megibow don't share Fukuyama's concerns about the wider social consequences of their medication, it's because they're more interested, quite reasonably, in feeling better and living a successful life.

What really worries critics like Satire and Fukuyama is that Prozac and Ritalin may be the neuropharmacological equivalent of bearskins and stone axes compared to the new drugs that

are coming. Probably the most critical mental function to be enhanced is memory. And this, it turns out, is where the most promising work is being done. At Princeton, biologist Joe Tsien's laboratory famously created smart mice by genetically modifying them to produce more NMDA brain receptors, which are critical for the formation and maintenance of memories. Tsien's mice were much faster learners than their unmodified counterparts. "By enhancing learning, that is, memory acquisition, animals seem to be able to solve problems faster," notes Tsien. He believes his work has identified an important target that will lead other researchers to develop drugs that enhance memory.

A number of companies are already hard at work developing memory drugs. Cortex Pharmaceuticals has developed a class of compounds called AMPA receptor modulators, which enhance the glutamate-based transmission between brain cells. Preliminary results indicate that the compounds do enhance memory and cognition in human beings. Memory Pharmaceuticals, co-founded by Nobel laureate Eric Kandel, is developing a calcium channel receptor modulator that increases the sensitivity of neurons and allows them to transmit information more speedily and a nicotine receptor modulator that plays a role in synaptic plasticity. Both modulators apparently improve memory. Another company, Targacept, is working on the nicotinic receptors as well.

All these companies hope to cure the memory deficits that some 30 million baby boomers will suffer as they age. If these compounds can fix deficient memories, it is likely that they can enhance normal memories as well. Tsien points out that a century ago the encroaching senility of Alzheimer's disease might have been considered part of the "normal" progression of aging. "So it depends on how you define normal," he says. "Today we know that most people have less good memories after age 40 and I don't believe that's a normal process."

Eight Objections

And so we face the prospect of pills to improve our mood, our memory, our intelligence, and perhaps more. Why would anyone object to that?

Eight objections to such enhancements recur in neuroethicists' arguments. None of them is really convincing.

- *Neurological enhancements permanently change the brain.* Erik Parens of the Hastings Center, a bioethics think tank, argues that it's better to enhance a child's performance by changing his environment than by changing his brain—that it's better to, say, reduce his class size than to give him Ritalin. But this is a false dichotomy. Reducing class size is aimed at changing the child's biology too, albeit indirectly. Activities like teaching are supposed to induce biological changes in a child's brain, through a process called *learning*.

Fukuyama falls into this same error when he suggests that even if there is some biological basis for their condition, people with ADHD "clearly . . . can do things that would affect their final degree of attentiveness or hyperactivity. Training, character, determination, and environment more generally would all play important roles." So can Ritalin, and much more expeditiously, too. "What is the difference between Ritalin and the Kaplan SAT review?" asks the Dartmouth neuroscientist Michael Gazzaniga. "It's six of one and a half dozen of the other. If both can boost SAT scores by, say, 120 points, I think it's immaterial which way it's done."

- *Neurological enhancements are anti-egalitarian.* A perennial objection to new medical technologies is the one Patens calls "unfairness in the distribution of resources." In other words, the rich and their children will get access to brain enhancements first, and will thus acquire more competitive advantages over the poor.

This objection rests on the same false dichotomy as the first. As the University of Virginia's Moreno puts it, "We don't stop people from giving their kids tennis lessons." If anything, the new enhancements might *increase* social equality. Moreno notes that neuropharmaceuticals are likely to be more equitably distributed than genetic enhancements, because "after all, a pill is easier to deliver than DNA."

- *Neurological enhancements are self-defeating.* Not content to argue that the distribution of brain enhancements won't be egalitarian enough, some critics turn around and argue that it will be too egalitarian. Parens has summarized this objection succinctly: "If everyone achieved the same relative advantage with a given enhancement, then ultimately no one's position would change; the 'enhancement' would have failed if its purpose was to increase competitive advantage."

This is a flagrant example of the zero-sum approach that afflicts so much bioethical thought. Let's assume, for the sake of argument, that everyone in society will take a beneficial brain-enhancing drug. Their relative positions may not change, but the overall productivity and wealth of society would increase considerably, making everyone better off. Surely that is a social good.

- *Neurological enhancements are difficult to refuse.* Why exactly would everyone in the country take the same drug? Because, the argument goes, competitive pressures in our go-go society will be so strong that a person will be forced to take a memory-enhancing drug just to keep up with everyone else. Even if the law protects freedom of choice, social pressures will draw us in.

For one thing, this misunderstands the nature of the technology. It's not simply a matter of popping a pill and suddenly zooming ahead. "I know a lot of smart people who don't amount to a row of beans," says Gazzaniga. "They're just happy under-achieving, living life below their potential. So a pill that pumps up your intellectual processing power won't necessarily give you the drive and ambition to use it."

Beyond that, it's not as though we don't all face competitive pressures anyway—to get into and graduate from good universities, to constantly upgrade skills, to buy better computers and more productive software, whatever. Some people choose to enhance themselves by getting a Ph.D. in English; others are happy to stop their formal education after high school. It's not

clear why a pill should be more irresistible than higher education, or why one should raise special ethical concerns while the other does not.

- *Neurological enhancements undermine good character.* For some critics, the comparison to higher education suggests a different problem. We should strive for what we get, they suggest; taking a pill to enhance cognitive functioning is just too easy. As Fukuyama puts it: "The normal, and morally acceptable, way of overcoming low self-esteem was to struggle with oneself and with others, to work hard, to endure painful sacrifices, and finally to rise and be seen as having done so."

"By denying access to brain-enhancing drugs, people like Fukuyama are advocating an exaggerated stoicism," counters Moreno. "I don't see the benefit or advantage of that kind of tough love." Especially since there will still be many different ways to achieve things and many difficult challenges in life. Brain-enhancing drugs might ease some of our labors, but as Moreno notes, "there are still lots of hills to climb, and they are pretty steep." Cars, computers, and washing machines have tremendously enhanced our ability to deal with formerly formidable tasks. That doesn't mean life's struggles have disappeared—just that we can now tackle the next ones.

- *Neurological enhancements undermine personal responsibility.* Carol Freedman, a philosopher at Williams College, argues that what is at stake "is a conception of ourselves as responsible agents, not machines." Fukuyama extends the point, claiming that "ordinary people" are eager to "medicalize as much of their behavior as possible and thereby reduce their responsibility for their own actions." As an example, he suggests that people who claim to suffer from ADHD "want to absolve themselves of personal responsibility."

But we are not debating people who might use an ADHD diagnosis as an excuse to behave irresponsibly. We are speaking of people who use Ritalin to change their behavior. Wouldn't it be more irresponsible of them to not take corrective action?

- *Neurological enhancements enforce dubious norms.* There are those who assert that corrective action might be irresponsible after all, depending on just what it is that you're trying to correct. People might take neuropharmaceuticals, some warn, to conform to a harmful social conception of normality. Many bioethicists—Georgetown University's Margaret Little, for example—argue that we can already see this process in action among women who resort to expensive and painful cosmetic surgery to conform to a social ideal of feminine beauty. Never mind for the moment that beauty norms for both men and women have never been so diverse. Providing and choosing to avail oneself of that surgery makes one complicit in norms that are morally wrong, the critics argue. After all, people should be judged not by their physical appearances but by the content of their characters.

That may be so, but why should someone suffer from society's slights if she can overcome them with a nip here and a tuck there? The norms may indeed be suspect, but the suffering is experienced by real people whose lives are consequently diminished. Little acknowledges this point, but argues that those who benefit from using a technology to conform have a moral obligation to fight against the suspect norm. Does this mean people should be given access to technologies they regard as beneficial only if they agree to sign on to a bioethical fatwa?

Of course, we should admire people who challenge norms they disagree with and live as they wish, but why should others be denied relief just because some bioethical commissars decree that society's misdirected values must change? Change may come, but real people should not be sacrificed to some restrictive bioethical utopia in the meantime. Similarly, we should no doubt value depressed people or people with bad memories just as highly as we do happy geniuses, but until that glad day comes people should be allowed to take advantage of technologies that improve their lives in the society in which they actually live.

Furthermore, it's far from clear that everyone will use these enhancements in the same ways. There are people who alter their bodies via cosmetic surgery to bring them closer to the norm, and there are people who alter their bodies via piercings and tattoos to make them more individually expressive. It doesn't take much imagination to think of unusual or unexpected ways that Americans might use mind-enhancing technologies. Indeed, the war on drugs is being waged, in part, against a small but significant minority of people who prefer to alter their consciousness in socially disapproved ways.

- *Neurological enhancements make us inauthentic.* Parents and others worry that the users of brain-altering chemicals are less authentically themselves when they're on the drug. Some of them would reply that the exact opposite is the case. In *Listening to Prozac*, Kramer chronicles some dramatic transformations in the personalities and attitudes of his patients once they're on the drug. The aforementioned Tess tells him it was "as if I had been in a drugged state all those years and now I'm clearheaded."

Cars, computers, and washing machines have tremendously enhanced our ability to deal with formerly formidable tasks. That doesn't mean life's struggles have disappeared—just that we can now tackle the next ones.

Again, the question takes a different shape when one considers the false dichotomy between biological and "nonbiological" enhancements. Consider a person who undergoes a religious conversion and emerges from the experience with a more upbeat and attractive personality. Is he no longer his "real" self? Must every religious convert be deprogrammed?

Even if there were such a thing as a "real" personality, why should you stick with it if you don't like it? If you're socially withdrawn and a pill can give you a more vivacious and outgoing manner, why not go with it? After all, you're choosing to take responsibility for being the "new" person the drug helps you to be.

Authenticity and Responsibility

"Is it a drug-induced personality or has the drug cleared away barriers to the real personality?" asks the University of Pennsylvania's Wolpe. Surely the person who is choosing to use the drug is in a better position to answer that question than some bioethical busybody.

This argument over authenticity lies at the heart of the neuro-ethicists' objections. If there is a single line that divides the supporters of neurological freedom from those who would restrict the new treatments, it is the debate over whether a natural state of human being exists and, if so, how appropriate it is to modify it. Wolpe makes the point that in one sense cognitive enhancement resembles its opposite, Alzheimer's disease. A person with Alzheimer's loses her personality. Similarly, an enhanced individual's personality may become unrecognizable to those who knew her before.

Not that this is unusual. Many people experience a version of this process when they go away from their homes to college or the military. They return as changed people with new capacities, likes, dislikes, and social styles, and they often find that their families and friends no longer relate to them in the old ways. Their brains have been changed by those experiences, and they are not the same people they were before they went away. Change makes most people uncomfortable, probably never more so than when it happens to a loved one. Much of the neuro-Luddites' case rests on a belief in an unvarying, static personality, something that simply doesn't exist.

It isn't just personality that changes over time. Consciousness itself is far less static than we've previously assumed, a fact that raises contentious questions of free will and determinism. Neuroscientists are finding more and more of the underlying automatic processes operating in the brain, allowing us to take a sometimes disturbing look under our own hoods. "We're finding out that by the time we're conscious of doing something, the brain's already done it," explains Gazzaniga. Consciousness, rather than being the director of our activities, seems instead to be a way for the brain to explain to itself why it did something.

Haunting the whole debate over neuroscientific research and neuroenhancements is the fear that neuroscience will undercut notions of responsibility and free will. Very preliminary research has suggested that many violent criminals do have altered brains. At the Stanford conference, *Science* editor Donald Kennedy suggested that once we know more about brains, our legal system will have to make adjustments in how we punish those who break the law. A murderer or rapist might one day plead innocence on the grounds that "my amygdala made me do it." There is precedent for this: The legal system already mitigates criminal punishment when an offender can convince a jury he's so mentally ill that he cannot distinguish right from wrong.

> **Like any technology, neurological enhancements can be abused. But critics have not made a strong case for why individuals should not be allowed to take advantage of breakthroughs.**

Of course, there are other ways such discoveries might pan out in the legal system, with results less damaging to social order but still troubling for notions of personal autonomy. One possibility is that an offender's punishment might be reduced if he agrees to take a pill that corrects the brain defect he blames for his crime. We already hold people responsible when their drug use causes harm to others—most notably, with laws against drunk driving. Perhaps in the future we will hold people responsible if they fail to take drugs that would help prevent them from behaving in harmful ways. After all, which is more damaging to personal autonomy, a life confined to a jail cell or roaming free while taking a medication?

The philosopher Patricia Churchland examines these conundrums in her forthcoming book, *Brainwise: Studies in Neurophilosophy.* "Much of human social life depends on the expectation that agents have control over their actions and are responsible for their choices," she writes. "In daily life it is commonly assumed that it is sensible to punish and reward behavior so long as the person was in control and chose knowingly and intentionally." And that's the way it should remain, even as we learn more about how our brains work and how they sometimes break down.

Churchland points out that neuroscientific research by scientists like the University of Iowa's Antonio Damasio strongly shows that emotions are an essential component of viable practical reasoning about what a person should do. In other words, neuroscience is bolstering philosopher David Hume's insight that "reason is and ought only to be the slave of the passions." Patients whose affects are depressed or lacking due to brain injury are incapable of judging or evaluating between courses of action. Emotion is what prompts and guides our choices.

Churchland further argues that moral agents come to be morally and practically wise not through pure cognition but by developing moral beliefs and habits through life experiences. Our moral reflexes are honed through watching and hearing about which actions are rewarded and which are punished; we learn to be moral the same way we learn language. Consequently, Churchland concludes "the default presumption that agents are responsible for their actions is empirically necessary to an agent's learning, both emotionally and cognitively, how to evaluate the consequences of certain events and the price of taking risks."

It's always risky to try to derive an "ought" from an "is," but neuroscience seems to be implying that liberty—i.e., letting people make choices and then suffer or enjoy the consequences—is essential for inculcating virtue and maintaining social cooperation. Far from undermining personal responsibility, neuroscience may end up strengthening it.

For Neurological Liberty

Fukuyama wants to "draw red lines" to distinguish between therapy and enhancement, "directing research toward the former while putting restrictions on the latter." He adds that "the original purpose of medicine is, after all, to heal the sick, not turn healthy people into gods." He imagines a federal agency that would oversee neurological research, prohibiting anything that aims at enhancing our capacities beyond some notion of the human norm.

"For us to flourish as human beings, we have to live according to our nature, satisfying the deepest longings that we as natural beings have," Fukuyama told the Christian review *Books & Culture* last summer. "For example, our nature gives us tremendous cognitive capabilities, capability for reason, capability to learn, to teach ourselves things, to change our opinions, and so forth. What follows from that? A way of life that permits such growth is better than a life in which this capacity is shriveled and stunted in various ways." This is absolutely correct. The trouble is that Fukuyama has a shriveled, stunted vision of human nature, leading him and others to stand athwart neuroscientific advances that will make it possible for more people to take fuller advantage of their reasoning and learning capabilities.

Like any technology, neurological enhancements can be abused, especially if they're doled out—or imposed—by an unchecked authority. But Fukuyama and other critics have not made a strong case for why *individuals*, in consultation with their doctors, should not be allowed to take advantage of new neuroscientific breakthroughs to enhance the functioning of their brains. And it is those individuals that the critics will have to convince if they seriously expect to restrict this research.

It's difficult to believe that they'll manage that. In the 1960s many states outlawed the birth control pill, on the grounds that it would be too disruptive to society. Yet Americans, eager to take control of their reproductive lives, managed to roll back those laws, and no one believes that the pill could be re-outlawed today.

Moreno thinks the same will be true of the neurological advances to come. "My hunch," he says, "is that in the United States, medications that enhance our performance are not going to be prohibited." When you consider the sometimes despairing tone that Fukuyama and others like him adopt, it's hard not to conclude that on that much, at least, they agree.

RONALD BAILEY is *Reason's* science correspondent and the editor of Global Warming and Other Eco-Myths: How the Environmental Movement Uses False Science to Scare Us to Death (Prima Publishing).

Getting Back on Track

Women who take career 'off ramps' to raise children often have trouble finding 'on ramps' when they are ready to work again. Now companies in need of talent are finally addressing the problem.

Daniel McGinn

It's 4:30 on a weekday afternoon and ordinarily Caterina Bandini would be tracking headlines, tweaking scripts and preparing to take her seat at the anchor desk for the 5 o'clock news at Boston's NBC affiliate. Instead, Bandini, 38, sits with her feet up in her Back Bay apartment, idly watching television as her station's broadcast begins. In October, Bandini will deliver twin girls. For most TV newswomen, childbirth brings only a brief maternity leave—Bandini's predecessor took six weeks—but she's made a different choice. In August, she quit her anchor job, intending to be a stay-at-home mom after her daughters are born. "I always thought it'd be important, at least for the first formative years, to spend as much time as I possibly could with my kids," she says. Bandini hopes someday to head back to a newsroom, but realizes there are no guarantees. "It's very difficult to get back into it—I took a huge risk doing this," she says.

A few years ago Bandini might have served as a prime example of the hot workplace trend: high-achieving women who were "opting out," quitting high-paying, sought-after jobs to raise children, care for aging parents or just escape from the chaos that often accompanies dual-income coupledom. Feminists decried the trend as a step backward, while skeptics questioned whether the statistics really showed women to be quitting in vast numbers. But lately, the debate over "Why Women Quit" has taken a subtle turn. The problem may not be that so many women take a break from salaried life; the more troubling issue is why it's so difficult for them to restart their careers when they're ready. Instead of persuading women not to leave their jobs and to stay on track toward leadership positions, lately the talk among work-family advocates has focused on finding ways to support women's "non-linear" career paths—and to build better "on ramps" for women wishing to return to work after career pauses.

For women who hope to make this transition, there are a growing number of highly visible role models. Last week Meredith Vieira, who famously quit "60 Minutes" to spend time with her children, slid into Katie Couric's old seat at NBC's "Today" show after nine years on ABC's "The View." Last year

Brenda Barnes, who quit a top job at PepsiCo in 1998 to reconnect with her kids, ascended to become CEO at Sara Lee. This month actress Calista Flockhart returns to network television after five years at home with her child. Meanwhile, a host of companies—investment banks, consulting firms, law firms—are trying to make it easier for nonfamous women to segue back to work as well. These businesses aren't motivated simply by altruism, but by the recognition that these off-ramped women may be an underutilized source of talent. Says Eliza Shanley, cofounder of the Women@Work Network: "There's a general sense among employers that whoever figures this out first wins."

The issue is hardly new: women have been talking about the ideal ways to integrate childbearing and family responsibilities into a high-stress career for decades. The growing focus on the issue—along with the vivid on-ramp/off-ramp metaphor—stem from a research study published last year in the Harvard Business Review. Based on a survey of midcareer women who hold graduate degrees or college degrees with honors, it found that 37 percent had taken extended breaks from work, with the average off-ramper staying home for 2.2 years. Most wanted to return to work, but just 40 percent regained full-time employment. The research put a spotlight on one reason so few women are advancing into corner offices. Says Sylvia Ann Hewlett, president of the Center for Work-Life Policy and the study's lead author: "The old idea was, all you needed to do was fill the pipeline with women and wait around for a couple of decades for them to move through the ranks. [But] there's an enormous amount of leakage from the pipeline—once women off-ramp even for a short while, it's incredibly difficult to get back in."

Since the study appeared, companies have begun rolling out new ways to address the problem. Last November Lehman Bros. invited 75 unemployed women who'd once worked on Wall Street to a back-to-work seminar. Part of the program, called Encore, dealt with technical banking issues, providing a sort of Cliffs Notes version of industry changes they've missed in the past few years. But much of it was focused on nuts-and-bolts concerns like how to talk about your years at home during an interview. Lehman hosted a similar event last spring, and will do another this November. So far, it's hired 16 of the women. Beyond the new hires, the program has helped Lehman portray itself as more family-friendly when visiting college campuses (where interest in Wall Street careers among young woman has been waning). It's also helped managers see beyond the firm's traditional MO of recruiting mostly new college grads, new M.B.A.s and employees of rival firms. Says Anne Erni, Lehman's chief diversity officer: "We've now created this fourth legitimate pool of talent."

The focus lately is on finding ways to support women's 'nonlinear' career paths.

Other firms are launching programs to help women ease back to work at a pace that suits them. At consulting firm Booz Allen Hamilton, more than 100 women who were once full-time employees now work in an "adjunct" program. The firm slices off discrete pieces of work—often research or proposal writing—for its adjuncts, who aren't on the payroll but have kept their Booz Allen e-mail addresses. The adjuncts (who include some men) can not only negotiate pay for each project, but also the terms under which they'll accept it. How many days a week must they work? Can they telecommute? Will it involve travel? Ani Singh, a 1997 Wharton M.B.A. who left the firm in 2002, now works as an adjunct in Virginia. She routinely turns down assignments that won't let her spend enough time with her child, but she never lacks for new opportunities. "I still feel like I'm making progress in my career whether I'm within the formal organization or not," Singh says. And the firm hopes that when she's ready to return to full-time work, she won't bother sending out résumés. "We want them to think only about coming back to us—that's why we put this in place," says senior VP DeAnne Aguirre.

Meanwhile, business schools are recognizing that helping women find on ramps could become a profitable market niche. This year several B-schools—Wharton, Harvard, Babson, Dartmouth, Pepperdine—have begun experimenting with on-ramping courses, ranging from Pepperdine's full-blown M.B.A. geared toward mothers with young children (starting in January), to Dartmouth's 11-day "Back in Business" executive education course, which launches next month. Ronna Reyes Sieh, a mother of three who earned her M.B.A. at Columbia in 1998 before logging three years at Morgan Stanley, will attend the Dartmouth program. She hopes not only to jump-start her job hunt, but to learn more about managing a fast-paced job without neglecting family responsibilities. "I want to be connected with other women in the same position," she says.

Amid the growing focus on helping women on-ramp, there's some fear that companies may view the issue as a magic bullet. Like diets, work-family programs can be faddish; long after firms showed bursts of enthusiasm for on-site day care or job-sharing, women still don't seem to be advancing in the numbers some advocates would like. "These are catchy phrases that are trying to give a simple explanation for a piece of what's very complex," says Ilene Lang, president of Catalyst, a research and advisory group focused on women in business. She fears that even women who make it back on track will still suffer from the larger problems facing female professionals, such as a lack of high-ranking role models and lack of access to informal networks.

It's also true that while progressive companies are rolling out on-ramping initiatives, most of the onus for successfully navigating this transition remains on the women themselves. Monica Samuels is an off-ramped Houston attorney and coauthor of "Comeback Moms," a book she conceived after meeting so many female law-school classmates who'd quit working and had no idea how to resume careers. She cites unexpected factors that intimidate would-be on-rampers, from the shift to business-casual dress to the never-ending rush of technology ("What's a BlackBerry?"). Some of these women also discover that their husbands grew content having them at home. To help overcome self-imposed hurdles—including lack of confidence—Samuels suggests small steps, like continuing to list "lawyer" or "accountant" (instead of "stay-at-home mom") on the "occupation" line when filling out paperwork at the pediatrician's office. "Sometimes women completely divorce themselves from people who are working and become isolated," she says. "That's not a good thing to do."

For Bandini, the newly unemployed news anchor, all thoughts of returning to work take a distant back seat to her soon-to-arrive babies. Financially, she's comfortable, thanks partly to her husband, who runs an aviation-equipment company. But even as she prepares for motherhood, her agent, Pam Pulner, will be making sure TV execs don't forget about her. Bandini may wait until her children are in school to begin working again, but Pulner says most of the TV women she represents resume their careers more quickly than they expected. "When she wants to come back, there will be a place for her," Pulner says. With luck and over time, more women will be able to find their places, too.

With Robbie Brown and Claudia Adrien

UNIT 6

Development During Middle and Late Adulthood

Unit Selections

Key Points to Consider

- Does laughter serve biological functions? If so, what are the uses of laughter that are regulated by our primitive instincts?

- How can parents successfully separate from adult children and encourage maturity and independence?

- Are the middle-adulthood years the best years of one's life? What new research suggests that this is true?

- Aging is inevitable. Should we fight off its signs and symptoms, or accept them gracefully?

- Why do adults who could live on their retirement incomes choose to continue to work? Why do some of them embark on entirely new careers?

- Why do some people live over 100 years and remain in good health? What are their secrets?

- People with Alzheimer's disease have lost many of their memories. Can new therapies help them rediscover some of their past knowledge?

- What are the ethics of terminal care? Who should prepare advance-care directives? When?

Student Web Site
www.mhcls.com/online

Internet References
Further information regarding these Websites may be found in this book's preface or online.

Alzheimer's Disease Research Center
http://alzheimer.wustl.edu/
Lifestyle Factors Affecting Late Adulthood
http://www.school-for-champions.com/health/lifestyle_elderly.htm
National Aging Information Center (NAIC)
http://www.aoa.dhhs.gov/naic/

Donna Day/Getty Images

Joseph Campbell, a twentieth-century sage, said that the privilege of a lifetime is being who you are. This ego-confidence often arrives during middle and late adulthood, even as physical-confidence declines. There is a gradual slowing of the rate of mitosis of cells of all the organ systems with age. This gradual slowing of mitosis translates into a slowed rate of repair of cells of all organs. By the 40s, signs of aging can be seen in skin, skeleton, vision, hearing, smell, taste, balance, coordination, heart, blood vessels, lungs, liver, kidneys, digestive tract, immune response, endocrine functioning, and ability to reproduce. To some extent, moderate use of any body part (as opposed to disuse or misuse) helps it retain its strength, stamina, and repairability. However, by middle and late adulthood persons become increasingly aware of the aging effects of their organ systems on their total physical fitness. A loss of height occurs as spinal disks and connective tissues diminish and settle. Demineralization, especially loss of calcium, causes weakening of bones. Muscles atrophy, and the slowing of cardiovascular and respiratory responses creates a loss of stamina for exercise. All of this may seem cruel, but it occurs very gradually and need not adversely affect a person's enjoyment of life.

Healthful aging, at least in part, seems to be genetically preprogrammed. The females of many species, including humans, outlive the males. The sex hormones of females may protect them from some early aging effects. Males, in particular,

experience earlier declines in their cardiovascular system. Diet and exercise can ward off many of the deleterious effects of aging. A reduction in saturated fat (low density lipid) intake coupled with regular aerobic exercise contributes to less bone demineralization, less plaque in the arteries, stronger muscles (including heart and lung muscles), and a general increase in stamina and vitality. An adequate intake of complex carbohydrates, fibrous foods, fresh fruits, fresh vegetables, unsaturated fats (high density lipids), and water also enhances good health.

Cognitive abilities do not appreciably decline with age in healthy adults. Research suggests that the speed with which the brain carries out problems involving abstract (fluid) reasoning may slow but not cease. Complex problems may simply require more time to solve with age. On the other hand, research suggests that the memory banks of older people may have more crystallized (accumulated and stored) knowledge and more insight. Creativity also frequently spurts after age 50. One's ken (range of knowledge) and practical skills (common sense) grow with age and experience. Older human beings also become expert at the cognitive tasks they frequently do. Many cultures celebrate these abilities as the "wisdom of age."

The first article about middle adulthood speaks to the urge to laugh. New brain research reported in "Emotions and the Brain: Laughter" suggests that laughing is a form of instinctive social bonding. We do not make a conscious decision to laugh. We are often unaware that we are laughing. And laughter is contagious. It makes us healthier by enhancing our immune responsivity and reducing our stress hormones. The "wisdom of age" may allow us to be more frivolous, and to take more pleasure in happy friendships within our families and communities. Children laugh freely. Somehow many adults learn to suppress laughter and to be more serious. Perhaps some wisdom and maturity is evidenced by not trying to suppress this important biological response.

"The Fine Art of Letting Go" addresses the angst of launching adult children into independent lives. The anxiety of leaving offspring at college can be overwhelming. Some parents hover with too many phone calls and/or e-mails, text messages, and so on. Barbara Kantrowitz and Peg Tyre present a short quiz about "helicopter parents," and a list of twelve steps to foster independence in both adult children and their detaching parents.

The last middle-adulthood selection, "The Myth of the Midlife Crisis," dismisses midlife as the beginning of a downward spiral towards death. New research evidence is presented that suggests increased creativity, a new sense of self, deeper knowledge, and better judgment in the second half of life. It makes one anticipate aging with hope and joy.

Erik Erikson suggested that the most important psychological conflict of late adulthood is achieving a sense of ego integrity. This is fostered by self-respect, self-esteem, love of others, and a sense that one's life has order and meaning. The articles in the subsection on late adulthood reflect Erikson's concern with experiencing ego integrity rather than despair.

The first late-adulthood article, "Second Time Around," deliberates opinions about second (or third or fourth) careers begun at the age of retirement. Daniel McGinn offers amicable and constructive judgments and conclusions about the benefits of meaningful work in old age. For many people, retirement is the perfect time to begin a new business adventure. It can be an exciting time to pursue one's dreams, with the fall-back security of a guaranteed retirement income.

In "Secrets of the Centenarians," Maya Pines portrays the lives of several people who are over age 100 but who appear to be in their 70s or early 80s. Researchers have identified genetic markers on the fourth pair of chromosomes that may contribute to longevity and good health. It may be possible in the future to manipulate the single-nucleotide polymorphisms (SNPs) to allow everyone to live as long as the centenarians being studied.

The third late-adulthood selection, "Lost and Found," deals with people with Alzheimer's disease. The author, Barbara Basler, describes new therapeutic methods devised by Cameron Camp, the head of the Myers Research Institute in Ohio. Dr. Camp's methods, deemed valid and reliable by researchers, help draw patients out of their confusion and recapture some of their basic skills and knowledge.

The fourth article deals with end-of-life care and decisions and addresses steps that can be taken to improve the quality of life that is near its end.

The last article describes end-of-life care. The author, Helen Sorenson, discusses the conflicting opinions that create turmoil for patients, family, friends, and health care professionals when death is imminent. "Navigating Practical Dilemmas in Terminal Care" gives useful information on how to reduce such conflicts. Family conferences should occur well ahead of the end of life to discuss the terms of advance-care directives. Asking questions and communicating openly can prevent misunderstandings.

Emotions and the Brain: Laughter

If evolution comes down to survival of the fittest, then why do we joke around so much? New brain research suggests that the urge to laugh is the lubricant that makes humans higher social beings.

Steven Johnson

Robert Provine wants me to see his Tickle Me Elmo doll. Wants me to hold it, as a matter of fact. It's not an unusual request for Provine. A professor of psychology and neuroscience at the University of Maryland, he has been engaged for a decade in a wide-ranging intellectual pursuit that has taken him from the panting play of young chimpanzees to the history of American sitcoms—all in search of a scientific understanding of that most unscientific of human customs: laughter.

The Elmo doll happens to incorporate two of his primary obsessions: tickling and contagious laughter. "You ever fiddled with one of these?" Provine says, as he pulls the doll out of a small canvas tote bag. He holds it up, and after a second or two, the doll begins to shriek with laughter. There's something undeniably comic in the scene: a burly, bearded man in his mid-fifties cradling a red Muppet. Provine hands Elmo to me to demonstrate the doll's vibration effect. "It brings up two interesting things," he explains, as I hold Elmo in my arms. "You have a best-selling toy that's a glorified laugh box. And when it shakes, you're getting feedback as if you're tickling."

Provine's relationship to laughter reminds me of the dramatic technique that Bertolt Brecht called the distanciation effect. Radical theater, in Brecht's vision, was supposed to distance us from our too-familiar social structures, make us see those structures with fresh eyes. In his study of laughter, Provine has been up to something comparably enlightening, helping us to recognize the strangeness of one of our most familiar emotional states. Think about that Tickle Me Elmo doll: We take it for granted that tickling causes laughter and that one person's laughter will easily "infect" other people within earshot. Even a child knows these things. (Tickling and contagious laughter are two of the distinguishing characteristics of childhood.) But when you think about them from a distance, they are strange conventions. We can understand readily enough why natural selection would have implanted the fight-or-flight response in us or endowed us with sex drives. But the tendency to laugh when others laugh in our presence or to laugh when someone strokes our belly with a feather—what's the evolutionary advantage of that? And yet a quick glance at the Nielsen ratings or the personal ads will tell you that laughter is one of the most satisfying and sought-after states available to us.

Funnily enough, the closer Provine got to understanding why we laugh, the farther he got from humor. To appreciate the roots of laughter, you have to stop thinking about jokes.

There is a long, semi-illustrious history of scholarly investigation into the nature of humor, from Freud's *Jokes and Their Relation to the Unconscious,* which may well be the least funny book about humor ever written, to a British research group that announced last year that they had determined the World's Funniest Joke. Despite the fact that the researchers said they had sampled a massive international audience in making this discovery, the winning joke revolved around New Jersey residents:

A couple of New Jersey hunters are out in the woods when one of them falls to the ground. He doesn't seem to be breathing; his eyes are rolled back in his head. The other guy whips out his cell phone and calls the emergency services. He gasps to the operator: "My friend is dead! What can I do?"

The operator says: "Take it easy. I can help. First, let's make sure he's dead." There is silence, then a shot is heard. The guy's voice comes back on the line. He says, "OK, now what?"

This joke illustrates that most assessments of humor's underlying structure gravitate to the notion of controlled incongruity: You're expecting x, and you get y. For the joke to work, it has to be readable on both levels. In the hunting joke there are two plausible ways to interpret the 911 operator's instructions—either the hunter checks his friend's pulse or he shoots him. The context sets you up to expect that he'll check his friend's pulse, so the—admittedly dark—humor arrives when he takes the more unlikely path. That incongruity has limits, of course: If the hunter chooses to do something utterly nonsensical—untie his shoelaces or climb a tree—the joke wouldn't be funny.

A number of studies in recent years have looked at brain activity while subjects were chuckling over a good joke—an attempt to locate a neurological funny bone. There is evidence that the frontal lobes are implicated in "getting" the joke while the brain regions associated with motor control execute the physical response of laughter. One 1999 study analyzed patients with damage to the right frontal lobes, an integrative region of the brain where emotional, logical, and perceptual data converge. The brain-damaged patients had far more difficulty than control subjects in choosing the proper punch line to a series of jokes, usually opting for absurdist, slapstick-style endings rather than traditional ones. Humor can often come in coarse,

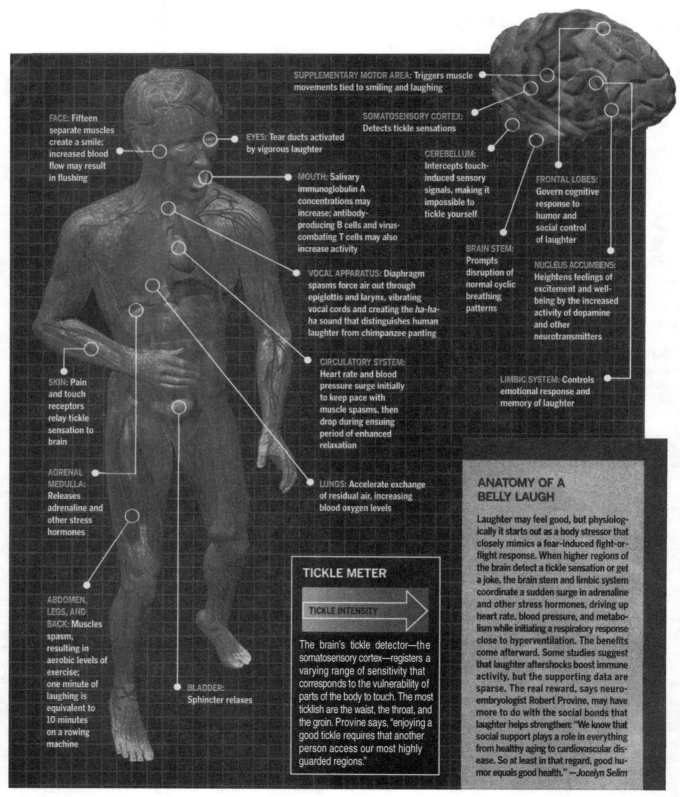

SUPPLEMENTARY MOTOR AREA: Triggers muscle movements tied to smiling and laughing

SOMATOSENSORY CORTEX: Detects tickle sensations

FACE: Fifteen separate muscles create a smile; increased blood flow may result in flushing

EYES: Tear ducts activated by vigorous laughter

CEREBELLUM: Intercepts touch-induced sensory signals, making it impossible to tickle yourself

FRONTAL LOBES: Govern cognitive response to humor and social control of laughter

MOUTH: Salivary immunoglobulin A concentrations may increase; antibody-producing B cells and virus-combating T cells may also increase activity

VOCAL APPARATUS: Diaphragm spasms force air out through epiglottis and larynx, vibrating vocal cords and creating the ha-ha-ha sound that distinguishes human laughter from chimpanzee panting

BRAIN STEM: Prompts disruption of normal cyclic breathing patterns

NUCLEUS ACCUMBENS: Heightens feelings of excitement and well-being by the increased activity of dopamine and other neurotransmitters

SKIN: Pain and touch receptors relay tickle sensation to brain

CIRCULATORY SYSTEM: Heart rate and blood pressure surge initially to keep pace with muscle spasms, then drop during ensuing period of enhanced relaxation

LIMBIC SYSTEM: Controls emotional response and memory of laughter

ADRENAL MEDULLA: Releases adrenaline and other stress hormones

LUNGS: Accelerate exchange of residual air, increasing blood oxygen levels

ABDOMEN, LEGS, AND BACK: Muscles spasm, resulting in aerobic levels of exercise; one minute of laughing is equivalent to 10 minutes on a rowing machine

BLADDER: Sphincter relaxes

TICKLE METER

TICKLE INTENSITY →

The brain's tickle detector—the somatosensory cortex—registers a varying range of sensitivity that corresponds to the vulnerability of parts of the body to touch. The most ticklish are the waist, the throat, and the groin. Provine says, "enjoying a good tickle requires that another person access our most highly guarded regions."

ANATOMY OF A BELLY LAUGH

Laughter may feel good, but physiologically it starts out as a body stressor that closely mimics a fear-induced fight-or-flight response. When higher regions of the brain detect a tickle sensation or get a joke, the brain stem and limbic system coordinate a sudden surge in adrenaline and other stress hormones, driving up heart rate, blood pressure, and metabolism while initiating a respiratory response close to hyperventilation. The benefits come afterward. Some studies suggest that laughter aftershocks boost immune activity, but the supporting data are sparse. The real reward, says neuro-embryologist Robert Provine, may have more to do with the social bonds that laughter helps strengthen: "We know that social support plays a role in everything from healthy aging to cardiovascular disease. So at least in that regard, good humor equals good health." —*Jocelyn Selim*

Graphics by Don Foley

lowest-common-denominator packages, but actually getting the joke draws upon our higher brain functions.

When Provine set out to study laughter, he imagined that he would approach the problem along the lines of these humor studies: Investigating laughter meant having people listen to jokes and other witticisms and watching what happened. He began by simply observing casual conversations, counting the number of times that people laughed while listening to someone speaking. But very quickly he realized that there was a fundamental flaw in his assumptions about how laughter worked. "I started recording all these conversations," Provine says, "and the numbers I was getting—I didn't believe them when I saw them. The speakers were laughing more than the listeners. Every time that would happen, I would think, 'OK, I have to go back and start over again because that can't be right.'"

Speakers, it turned out, were 46 percent more likely to laugh than listeners—and what they were laughing at, more often than not, wasn't remotely funny. Provine and his team of undergrad students recorded the ostensible "punch lines" that triggered laughter in ordinary conversation. They found that only around 15 percent of the sentences that triggered laughter were traditionally humorous. In his book, *Laughter: A Scientific Investigation,* Provine lists some of the laugh-producing quotes:

I'll see you guys later./Put those cigarettes away./I hope we all do well./It was nice meeting you too./We can handle this./I see your point./I should do that, but I'm too lazy./I try to lead a normal life./I think I'm done./I told you so!

The few studies of laughter to date had assumed that laughing and humor were inextricably linked, but Provine's early research suggested that the connection was only an occasional one. "There's a dark side to laughter that we are too quick to overlook," he says. "The kids at Columbine were laughing as they walked through the school shooting their peers."

As his research progressed, Provine began to suspect that laughter was in fact about something else—not humor or gags or incongruity but our social interactions. He found support for this assumption in a study that had already been conducted, analyzing people's laughing patterns in social and solitary contexts. "You're 30 times more likely to laugh when you're with other people than you are when you're alone—if you don't count simulated social environments like laugh tracks on television," Provine says. "In fact, when you're alone, you're more likely to talk out loud to yourself than you are to laugh out loud. Much more." Think how rarely you'll laugh out loud at a funny passage in a book but how quick you'll be to make a friendly laugh when greeting an old acquaintance. Laughing is not an instinctive physical response to humor, the way a flinch responds to pain or a shiver to cold. It's a form of instinctive social bonding that humor is crafted to exploit.

Provine's lab at the Baltimore county campus of the University of Maryland looks like the back room at a stereo repair store—long tables cluttered with old equipment, tubes and wires everywhere. The walls are decorated with brightly colored pictures of tangled neurons, most of which were painted by Provine. (Add some Day-Glo typography and they might pass for signs promoting a Dead show at the Fillmore.) Provine's old mentor, the neuroembryologist Viktor Hamburger, glowers down from a picture hung above a battered Silicon Graphics workstation. His expression suggests a sense of concerned bafflement: "I trained you as a scientist, and here you are playing with dolls!"

The more technical parts of Provine's work—exploring the neuromuscular control of laughter and its relationship to the human and chimp respiratory systems—draw on his training at Washington University in St. Louis under Hamburger and Nobel laureate Rita Levi-Montalcini. But the most immediate way to grasp his insights into the evolution of laughter is to watch video footage of his informal fieldwork, which consists of Provine and a cameraman prowling Baltimore's inner harbor, asking people to laugh for the camera. The overall effect is like a color story for the local news, but as Provine and I watch the tapes together in his lab, I find myself looking at the laughters with fresh eyes. Again and again, a pattern repeats on the screen. Provine asks someone to laugh, and they demur, look puzzled for a second, and say something like, "I can't just laugh." Then they turn to their friends or family, and the laughter rolls out of them as though it were as natural as breathing. The pattern stays the same even as the subjects change: a group of high school students on a field trip, a married couple, a pair of college freshmen.

At one point Provine—dressed in a plaid shirt and khakis, looking something like the comedian Robert Klein—stops two waste-disposal workers driving a golf cart loaded up with trash bags. When they fail to guffaw on cue, Provine asks them why they can't muster one up. "Because you're not funny," one of them says. They turn to each other and share a hearty laugh.

"See, you two just made each other laugh," Provine says.

"Yeah, well, we're coworkers," one of them replies.

The insistent focus on laughter patterns has a strange effect on me as Provine runs through the footage. By the time we get to the cluster of high school kids, I've stopped hearing their spoken words at all, just the rhythmic peals of laughter breaking out every 10 seconds or so. Sonically, the laughter dominates the speech; you can barely hear the dialogue underneath the hysterics. If you were an alien encountering humans for the first time, you'd have to assume that the laughing served as the primary communication method, with the spoken words interspersed as afterthoughts. After one particularly loud outbreak, Provine turns to me and says, "Now, do you think they're all individually making a conscious decision to laugh?" He shakes his head dismissively. "Of course not. In fact, we're often not aware that we're even laughing in the first place. We've vastly overrated our conscious control of laughter."

The limits of our voluntary control of laughter are most clearly exposed in studies of stroke victims who suffer from a disturbing condition known as central facial paralysis, which prevents them from voluntarily moving either the left side or the right side of their faces, depending on the location of the neurological damage. When these individuals are asked to smile or laugh on command, they produce lopsided grins: One side of the mouth curls up, the other remains frozen. But when they're told a joke or they're tickled, traditional smiles and laughs animate their entire faces. There is evidence that the physical mechanism of laughter itself is generated in the brain stem, the most ancient region of the nervous system, which is also responsible for fundamental functions like breathing. Sufferers of amyotrophic lateral sclerosis—Lou Gehrig's disease—which targets the brain stem, often experience spontaneous bursts of uncontrollable laughter, without feeling mirth. (They often undergo a comparable experience with crying as well.) Sometimes called the reptilian brain because its basic structure dates back to our reptile ancestors, the brain stem is largely devoted to our most primal instincts, far removed from our complex, higher-brain skills in understanding humor. And yet somehow, in this primitive region of the brain, we find the urge to laugh.

We're accustomed to thinking of common-but-unconscious instincts as being essential adaptations, like the startle reflex or the suckling of newborns. Why would we have an unconscious propensity for something as frivolous as laughter? As I watch them on the screen, Provine's teenagers remind me of an old Carl Sagan riff, which begins with his describing "a species of primate" that likes to gather in packs of 50 or 60 individuals, cram together in a darkened cave, and hyperventilate in unison, to the point of almost passing out. The behavior is described in such a way as to make it sound exotic and somewhat foolish, like salmon swimming furiously upstream to their deaths or butterflies traveling thousands of miles to rendezvous once a year. The joke, of course, is that the primate is *Homo sapiens,* and the group hyperventilation is our fondness for laughing together at comedy clubs or theaters, or with the virtual crowds of television laugh tracks.

I'm thinking about the Sagan quote when another burst of laughter arrives through the TV speakers, and without realizing what I'm doing, I find myself laughing along with the kids on the screen, I can't help it—their laughter is contagious.

We may be the only species on the planet that laughs together in such large groups, but we are not alone in our appetite for laughter. Not surprisingly, our near relatives, the chimpanzees, are also avid laughers, although differences in their vocal apparatus cause the laughter to sound somewhat more like panting. "The chimpanzee's laughter is rapid and breathy, whereas ours is punctuated with glottal stops," says legendary chimp researcher Roger Fouts. "Also, the chimpanzee laughter occurs on the inhale and exhale, while ours is primarily done on our exhales. But other than these small differences, chimpanzee laughter seems to me to be just like ours in most respects."

Chimps don't do stand-up routines, of course, but they do share a laugh-related obsession with humans, one that Provine believes is central to the roots of laughter itself: Chimps love tickling. Back in his lab, Provine shows me video footage of a pair of young chimps named Josh and Lizzie playing with a human caretaker. It's a full-on ticklefest, with the chimps panting away hysterically when their bellies are scratched. "That's chimpanzee laughter you're hearing," Provine says. It's close enough to human laughter that I find myself chuckling along.

Parents will testify that ticklefests are often the first elaborate play routine they engage in with their children and one of the most reliable laugh inducers. According to Fouts, who helped teach sign language to Washoe, perhaps the world's most famous chimpanzee, the practice is just as common, and perhaps more long lived, among the chimps. "Tickling. . . seems to be very important to chimpanzees because it continues throughout their lives," he says. "Even Washoe at the age of 37 still enjoys tickling and being tickled by her adult family members." Among young chimpanzees that have been taught sign language, tickling is a frequent topic of conversation.

Like laughter, tickling is almost by definition a social activity. Like the incongruity theory of humor, tickling relies on a certain element of surprise, which is why it's impossible to tickle yourself. Predictable touch doesn't elicit the laughter and squirming of tickling—it's unpredictable touch that does the trick. A number of tickle-related studies have convincingly shown that tickling exploits the sensorimotor system's awareness of the difference between self and other: If the system orders your hand to move toward your belly, it doesn't register surprise when the nerve endings on your belly report being stroked. But if the touch is being generated by another sensorimotor system, the belly stroking will come as a surprise. The pleasant laughter of tickle is the way the brain responds to that touch. In both human and chimpanzee societies, that touch usually first appears in parent-child interactions and has an essential role in creating those initial bonds. "The reason [tickling and laughter] are so important," Roger Fouts says, "is because they play a role in maintaining the affinitive bonds of friendship within the family and community."

A few years ago, Jared Diamond wrote a short book with the provocative title *Why Is Sex Fun?* These recent studies suggest an evolutionary answer to the question of why tickling is fun: It encourages us to play well with others. Young children are so receptive to the rough-and-tumble play of tickle that even pretend tickling will often send them into peals of laughter. (Fouts reports that the threat of tickle has a similar effect on his chimps.) In his book, Provine suggests that "feigned tickle" can be thought of as the Original Joke, the first deliberate behavior designed to exploit the tickling-laughter circuit. Our comedy clubs and our sitcoms are culturally enhanced versions of those original playful childhood exchanges. Along with the suckling and smiling instincts, the laughter of tickle evolved as a way of cementing the bond between parents and children, laying the foundation for a behavior that then carried over into the social lives of adults. While we once laughed at the surprise touch of a parent or sibling, we now laugh at the surprise twist of a punch line.

Bowling Green State University professor Jaak Panksepp suggests that there is a dedicated "play" circuitry in the brain, equivalent to the more extensively studied fear and love circuits. Panksepp has studied the role of rough-and-tumble play in cementing social connections between juvenile rats. The play instinct is not easily suppressed. Rats that have been denied the opportunity to engage in this kind of play—which has a distinct choreography, as well as a chirping vocalization that may be the rat equivalent of laughter—will nonetheless immediately engage in play behavior given the chance. Panksepp compares it to a bird's instinct for flying. "Probably the most powerful positive emotion of all—once your tummy is full and you don't have bodily needs—is vigorous social engagement among the young," Panksepp says. "The largest amount of human laughter seems to occur in the midst of early childhood—rough-and-tumble play, chasing, all the stuff they love."

Playing is what young mammals do, and in humans and chimpanzees, laughter is the way the brain expresses the pleasure of that play. "Since laughter seems to be ritualized panting, basically what you do in laughing is replicate the sound of rough-and-tumble play," Provine says. "And you know, that's where I think it came from. Tickle is an important part of our primate heritage. Touching and being touched is an important part of what it means to be a mammal."

There is much that we don't know yet about the neurological underpinnings of laughter. We do not yet know precisely why laughing feels so good; one recent study detected evidence that stimulating the nucleus accumbens, one of the brain's pleasure centers, triggered laughter. Panksepp has performed studies that indicate opiate antagonists significantly reduce the urge to play in rats, which implies that the brain's endorphin system may be involved in the pleasure of laughter. Some anecdotal and clinical evidence suggest that laughing makes you healthier by suppressing stress hormones and elevating immune system antibodies. If you think of laughter as a form of behavior that is basically synonymous with the detection of humor, the laughing-makes-you-healthier premise seems bizarre. Why would natural selection make our immune system respond to jokes? Provine's approach helps solve the mystery. Our bodies aren't responding to wisecracks and punch lines; they're responding to social connection.

In this respect, laughter reminds us that our emotional lives are as much outward bound as they are inner directed. We tend to think of emotions as private affairs, feelings that wash over our subjective worlds. But emotions are also social acts, laughter perhaps most of all. It's no accident that we have so many delicately choreographed gestures and facial expressions—many of which appear to be innate to our species—to convey our emotions. Our emotional systems are designed to share our feelings and not just represent them internally—an insight that Darwin first grasped more than a century ago in his book *The Expression of the Emotions in Man and Animals.* "The movements of expression in the face and body, whatever their origin may have been, are in themselves of much importance for our welfare. They serve as the first means of communication between mother and infant; she smiles approval, and thus encourages her child on the right path. . . . The free expression by outward signs of an emotion intensifies it."

And even if we don't yet understand the neurological basis of the pleasure that laughing brings us, it makes sense that we should seek out the connectedness of infectious laughter. We are social animals, after all. And if that laughter often involves some pretty childish behavior, so be it. "I mean, this is why we're not like lizards," Provine says, holding the Tickle Me Elmo doll on his lap. "Lizards don't play, and they're not social the way we are. When you start to see play, you're starting to see mammals. So when we get together and have a good time and laugh, we're going back to our roots. It's ironic in a way: Some of the things that give us the most pleasure in life are really the most ancient."

From *Discover*, April 2003, pp. 63–69. Copyright © 2003 by Steven Johnson. Reprinted by permission of the author.

The Fine Art of Letting Go

As parents, boomers face their final frontier: how to stand aside as their children become independent adults. Where's the line between caring and coddling?

BARBARA KANTROWITZ AND PEG TYRE

I magine tears, lots of tears. Imagine a trail of tears trickling across upstate New York. Judie Comerford and her husband, Michael, are in their minivan on a highway somewhere between Potsdam and their home in Buffalo. They've just bid farewell to their oldest child, Meghan, who's starting college. "I cried, and then I cried some more, and then I cried again," Judie recalls. "I didn't think it was possible for someone to cry for going on five hours." The Comerfords were so distraught that they failed to notice the speedometer hitting 92 miles an hour. "The next thing I knew, there were these flashing red lights," Judie says. They pulled over to the side, but the tears kept coming. The trooper asked, "Is there a problem here?"

Judie couldn't speak. Michael was no help; he was bawling, too. Finally, Judie blurted out, "We just took my daughter to college. My life is over. She's my little girl."

The cop got it. "I have a little girl," he said. (Perhaps that's why the Comerfords escaped with only a $15 ticket.) Since that difficult day in 1993, Judie and Michael have said goodbye to three other kids—all now out of school and living successfully on their own. And each time, Judie, a 52-year-old medical receptionist, was inconsolable. With all the birds out of the nest, Judie can joke about her overly emotional goodbyes—and about the solace she still gets from talking to her kids on the phone "oh, about 40 times a week." She laughs. "And then there's text messaging, too."

Letting go. Are there two more painful words in the boomer-parent lexicon? One minute, there's an adorable, helpless bundle in your arms. Then, 18 years go by in a flash, filled with Mommy and Me classes, Gymboree, Little League, ballet, drama club, summer camp, traveling soccer teams, piano lessons, science competitions, SAT prep classes and college visits. The next thing you know, it's graduation. Most boomers don't want to be "helicopter parents," hovering so long that their offspring never get a chance to grow up. Well versed in the psychological literature, they know that letting go is a gradual process that should begin when toddlers take their first steps without a parental hand to steady them. And hovering is certainly not a new phenomenon; both Gen. Douglas MacArthur and President Franklin Delano Roosevelt had mothers who moved to be near them when they went to college. But with cell phones and e-mail available 24/7, the temptation to check in is huge. Some boomer parents hang on, propelled by love (of course) and insecurity about how the world will treat their children. After years of supervising homework, they think nothing of editing the papers their college students have e-mailed them. A few even buy textbooks and follow the course syllabi. Later they're polishing student résumés and calling in favors to get summer internships.

Alarmed by these intrusions into what should be a period of increasing independence, colleges around the country have set up parent-liaison offices to limit angry phone calls to professors and deans. Parent orientations, usually held alongside the student sessions, teach how to step aside.

Letting go is the final frontier for boomer parents, who've made child rearing a major focus of their adult lives. The 76,957,164 Americans born between 1946 and 1964 are the wealthiest and best-educated generation of parents in human history, and they've had unparalleled resources to aid them as they've raised an estimated 80 million children. Although there have been some economic ups and downs, unemployment has been generally low, and the rise of two-career families has meant more for all. While their incomes grew, boomers kept family sizes small, thanks to the availability of birth control and abortion. "In the old days, parents thought of kids like waffles," says William Damon, director of the Stanford University Center on Adolescence. "The first couple might not turn out just right, but you could always make more. Now many families have only one or two kids to work with, so they focus all their attention and energy on one or two and want them to do well." An explosion of child-development research stressing the importance of the early years reinforces boomers' determination to give their kids the best. They've carefully followed expert advice on everything from music that nurtures the developing brain in utero to gaming the college-admissions process.

By many standards, all that effort has paid off. More students than ever are entering college, and rates of teen pregnancy, crime and drug abuse are all down. And the recipients of that guidance certainly appear to be grateful. "Their connection to their parents is deep and strong," says Barbara Hofer, an associate professor of psychology at Middlebury College who studies the transition to college. "They say, 'My parents are my best friends.' People would have seen that as aberrant a generation ago, as pathological." Hofer and her student Elena Kennedy recently surveyed Middlebury freshmen and found that students and parents reported an average of 10.41 communications per week over cell phone, e-mail, Instant Messenger, dorm phone, text messaging and postal mail. Parents initiate most of this contact, Hofer found, but their children don't seem to mind; most students said they were satisfied with the amount of communication they had with their parents and 28 percent wanted even more with their fathers.

But that closeness is a double-edged sword. When admissions directors get together, sharing horror stories of overinvolved parents is one of their favorite pastimes. "There are cases where the parent tells the adviser that their son wants to be a doctor," says one Midwestern dean, "and these are the classes he wants to take, and then, when the parent leaves the room, the students say, 'I'm not sure I want to be a doctor at all. English and art are more interesting to me'."

Parents who hover risk crippling their children's fledgling sense of self-sufficiency. Missa Murry Eaton, an assistant professor at Penn State University Shenango who studies parent-child relationships, says she's seen a number of parents who think it's OK to call their freshman sons or daughters early in the morning to make sure they wake up or check in late at night to see if they're studying. "They don't allow their children to deal with the consequences of their decisions," says Eaton. "So when a decision goes badly, they just fix it." Children and young adults build up confidence by tackling things that are hard, says Damon. "When they do succeed, they earn real self-esteem."

In fact, it's not the number of e-mails or phone calls that really matter, but the content of the connection. Here, boomers run into trouble. Chatting about the weather or politics is one thing; micromanaging decisions about courses or majors is quite another. But many parents think that economic pressures compel them to intervene. Sending a child to college these days is a huge financial commitment, more than $40,000 a year at elite private schools. For a lot of parents, that means substantial sacrifices like taking out a second mortgage or cutting into retirement savings. "Parents feel this is an economic investment, and they want that investment to pay off," says Hofer.

What's helpful and what's hovering? At Washington University in St. Louis, Karen Coburn, the assistant vice chancellor for students, says helping parents understand the challenges their students will face is a major part of her job. One important lesson: "No one was ever happy all the time between 18 and 22, and your kids aren't going to be, either." She tells parents to take tearful calls in stride. Walking across campus, she often hears students on the phone with a parent, complaining about a cold or a bad grade. "Then I see them click off the phone and go running over to a friend and say, 'Hi, how are you? Things are great!' And I think of those poor parents, sitting in their offices."

As graduation approaches, there's even more pressure on college career offices and prospective employers. "We have parents calling us to ask why little Johnny wasn't accepted to interview at Goldman," says Jennifer Floren, CEO of experience.com, a Web site that connects 3,800 universities with employers. "They're demanding passwords so they can get into the student's account. It's just bizarre." In an experience.com survey of career-center offices, respondents said parents were substantially more involved than even five years ago and that this trend cut across all regions of the country and all incomes.

Parents worry that their kids will never get jobs and end up home after graduation, living in the basement. It's not an unreasonable fear. Many kids graduate with debt from student loans, which makes it difficult to find affordable housing even if they do find work. According to the 2000 Census, 10.5 percent of Americans 25 to 34 were living in their parents' houses, compared with 8 percent in 1970, the low point for young adults moving home.

It takes will power to hold back. Rosalie Fuller knew what she had to do when her oldest son, Brinson, 20, left for Appalachian State University. "I'm trying very hard to force them to leave the nest," she says. Fuller, 48, who lives in New Bern, N.C., and her husband, Walt, 53, a timber buyer for Weyerhaeuser, have agreed to pay for Brinson's tuition, room and board, but he is supposed to pay for fraternity dues, car insurance and general expenses. In the middle of sophomore year, Brinson ran out of cash and the Fullers decided to take over his car-insurance payments but nothing else. Then his grades took a plunge—all C's and D's. The reason: too much partying and not enough studying. In an e-mail, Rosalie told him how many hours a week she spent working for a company that sells aviation fuel in order for him to go to college. "I told him that I would never again pay for a semester like this." Brinson got the message. He wrote her back a three-page mission statement laying

Leaving the Nest

85% of parents helped or expect to help their children decide which schools they will apply to.
69% of parents report that they helped or expect to help their children fill out college applications.
19% arranged or expect to arrange for their children to take an SAT/ACT prep course before the test.

Source: Based on a March 2006 survey by College Parents of America.

Paying Their Bills

55% of college students get help from their parents to pay expenses other than housing and tuition.
14% of college students report that their parents help them settle their credit-card debts.
17% receive a monthly allowance from their parents (the average allowance for this group is $869).

Source: NCES, NPSAS

Other Assistance

57% of 18- to 20-year-olds get help from parents with chores (averaging 527 hours a year).
48% of students graduating in 2006 say they will move back into their parents' home after graduation.
44% of last year's grads are still living with their parents (fewer than half say it's due to financial reasons).

Source: "On the Frontier of Adulthood: Theory Research, and Public Policy" by Bob Schoeni and Karen Ross, Monstertrak's 2006 entry-level job survey.

Why Parents Worry

22% of parents say their greatest concern regarding their college-age child is health and safety.
20% say that the issue troubling them the most is their college-age child's performance in school.
18% of parents report that career planning is their biggest worry about their college student.

Source: Based on University of Minnesota's parents survey.

Reaching Adulthood

81% of people say that, to be an adult, you have to choose values independently of parents.
74% of people say you must be able to support yourself financially to be considered an adult.
55% of people say you have to move out of your parents' household in order to achieve adulthood.

Source: "Emerging Adulthood: The Winding Road from the Late Teens Through the Twenties" by Jeffery Jensen Arnett

Markers of Maturity

46% of women had left home, married and had kids by 30 in 2000. It was 77 percent in 1960.
27 was the median age of marriage for men and 25 for women in the U.S. in 2000. In 1950 it was 22 and 20.

Source: USA Today; "Emerging Adulthood: The Winding Road from the Late Teens Through the Twenties" by Jeffery Jensen Arnett

out his plan of action to get better grades. "First and foremost," he wrote, "I will attend every class." Brinson followed up on his promise—his grades are up—and he's leaning toward an accounting major.

Closeness to their kids doesn't mean boomers are lenient. Sheila Walker, 51, a grocery clerk from Cleveland, doesn't think there's anything wrong with being in the face of her son, Ronald, 17. "He's a good boy, but I'm the mom," she says. "Part of our responsibility as parents is to know who your kids are with. Technology, like cell phones, makes it easier for us to monitor our kids." This fall, Ronald heads off to college. "Sure, I'm going to miss him," she says, "but I want him to be a man."

Many parents say letting go is hard because the stakes seem so much higher than when they were starting out. At every stage of their parenting careers, they've felt the pressure of competition—whether it's getting their kids into a good preschool, summer camp or college. Boomers might have spent their young-adult years shuffling from major to major or job to job, but many say they'd never condone that behavior in their kids. In fact, experimentation can be critical to real accomplishment, while following lockstep in a preordained path is often deadening. "The idea of taking good risks and doing your best and then learning from whatever happens is a necessary part of becoming a successful person," says Dave Verhaagen, a child and adolescent psychologist in North Carolina and author of "Parenting the Millennial Generation."

Barrie Smith, 45, of Old Westbury, N.Y., concedes that her son, Chase Steinlauf, about to turn 18, who just finished his freshman year at Duke University, has been at the center of her life. "Raising him was my career," she says proudly. She scheduled her days chauffeuring him to tennis, chess and math team. Things really ramped up when the college-admissions race started. She admits she pushed him to apply to the best schools. "You want that Harvard sticker on your car," she says. "They make a lot of connections at these schools."

Chase was a National Merit Scholar and graduated at the top of his class. Still, says Smith, "there was a lot of stress and fighting." She wanted Harvard. "I could see myself there," she says. Chase liked Yale. "He was trying to assert his independence," she says. He didn't succeed. Smith made him apply early to Harvard and he was deferred. He was rejected by Yale and got into Duke. "It was my mistake," Smith says. "I should have let him apply to the college of his choice."

She channeled her anxiety about his leaving into preparing his dorm room. Smith bought Ralph Lauren sheets, a cashmere throw, leather slippers, a sisal rug. "He lives like that at home," she explains. "I wanted to make it homey." Chase says he stuffed the decorative pillows, comforter and cashmere throw into his suitcase. "She likes things formal in a way that I find cluttered," he says diplomatically. Smith nearly passed out from anxiety about Chase's well-being after she dropped him off, but soon afterward, she started a Web site for equally worried moms of freshmen called mofchat.com. "It became a kind of catharsis," she says. When Chase talks about the Web site, he sounds more like the proud parent. "It was a lot more professional than I had anticipated," he says. "It's good to have a place where [parents] can talk to each other."

12 Steps to Independence

Your child's departure for college is a big step. But the journey from cradle to campus is filled with countless little steps—each an opportunity to prepare for letting go. Here, Karen Levin Coburn and Madge Lawrence Treeger, authors of "Letting Go: A Parents' Guide to Understanding the College Years," offer mantras for parents at every phase of the journey.

1. **Take a deep breath.** Give your child a chance to work things out. Even a crying infant eventually learns to fall asleep without being held.

2. **Help your child learn to negotiate conflicts.** Encouraging your toddler to use words rather than grab her shovel back from another child in the sandbox may be the first lesson in the art of conflict resolution.

3. **Help your child learn to cope with disappointment.** Empathize with your grade-school-age child when she isn't invited to a birthday party. Instead of trying to "fix it," help her to move on.

4. **Support your child's interests and passions.** You may have been hoping for a home filled with the sound of music, but your son is mad about metalsmithing. Praise your child for who he is becoming, not who you thought he would be.

5. **Help your child learn to advocate for herself.** The Little League dad who yells at the umpire for a bad call doesn't help the child learn to solve problems or gain confidence.

6. **Encourage your child to dream big dreams and set achievable goals.** Support your middle-schooler's dreams of running a marathon, but help her first achieve her 5K goal.

7. **Loosen the reins a little at a time.** Increase your child's freedom and responsibility a bit more each year.

8. **Teach your child to manage money.** During the early years piggy banks, allowances and household jobs are tools to teach about money management. When teenagers are allowed to make choices about the money they've saved, reality sets in.

9. **Help your child learn to manage time.** The college student who understands the consequences of too little sleep or being late has a big advantage.

10. **Be a coach.** Young people often need encouragement to seek the help they need. Support your child's emerging independence by helping him to take action on his own behalf.

11. **Remain an anchor.** Encourage your child to turn to you in good times and bad. Stay steady even when your child is shaky. And as the parent of a college student you can provide a familiar and safe haven, an anchor in a new and unfamiliar sea, a place for solace and encouragement and admiration.

12. **Finally,** when you drop your "emerging adult" at college, remember she is taking you with her. Though she may not admit it to you, she will quote things you've said—and recount things you've shown her. Resist your temptation to give one last lecture on all the things you fear you have forgotten to teach her during the past 18 years. She has been listening more than she will let you know.

During college and the first years after graduation, young adults should be learning to make decisions for themselves and dealing with the consequences. Parents can help or hinder that process. "You have to go from manager to consultant, from onsite supervisor to mentor," says Helen Johnson, coauthor of "Don't Tell Me What to Do, Just Send Money." "You have to let them fail and face those tough situations. It's not easy to do. But if you don't, think about the message you are conveying to your son or daughter—that they're not able to handle their own life."

That means a period of adjustment for both parent and child. Tom and Pam Burkardt, who live in suburban Boston, are getting ready for the day their youngest child, Colin, 17, goes to college. "We just told Colin the other day to 'Pick any college and we'll follow you'," says Pam, 52. "We were joking … sort of." Their older sons—Michael, 22, and Sean, 20—are both in college, but Tom, 47, says he talks to them "all the time," via cell phone, e-mail and instant messaging. When Colin leaves, Tom anticipates "a tough, tough time." But he knows that encouraging his sons' independence is the only way to help them lead happy and productive adult lives. All his sons worked during high school and summers between college semesters even though the family's bank account expanded considerably after Tom sold his telecommunications business. "Just because we have money doesn't mean we're going to spoil them," Tom says. "You have to learn the value of a dollar." Tom's personal measure of success? "Man, it warms my heart when one calls and says, 'Hey Dad, want to play some golf?' "

In the early years of the 20th century, parents hung on to their kids for as long as possible because children, who often started working at a young age, were an important source of income. "The kid would finally have to break away if they wanted to keep any of their own money," says Stephanie Coontz, a family historian at the Evergreen State College in Olympia, Wash. By the time the oldest baby boomers were born, parents expected their kids to grow up and move out—period. Half of all women were married by the age of 20, a move parents generally supported because they thought marriage promoted maturity.

As the older boomers were coming of age in the 1960s and '70s, ideas about leaving home shifted again. Young adults thought they had to rebel against their parents in order to achieve independence, Coontz says. Younger boomers were more likely to suffer from the sharp rise in divorce rates beginning in the late 1960s, which meant that sometimes parents left home before the kids. So both older and younger boomers entered parenthood with strong reasons to find a better way to raise their own children.

Jim Tully, 44, a sales manager for a beef company, was the youngest of six kids. His mother died when he was 9 and his father was working all the time. "There was no helicopter in my house when I was growing up," says Jim, who lives in Brockton, Mass. His wife, Sharon, 43, was the youngest of seven. "Everything is completely different from the way that I grew up," says Jim. "My wife and I dedicate our lives to our children." The four Tully children are now ages 21 to 8. "We talk about the sex, the drugs, the rock and roll," says Jim. In many ways, he says he feels close to his kids because he shares some of their interests and tastes. "I still love Jimi Hendrix and Aerosmith," says Jim. His daughter Jill, 18, who's going off to college in the fall, says the open relationship she has with her parents keeps her out of trouble. "Because my parents listen to me," she says, "I don't have any secrets from them. We can talk." They have, for example, talked about parties where there might be some drinking. Jill knows that if she did decide to drink, all she would have to do is call home and someone would come and get her. "Because we talk about things so much, I don't even want to drink," she says. "It's the kids whose parents don't talk to them who sneak around and do dumb things." Her parents are her role models. "That's the kind of relationship I want to have with my children in the future," she says.

But to get to that place of mutual trust and respect, parents do have to let go a little. "It is good and healthy for parents to want their kids to be successful, but there are many ways to get there," says Laurence Steinberg, a Temple University psychology professor and the author of "The Ten Basic Principles of Good Parenting." "Part of good parenting is facilitating your child's personal development, not just their accomplishments." Julia Cruz, 58, and her husband, Allen Russell Chauvenet, are both doctors who live in Winston-Salem, N.C. They chose their house because it is just a mile from the hospital where they work and they could be home for dinner with their kids, Nicholas, now 21, and Christina, 19.

As their kids grew older, Julia and Allen worked hard to encourage their independence, but the final goodbyes were wrenching. Julia will never forget the day she dropped Nicholas off at the University of North Carolina at Chapel Hill. As she helped him set up his room, she was crying. Before she left to go home, she told her son she was going off to the other end of campus to get a copy of the parent handbook. Nicholas said he was going to visit a friend. As they walked outside together in the sunny, late August weather, Julia tried to gather her composure. Nicholas said, "Are you going to be all right?" Julia said, "Yes, and you're going to be all right, too." They tearfully embraced. He started walking away. Julia didn't move. She just watched him—her baby—and then watched the girls watching him and suddenly saw him for who he had become, a handsome young man firmly in adulthood. She wanted to cry out a warning: be careful, wear clean clothes, don't fall in love with someone who will break your heart. But she remained silent.

And then her son turned and headed back to his dorm. She stood rooted to the spot while he walked past without seeing her. He was in his new world now.

With Joan Raymond, Pat Wingert and Marc Bain.

The Myth of the Midlife Crisis

It's time we stopped dismissing middle age as the beginning of the end. Research suggests that at 40, the brain's best years are still ahead.

GENE COHEN, M.D., PH.D.

I was taken by surprise several years ago when my colleagues started to worry that I was going through some sort of midlife crisis. I was in my late 40s, and after two decades as a gerontologist I was pursuing a new passion: designing games for older adults. My first game, a joint effort with artist Gretchen Raber, was a finalist in an internationally juried show on games as works of art. Though I still had a day job directing George Washington University's Center on Aging, Health & Humanities, I was now working hard on a second game.

"Are you turning right on us?" one friend, a neuroscientist, kidded me. He wasn't talking about politics. He was asking whether I'd scrapped the logical, analytical tendencies of the brain's left hemisphere to embrace the more creative, less disciplined tendencies of the right brain. But I wasn't scrapping anything. As a researcher, I had spent years documenting the psychological benefits of intergenerational play. Now I was using both sides of my brain to create new opportunities for myself. Instead of just measuring and studying the benefits of mental stimulation, I was finding creative ways to put my findings to work. What my friends perceived as a crisis was, in truth, the start of a thrilling new phase of my life.

The mature mind gets better at reconciling thoughts and feelings.

In thinking about this experience, I realized that our view of human development in the second half of life was badly outmoded. We tend to think of aging in purely negative terms, and even experts often define "successful" aging as the effective management of decay and decline. Rubbish. No one can deny that aging brings challenges and losses. But recent discoveries in neuroscience show that the aging brain is more flexible and adaptable than we previously thought. Studies suggest that the brain's left and right hemispheres become better integrated during middle age, making way for greater creativity. Age also seems to dampen some negative emotions. And a great deal of scientific work has confirmed the "use it or lose it" adage, showing that the aging brain grows stronger from use and challenge. In short, midlife is a time of new possibility. Growing old can be filled with positive experiences. The challenge is to recognize our potential—and nurture it.

Until recently, scientists paid little attention to psychological development in the second half of life, and those who did pay attention often drew the wrong conclusions. "About the age of 50," Sigmund Freud wrote in 1907, "the elasticity of the mental processes on which treatment depends is, as a rule, lacking. Old people are no longer educable." Freud—who wrote those words at 51 and produced some of his best work after 65—wasn't the only pioneer to misconstrue the aging process. Jean Piaget, the great developmental psychologist, assumed that cognitive development stopped during young adulthood, with the acquisition of abstract thought. Even Erik Erikson, who delineated eight stages of psychosocial development, devoted only two pages of his classic work "Identity and the Life Cycle" to later life.

My own work picks up where these past giants left off. Through studies involving more than 3,000 older adults, I have identified four distinct developmental phases that unfold in overlapping 20-year periods beginning in a person's early 40s: a midlife re-evaluation (typically encountered between 40 and 65) during which we set new goals and priorities; a liberation phase (55 to 75) that involves shedding past inhibitions to express ourselves more freely; a summing-up phase (65 to 85) when we begin to review our lives and concentrate on giving back, and an encore phase (75 and beyond) that involves finding affirmation and fellowship in the face of adversity and loss. I refer to "phases" instead of "stages" because people vary widely during later life. We don't all march through these phases in lock step, but I've seen thousands of older adults pass through them—each person driven by a unique set of inner drives and ideals.

What sparks this series of changes? Why, after finding our places in the world, do so many of us spend our 40s and 50s re-evaluating our lives? The impulse stems partly from a growing awareness of our own mortality. As decades vanish behind us, and we realize how relatively few we have left, we gain new perspective on who we are and what we really care about. This awakening isn't always easy—it often reveals conflicts between the lives we've built and the ones we want to pursue—but only 10 percent of the people I've studied describe the midlife transition as a crisis. Far more say they're filled with a new sense of quest and personal discovery. "I'm looking forward to pursuing the career I always wanted," one 49-year-old woman told me. "I'm tired of just working on other people's visions, rather than my own, even if I have to start on a smaller scale."

While changing our perspective, age also remodels our brains, leaving us better equipped to fulfill our own dreams. The most important difference between older brains and younger brains is also the easiest to overlook: older brains have learned more than young ones. Throughout life, our brains encode thoughts and memories by forming new connections among neurons. The neurons themselves may lose some processing speed with age, but they become ever more richly intertwined. Magnified tremendously, the brain of a mentally active 50-year-old looks like a dense forest of interlocking branches, and this density reflects both deeper knowledge and better judgment. That's why age is such an advantage in fields like editing, law, medicine, coaching and management. There is no substitute for acquired learning.

Knowledge and wisdom aren't the only fruits of age. New research suggests that as our brains become more densely wired, they also become less rigidly bifurcated. As I mentioned earlier, our brains actually consist of two separate structures—a right brain and a left brain—linked by a row of fibers called the corpus callosum. In most people, the left hemisphere specializes in speech, language and logical reasoning, while the right hemisphere handles more intuitive tasks, such as face recognition and the reading of emotional cues. But as scientists have recently discovered through studies with PET scans and magnetic resonance imaging, this pattern changes as we age. Unlike young adults, who handle most tasks on one side of the brain or the other, older ones tend to use both hemispheres. Duke University neuroscientist Robert Cabeza has dubbed this phenomenon Hemispheric Asymmetry Reduction in Older Adults—HAROLD for short—and his research suggests it is no accident.

In a 2002 study, Cabeza assigned a set of memory tasks to three groups of people: one composed of young adults, one of low-performing older adults and one of high-performing older adults. Like the young people, the low-performing elders drew mainly on one side of the prefrontal cortex to perform the assigned tasks. It was the high-scoring elders who used both hemispheres. No one knows exactly what this all means, but the finding suggests that healthy brains compensate for the depredations of age by expanding their neural networks across the bilateral divide. My own work suggests that, besides keeping us sharp, this neural integration makes it easier to reconcile our thoughts with our feelings. When you hear someone saying, "My head tells me to do this, but my heart says do that," the person is more likely a 20-year-old than a 50-year-old. One of my patients, a 51-year-old man, remembers how he agonized over decisions during his 20s, searching in vain for the most logical choice. As he moved through his 40s and into his 50s, he found himself trusting his gut. "My decisions are more subjective," he said during one session, "but I'm more comfortable with many of the choices that follow."

As our aging brains grow wiser and more flexible, they also tend toward greater equanimity. Our emotions are all rooted in a set of neural structures known collectively as the limbic system. Some of our strongest negative emotions originate in the amygdalae, a pair of almond-shaped limbic structures that sit near the center of the brain, screening sensory data for signs of trouble. At the first hint of a threat, the amygdalae fire off impulses that can change our behavior before our conscious, thinking brains have a chance to weigh in. That's why our hearts pound when strangers approach us on dark sidewalks—and why we often overreact to slights and annoyances. But the amygdalae seem to mellow with age. In brain-imaging studies, older adults show less evidence of fear, anger and hatred than young adults. Psychological studies confirm that impression, showing that older adults are less impulsive and less likely to dwell on their negative feelings.

An editor I know at a New York publishing company provides a case in point. He was in his 60s, and contemplating retirement, when he realized that he had finally matured into his job. Despite a sharp intellect and a passion for excellence, this man had spent much of his career alienating people with brusque, critical comments and a lack of sensitivity. Now, he told me over lunch, he was finally beginning to master interpersonal communication. As his emotional development caught up to his intellectual development, he morphed from a brilliant but brittle loner into a mentor and a mediator of conflicts. "I feel like a changed man," he said with a bemused smile. His best work was still ahead of him.

Clearly, the aging brain is more resilient, adaptable and capable than we thought. But that doesn't mean we can sit back and expect good things to happen. Research has identified several types of activity that can, if practiced regularly, help boost the power, clarity and subtlety of the aging brain.

Exercise physically. Numerous studies have linked physical exercise to increased brainpower. This is particularly true when the exercise is aerobic—meaning continuous, rhythmic exercise that uses large muscle groups. The positive effects may stem from increased blood flow to the brain, the production of endorphins, better filtration of waste products from the brain and increased brain-oxygen levels.

Exercise mentally. The brain is like a muscle. Use it and it grows stronger. Let it idle and it will grow flabby. So choose something appealing and challenging—and don't be surprised if, once you start, you want to do more. One of the programs I co-chair, the Creativity Discovery Corps, strives to identify unrecognized, talented older adults in the community. A 93-year-old woman we recently interviewed advised us that she might find scheduling the next interview difficult because she was very busy applying for a Ph.D. program.

Pick challenging leisure activities. Getting a graduate degree isn't the only way to keep your brain fit. An important 2003 study identified five leisure activities that were associated with a lower risk of dementia and cognitive decline. In order of impact (from highest to lowest), the winners were dancing, playing board games, playing musical instruments, doing crossword puzzles and reading. Risk reduction was related to the frequency of participation. For example, older persons who did crossword puzzles four days a week had a risk of dementia 47 percent lower than subjects who did puzzles only once a week.

Achieve mastery. Research on aging has uncovered a key variable in mental health called "sense of control." From middle age onward, people who enjoy a sense of control and mastery stay healthier than those who don't. The possibilities for mastery are unlimited, ranging from playing a musical instrument to learning a new language to taking up painting or embroidery. Besides improving your outlook, the sense of accomplishment may also strengthen the immune system.

Establish strong social networks. Countless studies have linked active social engagement to better mental and physical health and lower death rates. People who maintain social relationships during the second half of life enjoy significantly lower blood pressure, which in turn reduces the risk of stroke and its resulting brain damage. Social relationships also reduce stress and its corrosive effects, including anxiety and depression.

The brain is like the foundation of a building—it provides the physical substrate of our minds, our personalities and our sense of self. As we've seen, our brain hardware is capable of adapting, growing and becoming more complex and integrated with age. As our brains mature and evolve, so do our knowledge, our emotions and our expressive abilities. In turn, what we do with those abilities affects the brain itself, forging the new connections and constellations needed for further psychological growth. This realization should embolden anyone entering the later phases of life. If we can move beyond our stubborn myths about the aging brain, great things are possible. Successful aging is not about managing decline. It's about harnessing the enormous potential that each of us has for growth, love and happiness.

GENE COHEN is founding director of the Center on Aging, Health & Humanities at George Washington University Medical Center. This article is adapted from "The Mature Mind: The Positive Power of the Aging Brain," published this month by Basic Books, a member of the Perseus Book Group.

Second Time Around

After pink slips and midlife crises, a generation of seekers is beginning to create Career 2.0. In doing so, they may redefine the idea of retirement.

DANIEL McGINN

They were the children of the Organization Men, those gray-flannel-clad climbers whose zeal for corporate life remains a defining image of the 1950s. But by the time the first baby boomers began entering the work force in the late 1960s, times were changing. College degrees had become more prevalent. Women were seeking out careers that were once off-limits. Industrial jobs were giving way to even more office work. And America's postwar fascination with materialism—look, there's another new car in the driveway of another newly built suburban home!—was on the wane. When it came to work, baby boomers wanted something more than steady paychecks, predictable promotions and the gold watch. Many wanted their work to be, above all, meaningful.

That quest continues today. Boomers are a wide demographic: the oldest, at 60, are nearing the age when their parents probably thought about retiring, while the youngest, at 42, are just hitting the sweet spot of their careers. Some are fantastically wealthy; some struggle in poverty. But most have approached their working lives with a self-determination unlike any previous generation—and for many, that means starting a whole new career in midlife. "There are tens of millions of people involved here, [asking], 'What am I going to do with the rest of my life?' " says Richard Fein, author of "The Baby Boomer's Guide to the New Workplace." Every day, a few more boomers blast those "new contact info" e-mails out as they pursue new professional adventures. Some are trading high-paying jobs to move into nonprofits or government positions. Some are starting businesses—or trying to parlay an individual passion (for quilting, say) into a way to make a living. Not all these moves are voluntary: for many people nowadays, the journey toward a new career begins with the pain of a pink slip.

And not everyone will find what they're seeking. Harvard political scientist Russell Muirhead, author of "Just Work," says the notion that one's occupation should deliver something more meaningful than a paycheck began with the 19th-century Romantics, but it's boomers who've truly embraced this ideal. "They expect in some sense that their careers will help them realize their authentic self," he says. Muirhead thinks it's an attitude that's a bit overblown; while many of us whine that our jobs just don't *excite* us, it's worth recalling how happy our Depression-era grandparents were to have any job that delivered a reliable paycheck. But for a generation that invented the midlife crisis, career changes will no doubt continue.

Many of these job changes are driven by altruism. For 28 years, Bruce Pasternack worked at Booz Allen, a management-consulting firm. He counseled CEOs and wrote two books on management. But in the late 1990s, he began doing pro bono consulting work for the Special Olympics, the charity that encourages athletic competition for mentally impaired individuals. Soon Pasternack was on the Special Olympics board. Last year, as the group began to hunt for a new CEO, he mentioned his potential interest to the then CEO Tim Shriver. "What else could you do with your life in the next few years that would have as great an impact on the world?" Shriver asked him. This week marks Pasternack's first anniversary as CEO. He's taken a big pay cut, endured a heavy travel schedule and posed for hundreds of photos with Special Olympians. But at 59, he's happy. "It's more than met my expectations with respect to the personal satisfaction," he says.

For some career-changers, public-sector jobs are also a way to give back. This fall Waynewright Malcolm, 42, will begin teaching pre-algebra to eighth graders in Pembroke Pines, Fla., earning $38,000 a year. He can afford the meager paycheck because in his last job, as treasurer at the home-building giant Lennar, he made millions in salary and stock options. "A part of me has always wanted to teach—it's been in my heart a long time," he says. "My wife was very supportive when I told her what my plans were, but she challenged me—she wanted to make sure I was doing this for all the right reasons." Looking ahead to the fall, he's confident he is.

Traditionally, making a career change required finding another job. But for the generation that counts iconic company founders like Bill Gates and Michael Dell among its members, there's often a smarter route: creating a job of your own by starting a new business. David Thompson got a taste of start-up life when he was chief marketing officer at WebEx, a hot Web-conferencing firm. In 2000, WebEx was slated to go public—potentially making Thompson and his colleagues rich—but as the tech market softened, the IPO was delayed. "I had this huge emotional reaction," says Thompson, now 44. Reappraising his lifestyle, he saw a guy who ate horribly, slept too little and rarely exercised. So he took a nine-month sabbatical, doing yoga and losing 40 pounds. Soon afterward he launched his own firm, Genius.com, Inc., which develops software to support sales-people. As his own boss, he often works from home and sched-ules time for quiet reflection. "Everybody is so damn busy, no one thinks about what they really want," he says. Now, after years of craziness, he says, "my life finally has some balance."

That serenity is hardly the norm among folks who Inc. them-selves. Many say their transition from having a well-defined job to being master of everything (from fixing the copy machine to balancing the books) adds to their stress, at least initially. Seven months ago, when Larry Spear, the 45-year-old vice president of sales and marketing for a Florida utility, left to create his own telecom start-up, he knew he'd miss his prestigious title and his six-figure salary. But at BFE Telecom (it stands for Black Finan-cial Empowerment), he's launching projects like the Black 411, which lets callers throughout the United States dial a special number to locate black-owned businesses they can patronize. "I feel alive—I feel like what I'm doing matters," he says. "I'd like my kids to think, 'Hey, my dad did something more than make money. He did something very cool'."

Entrepreneur Randy Boudouris has found the fulfillment he lacked in the early years of his career. Boudouris, 50, studied art and music in college and hoped to be a rock star. But soon he was married with kids and needed a real job, so he signed on with a family printing business. He left after a dispute in 1998, and now he heads his own company, inventing products like wafer-thin magnetic coatings. "This is the most fun I've ever had," Boudouris says. "As far as I'm concerned, the second half of my life is the best part . . . You're never too old to change."

For some, career change is driven by the sense that they've been doing the same thing for far too long. Jean Blosser, 59, spent 35 years in academia as a speech-pathology professor and administrator. "I was kind of dying on the vine—I needed something more," she says. One day she read a newspaper story about Progressus Therapy, a speech-therapy firm. "That was that 'aha' event," she says, and she began researching how to apply for a job that didn't necessarily even exist. Convinced that her specialized training and leadership skills made her a perfect fit, she persisted in asking for meetings to explain why the firm needed her. Today she's VP for therapy programs and quality. "We created something that was a perfect fit for me and for the company," she says. "My move was risky, but it was worth it."

Some job changes begin with an ominous summons to a conference room, where an HR executive dispatches workers to the purgatory of unemployment. These corporate executions were rare when boomers' parents ruled the workplace; back then, companies "furloughed" manufacturing workers when times were slow but brought them back when sales picked up. Today, in contrast, many companies slice the white-collar head count in good times and bad. "Over the years, the permanent separation of people from their jobs, abruptly and against their wishes, gradually became a standard management practice," writes New York Times economics reporter Louis Uchitelle in

Boomer Jobs
Starting Fresh

For many boomers, retirement will be the perfect time to begin a second career. Some of the most popular fields, according to a recent survey:

Consultant	27%
Teacher or professor	20%
Customer greeter	15%
Tour guide	13%
Retail-sales clerk	13%
Bookkeeper or auditing clerk	10%
Home handyman	10%
B&B owner or manager	9%
Security screener	8%
Real-estate agent	7%

Source: 2006 Merrill Lynch New Retirement Study

his new book, "The Disposable American: Layoffs and Their Consequences." Since the 1980s, he figures, more than 30 million workers have been downsized—the majority of them baby boomers.

For some of these folks, the new gigs they land don't quite get them back to even. Bob Dew, 52, was laid off as a welder at a Fortune 500 company in Cleveland in 2002. After 30 years there, he draws a $1,300-a-month pension, but to supplement that income he works as a $7-an-hour shift supervisor at a drug-store; during baseball season he works a second job as an usher at a minor-league park. "It's actually a lot of fun," he says, and since neither job is physically demanding, he can probably do both into old age. But he now eschews name-brand products for generic and has put off his hopes to travel. His retirement plans are "dramatically different" since his layoff, he says. "Every-thing fell apart, and now I'm very guarded with cash."

Some boomers deal with a layoff by trying to turn their pas-sions into careers. Ellen Satter, 44, spent more than 18 years as a computer programmer for NASDAQ before being laid off on April 25. "I could see the writing on the wall," she says, describ-ing how her team had been cut back over time, with more work piled on survivors like her. To prepare for the inevitable, Sat-ter took night classes to earn an M.B.A. Now, with a generous severance package as a cushion, she's set out to create Career 2.0. "I realized I could do anything," she says. "I'm thrilled." She is about to lease a storefront space, and in October she'll open a scrapbooking store. "I can't see how I can get bored with scrapbooking," she says.

Most of the newbie entrepreneurs who are making these leaps say they have no illusions about the economics involved. Yes, there's more upside if a new business flourishes, but the trade-off is less financial security. Russ Klettke, 47, escaped a job as a corporate-communications executive to become a certified fit-ness trainer and research assistant at Northwestern University. On any given day he may be studying how strength training affects hardening of the arteries, or teaching a spin class, training clients one-on-one or working on a follow-up to his 2004 men's diet book. "Being split up between different gigs is exciting," he says. Financially, his new life feels more precarious, "but I wake up every morning and a list pops into my head of all the things I have to do that day, and I like that."

Of course, the people who make these career segues aren't the only ones affected—many have spouses and families who share the joys, pains and risks. Jay and Kendra Jeffcoat have been married for 38 years, but for the past two they've had a commuter marriage so that Jay, a 60-year-old lawyer, can stay in San Diego and work for the Sidney Kimmel Cancer Center, while Kendra works two hours east as a VP of academic affairs at Imperial Valley College. They see each other on weekends and have one "date night" each week midway between their homes. "She supports me and I support her," says Jay, who's looking forward to Kendra's full-time return to San Diego in July. For Tina Thompson, her husband's job transfer from Los Angeles to northern California in 2002 gave her the chance to ditch her teaching career to open an organic-kosher-vegetarian bakery in Pacific Grove. Now her goal is to "make others happy with my cooking," she says.

With life expectancies rising and traditional pension plans evaporating, these folks may need to keep their new careers going for years to come. Most experts predict baby boomers will work longer than their parents, and not just for financial necessity, but also to prevent boredom. According to a report called "The Future of Retirement" by the HSBC bank, "later life is increasingly seen as a time of opportunity and reinvention, rather than of rest and relaxation." The AARP says close to 70 percent of Americans plan to work at least part time during their "retirement" years—for money as well as a sense of purpose. Among human-resource pros, there are countless task forces studying ways that companies can better accommodate seniors.

The AARP even gives annual awards to the Best Employers for Workers Over 50; last year's winners included Volkswagen, Michelin and Whirlpool.

Aside from targeting firms with a senior-friendly track record, there are other steps aspiring career-changers can take. Fein says that just as college students routinely do internships to explore careers, older adults should test-drive new jobs, too. "It's important for people who are thinking about doing something new to try it out in a low-cost, low-risk environment," he says, which often means keeping your day job in the meantime. Sometimes the results will surprise you. Fein recalls a woman intent on opening her own greeting-card store. After working weekends in a similar shop, she realized she didn't really like dealing with customers. Fein says the happiest career changers are those who are jumping *toward* a new job, rather than trying to escape an existing one.

Embracing this advice has helped Janice Stein as she's moved through more careers than she ever expected to have. Stein, 47, has worked as an engineer for Northrop, then as a marketer with several Silicon Valley companies and a Norwegian videoconferencing firm. Two years ago, tired of nonstop travel and her constantly ringing cell phone, she quit to start a business finishing quilts that hobbyists had sewn. "At some point, you have to step back and decide to have a life," she says. She's enjoyed that self-created gig, but now she wants health benefits and more security, so she's going back to school to become certified in medical imaging. She'll be using technology that didn't exist when she came out of college a generation ago—just the kind of adventure these self-determined boomers have grown to welcome.

With Karen Springen, in Chicago, Joan Raymond, in Cleveland and Jamie Reno, in San Diego

Secrets of the Centenarians

In certain families, small genetic variations bring good health and long life. Can researchers apply this knowledge to benefit us all?

MAYA PINES

Is there a formula for living to the age of 100 or beyond? HHMI investigator Louis M. Kunkel believes there is, and he's working hard to define it.

Besides a healthy dose of good luck (Kunkel says it helps to not be killed in a war or a traffic accident), one key to longevity is a highly unusual combination of gene variants that protects against the customary diseases of old age. Several research teams are now in the process of uncovering these genes.

Kunkel, director of the Genomics Program at Children's Hospital in Boston, and his associates recently identified a genetic variant that is particularly prominent among sibling pairs in the New England Centenarian Study, perhaps the world's largest pool of centenarians. They are seeking additional genetic variants that might retard—or perhaps even prevent—many of the diseases that debilitate the old. "People with this rare combination of genes clearly age more slowly," Kunkel says. "When they reach 90, they don't look any older than 70."

Hundreds of centenarians around the world are now contributing their blood and medical histories to the search for these precious genes. They have become a key resource for researchers who hope that as these genes are revealed, their good effects may be reproduced in other people with the help of new drugs.

Clustered in Families

Kunkel was drawn to the hunt for longevity genes about six years ago, through a chance encounter with Thomas T. Perls, a Boston University Medical School geriatrician who had enrolled a large group of centenarians for his New England Centenarian Study. Kunkel's own research was focused on a deadly genetic disorder called Duchenne muscular dystrophy, which affects mostly boys. In 1986, he discovered a mutation that causes this muscle-wasting disease, and he is still working on a therapy for it (see Cures for Muscle Diseases?). But he could not resist the opportunity to also apply his knowledge of genetics to what he heard from Perls.

The two men were acquainted through Perls's wife, Leslie Smoot, who happened to be a postdoc in Kunkel's lab. When they met on a street in Cambridge, Massachusetts, in 1997 and

started talking about their work, "Tom told me that many of the centenarians whose lineage he was examining were clustered in families," Kunkel recalls. "I realized that's just got to be genetics. We soon started a collaboration."

For his part, Perls remembers that at the beginning of his study he thought the centenarians had little in common except for their age. But he soon realized that many of them had an unusually large number of equally aged relatives. "We had a 108-year-old man who blew out his birthday candles next to his 102-year-old sister," Perls recalls. "They told us they had another sibling who was 103, and yet another who was only 99. Two other siblings—also centenarians—had passed away. Four siblings had died in childhood. So here was an incredible clustering, 5 or maybe 6 siblings out of 10! We've since found about 7 families like that." This implied that all these families carried especially protective genes. Shortly after the two scientists met, a new postdoc arrived in Kunkel's lab—Annibale A. Puca, a young Italian neurologist who wanted to work in genetics—and Kunkel suggested he take on this new project. "I warned him it was going to be a lot of work and high risk, but he said okay," Kunkel says, "and he spearheaded the whole program."

Puca and Perls rapidly expanded the group of centenarians, recruiting them through alumni associations, newspaper clippings, and state census lists. After taking samples of the centenarians' blood, the researchers extracted DNA from it and started looking for genetic markers—specific stretches of DNA that might occur more frequently among these extremely old men and women than among a group of younger people who were the study's controls. Most scientists believed that human longevity is far too complicated a trait to be influenced by only a few genes. There are so many independent mechanisms of aging that "the chance that only a few major genes control longevity in man is highly unlikely," wrote a self-styled "pessimist" on this issue, George M. Martin of the University of Washington in Seattle, in the journal *Mechanisms of Ageing and Development* in 2002. But Kunkel's lab took a different view. "In lower organisms, such as nematodes, fruit flies, and yeast, there are only a few genes that need to be altered to give a longer life span," Kunkel says. "My feeling was that there were

Who Are These Centenarians?

"Centenarians tend to be independent, assertive, funny, and gregarious," says Boston University Medical School geriatrician Thomas T. Perls, who at 43 has probably met more people over the age of 100 than anybody else. "They also seem to manage stress very well, which makes sense, since we know that not handling stress predisposes you to cardiovascular disease and high blood pressure."

During a fellowship in geriatrics at Harvard Medical School in the early 1990s, Perls took care of 40 patients at Boston's Hebrew Rehabilitation Center for the Aged. Two of his healthiest patients, who looked as if they were in their seventies, were actually over 100 years old. "They were in really terrific shape," he says. "It was so different from what I expected! This sparked my interest."

As a result, Perls founded the New England Centenarian Study in 1994, becoming one of only a few researchers studying the very old at that time. He started out by looking for people over 100 in eight towns around Boston, using census records, voter registration files, and the media. Later, he expanded the study by adding centenarians from all over the United States. Now it includes 1,600 centenarians and 500 of their children. About 20 percent of the centenarian women in his study had given birth after the age of 40, Perls found, compared to a national average of only 3 percent of mothers. "It showed that these women were aging very slowly," he says.

He also studied the centenarians' siblings and concluded that their chances of living to their early nineties were four times greater than average. More recently, Perls examined the centenarians' children. At the age of 70, he found, they had a 24 percent reduction in mortality compared to the general population, as well as about a 60 percent reduction in the risk of heart disease, hypertension, and diabetes.

More than 90 percent of the centenarians had been in good health and completely independent until their early to mid-90s, Perls says. "They lived the vast majority of their lives with good function," he emphasizes. "So it's not a matter of 'the older you get, the sicker you get' but rather 'the older you get, the healthier you've been.' This is a different way of thinking about aging."

By the time people reach the century mark, however, the healthy ones are in the minority. "We found that 25 percent of the centenarians were doing well, but the remaining 75 percent had mild to severe impairment," Perls reports. "In the end, they die of cardiovascular disease or something that's related to frailty, such as pneumonia."

This fits in well with the theories of Leonard Hayflick, of the University of California, San Francisco, who showed in 1961 that there are limits to the number of times a normal human cell can divide. Even under the most favorable conditions, he said, noncancerous human cells die after about 50 cell divisions (this is now called the "Hayflick limit"). Eliminating the leading causes of death in old age—cardiovascular diseases, stroke, and cancer—"will only result in an increase of about 15 years in human life expectancy," Hayflick declared in the November 9, 2000, issue of *Nature*. Although these 15 years would be a great gift, assuming that people remained healthy during that time, nothing could stop "the inevitable increase in errors and disorders in the cells of vital organs" that results from age, he pointed out. Even the cells' repair processes would become disordered, leading to extreme vulnerability and death.

Then would it be a good thing for more people to live to 100? "Absolutely," says Perls. "Centenarians are sentinels of the health of older people. Our goal is not to get a bunch of individuals to be 120 or 130, but to discover which genes are most protective and then use this information to get a majority of people living almost all their lives in good health, as centenarians generally do."

---

only a few genes, perhaps four to six, in humans that would do the same."

The team proceeded to examine genetic markers for the entire genomes of 308 people, selected because they belonged to 137 sibships (sets of siblings) in which at least one member was over 98 and the others were over 90. "From early on, we saw a blip of a peak on chromosome 4," says Kunkel. "Eventually, in 2001, we found a linkage between one region of this chromosome and longevity."

Search for a SNP

It was "phenomenal" to get a real linkage from such a slight hint in the original data, Kunkel declares. But that didn't mean further research would be easy. This stretch of DNA was so large—12 million DNA base pairs long—that it seemed it could contain as many as 200 genes. Furthermore, the researchers knew that within these genes they would have to look for variations in single bases of DNA—"single-nucleotide polymorphisms," or SNPs (pronounced "snips"). "SNPs really represent the

difference between individuals," Kunkel explains. "Everybody's DNA is 99.9 percent identical—it's the SNPs that make us unique and allow certain people to live longer. Even though most of our DNA is alike, the 0.1 percent variation means that we have more than 10 million SNPs across the genome. And we're on the verge of being able to map them." For Kunkel, the critical question was "how would we find the one SNP in a single gene that might help a person to live much longer than average?"

The groundbreaking work of the Human Genome Project had not yet been completed at that time, and Kunkel realized that finding this particular SNP would be both expensive and time-consuming. It would also be quite different from zeroing in on a missing or severely garbled gene, as had been done for cystic fibrosis, muscular dystrophy, and other single-gene disorders. The widespread diseases of aging—heart disease, stroke, diabetes, cancer, and Alzheimer's disease—are much more complex and are triggered by subtle gene variations that produce only slightly altered proteins, Kunkel says. These proteins may either work a little better or be less active than those in the

Cures for Muscle Diseases?

Ever since Louis M. Kunkel discovered the cause of Duchenne muscular dystrophy (DMD) in 1986, he has been laboring to find a cure for this muscle-wasting disease. DMD—the result of an error in a single gene—attacks 1 out of every 4,000 newborn boys, progressively crippling and then killing them at an early age.

Kunkel saw that patients with DMD lacked a protein, dystrophin, which this gene would have produced if it were functioning normally. So he knew he had to replace the protein somehow. He and others tried many methods—gene therapy to deliver a normal gene to the defective muscle cell, drugs to help restore the mission protein, and cell therapy to inject normal cells into muscle or blood—but despite some partial successes in animals, nothing really worked.

Kunkels lab worked mostly with *mdx* mice, a naturally mutant strain that lack dystrophin. When he and his colleagues attempted to cure these crippled mice with injections of muscle stem cells from normal mice, "some of the donor cells did go into the damaged muscles." he recalls, "but we never got more then 1 to 2 percent of the muscles repaired. Part of the problem was that when you inject cells into a mouses tail vein, which is the most accessible part of its circulation, the donor cells to through all the organs—the lungs, liver, heart, and so on—and out through the arterial system. Most of the cells get filtered and lost, and don't contribute to the therapy."

Today, however, Kunkel feels he is on the verge of success. The big breakthrough came last summer when a team of Italian scientists headed by Giulio Cossu of Milan's Stem Cell Research Institute announced it had found a new route for the injection of stem cells into dystrophic mice directly into an artery. The cells seemed to lodge within the capillary system near the injection site. From there, about 30 percent of them migrated to the diseased muscles. Not only did the cells get there, he says, but at later time points, you could see a larger number of donor cells than at the earliest point, as if they were trying to divide.

"Can we improve on this?" asks Kunkel with a glint in his eye. "If we can get the stem cells into 50 percent of the dystrophic muscles, that's basically a cure."

They had trouble at first because "the mouse artery was 10 times smaller than our smallest injection needles—it was like trying to hit it with a hammer!" Kunkel says. Though a tail vein is even smaller than an artery, it can be hit much more easily because it is right under the surface of the skin and can be made to swell up by warming it. In the new system, the mouse had to be anesthetized and opened up to expose its artery, which was lifted out—a complex procedure.

"It wasn't until we started collaborating with some vascular surgeons who had been doing heart transplants in mice that we were able to get the stem cells into the mouse arteries efficiently," he says. In humans, of course, reaching an artery would not be a problem given that human arteries are so much larger.

Getting the stem cells into the muscles was just the first step. Unless these cells supplied enough dystrophin, the diseased muscles would not be repaired. So Kunkel also tried to find different stem cells that could do the job more effectively. In 1999 his lab and that of his colleague Richard Mulligan announced they could restore some of the missing dystrophin in mdx mice with the aid of a new kind of stem cells called "side population" (SP) cells, which seemed to work much better. These SP cells had to be taken from muscle tissue, however. Last year Kunkel's lab succeeded in deriving similar SP cells from adult skin, which is easier to obtain. Since they originate in adult tissue, both kinds of SP cells will be much less controversial then embryonic stem cells.

"It's my belief that you can do a lot of therapeutic intervention with adult-derived cells," says Kunkel. He notes that the new stem cells seem ready to differentiate into every type of muscle tissue, which implies that they have the potential to treat many forms of muscle disease.

The combination of new cell type and a new delivery system "may revolutionize how one does therapy for muscle diseases," Kunkel suggests. "When we get it perfected in mice, we'll go to humans." He thinks this might happen in a couple of years.

normal population, and several of them may work in concert. Searching for a single SNP would require doing thousands of genetic analyses on each of his subjects (now numbering 653) and comparing the results with the control group. "We estimated it would cost at least $5 million," Kunkel said. "It finally cost $8 million and took one-and-a-half years."

Ultimately, all that painstaking work paid off. The paper announcing the discovery of a SNP that contributes to longevity was published in the November 25, 2003, issue of the *Proceedings of the National Academy of Sciences*.

Now for the Others

The long-sought SNP turned out to lie within the gene for microsomal transfer protein, or MTP, which had been known since the mid-1980s to be involved in cholesterol metabolism.

"It's quite clear that to live to be 100, you've got to maintain your cholesterol at a healthy level," says Kunkel. "It makes perfect sense. We know that increased LDL (the 'bad' cholesterol) and lowered HDL (the 'good' cholesterol) raise your cardiovascular risk and that cardiovascular diseases account for a large percentage of human mortality. So variations in the genes involved in cholesterol packaging will influence your life span. It's as if these centenarians had been on Lipitor [a cholesterol-lowering drug] from birth!"

This discovery might lead to drugs that are tailored to intervene in the cholesterol pathway. Because the MTP gene was already in the public domain, however, it could not be patented, much to the disappointment of the former Centagenetix Corporation (founded by Puca, Perls, and Kunkel and now a part of Elixir Pharmaceuticals of Cambridge, Massachusetts), which had bankrolled most of the study.

In any event, this SNP "cannot be the whole story," Kunkel declares. "There must be other gene variations that enable people to avoid age-related diseases. Some of our original families did not show linkages to chromosome 4." Nor did a group of centenarians who were tested in France.

Determined to find some of the other SNPs that produce longevity, Kunkel says he's going back to his sample and will redo the whole study. "We now have 310 sibships," he says. "Our genetic markers are much denser. I believe we can get 10 times the power in our next screen than we had in the first."

Moreover, the work can be done much more rapidly and inexpensively than last time, he notes, given the giant strides that have been made recently in human genetics. Not only has the entire human genome been sequenced, but many of the errors in the original draft have been corrected. Equally important, all the known genes in the genome are now available on a single Affymetrix DNA chip, allowing researchers to promptly identify which genes are activated and which are damped down in any given situation. In addition, as many as 10,000 different human SNPs have been placed on a single chip.

Similar tools have already turned up new gene variants in yeast, worms, and flies. But Kunkel will use the chips to analyze the DNA of humans. Once his lab gets started on the new longevity project, he believes, it will not take very long to get some definitive answers. He hopes these will lead to drugs that could mimic the protective effects of the centenarians' genes.

Gold Standard

In fact, these studies foreshadow a far-reaching attack on all complex diseases—not just those of the aged but others, such as autism and hypertension. None of these ills could be tackled efficiently in the past. "The centenarians are the ideal control group for such research," Kunkel says. "To reach 100, you must have good alleles [versions of the genes] at all points. So if one wants to find the genes that are connected with hypertension, for instance, one can look across the genome for genes that are highly active in the hypertensive population but down-regulated in centenarians. Ultimately, that's what the centenarians' genes will be used for."

He believes that in the future, "every person who comes to our genetic clinic—or goes through any type of care system—with what appears to be a complex disease should be analyzed in detail. I mean that we should gather all the information we can about each patient's symptoms, the family history of these symptoms, any environmental insults the patient suffered, any learning disability—anything that would allow us to categorize the patient and [the patient's] family into subtypes of the disease which could be more related to one another and thus more likely to involve the same gene." To make this happen, Kunkel has just appointed a director of phenotyping (the Greek roots of this word mean "classifying phenomena into specific types") who will collect, categorize, and catalogue such patient information.

"We will also analyze the patients' genes but only in the context of the category of symptoms they exhibit," he says. "The samples we collect—under appropriate protocols—will be available to the national groups of patients and researchers that are organizing to find the underlying genetic bases of specific diseases." Eventually, he hopes, many complex disorders such as heart disease, diabetes, and autism will be broken down into more specific categories, which in turn may lead to more precise treatments or ways of preventing the disorder. Kunkel expects this process to accelerate in the near future as more patients' genes are compared with those of the gold standard for humans—the centenarians.

Lost & Found

Promising therapy for Alzheimer's draws out the person inside the patient

BARBARA BASLER

The woman wore a plain housedress and a big apron, its pockets stuffed with plastic checkers. Head down, eyes blank, she shuffled aimlessly around the activity room. Cameron Camp, a research psychologist who was visiting this assisted living home in Kentucky, watched the 70-year-old woman for a moment. Then, he recalls, "I went up to her and gave her one of our books—the one on Gene Kelly, the dancer—and asked her to please read a page."

He pauses, remembering the woman and the skeptical staff—and the very next moment.

"She took the book and read aloud—clear as a bell," Camp says with a smile. "A shocked staffer turned to me and said, 'I didn't even know she could speak. That's a miracle.'"

Camp heads the Myers Research Institute in Beachwood, Ohio, and his cutting-edge work with patients in all stages of Alzheimer's has left him improbably upbeat—because he sees miracles like this day after day.

His research is part of a sea change in the care of Alzheimer's patients who are in the later stages of the disease: "Ten to 15 years ago these people were institutionalized, and their care involved physical or chemical restraints," says Kathleen O'Brien, vice president of program and community services for the Chicago-based Alzheimer's Association, which, with the National Institutes of Health, has helped fund Camp's work.

> **Psychologist Cameron Camp says patients live in the moment. "Our job is to give them as many good moments as we can."**

"Today," she says, "more than 70 percent of those with Alzheimer's are cared for in the family home, and we talk about controlling the disease and enhancing daily life for those who have it."

Alzheimer's, the most common form of dementia in people over the age of 65, affects 4.5 million Americans. An irreversible brain disorder, the disease robs people of their memory and eventually impairs most of their mental and physical functions.

While research typically focuses on preventing Alzheimer's or delaying its progress in the early stages, some medical specialists and long-term care professionals are investigating activities that will help patients in the later stages.

"We can't stop cell death from Alzheimer's," Camp explains. "But at any stage of dementia there is a range of capability. If you give people a reason to get out of bed, activities that engage them and allow them to feel successful, they will be at the top of their game, whatever it is."

Camp, 53, began his research 10 years ago when he looked at the activities developed for young children by the educator Maria Montessori, whose "method" is followed today in Montessori schools around the world. There, children learn by manipulating everyday objects like balls, seashells and measuring spoons in highly structured activities that engage children but rarely allow them to fail.

Camp adapted these kinds of exercises for older people with dementia, tailoring them to the individual's background and interests, and found he could draw out the person inside the patient.

"Suddenly, they just wake up, come alive for the moment," he says.

That happened to Mary Anne Duffy's husband when they took part in Camp's research. James Duffy, 77, has Parkinson's disease and dementia and is confined to a wheelchair in a nursing home in Mentor, Ohio.

"James loved woodworking," Duffy says, "and he liked fixing things, so the researcher brought him a small box to paint, nuts and bolts to put together, puzzles." Before her husband began the activities, she says, he "just sat there, nodding off."

But when he was working a puzzle or painting a box, "James actually smiled—something I hadn't seen for a long time," Duffy says. "And he would talk. That was amazing."

People with Alzheimer's "live in the moment, and our job is to give them as many good moments as we can," Camp says. "We need to be thinking about these people in a new way. Instead of focusing on their problems and deficits, we need to ask what strengths and abilities remain."

People had assumed, for instance, that the woman with the checkers in her apron pockets was too impaired to read. But studies have found that reading is one of the very last skills to fade away. "It's automatic, almost a reflex," Camp says.

"If the print is right," he says as he flips through one of his specially designed books with big, bold letters, many Alzheimer's patients can read.

One goal of Camp's work has been to turn his research into practical how-to guides for professional and family caregivers. Published by the Myers Research Institute, the guides have been translated into Chinese, Japanese and Spanish.

While long-term care residences may have some activities for dementia patients—like coloring in a picture or listening to a story—often they don't have activities "that are meaningful, that call on an adult's past," Camp says. "And even people with Alzheimer's are bored if an activity isn't challenging or interesting."

Much of Camp's research is with residents at Menorah Park Center for Senior Living in Beachwood, which is affiliated with Myers Research. After Alzheimer's patients were given the large-print books that he and his colleagues developed, many could read aloud and discuss the books.

A brief biography of Leonardo da Vinci, for instance, talks about some of his wildly imaginative inventions, like a machine that would let soldiers breathe underwater so they could march underneath enemy ships, drill holes in their hulls and sink them.

"It's a wonderful, wacky idea," Camp says. "Dementia patients react to it just as we do. They love it. They laugh, they shake their heads. They talk about it."

Education Director Lisa P. Gwyther of the Bryan Alzheimer's Disease Research Center at Duke University Medical Center recalls visiting a facility where she saw Alzheimer's patients themselves teaching some of the simple activities they had learned to preschool children. "I was so impressed with the dignity and the purpose and the fun that was observable between the older person and younger child," she says. Camp's work has been rigorously studied in a number of small pilot projects, she adds, "which means this is a reliable, valid method."

At Menorah Park, Camp and his team look at what basic skills remain in those with dementia: Can the person read, sort, categorize, manipulate objects? Then they customize activities for those skills.

"We had one man who loved baseball," Camp says. "We had him sort pictures of baseball players into American and National leagues. Another man who loved opera sorted titles into operas by Puccini and operas by Verdi."

The activities help patients maintain the motor skills needed to feed themselves or button buttons. They also trigger memories, then conversations that connect the patient and the caregiver.

People with dementia won't consciously remember the activity from one session to the next. But, Camp says, "some part of them does remember, and eventually they will get bored. So you can't have them match the same pictures each time."

It doesn't matter if patients make mistakes, Camp adds. "What's important is that they enjoy the process."

Mike Skrajner, a project manager for Myers Research who monitored an Alzheimer's reading group at Menorah Park, recalls one morning when the group was reading a biography of Gene Kelly and came to the part where Kelly tells his father he is quitting law school—to take ballet lessons. "They stopped right there and had a great conversation about how they would react to that news," he says. "It was a wonderful session, and at the end they all wound up singing 'Singin' in the Rain.'"

Manipulating everyday objects helps patients maintain skills for feeding themselves or brushing their teeth.

Camp's research shows that people who engage in such activities tend to exhibit fewer signs of agitation, depression and anxiety.

George Niederehe, acting chief of the geriatrics research branch of the National Institute of Mental Health, which is funding some of Camp's work, says a large study of patients in long-term care facilities is needed for definitive proof of the effectiveness of Camp's approach. But his method could be as helpful to caregivers as it is to people with Alzheimer's, he says, because it would improve "staff morale, knowing they can do something useful for these patients." And that, he adds, would enhance the overall environment for staff and residents alike.

One vital part of Camp's theory—like Montessori's—is that residents need activities that give them a social role, whether it's contributing at a book club or stirring lemonade for a party.

The Menorah Park staff worked with one patient, a former mailman, who loved folding pieces of paper stamped with "Have a Nice Day!" He stuffed the notes into envelopes and delivered them to other residents.

"What we try to do," Camp says, "is let the person you remember shine through the disease, even if it's only a few moments a day."

To Learn More

- To download samples of Cameron Camp's activities for dementia patients, go to www.aarp/bulletin/longterm.
- The caregiver's manual "A Different Visit" costs $39.95 plus shipping, and the special large-print books for Alzheimer's patients cost $5.95 each (or six copies for the price of five) plus shipping. To order, go to www.myersresearch.org, or write Myers Research Institute, 27100 Cedar Road, Beachwood, OH 44122.
- For general information, go to the Alzheimer's Association Web site at www.alz.org.

For nine simple habits you can adopt that may delay dementia, see the September-October issue of *AARP The Magazine*.

Start the Conversation

The Modern Maturity guide to end-of-life care

The Body Speaks

Physically, dying means that "the body's various physiological systems, such as the circulatory, respiratory, and digestive systems, are no longer able to support the demands required to stay alive," says Barney Spivack, M.D., director of Geriatric Medicine for the Stamford (Connecticut) Health System. "When there is no meaningful chance for recovery, the physician should discuss realistic goals of care with the patient and family, which may include letting nature take its course. Lacking that direction," he says, "physicians differ in their perception of when enough is enough. We use our best judgment, taking into account the situation, the information available at the time, consultation with another doctor, or guidance from an ethics committee."

Without instructions from the patient or family, a doctor's obligation to a terminally ill person is to provide life-sustaining treatment. When a decision to "let nature take its course" has been made, the doctor will remove the treatment, based on the patient's needs. Early on, the patient or surrogate may choose to stop interventions such as antibiotics, dialysis, resuscitation, and defibrillation. Caregivers may want to offer food and fluids, but those can cause choking and the pooling of dangerous fluids in the lungs. A dying patient does not desire or need nourishment; without it he or she goes into a deep sleep and dies in days to weeks. A breathing machine would be the last support: It is uncomfortable for the patient, and may be disconnected when the patient or family finds that it is merely prolonging the dying process.

The Best Defense Against Pain

Pain-management activists are fervently trying to reeducate physicians about the importance and safety of making patients comfortable. "In medical school 30 years ago, we worried a lot about creating addicts," says Philadelphia internist Nicholas Scharff. "Now we know that addiction is not a problem: People who are in pain take pain medication as long as they need it, and then they stop." Spivack says, "We have new formulations and delivery systems, so a dying patient should never have unmet pain needs."

In 1999, the Joint Commission on Accreditation of Healthcare Organizations issued stern new guidelines about easing pain in both terminal and nonterminal patients. The movement

---

In Search of a Good Death

If we think about death at all, we say that we want to go quickly, in our sleep, or, perhaps, while fly-fishing. But in fact only 10 percent of us die suddenly. The more common process is a slow decline with episodes of organ or system failure. Most of us want to die at home; most of us won't. All of us hope to die without pain; many of us will be kept alive, in pain, beyond a time when we would choose to call a halt. Yet very few of us take steps ahead of time to spell out what kind of physical and emotional care we will want at the end.

The new movement to improve the end of life is pioneering ways to make available to each of us a good death—as we each define it. One goal of the movement is to bring death through the cultural process that childbirth has achieved; from an unconscious, solitary act in a cold hospital room to a situation in which one is buffered by pillows, pictures, music, loved ones, and the solaces of home. But as in the childbirth movement, the real goal is choice—here, to have the death you want. Much of death's sting can be averted by planning in advance, knowing the facts, and knowing what options we all have. Here, we have gathered new and relevant information to help us all make a difference for the people we are taking care of, and ultimately, for ourselves.

---

intends to take pain seriously: to measure and treat it as the fifth vital sign in hospitals, along with blood pressure, pulse, temperature, and respiration.

The best defense against pain, says Spivack, is a combination of education and assertiveness. "Don't be afraid to speak up," he says. "If your doctor isn't listening, talk to the nurses. They see more and usually have a good sense of what's happening." Hospice workers, too, are experts on physical comfort, and a good doctor will respond to a hospice worker's recommendations. "The best situation for pain management," says Scharff, "is at home with a family caregiver being guided by a hospice program."

The downsides to pain medication are, first, that narcotics given to a fragile body may have a double effect: The drug may ease the pain, but it may cause respiratory depression and possibly death. Second, pain medication may induce grogginess or unconsciousness when a patient wants to be alert. "Most people seem to be much more willing to tolerate pain than mental confusion," says senior research scientist M. Powell Lawton, Ph.D., of the Philadelphia Geriatric Center. Dying patients may choose to be alert one day for visitors, and asleep the next to cope with pain. Studies show that when patients control their own pain medication, they use less.

Final Symptoms

Depression This condition is not an inevitable part of dying but can and should be treated. In fact, untreated depression can prevent pain medications from working effectively, and anti-depressant medication can help relieve pain. A dying patient should be kept in the best possible emotional state for the final stage of life. A combination of medications and psychotherapy works best to treat depression.

Anorexia In the last few days of life, anorexia—an unwillingness or inability to eat—often sets in. "It has a protective effect, releasing endorphins in the system and contributing to a greater feeling of well-being," says Spivack. "Force-feeding a dying patient could make him uncomfortable and cause choking."

Dehydration Most people want to drink little or nothing in their last days. Again, this is a protective mechanism, triggering a release of helpful endorphins.

Drowsiness and Unarousable Sleep In spite of a coma-like state, says Spivack, "presume that the patient hears everything that is being said in the room."

Agitation and Restlessness, Moaning and Groaning The features of "terminal delirium" occur when the patient's level of consciousness is markedly decreased; there is no significant likelihood that any pain sensation can reach consciousness. Family members and other caregivers may interpret what they see as "the patient is in pain" but as these signs arise at a point very close to death, terminal delirium should be suspected.

The Ultimate Emotional Challenge

A dying person is grieving the loss of control over life, of body image, of normal physical functions, mobility and strength, freedom and independence, security, and the illusion of immortality. He is also grieving the loss of an earthly future, and reorienting himself to an unknowable destiny.

At the same time, an emotionally healthy dying person will be trying to satisfy his survival drive by adapting to this new phase, making the most of life at the moment, calling in loved ones, examining and appreciating his own joys and accomplishments. Not all dying people are depressed; many embrace death easily.

Facing the Fact

Doctors are usually the ones to inform a patient that he or she is dying, and the end-of-life movement is training physicians to bring empathy to that conversation in place of medspeak and

---

Hospice: The Comfort Team

Hospice is really a bundle of services. It organizes a team of people to help patients and their families, most often in the patient's home but also in hospice residences, nursing homes, and hospitals:

- Registered nurses who check medication and the patient's condition, communicate with the patient's doctor, and educate caregivers.
- Medical services by the patient's physician and a hospice's medical director, limited to pain medication and other comfort care.
- Medical supplies and equipment.
- Drugs for pain relief and symptom control.
- Home-care aides for personal care, homemakers for light housekeeping.
- Continuous care in the home as needed on a short-term basis.
- Trained volunteers for support services.
- Physical, occupational, and speech therapists to help patients adapt to new disabilities.
- Temporary hospitalization during a crisis.
- Counselors and social workers who provide emotional and spiritual support to the patient and family.
- Respite care—brief noncrisis hospitalization to provide relief for family caregivers for up to five days.
- Bereavement support for the family, including counseling, referral to support groups, and periodic check-ins during the first year after the death.

Hospice Residences Still rare, but a growing phenomenon. They provide all these services on-site. They're for patients without family caregivers; with frail, elderly spouses; and for families who cannot provide at-home care because of other commitments. At the moment, Medicare covers only hospice services; the patient must pay for room and board. In many states Medicaid also covers hospice services (see How Much Will It Cost?). Keep in mind that not all residences are certified, bonded, or licensed; and not all are covered by Medicare.

Getting In A physician can recommend hospice for a patient who is terminally ill and probably has less than six months to live. The aim of hospice is to help people cope with an illness, not to cure it. All patients entering hospice waive their rights to curative treatments, though only for conditions relating to their terminal illness. "If you break a leg, of course you'll be treated for that," says Karen Woods, executive director of the Hospice Association of America. No one is forced to accept a hospice referral, and patients may leave and opt for curative care at any time. Hospice programs are listed in the Yellow Pages. For more information, see Resources.

---

time estimates. The more sensitive doctor will first ask how the patient feels things are going. "The patient may say, 'Well, I don't think I'm getting better,' and I would say, 'I think you're right,'" says internist Nicholas Scharff.

Survival Kit for Caregivers

A study published in the March 21, 2000, issue of **Annals of Internal Medicine** shows that caregivers of the dying are twice as likely to have depressive symptoms as the dying themselves.

No wonder. Caring for a dying parent, says social worker Roni Lang, "brings a fierce tangle of emotions. That part of us that is a child must grow up." Parallel struggles occur when caring for a spouse, a child, another relative, or a friend. Caregivers may also experience sibling rivalry, income loss, isolation, fatigue, burnout, and resentment.

To deal with these difficult stresses, Lang suggests that caregivers:

- Set limits in advance. How far am I willing to go? What level of care is needed? Who can I get to help? Resist the temptation to let the illness always take center stage, or to be drawn into guilt-inducing conversations with people who think you should be doing more.
- Join a caregiver support group, either disease-related like the Alzheimer's Association or Gilda's Club, or a more general support group like The Well Spouse Foundation. Ask the social services department at your hospital for advice. Telephone support and online chat rooms also exist (see Resources).
- Acknowledge anger and express it constructively by keeping a journal or talking to an understanding friend or family member. Anger is a normal reaction to powerlessness.
- When people offer to help, give them a specific assignment. And then, take time to do what energizes you and make a point of rewarding yourself.
- Remember that people who are critically ill are self-absorbed. If your empathy fails you and you lose patience, make amends and forgive yourself.

At this point, a doctor might ask if the patient wants to hear more now or later, in broad strokes or in detail. Some people will need to first process the emotional blow with tears and anger before learning about the course of their disease in the future.

"Accept and understand whatever reaction the patient has," says Roni Lang, director of the Geriatric Assessment Program for the Stamford (Connecticut) Health System, and a social worker who is a longtime veteran of such conversations. "Don't be too quick with the tissue. That sends a message that it's not okay to be upset. It's okay for the patient to be however she is."

Getting to Acceptance

Some patients keep hoping that they will get better. Denial is one of the mind's miracles, a way to ward off painful realities until consciousness can deal with them. Denial may not be a problem for the dying person, but it can create difficulties for the family. The dying person could be leaving a lot of tough decisions, stress, and confusion behind. The classic stages of grief outlined by Elisabeth Kübler-Ross—denial, anger, bargaining, depression, and acceptance—are often used to describe post-death grieving, but were in fact delineated for the process of accepting impending loss. We now know that these states may not progress in order. "Most people oscillate between anger and sadness, embracing the prospect of death and unrealistic episodes of optimism," says Lang. Still, she says, "don't place demands on them to accept their death. This is not a time to proselytize." It is enough for the family to accept the coming loss, and if necessary, introduce the idea of an advance directive and health-care proxy, approaching it as a "just in case" idea. When one member of the family cannot accept death, and insists that doctors do more, says Lang, "that's the worst nightmare. I would call a meeting, hear all views without interrupting, and get the conversation around to what the patient would want. You may need another person to come in, perhaps the doctor, to help 'hear' the voice of the patient."

What Are You Afraid Of?

The most important question for doctors and caregivers to ask a dying person is, What are you afraid of? "Fear aggravates pain," says Lang, "and pain aggravates fear." Fear of pain, says Spivack, is one of the most common problems, and can be dealt with rationally. Many people do not know, for example, that pain in dying is not inevitable. Other typical fears are of being separated from loved ones, from home, from work; fear of being a burden, losing control, being dependent, and leaving things undone. Voicing fear helps lessen it, and pin-pointing fear helps a caregiver know how to respond.

How to Be with a Dying Person

Our usual instinct is to avoid everything about death, including the people moving most rapidly toward it. But, Spivack says, "In all my years of working with dying people, I've never heard one say 'I want to die alone.'" Dying people are greatly comforted by company; the benefit far outweighs the awkwardness of the visit. Lang offers these suggestions for visitors:

- Be close. Sit at eye level, and don't be afraid to touch. Let the dying person set the pace for the conversation. Allow for silence. Your presence alone is valuable.
- Don't contradict a patient who says he's going to die. Acceptance is okay. Allow for anger, guilt, and fear, without trying to "fix" it. Just listen and empathize.
- Give the patient as much decision-making power as possible, as long as possible. Allow for talk about unfinished business. Ask: "Who can I contact for you?"
- Encourage happy reminiscences. It's okay to laugh.
- Never pass up the chance to express love or say goodbye. But if you don't get the chance, remember that not everything is worked through. Do the best you can.

Taking Control Now

Sixty years ago, before the invention of dialysis, defibrillators, and ventilators, the failure of vital organs automatically meant death. There were few choices to be made to end suffering, and when there were—the fatal dose of morphine, for example—these decisions were made privately by family and doctors who knew each other well. Since the 1950s, medical technology has been capable of extending lives, but also of prolonging dying. In 1967, an organization called Choice in Dying (now the Partnership for Caring: America's Voices for the Dying; see Resources) designed the first advance directive—a document that allows you to designate under what conditions you would want life-sustaining treatment to be continued or terminated. But the idea did not gain popular understanding until 1976, when the parents of Karen Ann Quinlan won a long legal battle to disconnect her from respiratory support as she lay for months in a vegetative state. Some 75 percent of Americans are in favor of advance directives, although only 30–35 percent actually write them.

Designing the Care You Want

There are two kinds of advance directives, and you may use one or both. A Living Will details what kind of life-sustaining treatment you want or don't want, in the event of an illness when death is imminent. A durable power of attorney for health care appoints someone to be your decision-maker if you can't speak for yourself. This person is also called a surrogate, attorney-in-fact, or health-care proxy. An advance directive such as Five Wishes covers both.

Most experts agree that a Living Will alone is not sufficient. "You don't need to write specific instructions about different kinds of life support, as you don't yet know any of the facts of your situation, and they may change," says Charles Sabatino, assistant director of the American Bar Association's Commission on Legal Problems of the Elderly.

The proxy, Sabatino says, is far more important. "It means someone you trust will find out all the options and make a decision consistent with what you would want." In most states, you may write your own advance directive, though some states require a specific form, available at hospital admitting offices or at the state department of health.

When Should You Draw Up a Directive?

Without an advance directive, a hospital staff is legally bound to do everything to keep you alive as long as possible, until you or a family member decides otherwise. So advance directives are best written before emergency status or a terminal diagnosis. Some people write them at the same time they make a will. The process begins with discussions between you and your family and doctor. If anybody is reluctant to discuss the subject, Sabatino suggests starting the conversation with a story. "Remember what happened to Bob Jones and what his family went through? I want us to be different. . . ." You can use existing tools—a booklet or questionnaire (see Resources)—to keep the conversation moving. Get your doctor's commitment to support your wishes. "If you're asking for something that is against your doctor's conscience" (such as prescribing a lethal dose of pain medication or removing life support at a time he considers premature), Sabatino says, "he may have an obligation to transfer you to another doctor." And make sure the person you name as surrogate agrees to act for you and understands your wishes.

Filing, Storing, Safekeeping. . .

An estimated 35 percent of advance directives cannot be found when needed.

- Give a copy to your surrogate, your doctor, your hospital, and other family members. Tell them where to find the original in the house—not in a safe deposit box where it might not be found until after death.
- Some people carry a copy in their wallet or glove compartment of their car.
- Be aware that if you have more than one home and you split your time in several regions of the country, you should be registering your wishes with a hospital in each region, and consider naming more than one proxy.
- You may register your Living Will and health-care proxy online at uslivingwillregistry.com (or call 800-548-9455). The free, privately funded confidential service will instantly fax a copy to a hospital when the hospital requests one. It will also remind you to update it: You may want to choose a new surrogate, accommodate medical advances, or change your idea of when "enough is enough." M. Powell Lawton, who is doing a study on how people anticipate the terminal life stages, has discovered that "people adapt relatively well to states of poor health. The idea that life is still worth living continues to readjust itself."

Assisted Suicide: The Reality

While advance directives allow for the termination of life-sustaining treatment, assisted suicide means supplying the patient with a prescription for life-ending medication. A doctor writes the prescription for the medication; the patient takes the fatal dose him- or herself. Physician-assisted suicide is legal only in Oregon (and under consideration in Maine) but only with rigorous preconditions. Of the approximately 30,000 people who died in Oregon in 1999, only 33 received permission to have a lethal dose of medication and only 26 of those actually died of the medication. Surrogates may request an end to life support, but to assist in a suicide puts one at risk for charges of homicide.

Good Care: Can You Afford It?

The ordinary person is only one serious illness away from poverty," says Joanne Lynn, M.D., director of the Arlington, Virginia, Center to Improve Care of the Dying. An ethicist, hospice physician, and health-services researcher, she is one of the founding members of the end-of-life-care movement. "On the

Five Wishes

Five Wishes is a questionnaire that guides people in making essential decisions about the care they want at the end of their life. About a million people have filled out the eight-page form in the past two years. This advance directive is legally valid in 34 states and the District of Columbia. (The other 16 require a specific state-mandated form.)

The document was designed by lawyer Jim Towey, founder of Aging With Dignity, a nonprofit organization that advocates for the needs of elders and their caregivers. Towey, who was legal counsel to Mother Teresa, visited her Home for the Dying in Calcutta in the 1980s. He was struck that in that haven in the Third World, "the dying people's hands were held, their pain was managed, and they weren't alone. In the First World, you see a lot of medical technology, but people die in pain, and alone." Towey talked to MODERN MATURITY about his directive and what it means.

What are the five wishes? Who do I want to make care decisions for me when I can't? What kind of medical treatment do I want toward the end? What would help me feel comfortable while I am dying? How do I want people to treat me? What do I want my loved ones to know about me and my feelings after I'm gone?

Why is it so vital to make advance decisions now? Medical technology has extended longevity, which is good, but it can prolong the dying process in ways that are almost cruel. Medical schools are still concentrating on curing, not caring for the dying. We can have a dignified season in our life, or die alone in pain with futile interventions. Most people only discover they have options when checking into the hospital, and often they no longer have the capacity to choose. This leaves the family members with a guessing game and, frequently, guilt.

What's the ideal way to use this document? First you do a little soul searching about what you want. Then discuss it with people you trust, in the living room instead of the waiting room—before a crisis. Just say, "I want a choice about how I spend my last days," talk about your choices, and pick someone to be your health-care surrogate.

What makes the Five Wishes directive unique? It's easy to use and understand, not written in the language of doctors or lawyers. It also allows people to discuss comfort, dignity, and forgiveness, not just medical concerns. When my father filled it out, he said he wanted his favorite afghan blanket in his bed. It made a huge difference to me that, as he was dying, he had his wishes fulfilled.

For a copy of Five Wishes in English or Spanish, send a $5 check or money order to Aging With Dignity, PO Box 1661, Tallahassee, FL 32302. For more information, visit www.agingwithdignity.org.

to afford is at-home medication, monitoring, daily help with eating and walking, and all the care that will go on for the rest of the patient's life.

"When people are dying," Lynn says, "an increasing proportion of their overall care does not need to be done by doctors. But when policymakers say the care is nonmedical, then it's second class, it's not important, and nobody will pay for it."

Bottom line, Medicare pays for about 57 percent of the cost of medical care for Medicare beneficiaries. Another 11 percent is paid by Medicaid, 20 percent by the patient, 10 percent from private insurance, and the rest from other sources, such as charitable organizations.

Medi-What?

This public-plus-private network of funding sources for end-of-life care is complex, and who pays for how much of what is determined by diagnosis, age, site of care, and income. Besides the private health insurance that many of us have from our employers, other sources of funding may enter the picture when patients are terminally ill.

- **Medicare** A federal insurance program that covers health-care services for people 65 and over, some disabled people, and those with end-stage kidney disease. Medicare Part A covers inpatient care in hospitals, nursing homes, hospice, and some home health care. For most people, the Part A premium is free. Part B covers doctor fees, tests, and other outpatient medical services. Although Part B is optional, most people choose to enroll through their local Social Security office and pay the monthly premium ($45.50). Medicare beneficiaries share in the cost of care through deductibles and co-insurance. What Medicare does not cover at all is outpatient medication, long-term nonacute care, and support services.
- **Medicaid** A state and federally funded program that covers health-care services for people with income or assets below certain levels, which vary from state to state.
- **Medigap** Private insurance policies covering the gaps in Medicare, such as deductibles and co-payments, and in some cases additional health-care services, medical supplies, and outpatient prescription drugs.

Many of the services not paid for by Medicare can be covered by private long-term-care insurance. About 50 percent of us over the age of 65 will need long-term care at home or in a nursing home, and this insurance is an extra bit of protection for people with major assets to protect. It pays for skilled nursing care as well as non-health services, such as help with dressing, eating, and bathing. You select a dollar amount of coverage per day (for example, $100 in a nursing home, or $50 for at-home care), and a coverage period (for example, three years—the average nursing-home stay is 2.7 years). Depending on your age and the benefits you choose, the insurance can cost anywhere from around $500 to more than $8,000 a year. People with pre-existing conditions such as Alzheimer's or MS are usually not eligible.

whole, hospitalization and the cost of suppressing symptoms is very easy to afford," says Lynn. Medicare and Medicaid will help cover that kind of acute medical care. But what is harder

How Much Will It Cost?

Where you get end-of-life care will affect the cost and who pays for it.

- **Hospital** Dying in a hospital costs about $1,000 a day. After a $766 deductible (per benefit period), Medicare reimburses the hospital a fixed rate per day, which varies by region and diagnosis. After the first 60 days in a hospital, a patient will pay a daily deductible ($194) that goes up (to $388) after 90 days. The patient is responsible for all costs for each day beyond 150 days. Medicaid and some private insurance, either through an employer or a Medigap plan, often help cover these costs.

- **Nursing home** About $1,000 a week. Medicare covers up to 100 days of skilled nursing care after a three-day hospitalization, and most medication costs during that time. For days 21–100, your daily co-insurance of $97 is usually covered by private insurance—if you have it. For nursing-home care not covered by Medicare, you must use your private assets, or Medicaid if your assets run out, which happens to approximately one-third of nursing-home residents. Long-term-care insurance may also cover some of the costs.

- **Hospice care** About $100 a day for in-home care. Medicare covers hospice care to patients who have a life expectancy of less than six months. (See Hospice: The Comfort Team.) Such care may be provided at home, in a hospice facility, a hospital, or a nursing-home. Patients may be asked to pay up to $5 for each prescription and a 5 percent co-pay for in-patient respite care, which is a short hospital stay to relieve caregivers. Medicaid covers hospice care in all but six states, even for those without Medicare.

  About 60 percent of full-time employees of medium and large firms also have coverage for hospice services, but the benefits vary widely.

- **Home care without hospice services** Medicare Part A pays the full cost of medical home health care for up to 100 visits following a hospital stay of at least three days. Medicare Part B covers home health-care visits beyond those 100 visits or without a hospital stay. To qualify, the patient must be homebound, require skilled nursing care or physical or speech therapy, be under a physician's care, and use services from a Medicare-participating home-health agency. Note that this coverage is for medical care only; hired help for personal nonmedical services, such as that often required by Alzheimer's patients, is not covered by Medicare. It is covered by Medicaid in some states.

- A major financial disadvantage of dying at home without hospice is that Medicare does not cover out-patient prescription drugs, even those for pain. Medicaid does cover these drugs, but often with restrictions on their price and quantity. Private insurance can fill the gap to some extent. Long-term-care insurance may cover payments to family caregivers who have to stop work to care for a dying patient, but this type of coverage is very rare.

Resources

Medical Care

For information about pain relief and symptom management:
Supportive Care of the Dying (503-215-5053; careofdying.org).

For a comprehensive guide to living with the medical, emotional, and spiritual aspects of dying:
Handbook for Mortals by Joanne Lynn and Joan Harrold, Oxford University Press.

For a 24-hour hotline offering counseling, pain management, downloadable advance directives, and more:
The Partnership for Caring (800-989-9455; www.partnershipforcaring.org).

Emotional Care

To find mental-health counselors with an emphasis on lifespan human development and spiritual discussion:
American Counseling Association (800-347-6647; counseling.org).

For disease-related support groups and general resources for caregivers:
Caregiver Survival Resources (caregiver911.com).

For AARP's online caregiver support chatroom, access **America Online** every Wednesday night, 8:30–9:30 EST (keyword: AARP).

Education and advocacy for family caregivers:
National Family Caregivers Association (800-896-3650; nfcacares.org).

For the booklet,
Understanding the Grief Process (D16832, EEO143C), e-mail order with title and numbers to member@aarp.org or send postcard to AARP Fulfillment, 601 E St NW, Washington DC 20049. Please allow two to four weeks for delivery.

To find a volunteer to help with supportive services to the frail and their caregivers:
National Federation of Interfaith Volunteer Caregivers (816-931-5442; nfivc.org).

For information on support to partners of the chronically ill and/or the disabled:
The Well Spouse Foundation (800-838-0879; www.wellspouse.org).

Legal Help

AARP members are entitled to a free half-hour of legal advice with a lawyer from **AARP's Legal Services Network.** (800-424-3410; www.aarp.org/lsn).

For **Planning for Incapacity,** *a guide to advance directives in your state,* send $5 to Legal Counsel for the Elderly, Inc., PO Box 96474, Washington DC 20090-6474. Make out check to LCE Inc.

For a **Caring Conversations** *booklet on advance-directive discussion:*
Midwest Bioethics Center (816-221-1100; midbio.org).

For information on care at the end of life, online discussion groups, conferences:
Last Acts Campaign (800-844-7616; lastacts.org).

Hospice

To learn about end-of-life care options and grief issues through videotapes, books, newsletters, and brochures:
Hospice Foundation of America (800-854-3402; hospice-foundation.org).

For information on hospice programs, FAQs, and general facts about hospice:
National Hospice and Palliative Care Organization (800-658-8898; nhpco.org).

For **All About Hospice: A Consumer's Guide** (202-546-4759; www.hospice-america.org).

Financial Help

For **Organizing Your Future,** *a simple guide to end-of-life financial decisions,* send $5 to Legal Counsel for the Elderly, Inc., PO Box 96474, Washington DC 20090-6474. Make out check to LCE Inc.

For **Medicare and You 2000** *and a* **2000 Guide to Health Insurance for People With Medicare** (800-MEDICARE [633-4227]; medicare.gov).

To find your State Agency on Aging: **Administration on Aging, U.S. Department of Health and Human Services** (800-677-1116; aoa.dhhs.gov).

General

For information on end-of-life planning and bereavement: (www.aarp.org/endoflife/).

For health professionals and others who want to start conversations on end-of-life issues in their community:
Discussion Guide: On Our Own Terms: Moyers on Dying, based on the PBS series, airing September 10–13. The guide provides essays, instructions, and contacts. From PBS, www.pbs.org/onourownterms Or send a postcard request to On Our Own Terms Discussion Guide, Thirteen/WNET New York, PO Box 245, Little Falls, NJ 07424-9766.

Funded with a grant from The Robert Wood Johnson Foundation, Princeton, N.J. *Editor* Amy Gross; *Writer* Louise Lague; *Designer* David Herbick

Navigating Practical Dilemmas in Terminal Care

Helen Sorenson, MA, RRT, FAARC

Introduction

It has been stated that one-fourth of a person's life is spent growing up and three-fourths growing old. The aging process is universal, progressive, irreversible and eventually decremental.[1] Cellular death is one marker of aging. When cells are not replaced or replicated at a rate constant enough to maintain tissue or organ function, the eventual result is death of the organism.

Although not an unexpected endpoint for any human being, death unfortunately is often fraught with turmoil and dilemmas. Patients, family, friends, caregivers and health care professionals often get caught up in conflicting opinions regarding how terminal care should be approached. For the patient, the result often is suboptimal symptom management, an increased likelihood of being subjected to painful and often futile therapy and the unnecessary prolonging of death. For the family and friends of the patient, the psychosocial consequences can be devastating. Conflict at the bedside of a dying loved one can result in long-lasting and sometimes permanent rifts in family relationships.

There are some complicated issues surrounding terminal care, such as fear, lack of trust, lack of understanding, lack of communication, and stubbornness on the part of both the physician's and family members. There are moral, ethical, economic, cultural and religious issues that must be considered. Some of the dilemmas in terminal care come up more frequently than others. This paper will discuss some of the more commonly encountered ones. And possible interventions and/or alternate ways of coming to concordance regarding end-of-life care will be presented for consideration by the reader.

Fear/Death Anxiety

A degree of fear is the natural response of most individuals to the unknown. Despite many attempts at conceptualization and rationalization, preparing for death involves coming to terms with a condition unknown in past or present experience. Fear of death has been referred to in the literature as death anxiety. Research indicates that younger people have a higher level of death anxiety than older people.[2] The reasons are not difficult to understand. Younger adults in our society are often shielded

from death. Many young adults may not have had close contact with individuals dying from a terminal or chronic disease. When younger people confront death, it is most likely that of a grandparent, a parent, a sibling or a friend. Death is commonly from an acute cause. Grief is intense, with many unanswered questions and psychological ramifications.

Older adults have had more experience with death, from having lost a spouse, colleagues, a friend or relatives over the years. They undoubtedly will have experienced grief and worked through loss at some time in their life. Older adults may be more apt to express the fear of dying alone.

When facing a terminal diagnosis and impending death older adults are more likely to be concerned with "mending fences" and seeking forgiveness for perceived wrongdoing. There is a need on the part of many adults to put their affairs in order and resolve any outstanding financial matters. Some interesting research on death anxiety and religiosity conducted by Thorson & Powell,[3] revealed that persons higher in religiosity were lower in death anxiety.

How can the potential dilemma caused by fear be circumscribed? Possibly allowing patients to discuss the issue may ease death anxiety, but patients may be advised not to talk about funeral arrangements, since "they're not going to die." While well intended, the statement may not be helpful. Instead of preventing the patient from discussing "depressing thoughts," encouraging frank discussions about end-of-life issues may ease death anxiety. Asking the patient to verbalize his or her fears may lead to understanding the fears and alleviate the anxiety they cause.

It is important to guard against treating dying patients as though they are no longer human. For example, asking if a person would like to talk to a minister, priest or rabbi does not impinge the religious belief of the patient—it simply allows another avenue to reduce death anxiety.

Issues of Trust

Patients who have been under the care of a personal physician for an extended period of time generally exhibit a high level of trust in the diagnosis, even when the diagnosis is that of a terminal disease. Good end-of-life care requires a measure of continuity among caregivers. The patient who has had the same physician from the onset of a serious illness to the terminal stages of the disease has a substantial advantage.[4]

Planning, family support and social services, coordinated to meet the patient's needs, can be more easily arranged if there is an atmosphere of trust and confidence.

Health care today however, has become increasingly fragmented. A physician unknown to the family and/or patient may be assigned to a case. It is difficult for very sick patients to develop new relationships and establish trust with an on-going stream of care providers.[5] When circumstances are of an immediate and critical nature, issues of trust become paramount. Lack of trust in the physician and/or the health care system can erode into a lack of confidence in a diagnosis, which often results in a conflict between the patient, the family and the health care system.

Navigating this dilemma can be challenging. Recommending that the services of a hospitalist or a palliative care team be requested may be beneficial. Patients and families that are versed in the standard of care for the specific terminal disease may be in a better position to ask questions and make suggestions. Trust is associated with honesty. Conversely, trust can be eroded by what is perceived as the incompetence of or duplicity by health care providers.

An increased, concerted effort to communicate effectively all pertinent information to a patient and family and members of the health care team caring for the patient may not instantly instill confidence, but it may forestall any further erosion of trust. It is a good feeling to think that everyone on the team is pulling in the same direction.

Issues of Communication

Communication, or lack of adequate communication is problematic. A recent article published in *Critical Care Medicine* stated, "In intensive care settings, suboptimal communication can erode family trust and fuel so called 'futility disputes'."[6] Lack of communication does not imply wrongdoing on the part of the caregivers, nor does it imply lack of comprehension or skills in patients and families. The message is delivered, but not always in language that is readily understandable. While the message may be received, at times it is not comprehended due to the nature of the message or the emotional state of the recipient.

A few years ago, during a conversation about end-of-life care, a nurse shared with the author a situation she had encountered. The patient, an elderly female, had undergone a biopsy of a tumor. The physician, upon receiving the biopsy report, asked the nurse to accompany him to the patient's room to deliver the results. The patient was told "the results of the biopsy indicate that the tumor was not benign, so I am going to refer you to Dr. ***, an oncologist, for further treatment." The physician asked for questions from the patient and, receiving none, left the room. The patient then got on the phone, called her family and stated: "Good news, I don't have cancer." The nurse left the room and called the physician, who expressed surprise that the patient had misunderstood the message. Reluctantly,

he returned to the patient's room and in simple terms told her that she did indeed have cancer and that Dr. *** was a cancer specialist who would discuss treatment options with her and her family. Did the physician, on the first visit, tell the patient she had cancer—of course. Did the patient receive the message—unfortunately, no.

Although anecdotal, the case demonstrates a situation in which there was poor communication. Had the nurse not intervened, how long would it have been before the patient was adequately apprised of her condition?

Because quality communication with patients and families is imperative, the dilemma deserves attention. Many articles have been written, discussing optimal times, situations and environments best suited for end-of-life care discussions. Unfortunately, end-of-life does not always arrive on schedule or as planned.

Because of the severity of some illnesses, intensive care units may be the environment where the futility of further care becomes apparent. Intensive care units are busy places, sometimes crowded, and replete with a variety of alarms and mechanical noises on a continual basis. About 50 percent of patients who die in a hospital are cared for in an intensive care unit within three days of their death. Over thirty percent spend at least ten days of final hospitalization in an intensive care unit.[7] This is a particularly sobering reality for patients with chronic lung disease. Many COPD patients have had serious exacerbations, have been admitted to intensive care units, and many have been on mechanical ventilation. Fortunately, the medications, therapeutic interventions, and disease management skills of physicians and therapists often can turn the exacerbation around. Unfortunately, the airway pathology may not be reversible.

How and when and with whom should communication about the gravity of a situation be handled? Ideally, it should occur prior to any crisis; realistically, when it becomes obvious that a patient is unlikely to survive. Regardless of the answer, effective communication is vitally important.

Because few intensive care unit (ICU) patients (less than 5%) are able to communicate with the health care providers caring for them at the time that withholding/withdrawing life support decisions are made,[8] there is a real need to share information with and seek input from the family.

A recent article published as a supplement to *Critical Care Medicine* reviewed the importance of talking with families about end-of-life care. Although few studies provide hard evidence on how best to initiate end-of-life discussions in an ICU environment, Curtis, et al[9] provides a framework that could serve as a model for clinicians and families alike. The proposed components of the conference would include: preparation prior to the conference, holding the conference, and finishing the conference.[9]

Preparing in Advance of the ICU-Family Conference

It is important for the participating clinician to be informed about the disease process of the patient, including: diagnosis, prognosis, treatment options, and probably outcomes of various treatments. It is important also for the clinician to identify areas of uncertainty or inconsistencies concerning the diagnosis, prognosis, or potential treatments. Any disagreements between sub-specialists involved in the care of the patient should be resolved before the family conference. Additionally, in preparing for the family conference, it is advantageous for the clinician to have some familiarity with the attitudes of the family and the patient toward illness, life-extending therapy, and death. When possible, the determination of who will attend the conference should be done advance of the conference. The location of the conference should also be pre-determined: a quiet private setting, with adequate comfortable seating is ideal. Asking all participants to turn off cell phones and pagers is appropriate and will prevent unwanted distraction. (If the patient is able to participate in the conference but is too ill to leave the ICU, then the conference should take place in the patient's room in the ICU.)

Holding the ICU Family-Conference about End-of-Life Care

Assuring that all participants are introduced and understand the reason for the conference will facilitate the process. It is also helpful to discuss conference goals and determine what the patient and his or her family understand about the prognosis. If the patient is unable to participate in the conference, it may be opportune to pose the question: "What would the patient want?" Explaining during the conference that withholding life-sustaining treatment is not withholding care is an important distinction. Another recommended approach to achieve concord in the conference is to tolerate silence. Giving the family time to absorb any information they have just received, and allowing them to formulate questions, will result in better and more goal-oriented discussions. When families are able to communicate the fears and emotions they may have, they are better able to cope with difficult decisions.

Finishing the Conference

After the patient and/or family have been provided with the facts and have achieved an understanding of the disease and the treatment issues, the clinician should make recommendations regarding treatment options. It is a disservice, for example, to give family members the impression that they are single-handedly making the decision to "pull the plug" on a loved on. Soliciting any follow-up questions, allowing adequate time, and making sure the family knows how to reach you, should end the conference on a positive note.

Understanding Choices

Another commonly encountered dilemma in terminal care is the number of choices involved, as well as the medical terminology that sometimes mystifies the choices. Advanced directives, living wills, health care proxies, durable powers of attorney for health care; what they are, what they mean, how much weight they carry, are they honored, and does everyone who needs them have them? Not long ago during a conversation with a chaplain at a hospital, the advice shared with me—to pass on to others—was to give family members the gift of knowledge. The final gift you give them may be the most important gift of all. Let them know your wishes.

When advanced directives became available in the late 1980's, it was presumed that the document would solve all the problems and that terminal care would adhere to the patient's wishes. The Study to Understand Prognoses and Preferences for Outcomes and Risks of Treatment (SUPPORT), initiated in 1988, however, showed severe shortcomings in end-of-life care.[10]

Advanced directives, as a legal document, have not necessarily lived up to expectations. A viable option is a Durable Power of Attorney for Health Care, in which a trusted individual is designated to make health care decisions when the patient cannot.

Another option is to have advanced planning sessions with family members. If the patient and his or her family can come to consensus about terminal care in advance, and the doctor is in agreement with any decisions, unnecessary suffering probably can be avoided. (When death becomes imminent and the patient's wishes are not followed, waste no time in seeking a meeting with the hospital ethics committee.)

Adaptive Techniques

There is no "recipe" that, if followed precisely, will allow for the successful navigation of all potential dilemmas. There is no way to prepare for each eventuality that accompanies terminal illness and death. Knowledge remains the safest shield against well-meaning advice-givers. Asking questions of caregivers is the best defense against misunderstanding and mismanagement of the patient.

The University of Iowa Research Center is working on an evidence-based protocol for advanced directives, which outlines in a step-by-step fashion assessment criteria that factor in the patient's age, primary language, and mental capacity for making health care treatment decisions. The protocol also provides a check-list format for health care providers, the documentation thereof is easily accessible and in a prominent position in the patient's chart.[11]

Another alternative health care benefit being proposed is called MediCaring, which emphasizes more home-based and supportive health care and discourages hospitalization and use of aggressive treatment.[12] While not specifically aimed at solving end-of-life care issues, there may be parts of MediCaring that mesh well with terminal care of the oldest old.

Whether in a home setting, a community hospital or an intensive care unit, terminal care can result in moral, ethical, economic, religious, cultural and/or personal/family conflict. Even when death is universally accepted as a normal part of the life cycle, there will be emotional dilemmas to navigate around. Additional education and research initiatives, however, may result in increased awareness that this currently is an unsolved problem, for the patient, the family, and the health care providers. Notwithstanding, however, the medical community should continue to persevere in trying to understand patients' and families' fears and needs, the need for quality communication with questions and answers in lay vocabulary. The clinician's task is to balance communication and understanding with medical delivery.

References

1. Thorson JA. *Aging in a Changing Society,* 2000. 2nd Ed. Taylor & Francis, Philadelphia, PA.
2. Thorson JA & Powell FC. Meaning of death and intrinsic religiosity. *Journal of Clinical Psychology.* 1990;46: 379–391.
3. Thorson JA & Powell FC. Elements of death anxiety and meanings of death. *Journal of Clinical Psychology.* 1998;44: 691–701.
4. Lynn J. Serving patients who may die soon and their families. *JAMA.* 2001;285(7): 925–932.
5. Pantilat SZ, Alpers A, Wachter RM. A new doctor in the house: ethical issues in hospitalist systems. *JAMA.* 1999;282: 171–174.
6. Fins JJ & Soloman MZ. Communication in the intensive care setting: The challenge of futility disputes. *Critical Care Medicine*: 2001;29(2) Supplement.
7. Quill TE & Brody H. Physician recommendations and patient autonomy: Finding a balance between physician power and patient choice. *Ann Internal Med.* 1996;25: 763–769.
8. Prendergast T.J. & Luce JM. Increasing incidence of withholding and withdrawal of life support from the critically ill. *Am J Respir Crit Care Med.* 1997;155: 15–20.
9. Curtis JR et al. The family conference as a focus to improve communication about end-of-life care in the intensive care unit: Opportunities for improvement. *Critical Care Medicine.* 2001;29(2) Supplement. PN26–N33.
10. Pioneer Programs in Palliative Care: Nine Case Studies (2000). The Robert Wood Johnson Foundation in cooperation with the Milbank Memorial Fund, New York, NY.
11. Evidence-based protocol: Advanced Directives. Iowa City, IA: University of Iowa Gerontological Nursing Interventions Research Center. 1999. Available; [http://www.guideline.gov/index.asp].
12. Lynn. J. et al. MediCaring: development and test marketing of a supportive care benefit for older people. *Journal of the American Geriatric Society.* 1999;47(9) 1058–1064.

HELEN SORENSON, Assistant Professor, Department of Respiratory Care, University of Texas Health Science Center at San Antonio in San Antonio, Texas. Ms. Sorenson is also Managing Editor of "Emphysema/COPD: The Journal of Patient Centered Care."

Index

Index

fear, 181; terminal care and, 176
feedback, immediate, infants and, 46
female celebrities, as role models for young
    girls, 107–111
fetal development, 23–31
fetal intervention, 32–33
fetal learning, 29–30
fetal memory, 30–31
fetal programming, 24
fetal surgery, 32–33
fetus: development, 23–31; learning, 29–30;
    memory and, 30–31; programming of, 24;
    surgery of, 32–33
first grade, placing pressure on children
    in, 81–85
fish, mercury and, 28–29
Five Wishes, terminal care and, 177, 178
flu, maternal, during pregnancy, 26
folic acid, 29
foreign languages, babies and, 46
FOXP2, 13, 15
free time, lack of, for young children, 39–43
Freud, Sigmund, 162
Fukuyama, Francis, 143, 144, 147
functional noncoding DNA, 14

G

games, infant, 48
gender, role models for children
    and, 121–129
gene variants, aging and, 168–171
genetic(s): differences in human DNA from
    primates and Neanderthals, 12–16;
    personality disorders and, 100, 101;
    prenatal development and, 24; research,
    100; technology, 17–22
germ-line modification, 17–18
Geron, embryonic stem cell research
    and, 10–11
God Gene, The (Hamer), 139
God Part of the Brain, The (Alper), 139
government, universal preschool and, 52

H

Harlem Renaissance, 90
Hawthorne Effect, homeless youths
    and, 134
Hayflick, Leonard, 169
Hayflick limit, 169
Head Start, 51–52, 54
health care, terminal care and costs
    of, 177–179
health-care proxies, 177
helicopter parents, 95, 98
Hemispheric Asymmetry Reduction in Older
    Adults, 163
High/Scope Perry Preschool Project, 50–53
higher-end learning, 63
high-stakes testing, 113; effects of No Child
    Left Behind Act and, 76–78
Hilton, Paris, role models for young girls
    and, 107–111
hitting, dealing with, 58–59
homeless youths, street culture
    and, 132–135

homelife, 42–43
hormones, fetal development and, 27
hospice, 175, 179
hovering parents, 95
human accelerated regions (HARS), 14
human embryonic stem cells, 6–11
Human Fertilisation and Embryology
    Authority (HFEA), 8, 9
Human Genome Project, 169
human nature, 89–93
humor, laughter and, 153–157
Hwang, Woo-Suk, 9
hypoplastic left heart syndrome (HLHS),
    32–33
hypothyroidism, 30

I

impulse control, of young children, 49
Incarceration Education Program, at
    Onondaga County Justice Center,
    136–138
inductive learning, 63
infants, language-enriching experiences
    of, 48–49; reading minds of, 44–47;
    as social learners, 45
infections, during pregnancy, 25–26
integration, schools and, 103–106
intelligence: fetal, 30–31; of infants, 44–47
Iran, runaway girls in, 132

J

joy, expressing, baby and, 49
Justice Center, at Onondaga County Justice
    Center, 136

K

kindergarten, placing pressure on children
    in, 81–85
Kingsolver, Barbara, 112
Kunkel, Louis M., 168–171

L

language learning, 67–69
Latino children, role models and, 125, 126,
    127, 128
laughter, evolution of, and social interaction,
    153–157
layoffs, career changes and, 166
learner choice, 70–75
Lee, Gypsy Rose, 109, 110
leisure activities, aging and, 164
Lewinsky, Monica, 110
living wills, terminal care and, 177
Locke, John, 90
Lohan, Lindsay, role models for young girls
    and, 107–111
longevity, genetic markers for, 169
Lou Gehrig's disease, laughter and, 156

M

Madonna, female role models and, 110

Martin, George M., 168
Marxism, 93
math, 83; No Child Left Behind Act and
    increased emphasis on, 55, 76, 82, 84
mealtime, baby and, 49
Medicaid, 178
Medicare, 178
MediCaring, 183
Medigap, 178
memory drugs, 144
Menorah Park Center for Senior Living, 173
mental health, preschools and the
    promotion of, 56–57
mercury, 28–29
methylmercury, 28
Microsomal transfer protein (MTP), 170
middle age, myth of crisis in, 162–164
minorities, Brown v. Board of Education and,
    103–106
Miseducation: Preschoolers at Risk
    (Alkind), 40
Monroe, Marilyn, 109, 110
Montessori, Maria, 172
moral development, 58–59
Moss, Kate, role model for young girls
    and, 107, 110
mother's voice, infant and, 30
motivational processes, 64
Mozart effect, 31
Murdock, Alison, cloned human embryos
    and, 8, 9
music television, role models for children
    and, 123
Myers Research Institute, 172, 173

N

nature-nurture, 3–5
Naxism, 93
Neanderthals, differences in human DNA
    from, 12, 15
neural synapses, 48–49
Neuroethics, 143
neurophamaceuticals, 143; eight objections
    to, 144–146; therapy vs. enhancement
    by, 146–147
New England Centenarian Study, 168, 169
nicotine receptor, 144
No Child Left Behind Act (NCLB), 54, 106;
    disruptive parents and, 96; effect of, on
    public schools, 82, 84, 76–78; language
    learning and, 67–68
nursing homes, costs of, 179

O

observation, infants and, 46
obsessive-compulsive disorder, 100, 101
Okarma, Tom, 10
open-heart surgery, infants and, 32–33
Our Posthuman Future (Fukuyama), 143
over-the-counter drugs, during
    pregnancy, 25

P

Pääbo, Svante, 12, 13, 15

186

Test Your Knowledge Form

We encourage you to photocopy and use this page as a tool to assess how the articles in *Annual Editions* expand on the information in your textbook. By reflecting on the articles you will gain enhanced text information. You can also access this useful form on a product's book support Web site at *http://www.mhcls.com/online/*.

NAME: DATE:

_____

TITLE AND NUMBER OF ARTICLE:

_____

BRIEFLY STATE THE MAIN IDEA OF THIS ARTICLE:

_____

LIST THREE IMPORTANT FACTS THAT THE AUTHOR USES TO SUPPORT THE MAIN IDEA:

_____

WHAT INFORMATION OR IDEAS DISCUSSED IN THIS ARTICLE ARE ALSO DISCUSSED IN YOUR TEXTBOOK OR OTHER READINGS THAT YOU HAVE DONE? LIST THE TEXTBOOK CHAPTERS AND PAGE NUMBERS:

_____

LIST ANY EXAMPLES OF BIAS OR FAULTY REASONING THAT YOU FOUND IN THE ARTICLE:

_____

LIST ANY NEW TERMS/CONCEPTS THAT WERE DISCUSSED IN THE ARTICLE, AND WRITE A SHORT DEFINITION:

We Want Your Advice

ANNUAL EDITIONS revisions depend on two major opinion sources: one is our Advisory Board, listed in the front of this volume, which works with us in scanning the thousands of articles published in the public press each year; the other is you—the person actually using the book. Please help us and the users of the next edition by completing the prepaid article rating form on this page and returning it to us. Thank you for your help!

ANNUAL EDITIONS: Human Development 08/09

ARTICLE RATING FORM

Here is an opportunity for you to have direct input into the next revision of this volume.
We would like you to rate each of the articles listed below, using the following scale:

1. **Excellent: should definitely be retained**
2. **Above average: should probably be retained**
3. **Below average: should probably be deleted**
4. **Poor: should definitely be deleted**

Your ratings will play a vital part in the next revision.
Please mail this prepaid form to us as soon as possible.
Thanks for your help!

RATING	ARTICLE	RATING	ARTICLE
	1. The Identity Dance		21. Parents Behaving Badly
	2. The Power to Divide		22. Where Personality Goes Awry
	3. What Makes Us Different?		23. *Brown v. Board:* A Dream Deferred
	4. The Age of Genetic Technology Arrives		24. Girls Gone Bad?
	5. The Mystery of Fetal Life: Secrets of the Womb		25. Disrespecting Childhood
	6. The Smallest Patients		26. Parents or Pop Culture? Children's Heroes and Role Models
	7. Not Always 'the Happiest Time'		27. A Peaceful Adolescence
	8. Who's Raising Baby?		28. Understanding Street Culture: A Prevention Perspective
	9. Reading Your Baby's Mind		30. How Spirit Blooms
	10. 20 Ways to Boost Your Baby's Brain Power		31. The Battle for Your Brain
	11. Long-Term Studies of Preschool: Lasting Benefits Far Outweigh Costs		32. Getting Back on Track
	12. Accountability Comes to Preschool		33. Emotions and the Brain: Laughter
	13. Raising a Moral Child		34. The Fine Art of Letting Go
	14. A Time and a Place for Authentic Learning		35. The Myth of the Midlife Crisis
	15. Why We Need "The Year of Languages"		36. Second Time Around
	16. Choosing to Learn		37. Secrets of the Centenarians
	17. Ten Big Effects of the No Child Left Behind Act on Public Schools		38. Lost and Found
	18. The Power of Teaching Students Using Strengths		39. Start the Conversation
	19. The New First Grade: Too Much Too Soon?		40. Navigating Practical Dilemmas in Terminal Care
	20. The Blank Slate		

BUSINESS REPLY MAIL
FIRST CLASS MAIL PERMIT NO. 551 DUBUQUE IA

POSTAGE WILL BE PAID BY ADDRESSEE

McGraw-Hill Contemporary Learning Series
2460 KERPER BLVD
DUBUQUE, IA 52001-9902

NO POSTAGE
NECESSARY
IF MAILED
IN THE
UNITED STATES

ABOUT YOU

Name   Date
_____   _____

Are you a teacher? ❑ A student? ❑
Your school's name
_____

Department
_____

Address   City   State   Zip
_____

School telephone #
_____

YOUR COMMENTS ARE IMPORTANT TO US!

Please fill in the following information:
For which course did you use this book?
_____

Did you use a text with this ANNUAL EDITION? ❑ yes ❑ no
What was the title of the text?
_____

What are your general reactions to the Annual Editions concept?
_____

Have you read any pertinent articles recently that you think should be included in the next edition? Explain.
_____

Are there any articles that you feel should be replaced in the next edition? Why?
_____

Are there any World Wide Web sites that you feel should be included in the next edition? Please annotate.
_____

May we contact you for editorial input? ❑ yes ❑ no
May we quote your comments? ❑ yes ❑ no